Brandon Taylor

Collage

THE MAKING OF MODERN ART

with 206 illustrations, 91 in color

Thames & Hudson

First published in 2004 in hardcover in the United States
of America by Thames & Hudson Inc., 500 Fifth Avenue,
New York, New York 10110

thamesandhudsonusa.com

Library of Congress Catalog Card Number 2004100752
ISBN 0-500-23816-2

Designed by Keith Lovegrove

Printed and bound in China by C&C Offset

Acknowledgments

I have to thank many friends and colleagues for kindly advice, the loan of books, or tips
and cues for further research: among these are Jean-Marc Poinsot, Steve Edwards, Jill
Carrick, Alex Potts, Serge Guilbaut, Sarah Wilson, Robin Spencer, Michel Rémy, Peter
Middleton, Aleksei Sinodov, Elizabeth Cowling, Derek Bunyard, Sue Malvern, Katařina
Průšová, Julie Lawson, Anna Peebles and Roddy Maude-Roxby. Among artists, I have
benefited from conversation with Dorothea Behrens, Peter Blake, Eduardo Paolozzi,
Gwyther Irwin, Richard Davies, David Ferry, Dennis Hopper, Peter Kennard, Robert
Rauschenberg, John Stezaker and Gee Vaucher, and from correspondence with Valie
Export, Ivo Medek, Joseph Nechvatal, and the writers Robin Blaser and Robert Creeley.
In the Czech Republic I sat at the feet of Karel Srp, Voitěch Lahoda and Lenka Bydžovská,
who taught me most of what I know. Collectors and gallerists have been especially
helpful, among them Peter and Margot Schubring in Berlin, Elizabeth Irwin in London,
Elizabeth Fairman and Maria Rossi at the Yale Centre for British Art in New Haven, and
Odyssia Skouros in New York. Holly Boerner of the Museum of Modern Art in that city
was a model of efficiency, as was my research assistant Zena Hughes. Earlier versions of
the manuscript were read by Peter Jones, David Evans and David Cottington, and I am
indebted to them for steering me towards important revisions. Both the Arts and
Humanities Research Board of the British Academy and the University of Southampton
supported a period of study leave in 2002–3, while the International Department of the
British Academy enabled me to travel to the pre-eminent European city of collage,
Prague, where the Academy of Sciences of the Czech Republic made me feel at home.

Contents

1 **Pablo Picasso** *The Dream* 1908
While not strictly a collage, Picasso's witty re-use of a found object combines rapidity, humour and low-cost fabrication in a manner that was substantially new in art.

Introduction

Early 1908. The twenty-six-year-old Pablo Picasso takes a brown cardboard sheet, perhaps the side of a packing box, bearing a paper label from the luxurious Magasins du Louvre department store in Paris. Turning the sheet upside down, he paints over the label in white gouache, re-emphasizing its white, rectangular form. Upon this new rectangle, approximately ten centimetres high by twenty across, he draws in black ink a sketch of a figure, seemingly a woman, bending over the side of a boat – maybe fishing or filling a bucket of water. Against the right-hand edge of this small cameo picture he draws a line, which becomes a tree trunk, which in turn supports and frames a larger standing female nude holding a towel in her left hand while lazily stretching her right arm above her head, as if asleep. The figure could be a homage to any one of Cézanne's standing bather figures, whom Picasso had already parodied and modernized in the great painting done in the previous year, the so-called *Demoiselles d'Avignon*. To complete his improvised picture, Picasso now draws a second, reclining figure, luxuriating across and around the cardboard's left-hand side: her bodily volumes rising to form an overarching tree with swooping branches. To pull off the playful demonstration, Picasso makes this figure's left hand gesture towards the painted label (or is she holding it aloft for the viewer to see?). Though the boating scene is spatially further back, the composite image could just about be a 'dreamt' memory of Manet's *Déjeuner sur l'herbe* of 1863, with its recumbent figures framing a separate background scene. Or it might refer to Matisse, or to Puvis de Chavannes. Finally, the words 'Au Louvre, Paris' are visible upside down at the base of the inner rectangle. What is implied? A 'found' scrap of cardboard destined for the Musée du Louvre? Picasso showing off his visual memory? A commercial label 'creating' a work of art?

The Dream begs the viewer's participation in a game of tease and impermanence, one to be played, it would seem, only at his or her expense. One part of that game involves recognition of how 'poor' material can be transformed into an object of interest, even of monetary value. *The Dream* was almost certainly not created for artistic display, such as a gallery or museum. More likely, Picasso would show it to studio guests. It may even have been created in their presence, as a demonstration of his improvisatory skill. And Picasso knew that his little improvised picture would carry a host of mutually competing meanings.

While not strictly a collage (Picasso did not, after all, paste the label on) this modest work contains the germ of an idea that was to flourish some four years later, in the formation and elaboration of the influential style we know today as Cubism. Collage in its first and usual meaning involves the pasting-on of scraps that originated beyond the studio, in the department store or on the street. It is apparent from the Eugène Atget photograph of Paris in the 1900s that the early twentieth-century European city was covered in printed ephemera in the form of commercial hand-bills, entertainment posters, political messages – and that they greeted the citizen as a medley, as a confusing and varied set of signs similar to those carried by the newspapers themselves. As the art critic Guillaume Apollinaire said of Picasso's collage works of the Cubist period, 'he did not hesitate to make use of actual objects, a two-penny song, a real postage stamp, a scrap of newspaper, a piece of oil-cloth imprinted with chair-caning'.[1] And that remark about Picasso's newly heterodox materials introduces a second principle. For even when the imported object is still whole (a department-store label or a two-penny song), it has to join another surface where it does not strictly belong. Typically, two things happen in this transfer. A new relationship is enacted between the 'low' culture of stamps and two-penny song, and the 'high' culture of professional art. Secondly, that relationship is felt to be inappropriate, jarring or wrong – yet interestingly so. For who in the frenetic world of the avant-garde would want to deny – or could – the frisson of excitement at the sight of a coupling which is illicit, discontinuous, at the very limits of aesthetic decency?

Composite imagery was not of course unknown before the twentieth century. The seventeenth-century Flemish painter Peter Paul Rubens freely added 'improvements' to the drawings of others, regardless of modern attitudes to originality. A little later William Hogarth took delight in the incongruous visual–verbal mixtures to be found in shop and inn-signs. The nineteenth century saw the advent of the scrapbook as a popular form, while picture-postcard humour, made possible by montaging disparate photographic elements against each other, was by the end of the century widespread. The appearance of collage in modern art, however, was substantially new. When Picasso and the Frenchman Georges Braque introduced the idea of *papier collé* (as this kind of collage was called) in the years leading up to the First World War, neither term was old enough to have any stable meaning. The term *collage* is the noun from the French *coller*, literally 'to glue' or 'to stick'. As in English, nineteenth-century French idiom allowed of ears being 'glued' to doors in listening, eyes being 'fastened' to women, the backsides of the lazy being 'stuck' to seats. In French, students could be absorbed (*collés*) in their books, while hunting dogs may have their noses *collés à la voie* or 'stuck to the path' in following a scent. To be *collé* to a woman was to be married to her, or, increasingly from the early twentieth century, to be living with her 'in sin'. *Papier collé* meanwhile took the everyday meaning of 'paper impregnated with glue to prevent it from soaking up moisture', as in wallpaper-hanging. Not until thirty or forty years later did the plural *papiers collés* acquire the meaning of the neutral-sounding 'composition [in the fine arts] made of different materials but principally glued papers'.[2]

Collage as indecency, paradox and perplexity – as impurity by any other name. Collage as invention. Collage as simple *fact*. For most of the period covered by this book, the technique of pasted paper had a special and even profound part to play in the expression of modern sensibility: a sensibility attuned to matter in the modern city, matter under the regime of capital. This implies that we negotiate the fine line between understanding collage fragments as 'flat, coloured, pictorial shapes…pieces of extraneous matter incorporated into the picture and emphasising its material existence' (as some formalists say[3]), and taking a more anthropological interest in the category of the discarded, the unwanted, the overlooked, as marks of modernity. We are pulled both ways. For while the terminology of used-ness may be clumsy and provisional, we may still legitimately ask (because we feel we need to know) how the biography of *that* fragment was formed; how its present disuse came out of a former use – one inspired by desire, exchange, competition, labour – by whom and from what it was produced; who paid for it and when. Modernity's fragments, some collages suggest, *are* its history, its residue; they are what is left over when the great feast of consumption has ended for the day, when trading and exchange have ceased and the people have gone home for a rest. Collage in the fine arts allows us to see that it is somewhere in the gulf between the bright optimism of the official world and its degraded material residue, that many of the exemplary, central experiences of modernity exist.

Or existed: that will be my argument. In Atget's Paris, even up until the 1930s, everyday material culture was rich in pieces of paper and their competitive juxtaposition; hence it was primarily through collage that the artist could maintain a relationship to commercial modernity that was philosophical and social in the broadest meaning of those ill-fated terms: sometimes satirical and parodic, but also reflective, aesthetic and above all experiential. And cutting and glueing belonged in this world as ordinary, domestic skills. On yet another level, collage deliberately evoked the cognitive and technical standards of the child, the playful, or the mad – suggesting that anyone can shape material this way, that anyone can practise in the field of the fine arts.

Yet throughout, we shall encounter a paradox in the relative *privacy* of collage: its experimental quality and also the marginality of its status. For remember that modern collage is rapid in execution compared to a painting or a sculpture: that things finished in an afternoon (then stored away for later inspection) are frequently numerous. And the size of modern collage is often small, limited by the dimensions of a sheet of paper or the area which can be conveniently pressed down upon a work-top surface. These material features have consequences. One is that the fragile and small-format object has often been assigned a status somewhere below that of the work of art itself – or else positioned as a thought-experiment for larger and grander work. In contrast to more public examples, we shall uncover several instances of how collage was practised without a public exhibition in mind, but rather kept archivally against the day when a reputation secured by 'finished' work had been successfully built. Some of this work is only now becoming known.

The question for today is how far those relations and affinities can survive the onset of electronic commerce of the later twentieth century – a world of very different paper surfaces and very different spaces for the organization of meaning. The chronology of later modernity becomes crucial: by the 1950s, screen-printed photographs; by 1970, photocopies; by the 1980s, computer technology; by the 1990s, the worldwide electronic web and the advent of the heavily vaunted 'paper-free' office. Nearly a century on we may now be 'after' collage in the sense that the material world of paper and cardboard played out in *The Dream* no longer exists: or not much of it. How collage and its restless offspring, montage, have weathered the blizzard of the digital age will be discussed towards the end of this book. For now, let us take our cue from Apollinaire, who was right about so much. Early in 1913, he was captivated by the sudden arrival of the 'truth' of real objects as they appeared inside the work of art. He called this process *énumération*, by which he meant the brute, material, 'this then that' quality of the collage fragment. He also meant the self-declaring objecthood of things, the statement an object or surface makes about its own material presence. 'People might say that from a plastic point of view we could have done without all this truth', he says, 'but once the truth appeared, it became essential.' 'One does not choose what is modern, one accepts it', he says a little later. He adds: 'It is impossible to foresee all the possibilities, all the tendencies, of an art so profound and painstaking.'[4]

2 **Eugène Atget** *Place Saint-André-des-Arts, Paris* 1903–4 Atget, the great documenter of *fin-de-siècle* Paris, captures the excitement and apparent randomness of the information environment of the modern city, emblazoned on a scale no sensitive eye could miss.

3 **Pablo Picasso** *Guitar, Sheet Music and Glass* 1912
Semantic units and musical notes lend voice and sound to
an already tactile collage composition – compounding the
complex interplay of drawn, pasted and simulated surfaces
present in the picture.

1

Inventing Collage

While *The Dream* might be considered the forerunner of the technique, the first genuine modernist collages emerged a few years later, in the middle of the artistic upheaval known today as Cubism. This wider, revolutionary assault on the picture surface, discussed and analysed at considerable length by others, had its roots in work that Braque and Picasso had been pursuing, independently, since at least 1906 or 1907. What concerns us in this chapter is a specific period in these developments, from around 1912, when these two pioneers of the 'pasted paper revolution' – the phlegmatic yet sturdy Norman, and the mischievous, inventive Spaniard – begin to employ pasted elements in the artwork in a rigorous yet playful way. As the contemporary poetess Gertrude Stein remarked – and she knew both artists well – Picasso was unusual among artists in that he 'liked paper'.[1]

Braque and Picasso
It is the second week of July, 1911. Picasso has arrived in the small town of Céret, in the French Pyrenees, to work for the summer. An untalented but loyal friend, Frank Burty Haviland, has loaned him a room in his large house to paint in – which he does intensively from the outset, even though the weather is stiflingly hot. For once he is working alone, a change from the spring, when he enjoyed the closest possible working relationship in Paris – partnership, even – with Braque. As Picasso reminisced later, 'almost every evening, either I went to Braque's studio, or Braque came to mine. Each of us *had* to see what the other had done during the day. We criticised each other's work. A canvas wasn't finished unless both of us felt it was.'[2]

   Then, on 16 July a letter from Braque arrives, saying that he would soon be joining Picasso in the mountains: the implication was that they would continue their aesthetic explorations in close proximity, if independently. In fact Braque did not arrive until 15 August, meaning that the two men were apart for a full five weeks, unable to check the tricks and devices developing in the other's work. That interval was surely significant. In the late spring in Paris Braque had made a large upright painting entitled *Le Portugais* [5], seemingly representing a character playing a guitar in a port-side bar, probably in Braque's home town of Le Havre.[3] And yet despite its delicate, austere appearance, little is visible of the figure and only something of the bar. Only the scale of the painting (an upright portrait in the grand manner) and a series of hints of body (a forearm, a cheek, a shoulder) tell you

5 Georges Braque *Le Portugais* 1911–12
At nearly 120 centimetres (47 inches) high, Braque's painting is nearly the same size as Picasso's *Accordionist*: both works have an austerity at odds with their ostensible subjects.

Opposite 4 **Pablo Picasso** *The Accordionist* 1911
The grand triangular structures that organize the painting also serve to dematerialize the accordionist and make her float in atmospheric space. The hands come into focus, and some details of the head – but that is all.

6 Pablo Picasso *Bust of a Céretan Woman* 1911
Notice the *céretane*'s bent left elbow and clasped hands: Picasso drew dozens of sketches for larger paintings on the notepaper of the Grand Café in Céret, south-west France.

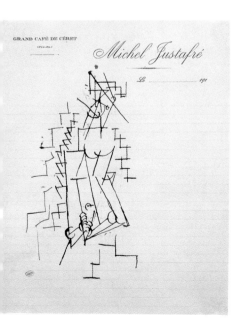

that a figure is there. In the background are some stencilled letters and numbers that could define panes of glass, a price, a time, the view from inside to somewhere further beyond; however, many regions of the painting are literally indecipherable, and probably intentionally so: Braque said later that some of the forms of his Cubist paintings 'had no literal meaning whatsoever'.[4] What Braque was reaching for is perhaps best summarized in the flickering obscurity of light upon dark, surface against shadow, full volume against empty shallow space. Or in the most marvellous of the stencils, the floating ampersand ('&') which has no alphabetic identity but stands as a visual sign for a word. It was this painting and above all this detail that set the standards for Picasso that summer.

During those five long weeks apart, Picasso occupied himself with various projects, including some paintings, now lost, for the library of Haviland's New York cousin Hamilton Field. Though intellectually close to Braque, Picasso's paintings and drawings from that interval are nevertheless significantly different from the Frenchman's. Picasso writes to Braque on 25 July a letter which provides a clue to this disparity. Thanking Braque for sending him a consignment of out-of-date cloche hats picked up cheaply, Picasso writes gaily: 'What a surprise, you can't have any idea how much I laughed [at the idea that the hats had been exported to Africa, then back to Le Havre, unsold].... We put them on with Manolo [Picasso's sculptor friend] last night to go to the café but with fake mustaches and side-whiskers applied with cork'.[5] That fondness for impersonation – for the feint, the seemingly innocent dissimulation, the clever reversal – underpinned more of Picasso's work than is usually recognized: it is, perhaps, the *characterological* determinant of many of his most serious and baffling ideas.

Take the painting known as *The Accordionist*, begun in Braque's absence and finished shortly before his arrival that summer: Picasso's ink drawing *Bust of a Céretan Woman*, quickly sketched on the front of a faintly ruled sheet of café notepaper, looks like a quick try-out for the structure and composition of *The Accordionist*, with its step-wise scaffolding and upright orientation, not to mention the graceful arc leading the ink hatchings to the café's letterhead, demonstrating Picasso's quick responsiveness to a print environment of a humble kind (he could, after all, have turned the paper over).

The drawing is also evidence of the give-and-take between printed paper and paint that he had tried out in *The Dream* three years before. One imagines Picasso sketching on the marble table-tops or café notepaper to fill time in the days before Braque's arrival, even while *The Accordionist* was under way in the studio. In that same 25 July letter he tells Braque that he began working on it soon after arriving in Céret: 'very liquid to start with and [then] Signac-style methodical treatment, smearings [*frottis*] only at the end'. Indeed the finished painting demonstrates his momentary disaffinity with the absent Braque. We know the 'accordionist' is a woman, since another sketch refers to the 'Pearl of Roussillon', as a popular song called the beautiful girls of the region. Certainly *The Accordionist* is visibly a cipher for a real human being with a head, face and other features, even though the language of representation is highly obscure. Picasso's biographer John Richardson has unlocked the sort of impersonation that the painting delivers: 'The genital positioning of the Pearl of Roussillon's instrument is the clue', Richardson suggests. 'Her "squeeze box", as the accordion is vulgarly known, with its little buttons and keys, not to mention the manual inflation and deflation that controls the emission of sound, turns out to be what the painting is about'.[6] We may add that the same playful expediency that utilizes a scrap of café notepaper is perhaps at work in the complicated geometry that obscures the 'accordionist' from our view. Why use a curve when a straight edge will do? Why depict a musician when a set of coded dabs, textures and facets will suffice? Why portray a figure directly when a ghostly mock-up, plus the occasional *double-entendre*, will perform the same roles? In any case, *bricolage* was a working-man's ethic, and Picasso was forever keen to demonstrate that aesthetic value can be contrived out of unlikely means.

Using a piece of café notepaper on the printed rather than the blank side raises a further question relevant to collage, namely why Picasso used lettering only very sparingly in his paintings at a time when to Braque it had become second nature. Partly, it must be due to that self-same penchant for impersonation, rather than any difficulty of obtaining stencils in a small Pyrenean town. But my suspicion is that Picasso wasn't confident about his handling of extraneous verbal matter until he had had time to experiment: or, specifically, to reflect how bluff and impersonation could aspire to something more philosophically far-reaching than a café joke or piece of wit. The profound question for Picasso at this stage was how the 'givens' of the contemporary graphic and commercial environment could function interchangeably with the stylistic units of ambitious art; how popular phrases or sayings could invade and re-figure the picture surface and hence alter the ways it could be read. And we know now that Picasso was a poet and writer as well as a purely 'visual' artist. But in the middle of 1911 he was not yet ready to plunder the whole of mass-printed culture in the way that he would shortly feel able to do.

A step, however, was taken in another Céret drawing, *Still Life with Glass, Cup or Bottle, with Two Straws*,[7] made on a sheet of notepaper from the Hotel and Café Gardes at nearby Arles-sur-Tech. This time, the printed letters and ruled surface of the paper form a more determining 'given', which the remainder of the still life drawing then elegantly confirms; the rising fluted column at left ends in the circular 'Hotel and Café' motif at the upper left, which circle is then echoed throughout the table-top scene, functioning sometimes as the elliptical base of a beaker, sometimes as a circular rim; while the letters of the word 'Gardes' complete a glass-like volume seen side on. As usual, the rapid execution tells its own story. Semi-consciously, Picasso's doodled still life has assimilated the promptings of the visual support, in so doing endowing his sketch with a 'voice' strongly evocative of leisure-time speculation, quotidian announcements, messages and labels. Yet for the time being, a full compromise with mass-culture is some way off – witness the small-ish *Bottle of Rum* (1911, Gelman Collection) which contains the letters 'L', 'E', 'T' and 'R' in the left-hand area and seems to want those letters to refer to themselves (yet they are wobbly and uncertain in execution, and evoke no distinctive contemporary typeface), and the same-sized *Still Life with Fan (L'Indépendant)*, also from the summer of 1911, whose gothic font word-fragment 'L'Indép' occupies an extraordinary advancing plane rushing into the nearground from some distant vanishing point. The local newspaper mast-head puns with the idea of *indépendance* (a cipher for Picasso and his project?) but the idea and the execution are surely weak. The letters themselves gyrate and slither, and define no stable space within the painting's otherwise rather mechanical fan-like structure.

Historians of Cubism are fond of emphasizing how inexorably one stage of discovery led to the next, and there is no denying a sense of 'evolution' at least up until 1914 or 1915. Yet given Picasso's powers of invention – and his skill with *bricolage*, or the expedient use of the 'wrong' materials – the mystery is how falteringly actual pasted paper made its way into Picasso's work, and how long it took. Three or more circumstances perhaps explain the delay. First, Braque was if anything the more audacious artist during the time at Céret, taking greater liberties with *sfumato*, with pure painterliness and with the dissolution of form. As an artist from a house-decorator's background he was not averse to decorativeness, even to abstraction. Picasso, on the other hand, wrestles with the very different problems of the relationship between drawing and form; the effects of a switch to *pointillisme* compared with rapid shading; and with the pros and cons of density versus light, opacity versus transparency. He also considers how to achieve expressiveness in painting by letting one object or effect impersonate another, a problem more or less foreign to Braque. Further, Picasso's domestic life was turbulent, and it may be that the need for thorough and even methodical work took precedence over the very different impulse to experimentation. On the other hand, the intensity of the brief stay in Céret was rudely

7 **Pablo Picasso** *Still Life with Glass, Cup or Bottle, with Two Straws* 1911
This remarkable sketch of a set of still-life objects begins and ends in the typographic environment of the paper itself, from its elegant typeface to its grid of ruled lines and the fold, running from top to bottom, which helps define the drawing's orientation and structure.

above, right 8 **Pablo Picasso** *The Scallop Shell ('Notre Avenir est dans l'Air')* 1912
The wobbly lettering and shifting geometry of this small picture also serve to dynamize the space and activate rhythms that the interval between seashore and aeroplane seems to demand. The world is a set of mobile metaphors, compressed into a small space.

above 9 **Pablo Picasso** *Still Life with Chair Caning* 1912
Here, it is the normally stable distinction between flat and elevated that is at risk. The viewer hovers, or lowers, according to the perceptual processes in play: it is a veritable game ('JOU') with the certainties of looking and knowing.

interrupted when Picasso had to race back to Paris on 4 September 1911 to answer malicious but unnerving charges of stealing statuettes from the Musée du Louvre, as well as to deal with his faltering relationship with Fernande Olivier and launch his next, and secretive, affair with Eva Gouel. The great work known as *Woman with Guitar (Ma Jolie)*, completed in Paris in the late part of 1911, was the result.[8]

And Picasso's skill as a *bricoleur* was soon to lead him in other directions. In the spring of 1912 we find him using house-decorators' paints called Ripolin (they are shiny and brightly coloured) in *The Scallop Shell ('Notre Avenir est dans l'Air')*. We find him applying a wide swathe of alien material and a rope border, in *Still Life with Chair Caning*: the first literally collaged work in modern Western art, this small oval picture-object is awkwardly claustrophobic in its structure, and unusual in being an oval work placed on its side. It is less of a painting than a thing: one which represents other things. And the spatial switching within the work, from flat to upright and back again is, if not new in Picasso's work, then supercharged here: either the chair-caning represents a chair seat, giving rise to a plan view; or it provides a general texture underpinning a still life table-top tableau, in which case it reads as flattened elevation. And yet the painting does not in fact contain chair caning but a piece of simulated caning made of oil-cloth that is pasted down, before being over-painted with shadows that turn it into a ground-plane for the cubified objects on top. The fact is that for both Picasso and Braque in the spring of 1912, the idea of including literal paper fragments was still a step too far. For Braque, already well-practised at *faux-bois* effects and stencilled lettering, the question of literal pasted paper was irrelevant, while Picasso, the anxious *bricoleur*, was more concerned with a breakthrough into relief-like volume, as several small sketches of standing objects from the same time clearly show. And it is striking how Picasso's painted lettering in the other early 1912 works – such as the magnificent vertical oval of the *Violin, Glass, Pipe and Inkstand* – are uneven, lop-sided notations maintaining no firm allegiance to an absolutely flat plane (notice how the 'A' of 'Avenir' in *The Scallop Shell* has been wittily turned into an ice-skating figure, its rear leg flying).

Yet something in Picasso's awareness was shifting that spring. When the usually supportive Willhelm Uhde expressed his disgust at his use of kitschy house-paints to Picasso's dealer Kahnweiler, who then passed it on, the artist retorted: 'Perhaps we'll

succeed in disgusting everybody: we have a lot more tricks up our sleeve'.[9] Ripolin oil paints signal an affinity for simple choices, for ready-made surfaces and sensations. Those bar-room letters and wood-grain textures which resonate with casual conversation, inebriated leisure and the working-man's off-duty ambience – these effects were supposed to work rapidly, even instantaneously, certainly without a narrative structure of 'first this, then that'. Picasso spoke later to William Rubin about the 'reality-effect' of analytic Cubism: 'It's not a reality you can take in your hand. It's more like a perfume – in front of you, behind you, to the sides. The scent is everywhere but you don't quite know where it comes from'.[10] Simultaneously, the word-play becomes more complex and allusive: in *The Scallop Shell* the painted lettering mockingly duplicates a patriotic leaflet in red, white and blue entitled *Notre Avenir est dans l'Air* (Our Future is in the Air). Flying was already a well-known metaphor for avant-gardist escape from conventionality; but since it was invented by the Futurists, who had come to challenge the dominance of Paris only a few weeks before, Picasso may have been playfully answering what he saw as their bombastic and inflated claims. There may be a personal reference too: the letters 'AVE' at the beginning of *Avenir* seem to represent Eva's name secretly. Picasso was increasingly comfortable with the language of concealment: bluffing one object as another, one sign as another, one texture or fabric as some other thing. The game of impersonation was gathering speed.

With a renovated love-life and a new technical confidence in the later spring of 1912, Picasso must have felt comfortably ahead in the competition of sheer inventiveness between himself and Braque, as well as with the other contenders, the Futurists and the Salon Cubists. Yet it is worth noticing that the experimental *élan* of *Still Life with Chair Caning* was not to be repeated, at least not in that form. Furthermore Braque also disapproved of the use of Ripolin paints, recognizing that, with it, Cubism in Picasso's hands might have irreversibly changed.[11] Yet they were still keen to work together, Picasso most of all. On 18 May 1912 he set off again to Céret, this time with Eva, hoping that Braque would join him and continue their working conversation. But no sooner had Picasso installed himself and begun work than he heard of Fernande's imminent arrival and hurriedly moved again, this time, and in secret to all but Braque and Kahnweiler, to the nondescript small town of Sorgues, north of Avignon. Such upheavals would be unsettling to a lesser artist – but to Picasso they presented a new chance to exploit the

above, left 10 **Pablo Picasso** *Violin ('Jolie Eva')* 1912
In describing his new paintings as 'robust' and 'clear', Picasso tells us something of the tough-minded carving quality of the forms he was now achieving. In making the violin 'lie down' (with Eva's name attached), he now elaborates a metaphor of the musical instrument as sexual that would recur many times again.

above 11 **Georges Braque** *Fruit Dish and Glass* 1912
Braque's pasted paper attachments play hide-and-seek with the viewer's understanding of what is real and what is depiction, what is flat and what is volume. The scale of the drawing is large, and displaces rather than prefigures a subsequent painting.

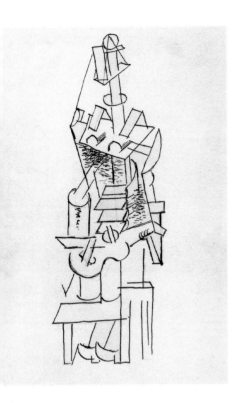

2 **Pablo Picasso** *Guitarist (Idea for construction)* 1912
In proposing constructions that could almost be made, Picasso
anticipates his later sculpture based on the standing figure.
Notice at the top of the structure the pyramidal form of the
head, while near the legs is a box-like arrangement necessary
for the object's stability.

see-saw of his private life in the context of the development of his art. Many of his works
of mid-1912 not only betray signs of abrupt changes of style or physical orientation, but
exploit those changes to the full. The marvellous *Violin and Grapes* or the *Violin ('Jolie
Eva')* have almost certainly been started in portrait format and switched to landscape, and
back again, perhaps several times. Their *faux-bois* passages especially look as if they were
painted in one orientation and then turned expediently to another, where they positively
sizzle with energy. Picasso proclaimed in a letter to Kahnweiler from Céret that his
paintings have 'gained in robustness and clarity…'.[12] Another example of a two-location
painting is the large Basel *Aficionado*, begun in Céret as a painting of a local bagpipe-
player, but finished in Sorgues as a swarthy bull-fighting fan with a mustache, a bottle and
a wide-brimmed Cordoban hat. This is not, it seems, a case of Picasso the 'social history'
painter reflecting the local bar clientele of Provence versus Roussillon, perhaps at the
expense of the former.[13] He was putting to good effect the accidents of his experience in
the formulation of a grand but complex art, one self-mocking enough to join 'high'
technique with 'low' subject-matter in a game of hide-and-seek with the playfully
disorientated viewer.

Braque arrived in Sorgues on 7 August 1912 for what proved another short but
concentrated collaboration on the problems of Cubist art. No more than three weeks would
elapse before Picasso would move again, this time back to Paris. From this distance we
have little way of knowing what the two men discussed, in what tone, manner or temper;
but as Braque later told Dora Vallier in an emotional recollection, they were exchanges that
'nobody but us would ever be able to understand'.[14]

Yet their talk must have ranged over their differences as well as the things they could
share. Both artists were united in a commitment to a 'high' art within the painting
tradition, hermetic in its difficulty and uncompromising in its demands; and both were
concerned with everyday 'reality', with the sensations and surfaces that made up their
world.[15] But other changes were afoot. By the end of the summer of 1912, Braque was
increasingly using *matière* – sand, cinders, sawdust, grit, metal filings, even coffee grounds
– to enrich the textures and effects in his paintings to a point hitherto unseen: a kind of
collage in all but name that was quite literally new to art.[16] Picasso meanwhile was
intensifying his search – not for the 'fourth dimension' as some contemporaries claimed,
but for the third. A series of extraordinary sketches done while closeted at Sorgues are
obviously designs for wobbly humanoid constructions that follow the logic of the painted
aficionados and accordionists through into actual materials such as cardboard or wood
(the scale of these constructions is in fact unimaginably large). Then, in the first fortnight
of September, came a *dénouement*. Braque was alone in Sorgues, Picasso having returned
to Paris to change studios. In an Avignon wallpaper store Braque spotted some wood-grain
wallpaper and immediately went in to buy it. Returning to the studio, he pasted
rectangular patches onto the surfaces of several large charcoal drawings, in such a way
that the drawing and the paper defined each other in a series of procedural and semantic
orderings that would have massive implications for what was to follow. The work on paper
known as *Fruit Dish and Glass*, for example, has three unequal patches at left, and right,
and lower down, probably attached *after* some initial drawing defined the main curve of
the fruit dish but *before* the drawing was continued over the wood-grain patches or
completed in recognition of the paper's rectangular edges. The relationship of this novel
format to Cubist painting is immediately challenging to the most radical degree. For not
only are these new drawings larger than some Cubist paintings, but they also carve out a
wholly new *métier* whose seriousness and ingenuity is the equal of any painting, even if for
the moment that quality was less easy to recognize. Paper and oil paint would never be
easy to mix, of course. But more than that, Braque's new inventions introduced a new
order of depiction which the painted pictures had only been able to imply, namely one in

13 Pablo Picasso *Guitar and Sheet Music* 1912
The appearance of the word 'Valse' (waltz) and the fragment of musical score lends to this collage a melancholy gaiety that is at once contemporary and slightly out-of-date – evocative of a claustrophobic bourgeois interior, rather than the jumbled studios of the avant-garde.

which pasted paper in its overlap of the ground upon which it rests operates both as literal surface as well as implied spatial supercession in terms of front-to-back. Which is to say that tactility and visuality are now combined, and often in abrupt tension with each other. 'After having made the [first] *papier collé*,' Braque recalled later, 'I felt a great shock, and it was an even greater shock for Picasso when I showed it to him'[17] – as he inevitably did on the Spaniard's return to Sorgues to collect his things.

Picasso, bricoleur

For Picasso it was as if the penny had dropped. Back in Paris in his new Montparnasse studio at boulevard Raspail, he immediately embarked on a phase of nearly a hundred *papiers collés* that would fully exploit the implications of Braque's extraordinary move. As so often with Picasso, it felt as if he had come across something he had known all along: as he said to Pierre Daix years later, 'I had always seen *collage*'. He was referring, perhaps, to Spanish popular religious images containing pasted elements, that he had seen as a child.[18]

We have no precise chronology for Picasso's first *papiers collés*, but it seems that the earliest, from the last week of September and the first week of October 1912, were done from coloured paper, available wallpaper scraps, and musical sheets, with minimal over-drawing and shading. 'I am using your latest papery and powdery methods,' he wrote appreciatively to Braque on 9 October,[19] referring both to *papier collé* as well as to sawdust and sand. 'I am in the process of imagining a guitar', he adds, perhaps referring to a complex cardboard construction that became important to him at about the same time. But look carefully at what is perhaps the earliest of Picasso's *papiers collés*, the *Guitar and Sheet Music*, to appreciate the materials to which Picasso as a new adept of artistic *bricolage* was becoming perfectly attuned. He now attaches pasted paper in ways that compete with the eye-fooling wood-grain drawing; layering planes by means of deft shading and implied (then often contradicted) structure. Like several early works it also employs a mustard-coloured diamond-patterned wallpaper, whose very ordinariness Christine Poggi has analysed as belonging to a rather precise category of middlebrow taste of the period. Wallpaper of this inoffensive kind decorated almost every home, and hung in tatters from the walls of Picasso's Montparnasse studio, where he occasionally tore pieces off. Poggi says that frequently 'it is in very poor condition and gives the impression that the artist has only remnants at his disposal…it gestured towards an appearance of luxury but fell short of achieving it' (an understatement indeed).[20] The other evidence is that such wallpapers were hard to find. When the British painter Duncan Grant visited Picasso a year and a half later, he wrote his friend Clive Bell that he had taken Picasso 'a roll of old wallpapers which I had found in my hotel and which excited him very much as he makes use of them frequently and finds them very difficult to get'.[21] Whatever their rarity, it does indeed seem that Picasso sought out wallpapers for the most part in the same browns, greys and tans that had been used in so-called 'analytic' Cubist painting of the previous years: perhaps such papers belonged to that category of the recently *passé* to which *bricoleurs* are so often drawn. Secondly, the earliest *papiers collés* are full of fragments of popular songs, fake wood-grain paper, and the usual armoury of visual *double-entendres* relating to reclining bodies, faces, musical instruments and table-top arrangements, whether 'found' or posed. But as much as the imagined constructions and the oval *Still Life with Chair Caning*, these *papiers collés* are also picture-objects in the sense of being assembled, constructed things: outside the category of *beaux arts* representations, they were intrusive new entities with a hybrid ontology all their own. The further possibility – it may be a remote one – that they were intended to hang (framed or otherwise) *against* the very wallpaper of which they were made, only enriches our understanding of Picasso's passion for switching identities, for clever bluff and counterfeit, for expedient and often jocular impersonation of the pictorial by the 'real'.[22]

The overall semantic quality of Picasso's early *papiers collés* is further complicated by an iconographic feature which has received much comment of late. The art-historian Patricia Leighten has worked out that of Picasso's fifty-two *papier collé* works of 1912 and early 1913 containing newspaper clippings, about half (hence a quarter of the total *papier collé* production) refer to the military conflict in the Balkans which broke out on 15 October 1912.[23] The question is why. Leighten's suggestion is that Picasso was showing us his anarchist-syndicalist sympathies; but the theory fails to account for the mood, the *ésprit*, with which these references were paraded. Picasso's close friend Gertrude Stein makes much of the fact that when the artist moved to Montparnasse in 1912 the 'gaiety' of the Montmartre period of Cubism ended: 'The gaiety was over…everything continued, everything always continues but Picasso was never again so gay, the gay moment of Cubism was over.'[24] But if the gaiety was lost, the sophisticated doubling was still there. For most likely Picasso used the Balkan 'reports' much like his other newspaper excerpts: sometimes to compose verbally clever messages for the delectation of companions and studio visitors, sometimes to lend the piece narrative 'colour', sometimes both. Hence in *Guitar, Sheet Music and Glass* [*3*] the sentence- or word-fragments 'LA BATAILLE S'EST ENGAGÉ[E]' and 'Constantinople' both occur beneath the word-fragment 'LE JOU': the reference is as likely to be to the 'battle' with his rivals in the avant-garde, notably Braque and Matisse, as it is to the Balkan War. As David Cottington has argued in a recent book, Picasso's Balkan War references and his more private artistic concerns are mutually connected: 'it is the anchoring of one pole of meaning in the public discourse that gives the other textual elements their resonance', he says. Without it, those puns and ambiguities 'would lose much of their allure of private, sub-cultural play'.[25]

Indeed, by the beginning of 1913 Picasso had become adept at sprinkling his *papiers collés* with references to all kinds of great and small events – wars and catastrophes on a global scale right down to the petty but heart-rending *fait divers* for which his favourite newspaper *Le Journal* was undoubtedly the best source. Furthermore most of the collages were not exhibited for at least a decade. Given to Kahnweiler for possible sale to private buyers, they were not intended to convey messages to an identifiable public in the way that Salon paintings were. And of course, many of Picasso's techniques were already latent in the culture. As Jeffrey Weiss has argued convincingly, the musical hall, the *revue* and the early cinema were already composed in the quick-change admixture that we now recognize in the earliest *papiers collés*: both *revue* and high-cultural collage were delivered in 'a period lexicon…specific to both: the *actualités*; the pun; the allusion and the *à peu près*; the *sous-entendu* and *entente*; irony, satire and *grivoiserie*; newspaper, advertising and song'.[26]

Of the last three named modalities, advertising and song brought to early *papiers collés* the worlds of commercial and popular culture that Picasso relished for their aural, musical and declarative voices – as well as for their sexual innuendo, their erotic *frisson* or black-humoured *blague*. They bristle with the colour of time spent at ease, in urban entertainment, or in observing the effects of commercial display. In the magnificent *Glass and Bottle of Suze* [*17*] of late 1912, we find a Balkan War report from *Le Journal* of 18 November, an account of an anarchist and socialist anti-war demonstration, and a fragment of a serialized novel, all circulating hotch-potch around a Suze label (*Aperitif à la Gentiane*) in a formal scheme suggestive at once of a table-top still life, a human figure with legs, a body and head, and a musical instrument such as a lute or mandolin. Moreover, this vast range of sensations and contemporary formal references were all cobbled together within one improvised structure, laid down 'at a stroke' and incapable of adjustment in the way that painting surfaces are – not to mention the variations in texture, density and colour carried by the paper fragments alone.[27] Subsequent *papiers collés* included newsprint references to murders, suicides, and tragi-comic domestic scenes that

right 15 **Juan Gris** *Bottle of Banyuls* 1914
The delicate geometrical structures of Gris's collages echoed, and were echoed by, those of his paintings. Here he interleaves plan and elevation, aligning shapes and volumes while modulating the medium in which they are presented.

above 14 **Gino Severini** *Still Life: Bottle, Vase and Newspaper on a Table* 1914
Italian Futurist collages invest the surface with 'lines of force' that suggest movement or the play of light: unlike Picasso's work, they seldom exploit devices of metaphor or black humour, welcoming instead the devices of simultaneity.

right 16 **Antonín Procházka** *Still Life with Fruit and Goblet* 1925
Procházka's balanced collage-paintings of the mid-1920s use encaustic wax to elevate some surfaces, stippling other planes to achieve tactility. Living and working in Brno, his first major exhibition was in 1932.

following pages
17 **Pablo Picasso** *Glass and Bottle of Suze* 1912
Picasso confirmed later that including the report of the anti-war demonstration in this statuesque and imposing work was 'my way of showing I was against the war', that he 'knew that people would find this later and understand'.

18 **Juan Gris** *Packet of Coffee* 1914
This large collage has the size and scale of an easel painting: its extraordinary visual complexity elevates to the status of history painting the modest table-top assembly of newspaper, bottle and packet of coffee, as if to dramatize everyday life in the idiom of the heroic.

constitute a sort of critical but also delighted burlesque of the contemporary world: a *mélange* of topical references that shared with the contemporary Parisian musical hall, or the new genre of popular cinema, the quality of being momentarily relevant, touching or spectacular – but quickly forgotten.

The Collage Diaspora: Severini, Gris and beyond

The discovery of *papier collé* spread widely through the Paris studios as soon as it became rumoured that Picasso – who never exhibited publicly in Paris at this time – was on to something extraordinary. But how were these works understood? At the end of 1912, so the Italian Futurist Gino Severini tells us, he had a studio conversation with Apollinaire, who mentioned to him that Picasso was using pasted elements in his pictures, somewhat as real objects such as jewels and pearls, crosses or keys, are embedded into the surface of Italian 'primitive' paintings.[28] Severini soon included pasted newspaper cuttings in his own paintings, especially those meeting Filippo Marinetti's call for references to the war: stories of trench warfare, some with photographic illustrations, occur in Severini's collages as early as late 1914. The other Italian Futurists, notably Umberto Boccioni, Carlo Carrà and Giacomo Balla followed suit: collage became a method of enriching the surface (Boccioni), or of including ready-made elements in so-called 'free word' pictures (Carrà), or of crafting visually mobile versions of three-dimensional constructions (Balla). The artist Ardengo Soffici, for his part, soon went beyond the celebration of war to assert the values of Latin order and rationality. The uses and applications of collage were suddenly legion. Aside from high-ranking Futurists, a stream of local and overseas visitors to Picasso's boulevard Raspail and later the rue Schoelcher studio (including dozens of 'bees' from the La Ruche ('The Beehive') studio complex in Montparnasse) all saw, or heard about, or themselves invented versions of, the paintings and the *papiers collés* that were being created by Picasso in those years.

The exception to every generalization was the Spaniard Juan Gris. Always and only a two-dimensional artist, the use of pasted paper in Gris's hands was from the beginning the most pictorially complex of its time. Supported generously in Paris by Gertrude Stein and by Kahnweiler, Gris devoted much time to the implications of simulated material effects in his works, both in 1913 and 1914. Always bolder in colour than Braque, his collage pictures generally revolve around a trapezoid central structure completely unlike the triangular motifs of Picasso. Their balance between 'picturing' and anti-illusionistic play with materials – not to mention the persistent play with chequerboard patterning – is always strenuously worked-at and in tight-knit geometrical balance. Compare for example the large and complex *Packet of Coffee* [*18*], now in the museum at Ulm, with the smaller and simpler *Bottle of Banyuls*, the latter made while staying in Collioure near the French Pyrenees in the middle part of the same year (Banyuls is just down the coast). The American critic Clement Greenberg would complain much later of the excess of decoration in the larger works; Greenberg's contemporary James Thrall Soby would call them 'among the most perfect works of art of our time'.[29] Following the experiments of 1912–13, the relation between pasted paper and the painted image became fundamental: we must acknowledge that Cubist *papier collé* triggered more imitators and opponents than can be contained within a single book. Some variations even now are too little known. In Prague, for example, collage was addressed not only by the Czech Cubists Emil Filla and Bohumil Kubišta. Picasso's contemporary Antonín Procházka, who saw Picassos and Braques almost as soon as they were made, used sand, encaustic and other materials in a light-hearted version of Cubism after the First World War, producing beautiful classical effects in works like the small *Still Life with Fruit and Goblet* of 1925. It is an example out of thousands that demonstrate how *papier collé* would rapidly become international modernism's most elegant and fertile style. It would become much more besides.

19 Installation of *papiers collés* in Picasso's boulevard Raspail studio, photograph no. 2, winter 1912
All of Picasso's three photographs of his studio wall were taken immediately prior to taking the works down – though the cardboard guitar remained hanging throughout, as a reminder of how real and depicted depth were almost the same.

2

Paths to Construction

For all its playful ephemerality, elegance and style, Picasso's *papier collé* method was underpinned by far deeper purposes. Even in the autumn of 1912 it was clear to some of those who visited Picasso's studio that his goal lay beyond the mere rearrangement of surfaces and texts. Indeed, out of that extraordinary crucible, to their surprise and perhaps also to Picasso's, emerged a new adventure, that of three-dimensional construction. Or rather, the discovery that the very distinction between flat and volumetric was no longer absolute, that through a process of unprecedented spatial and semantic complexity, something deeply unsettling was happening to art. 'He takes musical instruments to pieces as if they were clockwork, and tortures them like an inquisitor' was the verdict of the Russian critic Yakov Tugendkhold on seeing Picasso's works in the Moscow collection of Sergei Shchukin. He agreed with Apollinaire that Picasso 'studies the object as a surgeon dissects a corpse'.[1] Suggesting a rearrangement of categories as well as of physical matter, such reports capture well the timeliness, the strangeness, the excitement, of what Picasso was doing between the later part of 1912 and the beginning of 1914.

The Italian Futurists are partly relevant here. As we saw in Chapter 1, they had arrived in Paris early in 1912 with noisy proclamations and even noisier sound-performances, and, in three dimensions, the twisted dynamic volumes of Boccioni's spatial analyses of a bottle in space, a head and a window, a walking man. Picasso disliked all of this – but shared with them the intuition that the object and the experience of the object were in a state of profound change, even crisis. Futurist analyses of the object tended to unfold it dynamically in time, to narrativize it. Picasso's method was the opposite: there are photographs taken by him in his studio in the last weeks of 1912 which show him building literal space *into* the representation of objects on a single plane – either by making materials obtrude from the plane as in a sculptural relief, or by hanging simulated things against and upon such a plane. At almost the same time, Braque made sculptures in the corner of a room that both occupy and do not occupy real space. It was the beginning of a much larger concept of 'construction' that would resonate throughout the decades to come.

Paris: In the boulevard Raspail
'I am in the process of imagining a guitar', Picasso had said in the letter to Braque of 9 October 1912, soon after his return to Paris. Perhaps he was referring to the first *papiers*

collés that 'imagined' guitars out of wallpaper, card and sheet-paper; or, as I like to think, the guitar made of cardboard which he hung at the centre of a changing display of seventeen relatively austere newsprint collages on a large wall of the boulevard Raspail studio between the end of November and about 14 December 1912 [*19*]. The cardboard guitar seems to make literal the spatial play that the last paintings of 'analytic' Cubism had suggested. We know Picasso felt his new construction was a breakthrough: he joked later that he could 'sell the plan of the guitar so that every artisan would be able to make one'.[2] Photographing it seemed important to him too: he took three photographs altogether, whose sepia tonality seems to confirm that the *real* spatial intervals implied by cast shadows of up-standing cardboard and the *illusions* of pictorial space implied by newsprint texture or flat shading look more or less the same. At least, the photographs show a relationship between the 'virtual' guitar and the spatial intervals of the collages. A real shadow mimics a flat newsprint paste-up (and vice-versa), while elsewhere the same tonality produces 'volume', either as modelling or as texture alone. Signs are now 'circulating', to use Rosalind Krauss's term, not only between material qualities of the surface, but between depth and flatness itself. Depth and flatness, horizontal and vertical, line and texture, volume and shadow: these are no longer alternatives, but are becoming interdependent, symbiotic pairs.[3] Picasso's achievement, it might be said, was to remake art, not as new 'content' or a new type of illusion, but as a new category of thing. The language of two and three dimensions which upheld a professional division of labour between 'painters' and 'sculptors' looked suddenly archaic.

Two other features of the boulevard Raspail experiment call for attention. The first is the sudden arrival of newsprint, sometimes overlaid with charcoal or wood-grain effect, devoid of photographic images but sometimes including, for emphasis, a highly legible headline or title or a fragment thereof ('JOU' and 'RNAL' and so forth). These scraps are carefully selected from a newspaper pile, scissored into columnar strips or wedges, and matched against a template pre-drawn in charcoal. Their edges cut rapidly in succession, they read as instantaneous presence rather than as directionally elongated lines, such as might be created by a painter's brush. Declaring themselves as familiar scraps of no material value, they form a yellowish grey texture that offers itself simultaneously as something to read, or at least to scan fleetingly. (The dark-brown tonality that they possess today is an effect of ageing, but could it have been intentional?[4]) The newscuttings can also be said to evoke a graphic regime that reproduces a rational assembly-line accumulation of information. While summoning the illusory presence of wars, dramas and city life, not to mention weather forecasts and prices on the stock exchange, it is still order, rule, form, column, style and type, whose medium-as-message complexity Picasso quite evidently relished.[5]

The second feature of the experiment is an apparent plundering of artisanal skills previously unheard of within the fine arts. In constructing his guitar, for example, had Picasso taken stock of the methods of the celebrated guitar-maker Julián Gómez Ramírez, a neighbour of his and Eva's while they lived in Montmartre, and whose workshop was so small he worked on the street? And had Picasso learnt from observing the dress-making skills of Fernande and also Eva, both of whom liked to sew and both of whom pinned flat patterns of material onto templates while making garments that could be worn? There are pins galore in the *papier collé* works of this time: 'who but Eva would have shown him how to get the protruding sound hole he had contrived out of a cardboard tube to fit as snugly into his construction as a sleeve into a jacket?'[6] Or look back to the very top of the *Guitarist* construction of 1912 [*12*] and see how the small pyramid (which acts as a cipher for the head) reappears as collage in a group of small paper-and-card experiments of 1913. Long vertical rectangles of pasted paper, one topped by a small drawn circle representing an eye, now lean against each other within a 'D' representing the cranium in the most playfully reductive synonym of the human head ever attempted.[7] Here were fabricational methods

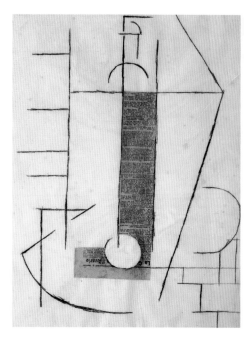

20 **Pablo Picasso** *Bottle on a Table* 1912
In the newsprint collage, careful inspection is needed to discern the order in which drawing, pasting and over-drawing were done.

opposite 22 **Pablo Picasso** *Bar Table with Guitar* 1913
Pinning rather than pasting paper lends an air of provisionality to the work, while absence of glue suggests efficiency and lightness: both qualities that Picasso enjoyed.

21 **Pablo Picasso** *Head* 1913
This small but extraordinary work was later acquired by André Breton, who saw in it confirmation of Picasso's 'surrealist' imagination, his transformatory powers.

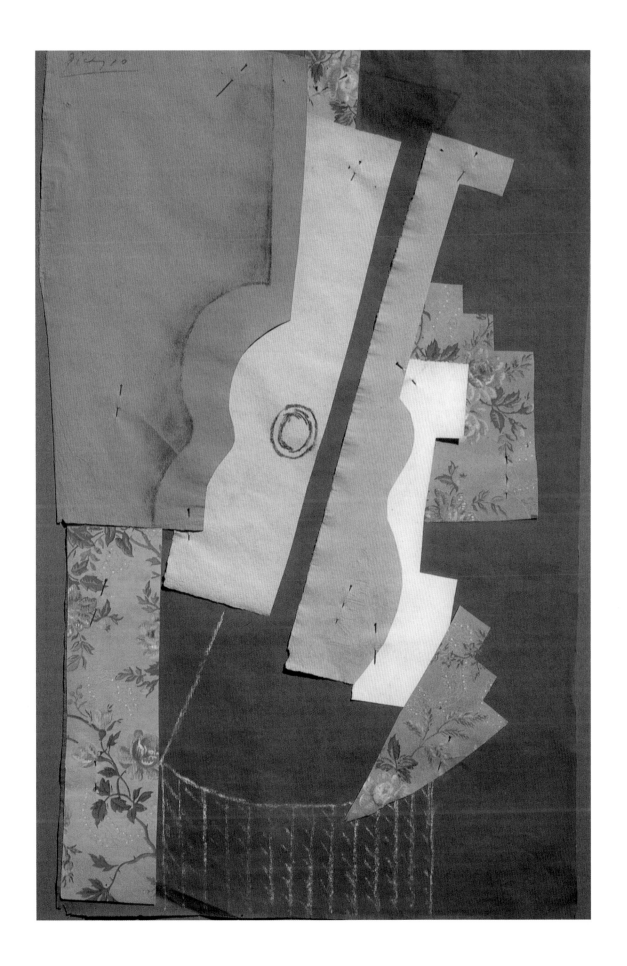

and conceptual blendings not previously considered the purview of a fine artist, let alone the *soi disant* genius of Paris's hectically competitive avant-garde. It seems legitimate to conclude that just as the cardboard 'guitar' and its associated *papiers collés* and *papiers epinglés* (pinned paper) undo and reorganize the distinctions between volume and line, literal and perceived depth, they also begin to erase the line between professional and amateur, artist and artisan, that had largely underpinned the edifice of Western art since at least the Renaissance. Collage had played the vital part in this new visual and cognitive invention – the *tableau-objet*, as it was sometimes known.[8] And not only had Picasso outflanked his rivals, he had risen above them in sheer inventive facility through a technique of homespun simplicity applied to the cheapest materials such as permanently to blur and to problematize relations between 'high' art and the lower commodities. The material and philosophical basis of Western art would never be the same.

That conclusion needs a further but important elaboration, one relating to the functioning of the sign in *papiers collés* and the constructions. For it is often said that the *papiers collés* in particular are the 'representation of representation'; that, like language, they are structured by means of arbitrary signs 'circulating' within a system of opposites.[9] It is a conclusion that is often traced to Picasso's involvement in African art. For commentators have had to reconcile the appearance of Africanized masks and other carved or striated material found in early Cubist paintings with Picasso's later assurance that 'there is no African art in the *Demoiselles*'; nor by implication in other paintings of the same character. Recent scholarship has insisted that *something* occurred in the explosive encounter between Picasso and the Trocadéro Museum in Paris where non-Western artifacts were stored and displayed. And Picasso's dealer Kahnweiler, one of the most thoughtful early historians of Cubism, later affirmed that 'the discovery [by Picasso] of the Grebo mask [from the Ivory Coast or Liberia] coincided with the end of analytic Cubism', in other words the summer and autumn of 1912, the exact moment of *papier collé*. It is true that the Grebo mask comprises a flat background plane with a protruding forehead, eyes and nose, all shorn off to define a frontal plane, while casting depth-implying shadows onto the plane behind. And there is no escaping the fact that its two-planed solidity with voids and solids just *is* the structure of Picasso's cardboard *Guitar*; that both mask and guitar hang frontally against an upright surface such as to offer to vision a pictorial thing which at the same time represents something else. And at 64 and 66 centimetres (25⅛ and 27 inches) in height respectively, the constructions are remarkably close in size. The mask acts as decoy for the face; while the guitar acts as surrogate for a universe of possible objects, including bodies, furniture, even a table-top tableau. It is with every justification then that Kahnweiler should say:

> These [Cubist] painters turned away from imitation because they had discovered that the true character of painting and sculpture is that of a *script*. The products of these arts are signs, emblems for the external world, not mirrors reflecting the external world in a more or less distorting manner…the [Grebo] masks bore testimony to the conception, in all its purity…that art aims at the creation of signs. The human face 'seen'…does not coincide at all with the details of the sign…. The epidermis of the face that is seen exists only in the consciousness of the spectator, who 'imagines'…the volume of this face *in front of* the plane surface of the mask…[10]

It is all the more unfortunate then that recent historians have read the 'signs' in question to be those of Ferdinand de Saussure in his *Cours de Linguistique Générale* of 1915, which promulgated the controversial notion of the 'arbitrariness' of the sign. 'From Grebo art', writes the Harvard art historian Yves Alain-Bois, 'Picasso received simultaneously the principle of the semiological arbitrariness and, in consequence, the non-substantial

23 Grebo Mask, from Ivory Coast or Liberia
The human face may be a prototype of all form: its visual arrangement reverberates in other objects and constructions, as Picasso was acute enough to realize in the *papier collé* phase.

character of the sign'.[11] Yet the conclusion is erroneous: not only is the visual (as opposed to the literary) sign not arbitrary, but it was not a Saussurian conception of the sign that Picasso felt he had discovered – and which with the help of the Grebo mask launched 'synthetic' Cubism and its progeny. Picasso's 'sign' was just what Kahnweiler first said it was: emblems, or a script, understood to mean hieroglyphs having iconic form. For it is not the *dissimilarity* of those emblems to the real that counted, but on the contrary the very *similarity* of those cylindrical eyes to actual eyes, of the wedge-shaped nose to an actual nose, of the organization of the mask to an actual face, that rendered those emblems attractive to an artist bent on achieving a first frenetic freedom from narrativity. It is the same with the cardboard guitar and the *papier collé* sheets. Neither volume nor plane, all now function on the basis of formal and visual similitudes with the entities they 'represent' as emblems. And like other emblems they signify quickly – this, it seems, was one of Picasso's purposes in making them.

Four smaller constructions by Picasso were published by Apollinaire in *Les Soirées de Paris* in November 1913, to an audience of readers astonished by their shoddiness, their strangeness, their emblematic force.[12] It would not be long before the original cardboard guitar was cast in metal, to become to later generations of sculptors a demonstration of how volume can be achieved without mass, how structure can be achieved without solidity. 'Construction' here had been achieved, not as rational manufacture, still less as narrative, but as immediacy, as semiotic 'speed'.

Sdvig *and* Za-um: *Moscow and St Petersburg*

We have seen already how Picasso's new vision of art travelled far and fast. Freedom from narrativity; emblematization; semiotic speed: to observers in the Russian cities these ideas proved both repellent and attractive. Mystical philosophers felt that the cosmos was collapsing. 'When I look at his pictures', wrote Nikolai Berdyaev in 1914, 'I think something is going wrong with the world…it seems that after Picasso's terrible winter nothing will ever blossom again – that this winter will not only destroy the veils of foliage but that the whole objective, physical world will be shaken to its foundations, in a mysterious disintegration of the universe'.[13] Younger artists who witnessed Picasso's works saw confirmation in them of their own revolutionary experiments – hermetic, provocative, primitivist – that were just then being unleashed upon the world. The major difference was that in Russia the collaboration was between *writers* and the visual arts, according to priorities long established in that country. If Picasso's battlefield in Paris was perceived to be space and matter, in Moscow and St Petersburg the primary terrain was that of the word.

It was David Burliuk's essay 'Kubism', as well as the manifesto 'A Slap in the Face of Public Taste' (both 1912), signed by Burliuk, Velimir Khlebnikov, Aleksei Kruchenykh and Vladimir Mayakovsky, that inaugurated the concept *sdvig* (shift), meaning the dislocation or displacement of parts. They had declared that 'hieroglyphics' were more comprehensible than Pushkin, that the poet had the right to invent words and to feel 'insurmountable hatred for the language existing before them'. Within months, that is by early 1913, Khlebnikov had formulated new visual and verbal principles: that he would stop considering word-formation according to grammatical rules, that he would ascribe 'content' to words 'according to their graphic and phonetic characteristics'. Punctuation would be abolished in order to emphasize 'the verbal mass', and so on.[14] An instructive example of how 'shift' worked in poetry and painting has been presented by Juliette Stapanian, who in early poems by Mayakovsky and contemporaneous paintings by Kasimir Malevich finds parallel concerns with urban movement and dislocation, taking place in both verbal and visual registers. Mayakovsky's poem 'From Street to Street' (1913) makes endless play with the unfolding perceptions of a tram traveller and the memories or associations so evoked – at the same time as he dramatizes these effects with word-inversions, syllabic mixing and reversal, recreating semantic ambiguity through methods akin to play. Repeated references to 'cutting', to vertical and horizontal movement, to the mixing of interior and exterior views, and the splicing together of several authorial voices, trigger spatial as well as semantic jumps that serve to destabilize the poem radically from within.[15] 'Versified Cubism' was Malevich's term for this new poetic idiom. Meanwhile his own Cubo-Futurist paintings *Woman At a Tramstop* (1913), and more particularly *Woman at a Poster Column* (1914) and a whole set of paintings from the same year incarnate methods of temporal dislocation and do so through a method which is essentially as well as literally that of collage.[16] Perhaps deriving at one remove from Picasso, *Woman at a Poster Column* uses collage elements to 'shift' the material and temporal coordinates of the image by references to *kvartira* (apartment), *razoshols'a byez* (sold without), *Chetverg* (Thursday), *Africanskiy* (African) and various floating letters jumbled up with impressions of war and civilian life. *Composition with Mona Lisa* contains the words *chastichnoye zatmenie* (partial eclipse, a reference to Kruchenykh's opera-play *Victory Over the Sun*), above a pasted image of the Mona Lisa crossed out, under which we read the words *peredayotsa kvartira* (apartment changing hands): at one time a cigarette was seen glued to the lips of the *gioconda*.[17] 'Shift' here serves to dramatize the simultaneity of disjoint times and places in what to a contemporary Russian audience must have appeared a startlingly dislocating (and dislocated) mix.

But the Russian progression from collage to 'construction' remains very different from that of West European Cubism. The very title of *Woman at a Poster Column* refers the picture to the human experience of *sdvig* in a way that the Parisian *papiers collés* or constructions were never intended to do. Further, Malevich's emphatic blocks of paint and his generally upright scrambled fragments maintain a relation to the picture's edges that gives a noticeboard effect very unlike the radical volumetric deconstruction practised in the boulevard Raspail. As a painter Malevich would use the format of block-like forms upon a rectangular ground right into his later, Suprematist phase: for him, quite long spatial distances replace Picasso's arm's-length relationship with table-top subjects – once more an effect of the linguistic orientation of the Russian avant-garde. But there is little doubt that Vladimir Tatlin enjoyed a greater instinctive affinity for the material discoveries of Picasso's work. Unlike Malevich, he visited Picasso's studio in the boulevard Raspail in early 1913 and must have seen both the cardboard *Guitar* and perhaps other small constructions too. By the time of his visit Tatlin had joined the avant-garde Union of Youth, had met the influential Khlebnikov, and had also done illustrations for Mayakovsky, notably for his poem 'Signboards'. Returning to Moscow, Tatlin begins work almost immediately on a set of what he called 'painterly reliefs' which deploy a wooden board as a ground-plane but which now figure table-top constellations of bottles, glasses and perhaps shafts of light that he had seen in Paris – and do so in terms of materials alone. It will be noticed immediately that the golden metal foil and wooden base evoke the rich patination of the Russian icon, whose pictorial instantaneity the Russian avant-garde universally admired. This and a group of other painterly reliefs by Tatlin were exhibited in Moscow in May 1914.[18] It was a short but audacious step on the way first to the 'counter-' or 'corner-reliefs' of 1915, then to Tatlin's subsequent leap into 'construction' proper. The Parisian *métier* of glueing paper now gave way to the nailing or fastening of strips of unused material to a surface. A colleague of both Tatlin and Malevich, the artist Ivan Kliun also developed a relief style of wood and metal remnants around 1915–16. 'The whole effort of a poet and a painter', the literary theorist Viktor Shklovsky wrote about such work, 'is aimed first and foremost at creating a continuous and thoroughly palpable object, an object with *faktura*'.[19]

It is to the brilliant Shklovsky of the St Petersburg *Opoyaz* group, himself a master of overstatement, literary inversion and ironic play, that we owe the most succinct

24 **Kasimir Malevich** *Woman at a Poster Column* 1914
Semantic units pass into and go out of focus amid a series of spatially unstable planes of colour, pulsing and mixing as in the flow of consciousness itself.

25 **Ivan Kliun** *Untitled* 1916
'We have arrived at an ideally simple form: straight and circular planes', Kliun wrote in 1915; or, in another formulation, 'the great task has arisen of creating a form *out of nothing*…we are the primitives of the twentieth century.'

opposite 26 **Vladimir Tatlin** *Painterly Relief* 1913–14
Tatlin's interest in relief is visible here in the bent metal foil and twisted wire, which together with the wooden surfaces are formally 'rich' in spite of their material poverty.

formulation of the basic idea of creative 'deformation' by which *cliché* is avoided and the world of images and words appears suddenly sharp and unfamiliar.[20] The twin processes of 'laying bare the device' (*obnazenie priema*) and 'making strange' (*ostraneniya*) function in Russian Formalist theory to separate both an image and its material from their habitual contexts. To Shklovsky, 'laying bare the device' meant both letting the commonplace infiltrate the sophisticated and vice-versa (examples were to be found in Tolstoy and Lawrence Sterne, as well as in French Cubist collage). The results were explosive: the invasion of the sophisticated by the simple provided a link with a European pastoral tradition reaching back to Virgil, while the overlaying of simplicity with complexity (of diction, rhythm or reference) brought with it the possibility of parody and the burlesque: a quantum leap from the routine concern with the metaphorical image that had suffused Russian symbolist art and literature for a generation. To Shklovsky, *faktura* was a quality of both poetic writing *and* visual art. 'Density [*faktura*]', wrote Shklovsky, 'is the principal characteristic of this peculiar world of deliberately constructed objects, the totality of which we call art'.[21]

Meanwhile the young Roman Jakobson had as an adolescent poet and language student in the years before the First World War enthusiastically discussed with Khlebnikov, Kruchenykh and Malevich how to transcend the perceived limitations of Symbolist poetry and art. 'With Khlebnikov', wrote Jakobson later, 'I discovered the innermost laws of glossolalia [speaking in tongues] recorded in the eighteenth century among Russian religious sects...while Kruchenykh suggested nagging questions of possible correlations and junctures between the rational and irrational in traditional and recent poetry'.[22] But it was the abstract and Cubist painters who sparked Jakobson's theoretical interests in the nature of the sign. Soon to become a member of the Moscow Linguistic Circle, he became acquainted with the Moscow abstract artists Sergei Bajdin and Isaak Kan and saw Cubist pictures by Picasso and Braque in the Moscow collection of Shchukin (he was taken there by Knave of Diamonds member Adolf Mil'man). He knew Mayakovsky, Filonov and Brik. But it was Jakobson's friendship with Malevich that played an especially important role. Already interested (like Kruchenykh) in the complementary roles played in poetry by signification and intonation, Jakobson relates how soon after their first meeting in 1913 Malevich 'was attracted by the fact that...I obstinately insisted on the avoidance of meaningful words in order to concentrate on the elementary components of the word, on the sounds of language in themselves...'.[23] Here, then, in *Woman at a Poster Column* and other Cubo-Futurist works we find sound-clusters (later called phonemes) as well as single or truncated words functioning alongside the colour-rectangles that were later to become the blocks and triangles of Suprematism. Malevich wrote to Mikhail Matiushin in 1916 about these 'phonic masses'. Freed from object-reference, he said, we can:

> tear the letter from its line...give it the possibility of free movement. Lines suit only the world of bureaucracy and domestic correspondence.... We came to the distribution of letter-sounds in space, just like Suprematism in painting. These phonic masses will be suspended in space and will produce for our consciousness the possibility of reaching ever further from Earth.[24]

Hence it is with the diverse phenomena of early Russian Futurism that Jakobson's interests in the cross-overs between poetry and visual art really begin.[25] In 1913 he had written to Kruchenykh, enthusing that his Futurist opera-play *Victory Over the Sun* had 'shattered' the pure glass of Symbolist poetry, leaving the way for new patterns to be made 'out of the splinters...in the name of liberation'.[26] Jakobson also tells of a visit to Matiushin's apartment in war-time Petrograd in 1914 or 1915 'where on the shelves and chests of drawers stood his sculptures. These were sculptures made from roots, from half-fossilised

opposite, above 27 **Varvara Stepanova** Fragment from her hand-made book *Gaust chaba*, 1919
Gaust chaba is a hand-made 'anti-book' of leaves of newspaper embellished with scrawled *za-um* words and pasted paper fragments: in Stepanova's words, 'breaking up the dead monotony of interconnected printed letters by means of painterly graphics.'

28 **Varvara Stepanova** Illustration for Kruchenykh's book *Gly-gly* 1918
The collage elements here are organized round a firm diagonal structure in a manner distinctive of the Russian avant-garde. Kruchenykh's book may not, in fact, have been published.

branches that he had found by the seashore, transrational sculptures, practically unworked'. 'Transrational' here refers to *za-um* (meaning 'beyond sense'), a preoccupation too of Malevich and Jakobson, who we know to have been writing transrational poems and declarations at the time (like Matiushin's sculptures, they are now lost). Jakobson also tells us how he and the painter David Burliuk would look at pictures together in the Hermitage, where Burliuk would play a game of imagining which Old Master pictures his friends might appear in: significantly, he assigned Jakobson to Rubens, whose drawings had often been cut-ups of his own or other painters' work.[27]

Constructivism: Rodchenko and Klutsis

Jakobson's anecdotes tell us too that cut-up, *za-um* and assemblage – not to mention *sdvig* and the shallow-planed relief – all functioned more or less simultaneously in war-time Russia as off-spring of a generic collage idea. Hence it comes as no particular surprise that by the time of Jakobson's 1919 essay 'Futurism', collage attracts no detailed comment: he simply records that Cubists are 'putting all kinds of things' into the surface of their paintings. By that time, of course, the Russian Revolution had taken place and the language of art was for ideological as well as pragmatic reasons becoming heavily politicized. Soon after October 1917 Aleksandr Rodchenko was identifying himself and other revolutionary artists with workers' culture: 'Our position is worse than the oppressed workers, since we are both workers for our own sustenance and creative artists at one and the same time', he announced. 'We have been opposed by the patrons, who forced us to carry out their whims…[But] we are proletarians of the brush!'[28] Virtually abandoning the brush as a drawing implement, Rodchenko did some planar paintings in 1918, whose aim was to articulate the plane by means of its colour-weight, form and interval from other planes: it was an experiment that reached its giddy climax at the Tenth State Exhibition, opening on 27 April 1919, 'Nonobjective Art and Suprematism'. 'Greetings to you all, comrades', write Rodchenko and his partner Varvara Stepanova on the occasion of the show, 'who fight for new ideas in art…. The Suprematists and Non-objectivists are the only true creators left on earth, playing with inventiveness as jugglers playing with balls…don't look back, but go forever onwards…. Objects died yesterday.'[29] Stepanova notes in her diary: 'In reality this exhibition is a contest between Anti [her pet name for Rodchenko] and Malevich, the rest are no good. Malevich has hung five white canvases, Anti black ones', the latter deriving their austere beauty and power, as Stepanova notes, 'from purely painterly effects without being obscured by incidental elements, not even colour…. In them he [Rodchenko] has demonstrated just what *faktura* is.'

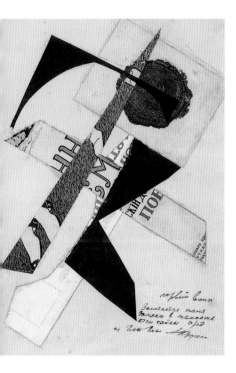

Stepanova's point is well-made: Rodchenko's black paintings show intersecting lozenges and arcs, all in differentiated degrees of black; from thick and dark to pale and evanescent. They constitute irreproachable proof that *faktura* could be achieved without 'depiction' and without associational, let alone descriptive, colour. 'There is nothing but painting in them', Stepanova notes correctly, 'and for this reason their *faktura* gains extraordinarily, it creates the impression that the work was painted with quite different materials. These lustrous, matt, flaky, uneven, smooth parts of the surface produce an extraordinarily powerful composition'.[30] But Stepanova was an artist in her own right: her own contribution to the exhibition consisted of new experiments in graphics and book-design, mostly dating from the year before. In the catalogue to 'Nonobjective Art and Suprematism' she writes in self-explanation: 'the new type of non-objective poetry, consisting of sound and typography, is combined in my works with painterly sensation, which fills the monotonous sounds of the verse with a new, live visual experience'. She refers to a series of 'sound books', *Zigra ar*, *Rtni khomle* and *Gaust chaba* (1919), in which *za-um* inventions are mixed with newsprint and (significantly) photo-fragments even more daringly than in Kruchenykh, as well as her illustrations for Kruchenykh's own book *Gly-gly* (1918) which deploy thin coloured papers (once more in armature style) to suggest dancing movements. Movement, words, sound and graphics are now being inventively mixed in what Stepanova sees as a crucial step towards 'a new art'.[31]

It took the example of Stepanova's boldness to spur Rodchenko finally to leap out of painting into construction. And for him, too, collage was the key, for it offered another strategy for opposing 'bourgeois' painting by taking real materials and placing them sharply and surprisingly in contrast. The fragments used for the half dozen or so small collages that Rodchenko made in 1919 create a self-supporting armature or 'spine', leaning to left or right and exemplifying on a desk-top scale the antinomies of old/new, distant/near, war/peace, past/present and colliding them within a format of connected, dissimilar forms. Within them one finds references to the war, envelopes, photos of a woman's head, elsewhere postcard views and commercial labels, and, in two or three of them (as here), entrance tickets for one of the several Knave of Diamonds exhibitions which had collected avant-garde energies several years before. Rodchenko's subtle conjunctions have transformed the dramas of Picassean still life with the daring announcement of a 'new world' of spatially and culturally disjoint elements, thrown into unfamiliar relations at the hands of the new artist-constructor. Indeed, Rodchenko and Stepanova's small mixed-media collages from 1918 and 1919 present the clearest possible expression in two dimensions of what the next year was to become Constructivism proper. 'All the former non-objectivists, now Constructivists or constructors, have begun to work *for* life and *in* life: the first task they set themselves was work on material structures', Rodchenko would write in the spring of 1921.[32] Originating in discussions within InKhuK's Objective Analysis Group, the so-called 'Programme of the Working Group of Constructivists', approved on 1 April 1921, began by 'setting itself the task of expressing the Communist idea in physical constructions according to...scientific Communism built on the theory of historical materialism'. The ideology of form would be based on the three principles, first of *tectonics*, or the functional use of industrial material; then *construction*, or the Communist functionality of tectonics; and finally *faktura*, now in the somewhat altered meaning of 'the conscious choice of material and its appropriate utilisation without impeding the dynamics of construction or of tectonics'. Aimed at the 'constructive realisation of projects, exhibitions, and establishing linkage with the Central Committees in charge of producing Communist forms of life', the declaration ends by valiantly criticizing the inadequacy of all past artistic culture and by 'declaring open war on art in general...the collective art of today is constructive life'.[33]

Then in 1923 comes Mayakovsky's epic poetic reverie *Pro Eto* (It), to which Rodchenko supplied a set of eight collateral collages of a very different kind. The two friends had collaborated on advertising posters the year before; and Mayakovsky's trip to Paris and Berlin in late 1922 had acquainted him with the wholesale recent shift from drawings to photos in a majority of commercial publications (a technical development we shall encounter again). In *Pro Eto*, for the first time, the unwavering use of same-size 'found' photographic fragments is abandoned, as Rodchenko buys himself an enlarger and commissions other photographers (notably Abram Shterenberg) to take photos of Mayakovsky and Lili Brik, which he then combines with the various colours and textures of photo-journalism and the background paper to form highly dispersed images both thematically and technically beyond the limits of Constructivism in its ideological form. The poem itself is a reverie on Mayakovsky and Lili Brik; it is shifting and restless, written during a period of voluntary separation undertaken in order to prevent their relationship settling into routine.[34] Its orthographic form is also new: no longer the *stolbik* (column) format but the highly novel *lesenka* (stepladder) formation in which lines are re-jigged by lowering successive portions into spaces below – thereby interrupting the grammar and producing emphatic breaks in the semantic flow.[35]

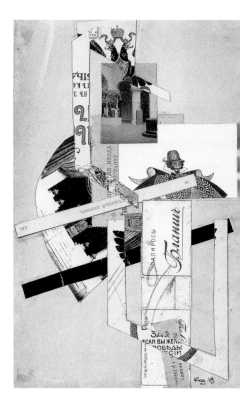

Significantly, too, Rodchenko's sources are *all* photographic: so we can distinguish for the first time perhaps between photo-collage (the actual maquette) and photomontage (the printed reproduction). The distinction is of general importance. A pupil of Malevich and hence for a time a Supremalist, the young Gustav Klutsis had seen *Woman at a Poster Column* and perhaps even Rodchenko's collages of 1919 before his own very early collage and montage experiments with photographs in the same year. He may also have known Berlin Dada (see Chapter 3).[36] Klutsis's *Dynamic City* of 1919 (the work was reproduced in the agitational journal *Izofront* in 1931) shows a cosmic disc onto which are placed rectangular and cubic structures resembling modern Constructivist-type architecture: they were probably intended to evoke the concrete wall-structures of American skyscrapers viewed as symbols of advanced technical rationality. In, or on, Klutsis's 'dynamic city' can just be seen the figures of three workmen, the class representatives of the new communist world. His even better-known design for *The Electrification of the Entire Country* poster of 1920 is again a circular cosmic structure with Lenin carrying what appears to be an electrical pylon, buildings attached, with his resounding electrification slogan on top. With the exception of Rodchenko's small works of 1919, it is perhaps the earliest Russian example to dramatically exploit the dynamic perspectives and changes of scale that arise out of conjoining previously distinct photographic fragments in a single design.

We are not overly concerned about priority; but Klutsis himself would see his incorporation of whole photographic fragments as announcing a broader discovery, one that would shortly be put into words in an early issue of the journal *LEF* (Left Front of the Arts). With covers and design layouts by Rodchenko, *LEF* from its 1923 beginnings became a platform for both the practice and theory of Constructivist photomontage – as it was now unequivocally called. *LEF* no. 4, for example, contains an unattributed article (it may be by Klutsis) explaining: 'By photomontage we mean the use of the photographic print as a *figurative* means. The combination of snapshots changes the composition of graphic images'. Here was a claim by Constructivists that photomontage had the means to combine 'content' with abstract design: It was also surely a statement that could placate the zealots of Soviet 'realist' easel painting, who since their conservative *Declaration* of 1922 had been attempting to relaunch nineteenth-century narrative painting with a Soviet theme.[37] For the avant-garde, on the other hand, it is a sudden and excited recognition that the new technology of the photograph has a direct relation to visual reality, that the viewer's recognition of this relation constructs a new and active relation to the image. *LEF* continues:

> The meaning of this change is that the photograph is not the drawing of a visual fact but the exact fixation of it. This precision and documentary quality give the photograph a power to influence the viewer that the drawn image is never able to attain.... An advertisement with a photograph of an object is more effective than a drawing. Photographs of cities, landscapes and faces give the viewer a thousand times more than paintings can of these subjects.

The author adds tellingly: 'Until recently...photographers assumed that the more a snapshot resembled a painting, the more artistic it was; in fact, the reverse is true: the more artistic, the worse it was'.[38]

3

Dada Dialectics

If 'construction' in some form was the goal of the French Cubists and Russian Constructivists, then a quite opposite impulse was at play in what came to be known as Dada. The political madness of the First World War was the main provocation that produced Dada and the Dada spirit: yet the combinatory methods of pasted paper were very similar to those of the Cubist phase. Furthermore, Dada collage and montage would have been impossible without Cubism. And Dada's links to Constructivism and eventually Surrealism make it pivotal in any understanding of modernism as a cultural force.

Zurich Collage: Hans Arp
In May 1915 a German revolutionary and writer in the Expressionist style called Hugo Ball arrived in Switzerland with his future wife Emmy Hennings. They travelled for a while in a variety troupe before placing an advertisement in the Zurich newspapers stating that: 'a group of young artists and writers has been formed with the idea of creating a centre for artistic entertainment. The idea of the cabaret is that visiting artists will hold musical recitals and readings at their daily meetings'. The name given to the cabaret was Voltaire: in Ball's words, 'the anti-poet, the king of jackanapes, prince of the superficial, anti-artist, preacher of the gate-keepers, the Papa Gigogne of the newspaper editors of the *siècle*'.[1]
In the rear room of a scruffy back-street bar called *Der Meierei* (The Dairy), Ball and his colleagues put on in the spring and summer of 1916 an impromptu mixture of acts: songs, a balalaika orchestra, a group of Dutch banjo and mandolin players, poetry readings and noisy declamations; Richard Huelsenbeck with his aggressive recitations, Tristan Tzara and Marcel Janco reading poems simultaneously, Negro chants, Bruitist poems, Laban dancers, drumming. In the high-speed prose of Tzara's 'Zurich Chronicle', published in Berlin in 1920:

> the dogs bay and the dissection of Panama on the piano and dock – shouted Poem – shouting and scuffles in the hall, first row approves second row declares itself incompetent the rest shout, who is the strongest, the big drum is brought in…the people protest shout smash windowpanes kill each other demolish fight here come the police interruption.[2]

32 **Raoul Hausmann** *Abstract Composition* 1918
Hausmann's brightly coloured painting with its unpainted areas and provisional construction is embellished with textual elements in many languages, implying an international range for the Dada impulse – at the same time retaining contact with an 'expressive' painting style.

Roman Jakobson, passing through Berlin en route for Prague in that year, confirms that Dadaists were above all eclectics: 'Not by chance was Dada born in a cabaret in Zurich: A little song of the Maoris takes turns with a Paris music-hall number, a sentimental lyric…"Nous voulons nous voulons nous voulons pisser en couleurs diverses", as Tzara said. "Me, I'm of many nationalities", says Picabia'.[5] Both accounts confirm Dada's liking for sensory overload – the remorseless piling up of sensations without reference to the distinctions between writing, painting, music, theatre and dance as separate arts. The collision of these forms in a chaotic interplay of free and raucous expression was entirely to Dada's purpose: 'an indefinable intoxication' was how Ball summarized it. The presence on the walls of the Cabaret Voltaire of works of visual art by Hans Arp, Marcel Slodki, Otto van Rees, Alberto Giacometti, Giorgio de Chirico, Amedeo Modigliani and Picasso, together with 'Negro sculptures' and children's art, worked to endorse that cacophonous assault and declare that 'representation' in the old manner was at an end. The eradication of the distance between the visual and the verbal was the other major principle that was important to Dada from the start. As in the Russian avant-garde, Dada poems were penned to be intoned emphatically from the written text:

> jolifanto bambla ô falli bambla
> grossiga m'pfa habla horem
> égiga goramen
> higo bloiko rusula huju
> hollaka hollala
> anlogo bung…

while the line-by-line switches of font in the printed version magnified the aleatory effect.[4]

Unlike Russian *za-um*, however, Zurich Dada had no theory other than its own love of nonsense, and little appetite for the primitive 'real'. Coming directly out of protest against the self-destruction of European humanism, Dada's very lack of interest in structure was its most powerful weapon as well as its greatest vulnerability. Perhaps adaptability was Dada's greatest asset: 'anti-everything' could function as a formula *both* as a slogan of protest applied haphazardly in a ludic and provocative fashion *and* as a move towards the occult. Take the early career of the young Hans Arp. Born in Strasbourg but soon a resident of Cologne, Arp had taken the train to Paris when Germany declared war on France in August 1914 in order to escape the military draft. Arriving with his brother in the French capital, he had become for a time caught up in Picasso's Montparnasse circle (where he must have seen *papiers collés*) as well as in the works of Jakob Böhme and Meister Eckhart, in the Theosophists, in drugs, and the taking of long walks at night in a city soon threatened by German attack. Arp and his friends rejected the technological civilization that from the Renaissance had exalted reason and above all the model of individual agency associated with 'great art'. We know that early in 1915 Arp used the dynamic formats of German Expressionism to create some diagonally composed paper collages (now lost), which his sister-in-law turned into embroideries, and that in the same year he was commissioned to produce mural decorations for the publishing house of the Paris periodical *Le Théosophie* (also lost, these were symmetrical designs of coloured paper, with curvilinear, flame-like forms). By November 1915 Arp and his brother had been accused of German espionage and had fled Paris for neutral Zurich. There, in the same month, he exhibited collages, drawings and textile designs at the Galerie Tanner, explaining in a catalogue that the works were 'structures of lines, forms and colours that attempt to achieve the infinite and the eternal – beyond the human realm. They are a denial of human egotism'.[5] To Tzara, who described the event, it was the first act of Zurich Dada and important for the 'uproar' it provoked for being 'neither art nor painting'.[6]

34 **Hans Arp** *Squares According to the Laws of Chance*
c. 1917
The removal of overt signs of human agency helps give the
appearance of paper fragments having arrived in the picture
all at once: simultaneity of effect then becomes the immediate
and striking index of 'chance'.

33 **Hans Arp** *Paper Picture (Construction with Planes and
Curves)* 1915
The relative anonymity of cuts of wallpaper and printed fabric
provided Arp with his escape from 'egotism' at the same time
as asserting colour and form *per se*: these collages have no
immediate anthropomorphic reference.

Arp's early creations were certainly compatible with the non-materialistic emphases of
the Cabaret Voltaire, where we find him two months later in the company of Huelsenbeck,
Hennings, Tzara and Janco. 'Despite the booming of remote artillery', Arp recollected, 'we
sang, painted, pasted, and wrote poetry with all our might and main. We were seeking an
elementary art to cure man of the frenzy of the times and a new order to restore the
balance between heaven and hell'.[7] Yet one observer noted that Arp remained at a distance
from the more rowdy events. Upset by the anti-German rhetoric of the Huelsenbeck group,
in a new set of collages based on the laws of chance he sought contact with the spirit of the
Chinese philosophy of Lao-Tzu: as Hans Richter reported, 'Arp had been working on a
drawing in his atelier…. Dissatisfied, the finally tore up the page and dropped the tatters on
the floor…somewhat later, he was surprised by their arrangement: it expressed precisely
what he had vainly attempted to achieve the whole time'.[8] Georges Hugnet gives a different
account: Arp 'put on a piece of cardboard pieces of paper that he had cut at random and
then coloured' before shaking the cardboard and pasting the scraps just as they were.[9]
Either way, Arp's idea was to produce works of trans-personal significance whose self-
created nature was expressive of a 'cosmic' principle, a point of mergence between object
and subject. 'We [Dadaists] sought an anonymous and collective art…', he wrote later, 'we
rejected all mimesis and description, giving free reign to the Elementary and Spontaneous.'
Chance was 'simply a part of an inexplicable reason, of an inaccessible order'.[10] And while
the resulting works were almost certainly 'adjusted' to meet certain formal requirements
(alignment, proximity, orientation), an appearance of randomness had perhaps been
achieved. There followed in 1917 and 1918 a set of almost regular grids of coloured paper
rectangles made jointly with Sophie Täuber, which expelled agency from the work by a
different route. Arp wrote of this group: 'Any element of chance was eliminated…for [these]
paper pictures we even discarded scissors, which all too readily betrayed the life of the
hand. We used a paper cutter instead…. I would like to call these works the art of silence.
It rejects the exterior world and turns towards stillness, inner being, and reality.' For Arp,
stillness was the route to a different reality. 'With rectangles and squares we built radiant
monuments to deepest sorrow and loftiest joy. We wanted our works to simplify and
transform the world and make it beautiful'[11] – a statement which foreshadows what Arp
was later to call 'concrete' art. But by this time Dada was spreading from Zurich to several
other cities. Indeed, early in 1917 the fiery and eloquent Huelsenbeck had travelled with
news of Dada to a city already receptive to revolution amid the detritus of war: Berlin.

Berlin: Towards the International Dada Fair
Huelsenbeck had performed in the city before, when in April 1915 he had read some
'Negro' poems there with Hugo Ball. By the time of his lecture of 22 January 1918 the ever-
active Huelsenbeck had brought together George Grosz, John Heartfield (he Americanized
his name from Helmut Herzfelde in 1915 in protest at German war policy) and his
publisher brother Wieland Herzfelde – all leftists associated with the magazine *Neue
Jugend* – with Franz Jung, Raoul Hausmann and Johannes Baader from the group around
Die freie Strasse. In the lecture Huelsenbeck announced a decisive break with Cubism,
Futurism and even the antics of the Zurich cabaret. 'It was a witches' Sabbath', he said, 'the
likes of which you cannot imagine, a hullabaloo from morning to night, a frenzy of kettle-
drums and tom-toms, an ecstasy of two-step and Cubist dances.' He also claimed that Dada
in Zurich was 'pro-war and Dadaism is still pro-war today. Collisions are necessary: things
are still not cruel enough'. He lists Tzara's simultaneous poems, his own vowel concerts
and Bruitist poems as examples of the 'collisions' he wanted the Berlin group to develop.
'We were fed up with Cubism', he adds pointedly. 'Dadaism has superseded the elements of
Futurism and the theorems of Cubism'. What was Dada to become, Huelsenbeck asks? It
should include 'real characters, people of destiny with a capacity for living. People with a

honed intellect, who understand they are facing a turning-point in history. It is a single step away from politics.'[12]

That association with politics was quickly guaranteed by the turn of events. The abdication of Willhelm II at the moment of Germany's defeat late in 1918 led to two main power bases in the closing months of 1918 and the beginning of 1919: the Social Democratic Party under Ebert and Scheidermann, and the far-left Spartacus League headed by Karl Liebknecht and Rosa Luxembourg. Strikes and street fighting between these and other left-wing groups presented the appearance of a virtual civil war, with Social Democrats generally forced into uncomfortable alliances with residual Wilhelmine elites to produce a turbulent atmosphere of political diversity mixed with economic chaos and, with the announcement of the Versailles Peace terms in August 1919, a sense of national shame. Already by the time the new Republic was launched in November 1918, Huelsenbeck together with Hausmann, Hausmann's girlfriend Hannah Höch, Grosz, Heartfield and Baader had formed a political platform based on social revolution and the overthrow of Social Democracy and the old bourgeoisie alike.

It was in this formation that collage was set to achieve its first explicitly political orientation. Of significance here was the ability of found material to generate metaphor, but very differently from Cubism. 'In Dada you will recognise your own true condition', wrote Hausmann in his *Synthetic Cino of Painting* pamphlet of 1918: 'Wonderful constellations in real materials, wire, glass, cardboard, textiles are the organic equivalents of your own complete brittleness, your own shoddiness'. 'Mankind is simultaneity,' he wrote in the same pamphlet, 'a monster of proper and improper parts, now, before, after and all at once.... Mankind's discovery of its enormous potential for experience is unfolding. Uncovering our psycho-sexual nature, we no longer need the ethical pirouettes of "art". Dada offers an incredible refreshment, an impulse to experience all possible relationships.'[13] Yet that same inclusiveness meant a life of hectic activity. Richard Huelsenbeck again: 'A Dadaist...can fling away his individuality like a lasso – and is resigned to the realization that the world at once and the same time includes Mohammedans, Zwinglians, fifth-formers, Anabaptists, pacifists, etc.'

Resigned (then) to the delirious motley of the world, the Dadaist according to Huelsenbeck is one who believes that all patterns of coherence have ended: 'You walk aimlessly along, devising a philosophy for supper, but before you have it ready, the postman brings you news that your pigs have died of rabies, your dinner jacket has been thrown off the Eiffel Tower, and your housekeeper has come down with the epizootic' – the bourgeois consciousness suddenly thrown asunder by a blizzard of information, by events. And Dada's radical heteronymy was convertible into verbal monstrosity: 'The bartender in the Manhattan bar who pours out Curaçao with one hand and fondles his gonorrhea with the other is a Dadaist'. Or as a general principle: 'The Dadaist is a man who has fully understood that one is entitled to have ideas only if one can transform them into life: he is a man of the completely active type, who lives only through action...'.[14] Dada collage and montage premised an extraordinarily inclusive attitude to the new media realities and their possible recombinations. While Arp's Zurich technique had aimed to transcend materiality, in Berlin the material to be used was from the very fabric of the new bourgeois life: magazine and newspaper photographs, advertising imagery, slogans – all now quickly readied for use *against* the bourgeoisie by the simple expedients of cutting, mixing and recombination in a variety of licentious, provocative ways. As Hans Richter said later, 'Berlin added a new dimension [to Zurich collage]: the "alienation" of photography.'[15]

That use of photographic fragments marked a watershed – semantically, aesthetically, politically. From the beginning, Dada montages (they used the word *montieren*, 'to fit', 'assemble') were designed to say in images what could not legally be said in words – or what would not easily escape the censorship of wartime. We can well believe John

Heartfield's claim that he began cutting and pasting photo-images in the trenches as early as 1915 – before he feigned illness to get himself removed from military service. This is the slightly different version that George Grosz tells:

> In 1916…Johnny Heartfield and I invented photomontage in my studio at the south end of town at five o'clock one May morning.… On a piece of cardboard we pasted a mish-mash of advertisements for hernia belts, students' song-books and dog food, labels from schnapps and wine-bottles, and photographs from picture papers, cut up at will in such a way as to say in pictures what would have been banned by the censors if we had said it in words. In this way we made postcards supposed to have been sent home from the front, or from home to the front.[16]

In 1918 Heartfield, his brother Wieland and George Grosz all joined the Berlin Club Dada with Huelsenbeck and became members of the German Communist Party. But it was not until the following year that they launched the political magazine *Die Pleite* (Bankruptcy) and energetically began to convert their inflammatory war-time jokes into a technique of negative art. The Grosz–Heartfield partnership produced a number of futuristically 'dynamic' compositions either yearning for American life (as in *Dadamerika* of 1919) or ironizing the heroism of military action and the hypocritical humanistic culture of old – as in the vortex-like *The Sunny Land*, also of 1919, a visual merry-go-round of incongruously overlapping images of German bourgeois life underscored by a mocking title. By his own rhetoric Heartfield was by now a new kind of artist. Having thrown all his youthful paintings away in 1915 at the time of his first montage discoveries, he could now style himself 'Der Monteurdada' in order to canonize the new role that he and Hausmann had devised for themselves. 'We called this process "photomontage"', said the latter, 'because it embodied our refusal to play the part of artist. We regarded ourselves as engineers, and our work as construction: we *assembled* [*montieren*] our work, like a fitter'.[17] *Klebebild* (glue-picture) was the term the Berlin Dadaists sometimes preferred.[18]

The new terminology mattered a great deal. *Papier collé* was perceived as too dainty a term – and too French. It suggested flat paper materials in the service of art, whereas Dada was concerned with art's cancellation and reversal, pending its continuation by other means. Raoul Hausmann meanwhile was producing his own merry-go-round images that combined headline fragments with a Dada repertoire of machine-parts, fashion plates and news photos. He had already done some large-scale easel paintings with scraps of newsprint and advertising attached [*32*]. Interestingly, Hausmann also claims to have invented photomontage, while on holiday with Hannah Höch in the Baltic, where he saw a framed oleograph of the Kaiser, his ancestors, his descendants, a young soldier, and the face of his landlord, all pasted in.[19] 'There, in the midst of his superiors, stood the young soldier, erect and proud amid the pomp and splendour of this world', reports Richter; 'This paradoxical situation aroused Hausmann's perennial aggressive streak'.[20] Back in Berlin, Hausmann made heads composed of typographic fragments and designed covers for some issues of *Der Dada*, beginning in June 1919, as well as the major set-pieces for which he is well-known – among them *The Art Critic* (1919–20), and *Elasticum* of 1920 [*36*], a work which, though often described as a 'collage' today, in fact owes little to the *papier collé* past. More accurately, it mounts a face, machine-parts, explosive letter-combinations and slang expressions like 'Pipicabia', 'popocabia' and 'merde', in the manner of the Futurist sound-poems Hausmann had made earlier with Johannes Baader. The technique is to 'mount' nearly-complete images against each other in the manner of a commercial advertisement gone seriously awry. Some historians have traced the technique's origins to late nineteenth-century forms such as the postcard, the family album or the *carte-de-visite*,[21] but in Dada's reinvention photo-fragments functioned as witness of the contemporary urban life.

osz-Heartfield mont.   Sonniges Land

5 George Grosz and John Heartfield *The Sunny Land* 1919
The collage combines dozens of obvious and obscure topical references from contemporary politics, culture and society – which the eye notices or passes over in entirely unpredictable ways. 'Away with these worker-councils!', reads one headline near the centre.

36 **Raoul Hausmann** *Elasticum* 1920
Contemporary automobile parts functioned importantly in the
Dada *Klebebild*, both as celebration of impersonal dynamic
energy, but also as a satire on the figurative tradition in art.
The French artist Francis Picabia, referred to twice here, had
recently taunted the Cubists with scandalous mechanical
analogies of his own.

Indexing the world directly, they lent themselves to dangerous political metaphorization through the devices of ribald or offensive juxtaposition. Cubism was never so daringly referential.

Yet the attentive reader will have noticed that Dada's relation to Cubist collage was dialectical, at least – notwithstanding Huelsenbeck's vigorous offensive against it. Hausmann especially took pains to organize his images pictorially: they still, in some sense, needed to be art. The spacing and intervals of Grosz and Heartfield's otherwise anarchic *The Sunny Land* are also carefully considered, even precise. An exception perhaps can be seen in the off-centre emphases of their *Life and Times in Universal City at 12.05 Noon* of c. 1919, a vortex of gyrating energy which foreshadows many another modernist composition based on the rushing visual information of a city street: in this case cinema, traffic, skyscrapers and showbiz headlines – in short, America. On the other hand even the most anarchic of Hausmann's images, say the *Dada Cino* of 1920, turns the explosive side of Futurist composition back into an almost classicizing image: its internal vectors seem to guide the eye always back towards the central diagonal armatures that anchor the viewer's gaze (notice the small rectangular base bearing Hausmann's name).

The public life of Dada needed a measure of anarchy, admittedly. This at least is clear from the angry cacophony institutionalized at the First International Dada Fair, held at 13 Lutzowufer in June and July 1920 and best seen as the climax of Berlin Dada in its most publicity-hungry mood [*39*]. All of the Berlin group, as well as Ernst, Arp, Picabia and Baargeld were included. By now Cubism and Futurism were definitely objects of ridicule: Grosz and Heartfield contrived two 'corrected' masterpieces – for one of which they took a reproduction of Picasso's *Head of a Girl* of the spring of 1913, turned it upside down and pasted image-fragments and the words 'Grosz' and 'Vollendete Kunst' (perfectly finished art) on top. Reproduced in the Fair's catalogue, a text nearby by Wieland Herzfelde explains that Cubism (along with Expressionism and Futurism) were all attempts to 'deny the factual'. Dadaists by contrast are saying: 'We now need only to take scissors and cut out what we need from among the paintings and photographic depictions of...things.' Above all: 'to produce pictures is no big deal' (since reproductions and found objects will do).[22] To pair Picasso's 'corrected' masterpiece they contrived another: on top of Henri Rousseau's painted *Self-Portrait*, Heartfield pasted his photographic own, adding a lace frill and other

bourgeois accoutrements.[23] In this its most scurrilous form Dada's new technique was pictorial in the simplest and crudest way: in line with the crowded *mise-en-scène* of the Fair, it had embraced the parodic spontaneity of the music-hall for its most caustic and provocative effects.

Enter Kurt Schwitters

A notable absence from the first Dada fair was the great Hanover artist Kurt Schwitters. Shortly after the end of Berlin Dada he wrote in a magazine, 'I compared Dadaism in its most serious form with *Merz*, and came to this conclusion: whereas Dadaism merely poses antitheses, *Merz* reconciles antitheses by assigning relative values to every element in the work of art. Pure *Merz* is art, pure Dadaism is non-art; in both cases deliberately so.'[24] The factors that underpinned this stand-off are seminal to the evolution of collage practice and indeed to all of subsequent modernism. Until 1917 Schwitters had been an expressionist painter. By 1918, however, paintings such as *Abstraction 9: The Bow Tie* are already showing signs of departing from the agitated, politicized expressions of the Der Sturm group (formed around Herwarth Walden in Berlin) that Schwitters had joined in that year. For though Der Sturm was a good home for Schwitters in view of his interests in poetry and publishing, we find his new paintings pushing in other directions: towards abstraction (an actual bow-tie, for example, is all but invisible) but equally towards the real matter of the picture surface, or even beyond the surface into actual physical space. As Schwitters wrote later of these saliences, 'the individual and specialised observation of nature…gives way to an increasingly objective and theoretical study of the picture and its laws.'[25]

The decisive break came in the latter part of 1918. Coinciding with the Armistice, the abdication of Wilhelm II, the announcement of the new Republic and the outbreak of the November Revolution, something clearly snapped in him. 'I felt myself freed', Schwitters wrote later of this epiphany, 'and wanted to shout my jubilation to the world…. One can shout with rubbish…. Everything had broken down in any case and new things had to be made out of the fragments.'[26] But what is the identity of these things? The paper pictures and shallow relief constructions that he now began to make used all kinds of detritus picked up on the street, but had no name, no category. Some contain passages of paint, and some refer glancingly to the chaotic political landscape of 1919, but generally they make

39 Opening of the First International Dada Fair, Burchard Gallery, Berlin, June 1920
This photograph of the opening on 5 June 1920 shows Hausmann, Höch (seated), Dr Burchard, Johannes Baader, Wieland Herzfelde and his wife, Grosz's brother-in-law, Grosz himself, and John Heartfield.

40 **Kurt Schwitters** *Abstraction 9: The Bow Tie* 1918
Here Schwitters expands the motif of the bow tie to a scale where its significance becomes overtaken by what Schwitters called 'pictorial problems', departing radically from representing nature in order to attain expression. The painting is some 74 centimetres (29 inches) high.

no explicit comment on it. The physically large *The Worker Picture* of 1919 [*41*], for example, is dominated by circular wooden or metal forms and a passable semblance of connecting rods – much like the interior of a clock – and yet *Arbeiter* ('worker') pasted in small red letters on the large circle at the top could as easily refer to the male world of the factory bench, as to the government crushing of the Bavarian Soviet on 1 and 2 May.[27] The scraps were collected according to a certain principle. Schwitters' method consisted of scouring the streets of Hanover, returning to his home in the Waldhauenstrasse with bags and pockets full of strips of wood, wire mesh, metal plates, scraps of card, cloth, or the odd mechanical part. More inclusive than the carefully selected fragments of Parisian *papiers collés*, Schwitters staged a kind of joyous descent into the material residuum of the gutter and the dustbin; fields that in Roger Cardinal's phrase were 'as fertile as they were disgusting'.[28] Such remnants could be read as the city's version of nature: *dejecta* that could be reassembled in the studio into something like an organic picture-object that echoed urban realities. Or – to attempt another explanation – such obsessive collecting and assembling looks psychologically like an effort to reintegrate the fragments of a shattered personal world: he had been traumatized in childhood when a garden he had made was destroyed before his eyes by local children.[29] Viewed still more widely, Schwitters' *bricolage* posture (in common with Picasso's) can be traced to the rag-picker motif in Baudelaire, to the modern man or woman as a celebrant of 'the ephemeral, the fugitive, and the contingent' in modernity.[30]

However judged, it is a measure of Schwitters' originality as well as his skill at self-promotion that from 1918 to about 1921 he managed to maintain two footholds in Berlin art circles, one in the Der Sturm camp and one in Berlin Dada: and the two groups were deeply opposed to one another. Der Sturm provided Schwitters with an exhibiting base; but it was the object of explicit attack in Huelsenbeck's 'First Dada Manifesto' of April 1918. Expressionist painters and their works, he declared, had

> a hatred of the press, a hatred of advertising, a hatred of sensationalism…[they] find their armchairs more important than the din of the streets…[whereas] the word 'Dada' symbolises the most primitive relation to surrounding reality. Life appears as a simultaneous confusion of noise, colours and spiritual rhythms…Dada demands the use of *new materials in painting* – a piece of cloth rips between one's fingers, one says yes to a life wishing to elevate itself by negation. Affirmation-negation: the gigantic hocus-pocus of being fires the nerves of the true Dadaist.

'Expressionism wanted inwardness', Huelsenbeck complained, 'while Dadaism is nothing but an expression of the times'.[31] Schwitters must have been attracted to at least some of this rhetoric. Yet Berlin Dada was inexorably different. 'I am a painter and I nail my pictures together', Schwitters is reported to have told Hausmann at their first meeting late in 1918. The next day, the Dada General Council met to discuss – among other things – Schwitters' application to join Club Dada. Huelsenbeck, who had already got to know Schwitters and had taken an aversion to him, turned him down.

The event is significant because it confirmed in Schwitters a sense that his early constructions and assemblages – which Huelsenbeck at the time might not even have seen – were truly aligned *neither* with Der Sturm *nor* with Dada. It is the best explanation for Schwitters' choice of a new concept, *Merz*, to describe his work when it was shown at Der Sturm in July 1919. Like Heartfield, he knew he could improve upon the terminology of *papier collé*.[32] As Schwitters himself explained, *Merz* as a word-fragment first came from *Kommerz* as it appeared in one of his works.: it might refer to the products of low-level commerce that Schwitters found in the gutter – or to the fact that these elements 'do commerce' with each other in the fabrication of the works. *Merz* as a part of the verb *ausmerzen* (to eradicate, expel) might be linked with the fact that those fragments have been thrown away or rejected, that at the point of recovery they are valueless, commerce-free. *Merz* also rhymes temptingly with *Schmerz* (pain). In Schwitters' own words of that July:

> The word *Merz* denotes essentially the combination of all conceivable materials for artistic purposes, and technically the principle of equal evaluation of the individual materials. *Merzmalerei* [*Merz* painting] makes use not only of paint and canvas, brush and palette, but all materials perceptible to the eye and of all required implements. Moreover it is unimportant whether or not the material used was already formed for some purpose or other. A perambulator wheel, wire netting, string and cotton wool are factors having equal rights with paint.... The metamorphosis of materials can be produced by their distribution over the picture surface. This can be reinforced by dividing, deforming, overlapping, or painting over. In *Merzmalerei* the box top, playing card and newspaper clipping become surfaces; string, brushstroke and pencil stroke become line; wire-netting becomes overpainting, pasted-on greaseproof paper becomes varnish, cotton becomes softness...[33]

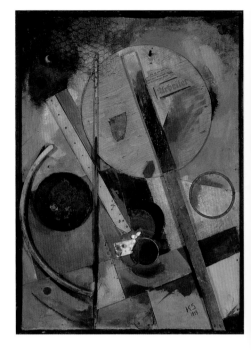

41 **Kurt Schwitters** *The Worker Picture* 1919
The word 'Arbeiter' (worker) may refer to the work of the picture maker as much as to the mechanism of the picture: Schwitters' refuse-gathering activity was new to art, as was his method of picture construction.

42 **Kurt Schwitters** *Merz 19* 1920
These subtle yet tough-minded smaller works, assembled while the paper is still wet, place commercial labels and other contemporary typefaces in a new framework of visibility, grand enough in its conception to inspire larger works.

Over the rest of his life Schwitters made some four thousand *Merz* drawings and pictures, and about an equal number of oil paintings.[34] In the larger *Merz* pictures such as *The Worker Picture* we saw how materials belonging to a single volatility (unbending materials like card or wood or metal) are assembled to provide an image of the almost flat surfaces of everyday labour in the workshop or the home. The very small *Merz* drawings, on the other hand, create a more abstract microcosm, galactic in scale despite being only a few inches square, out of surfaces made of wrapping-paper, card and other creatural fabrics assembled wet-against-wet in a sort of slippery mosh before being set aside to dry.[35]

Schwitters' third technique is abruptly juxtapositional: in *Merz 151: The Knave Child* (*Das Wenzelkind*) of 1921, an upright reproduction of Raphael's *Sistine Madonna* is startlingly overlaid by a modish young woman's head from a fashion plate and by a numbered machine diagram. The textual fragments above and below read: *Amerika ist angenehm berührt* (America is pleasantly touched), and *Gedankenvoll liess Viktor das Blatt sinken* (thoughtfully Viktor let the page fall), and small insertions referring to sport (a racehorse) and money (3 Pfennigs). Here, overt meanings are 'played off' against one another by image-substitution and interruption, in this case pointing provocatively to America as the new culture of the modern by gently alliterative means, as in a waking fantasy or a dream. A kind of mockery is taking place: to stick a modern fashion plate over Raphael's Madonna is to talk about the eclipse of piety by modishness (for better or worse). To have Saint Barbara (patron saint of soldiers) glance down at a piece of up-ended machinery rather than the pair of mischievous *putti* in the middle is to abuse holy sentiment in the name of modern irony. It is all amusingly nonsensical, but respectful too. The more salient fact perhaps lies in the technical and semantic distance of *Merz 151* from Cubist *papiers collés*: we are seeing Schwitters like other Dadaists constructing metaphors out of similar yet dissimilar units – a technique soon refined by the Surrealists – except that Schwitters typically has no political satire in mind, no social programme to pursue.

And that may *be* the point, for very few of Schwitters' works use language.[36] More generally, Schwitters' practice was to use materials or images less to refer them back to their real-world use than to counterpose them one against the other inside the pictorial frame. Indeed, throughout 1920 and 1921 Schwitters ranges across many moods both light and dark, geometric and irregular, topical and abstract; in fact with such elegance and profligacy as to force us to locate a common impulse not in his political allegiances nor in

op 43 **Kurt Schwitters** *Merz 151: The Knave Child* 1921
Schwitters pays homage to the Renaissance painting tradition
while at the same time corrupting it with fragments of
modernity which are his own. The piece of machinery at the
base is not contemporary, but from an older manual, perhaps
from the late nineteenth century.

44 **Kurt Schwitters** *Forms in Space* 1920
Another very small work, this *Merz* drawing constructs visual
analogies between printed type, including numbers and prices,
and the textures of fabric – all of which float diagonally, as in
a Suprematist work.

his occasional indebtedness to another artist, such as Arp or Malevich (the title of the *Merz* drawing *Forms in Space* seems to be an homage to Suprematist ideas) but in the spirit of a battered wartime culture, reassembled in discovery, beatitude or play. And the word 'beatitude' is to be taken at face value here: as Schwitters said, 'I felt myself free...and had to shout my jubilation to the world'. Meanwhile, the verticality of the easel painting had been redesigned as a picture-object that has been pressed flat on a table surface and only secondarily raised up vertically as an object of sight. The aim finally was to produce works of art that belonged to no literary or visual or theatrical or architectural category – and yet belonged to them all. 'My aim is the *Merz* composite work of art that embraces all branches of art in an artistic unit', says Schwitters: 'I drove nails into pictures in such a way as to produce a plastic relief aside from the pictorial quality of the painting. I did this in order to efface the boundaries between the arts.... At some future date perhaps we shall witness the birth of the *Merz* composite work of art, [but] we cannot create it, for we ourselves would only be parts of it. In fact we would be mere material.'[37]

The World of Hannah Höch

Hannah (she was born Anna) Höch had made pasted paper collages as a child, some time before registering as a student at the School of the Royal Museum of Applied Arts in Berlin (where George Grosz was also a pupil from 1915 to 1917). A little later she worked part-time in the handiwork division of the Ullstein Press making embroidery and dress designs for publications like *Die Dame* (The Lady) and *Die Praktische Berlinerin* (Practical Berlin Woman), two of the many photo-illustrated periodicals whose production Ullstein had pioneered. Such details are important in establishing Höch as temperamentally and by avocation a designer as much as an artist, and for lending support to the proposition that the Dada *Klebebilder* for which she is best known form only part of a much larger output. But it was through her largely destructive relationship with Hausmann (two abortions on her part and a string of broken promises on his) that she became caught up in the activities of Berlin Dada. It was after a row with Hausmann that she refused to take part in the first Dada-*soirée* in April 1918 at which Huelsenbeck read from his manifesto, Hausmann read from his 'The New Material of Painting', and Grosz bounced a football off the heads of his audience.[38] Given that history, the 'discovery' of montaged oleographs on the Baltic trip with Hausmann in August 1918 marks only a resumption by Höch of the collage method she had practised years before: soon, like Eva Gouel and Fernande Olivier before her, she would bring to the fine arts a flair for dress design based on paper patterns and cutting. Furthermore Höch had strong enough political convictions to join the revolutionary Novembergruppe at the end of 1918 – though not, like Grosz, Heartfield and Baader, the Communist party. Höch spoke later of the 'feeling of alienation' that afflicted the Dada group between 1917 and 1922: 'We were living in a world that nobody with any sensitivity could accept or approve'. Being allied with Communism or becoming a Communist was at least a gesture of support for pacifism, and for a set of doctrines they could hope promised 'a better future, a more equitable distribution of wealth, leisure, and power. We really believed', said Höch later, 'in the slogans of the Communists.'[39]

We assume then that Höch must have done Dada *Klebebilder* from late 1918, but the dozen or so earliest works that survive are from 1919, a year in which she also exhibited some abstract watercolours and published a short story.[40] Yet it must be partly due to the breadth of her talent that Höch's commitment to Dada was reckoned too tentative by Heartfield and Grosz, and it was only through Hausmann's intercession that she was eventually included in the First International Dada Fair, with eight works including her Dada-dolls, a work of 1919 entitled *Dada Panorama* [45] and the large and well-known *Cut With the Kitchen Knife Dada through the Last Weimar Beer-Belly Cultural Epoch of Germany* (1919–20).[41]

The question is how these photomontages were or should be read. Instant recognition of at least some of the visual jokes and caricatures must have been common at the time. Indeed, critics have exhausted whole books identifying the dozens of personages, photographs and floating semantic units that populate Höch's montages: here, for example, is a recent description of the *Dada Panorama* piece:

> Photographic fragments of mass demonstrations at the left, bottom and right edges reference the widespread nationalist opposition to the terms of the peace [of Versailles], while the newly emerging political order is parodied with ludicrous images of Reich President Friedrich Ebert and Defence Minister Gustav Noske in bathing suits…. By appending military boots to Ebert's figure and including, in the lower corner, a well-known image of a soldier atop the Brandenburg Gate during the brutal government suppression of the Spartacist revolt, Höch connects the representatives of the new, supposedly democratic Republic to the old militaristic order of the Empire, referenced at the lower left by a row of uniformed officers standing stiffly to attention.[42]

And yet the excited ambience of Dada must have worked against too systematic a reading. Visual formalities surely play a part too. For though sprinkled with obligatory Dada photo-portraits and word-fragments, both works marvellously combine two visual devices which are always deployed effectively in Höch's work. The first involves a renunciation of the Futurist vortex which makes visual elements swirl about centripetally and which is more typical of Hausmann or the early Heartfield: Höch favours a stabilizing grid which anchors the pictorial elements in an organizing framework of rectangles, sections, and planes. Secondly, Höch uses the child-like device of replacement (superposition), which functions to burlesque a given image by placing the wrong head on the wrong body, reversing or inverting the head, or detaching it altogether. While contemporary in their range of references, it is clear that Höch's montages are grounded in her pictorial and formal skills, and most display a far more elegant colour range than can be found in Hausmann or Heartfield. We can appreciate Höch's independence relative to the male Dadas by looking at *Dada-Ernst* (1920–1), with its sexual references, its air of glamour, its interest in clothing and revelation of the body; or *Untitled* of 1921 in which the Russian dancer Claudia Pavlova's image from the June 1921 issue of *Die Dame* is shockingly replaced by a pensive female gaze, a pointing male figure, machine parts and a sewing pattern which looks like a satire on the unequally gendered mechanization of labour in the post-war world. Both these and other early works register Höch's life-long concerns: the war between the genders (her battles with Hausmann), the feminine mask (culture versus nature), and the trans-gendered individual. Her later works returned insistently to the achievements of the Dada years.

Yet after the climactic summer of 1920 Höch felt increasingly free to strike out along independent paths. She left the hypocritical Hausmann in 1922 and liberated herself from subservience to Dada ethics and methodology, moving closer to Schwitters in the process. Indeed, so sympathetic was she to the method of *Merz* organicism that she helped build the first two grottos of the Hanover Merzbau that Schwitters spent from 1923 to 1937 constructing inside his home in the Waldhauenstrasse.[43] And it was through Schwitters that she met Arp, the Hungarian Constructivist Vilmos Huszár, and virtually the entire artistic population of Bauhaus Weimar and Surrealist Paris, not to mention the Punis from Russia, the van Doesburgs from Holland, and in 1926 the Dutch poet Til Brugman, with whom she had a close personal relationship until 1935–6. Like many Constructivists, Bauhaus artists and Surrealists, Höch's commitment to textile design, oil painting, short-story writing, poetry and stage design for avant-garde theatre (the latter with Schwitters) was almost natural: her *Klebebilder* formed just one peak of this impressive mountain of activity.

45 **Hannah Höch** *Dada Panorama* 1919
Other characters who appear in the Panorama include the American president Woodrow Wilson, and Anna von Giercke, elected to the National Assembly in 1919. Near the lower edge appear the words 'schrankenlose freiheit für H.H' (unlimited freedom for H[annah] H[öch]).

46 **Hannah Höch** *Dada-Ernst* 1920–1
Dada-Ernst can mean 'Dada serious' as well as alluding to Max Ernst, at this time based in Cologne. The image of the open legs with an eye pasted in the position of the vulva is one of the most undisguised sexual references in all modern art.

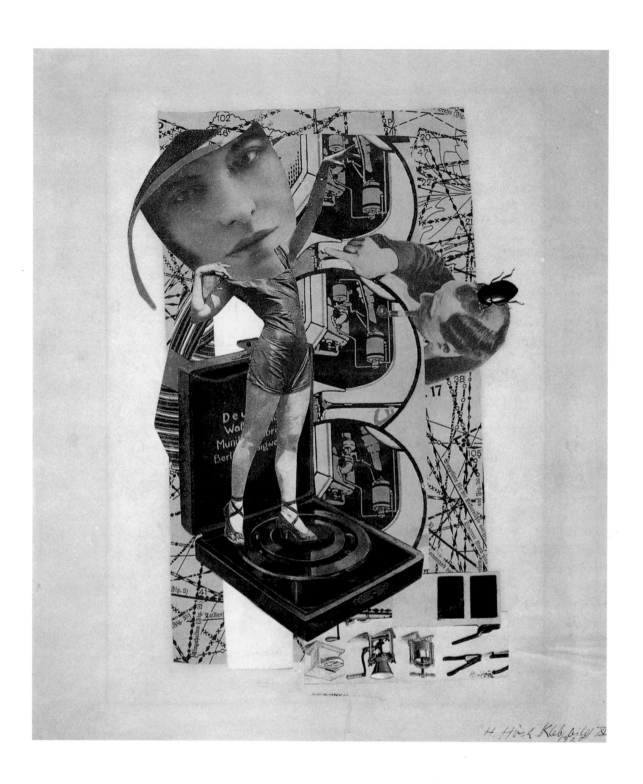

47 Hannah Höch *Untitled* 1921
The glamorous Pavlova is here placed in a crowded context
which includes a ball-bearing case, up-ended diagrams of
machinery, domestic utensils, and strangest of all, a pipe-
smoking man pictured from above with a beetle on his head:
the background pattern refers to Höch's work as a dress
designer.

4

Legacies of the Dada Mind

Dada's motivated use of worthless, expendable materials, the off-cuts and detritus of the modern world, the contingent comings-together of high and low, revered and useless, old and new, had several legacies, the first of which was the dazzling experiment known as Surrealism. Of late, it has become customary to locate Surrealism not in the 'high' arts of painting or sculpture, but in photography, magazine publication, theatre, performance or literature. Simultaneously, fresh attention has been paid to the psychoanalytical ideas out of which Surrealism was sometimes made – the dissection and exposure of a 'haunted self', in the words of a recent book.[1] In this double process, montage as a method of combining materials – one that echoes Lautréamont's description of 'the marvellous' as 'the chance meeting on a dissecting table of a sewing machine and an umbrella' – has been forced to take a back seat. Yet Lautréamont's formula is already both a verbal collage and an image which can be visualized in a collage-type way. It is an image, too, that is loaded with sexual meanings and hence a perfect one with which to ground the Surrealists' revolutionary attempts to 'unbind' the pathways of desire. Hence to understand how painting after Dada was given a new lease of life by the devices of folded, torn, cut and pasted paper, is to move beyond reading 'content' out of particular scenes, as if those scenes were texts and nothing more. It is to witness the grounding of a 'second' modernism standing foursquare against Cubism, and it is to raise the question how, if at all, the two streams of inquiry could be thought together – how 'modern art' could exist as one thing. Constructivism, too, as we shall see later on, would benefit from the Dada experiment.

Dada in Cologne: Ernst and Baargeld
In the years when Cubism was being elaborated in Paris, Céret and Sorgues, Max Ernst was a student at the University of Bonn, studying art history, language and literature, psychology and philosophy. His four years there between 1910 and 1914 were also occupied with practical photography, Christian iconography, drawing and sculpture – and with discussion among his friends of Nietzsche's *Gay Science* (1887), which he later described as 'a book which speaks to the future – the whole of Surrealism is in it, if you know how to read it.'[2] In the last two years of his studentship in Bonn, Ernst rejected the painstaking naturalism of academic painting, including the minutely exact style of his painter father (an amateur with a personality 'of almost numbing seriousness' according

8 **Max Ernst** *Fruit of a Long Experience* 1919
he phallic shapes and sexual cavities, together with the plus
nd minus wiring terminals, seem to point to a parody of
morous conjunction; the zodiacal sign points outwards to the
osmos, while the whole construction in true Dada style is
ade of rejected material remnants.

to a friend of the young Max[5]), in preference for an Expressionist idiom energized by 'a sensibility for the inherent life of line and colour, including line and colour divorced from actual objects': in other words a fairly typical avant-gardist posture of the day.[4] In a provocative exhibition review he wrote at the time, the twenty-one-year-old Ernst charges one artist (Gisela Zeitelman) of 'merely photographic fidelity', another with 'false motives' (Küppers); another (Karl Menser) he urges to 'look at Negro sculpture'. He ends: 'my advice to you all is to throw in the towel. I charge you all with insignificance.'[5] On a visit to Paris in the late summer of 1913 it is noteworthy that Ernst chose not to meet Braque or Picasso, preferring (as now seems likely) to spend his time exploring Paris's many alchemical sites. Cubism of a conventional kind hardly appears in Ernst's early paintings: it is the melancholy ambience and dislocated imagery of De Chirico and Chagall that proved more important to him at this stage.

49 **Johannes Baargeld** *Anthropophiliac Tapeworm* 1920
Baargeld enters into the spirit of Cologne Dada with a small work that, like the Baader tower of 1920 but on a different scale, anticipates 'assemblage' art of thirty years later. Ernst took to collage only after his collaboration with Baargeld in this year.

We place Max Ernst's development in relation to Cubism because Cubism was the crucible from which almost all other directions and definitions arose. There are only two (now lost) works recorded in the *Oeuvre Catalogue* which show Ernst tentatively exploring a Cubist–Constructivist idiom: the work known as *Fruit of a Long Experience* of 1913, a shallow relief with glazing as a front plane and having a single collage element, and a Cubist-type painting known as *Composition with the Letter E* of 1914. The former gets a reprise in a fine wooden relief of the same title made in the very different circumstances of Cologne Dada in 1919 [*48*]. This and two other lost reliefs of 1919 tell us most about Ernst's appetite for the formal rhythms of Cubism, but also that he seemed to feel at sea without the presence of little anthropomorphic elements in the form of rods, sticks, handles for turning, curious furniture spindles, wooden off-cuts and the occasional printed and pasted-on label. The work known as *Relief 123* (one of the lost pair), contains a paper fragment bearing the words 'Sculpto-Peintures', taken from an Archipenko show in Zurich from that year, and which would seem to indicate Ernst's preferred description of the work.[6]

We should remember that between the first and second versions of *Fruit of a Long Experience* fell the shattering events of the First World War, and (for many) the dismantling of any desire to adhere exclusively to strict formal discipline in art; at least for an artist like Ernst, whose head was already full of animal and human fantasies from a private childhood mythology and whose experience in the German Field Artillery had been to propel him out of the carnage of the Western Front to Berlin in 1916, where he briefly met George Grosz and Wieland Herzfelde, and into the orbit of *Der Sturm* Expressionism. During this interval it was difficult for Ernst to maintain real contact with events in Paris, or with those in Zurich at the Cabaret Voltaire. 'What to do against military life', Ernst wrote about his life on the Western front, 'its stupidity, its hideousness, its cruelty? To scream, swear, vomit and rage serves no purpose'.[7] But in the paintings he managed in off-duty hours, Ernst's imagination was already at work, not on new ways of articulating the picture-plane, but on man-machine and animal-machine metaphors relating to fish, aeroplanes, birds and violently clashing forms thrashing around in the undergrowth or on the sea-bed. Already he was devising metaphors that find a similarity between the brutality of nature and the violence of modern war.

Max Ernst's *entrée* into Dada began shortly after the war with the writer and activist Johannes Baargeld in Cologne, where in late 1919 the two men published with Angelica Hoerle and Otto Freundlich a provocative small magazine *Bulletin D*, and where we see for the first time the use of printer's blocks and little graphic ready-mades, sprinkled about a magazine otherwise devoted to scathing attacks on Cubism, Cézanne and Expressionism. By this time, news of events in Zurich and Berlin was starting to trickle through, and *Bulletin D* decided to sponsor what would be the first Dada exhibition in Cologne. Arp, Klee, Hans Bolz and some unknown Sunday painters were among the exhibitors in what by all accounts was a confrontational and highly playful show. The principle of designating ready-made objects 'works of art' was by no means confined to Marcel Duchamp (by now in New York): here in Cologne were mechanical instruments, African sculptures, umbrellas and assemblage sculptures, all framed by a large fraternity pipe hung over the door.[8] Ernst himself exhibited his relief assemblages of late 1919 (including *Relief 123*) and a sculpture made out of flower-pots. By this time he was also aware of the work of Kurt Schwitters.

All of which is to demonstrate how Ernst inclined towards two principles which will lead all but inevitably to his masterly adoption of collage. The first is a developing eye for found and 'poor' materials – wooden rods, spools and the like – such as to enable them to function as, or within, a pictorial framework. The second is the principle of variety, inspired perhaps by Schwitters' *Der Sturm* statement of 1919 that the *Merzbild* was 'the combination of all conceivable materials...all having equal rights with paint', a form of combination that threw together pictorial signifiers in unpredicted relationships as a means of stimulating the over-habituated eye, of 'defamiliarizing' and de-hierarchizing matter. By late 1919 Ernst had behind him some drawings of oddly tilting perspectives peopled by machine-like personages connected by dotted lines on artificial stages, essentially a meld of ideas from De Chirico and Picabia. By the spring of 1920 he was building bridges with a group in Paris comprised of Louis Aragon, Paul Éluard, André Breton, Philippe Soupault and Georges Ribemont-Dessaignes in the run-up to the launch of a magazine *Die Schammade* (*Scham* = genitals, *Made* = maggot) that Ernst was evolving with Baargeld. *Die Schammade* when it was published in April 1920 ridiculed the Berlin Dadaists for limiting their attacks on the bourgeoisie to ideological or political graphics: for not immersing themselves fully in nonsense. The artistically untrained Baargeld was Ernst's closest collaborator: his relief assemblage *Anthropophiliac Tapeworm*, now also lost, but reproduced in *Die Schammade*, demonstrates that for him as for Ernst, Dada was first and foremost an instrument of poetic transrationality and not a servant of political persuasion – even though Baargeld was the founder of the Communist Party of the Rhineland and brought it within the German Communist movement. The proof of the argument is perhaps best achieved through a comparison. The Berlin example would be Johannes Baader's five-storey *Plastic-Dada-Dio-Drama* exhibited at the Berlin Dada International Fair in June. Here was a physically and programmatically layered work for which Baader produced a complex narrative making clear that it was in fact a parody of Spengler's five developmental stages of *The Decline of the West*. The whole teetering structure with its '3 parks, 1 tunnel, 2 lifts and 1 cylinder cap' organizes the ascent upwards of Superdada (i.e. Baader) and the revelation that 'the World War is a newspaper war: in reality it never existed', the whole thing he asserted was a sort of baffling mystical plot.[9] By contrast, the surviving photograph of Baargeld's mischievous little relief seems to show a frying pan, a rack and a bell, and some unidentifiable domestic implements. Ernst also produced a small junk sculpture made of cog-wheels, bits of wire and cotton waste which had a vaguely anthropomorphizing presence.

This immersion in the techniques and possibilities of construction – both in relief and in three dimensions – was, at least in Cologne, the preferred expression of the Dada spirit. For Max Ernst, perhaps uniquely, it would eventually lead back into collage. And yet for the Cologne 'Dada Exhibition' of May 1920, a second show put on by Baargeld and Ernst (this time with Arp) and designed to coincide with the appearance of *Die Schammade*, such objects and constructions were designed to provoke, less an open attack on bourgeois morality, rather a sense of absurdity. The recollections of Georges Hugnet provide perhaps the most compelling account. In all of Dada, Hugnet recalls, 'I know of nothing stronger or more convincing':

> The centre of Cologne was chosen as being accessible to the public and its slander. Dada planned to insult, and to this end rented a little glassed-in court behind a café,

40 Johannes Baader *Plastic-Dada-Dio-Drama* 1920
Dada's most celebrated and provocative publicist, Baader was also a trained architect and a millennialist tract writer: here he parodies Tatlin's tower, by arranging the storeys as 'Preparation of Superdada', 'Metaphysical Test', 'Inauguration', 'World War', and 'World Revolution', with a 'penthouse' on top.

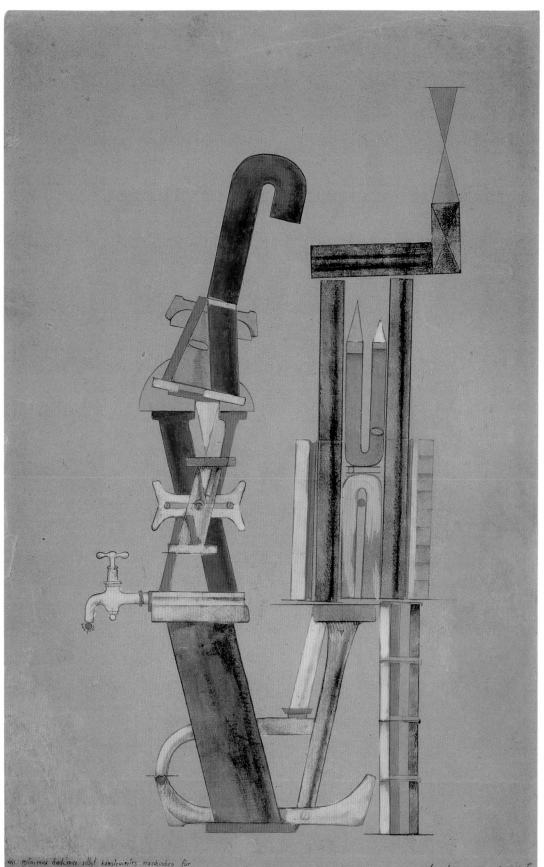

von minimax dadamax selbst konstruiertes maschinchen für
furchtlose bestäubung weiblicher saugnäpfe zu beginn der wechseljahre u. dergl. furchtlose verrichtungen

dadamax ernst

which was reached through a public urinal.... A young girl dressed for her first communion opened the exhibition...[and she] begins to recite obscene verses.... On the wall hung the drawings we know; on the floor were strewn objects by Arp and Ernst. In a corner was Baargeld's...aquarium filled with red-tinted water; with an alarm clock at the bottom; on the surface a magnificent head of a woman's hair floated as casually as the Milky Way, and an elegant arm of polished wood, such as glove makers use, protruded from the water. Beside it stood an object by Ernst in very hard wood, to which a hatchet was chained; any visitor who felt inclined was allowed to destroy the object, as one cuts down a tree.[10]

while another report tell us that 'on the way out, [visitors] pass a couple of open garbage cans full of eggshells and all kinds of junk, and cannot decide whether these belong to the exhibition or are natural originals'.[11] Ernst's drawings, which Hugnet mentions, were done by rubbing a printer's typeface blocks with ink, then building up pairs of totemic figures in precariously stacked layers, in a mildly bathetic reduction of human amorous functions to machine-like impotence. They clearly take their direction from Picabia's irreverent mechanical drawings of those years, but, unlike Picabia, Ernst had seen the horrors of trench warfare. Could they refer to the dysfunctional condition of human awareness under conditions of mechanized war? The long inscription referring to 'the dusting of female suckers' at the base of *Little Machine*, and the tap in the genital position, seem to parody the idea of sexual vitality.[12] The show drew the predictable outrage of Ernst's father: 'I curse you...you have dishonoured us,' he angrily wrote to his son.[13] It was the start of an illustrious career.

Max Ernst and Collage in Surrealist Paris

As frequently happens with the modernist avant-garde, the climactic events are also the last. The Cologne exhibition in May and the Berlin Fair in June 1920 marked a watershed. Afterwards, Baargeld went to earn money in the insurance business, while Ernst's attention turned to paper collages and the forging of a relationship with the French rather than the German sensibility. By the autumn of that year he had become fully attuned to ideas and sensations that would project him from German Dada to its Paris counterpart, and to Surrealism.

Ernst found that the mood among Paris Dadas was already fervently anti-painting – though the relationship to Cubism remained crucial. Dada's rhetoric on the subject was full of angry hostility: 'We have had enough Cubist and Futurist academies,' Tzara had thundered in his great March 1918 *Manifesto* that had appeared (in French) in *Dada 3*. 'Laboratories of formal ideas', he had called Cubist paintings, and with good reason. 'There is a great negative work of destruction to be accomplished. We must sweep and clean.' Above all, Cubist paintings were being sold to the bourgeoisie by dealers. 'Every group of artists has ended up at this bank...opening the door to the possibility of wallowing in comfort and food.... We Dadas are drunk with energy', Tzara had said, calling for a meltdown of art into a literature of nonsense: 'We are revenants thrusting the trident into heedless flesh.' 'Every page should explode', he had written approvingly of the Dada graphics he had seen, 'either because of its profound gravity, or its vortex, vertigo, newness, eternity, or because of its staggering absurdity...its typography'.[14] André Breton, Louis Aragon and Philippe Soupault had been publishing the monthly magazine *Littérature* since March 1919 (rather primly designed but still aligned with Dada ideas), and Picabia's *391* with its more visual appearance had been appearing since 1917. Walter Benjamin, shortly to publish *One-Way Street*, would observe that Dada typographics:

stemmed not from constructive principles but from the precise nervous reactions of

51 **Max Ernst** *Little Machine Constructed by Minimax Dadamax Himself c.* 1919–20
The full translation of Ernst's inscription is 'Little machine constructed by minimax dadamax himself for fearless dusting of female suckers at the beginning of the change of life and for similar fearless acts'. The words 'bon jour' below the dripping tap heighten the absurdity of Ernst's mordant joke.

these literati [such as] Mallarmé, who in the *Coup de Dés* was the first to incorporate the graphic tensions of the advertisement into the printed page…. Printing, having once found in the book a refuge in which to lead an autonomous existence, is pitilessly dragged out onto the street by advertisements and subjected to the brutal heteronomies of economic chaos.[15]

Benjamin also summarizes well the process whereby the pre-war printed commercial catalogues of the Wilhelmine era now became relevant to art, in so far as they dramatize the abrupt dislocation of the post-war world from its pre-war existence ('brutal heteronomies of economic chaos'). Indeed, in preparation for an exhibition organized by Breton in the spring of 1921 Max Ernst now himself assembles imagery of a new type. In his later recollections he wrote that it was in 1919 when:

> One rainy day in Cologne on the Rhine, the pages of an illustrated catalogue [the *Biblioteca Paedagogica* of 1914] showing objects for mathematical, geometrical, anthropological, zoological, botanical, anatomical, mineralogical, paleontological demonstrations, caught my attention – elements of such a diverse nature that the absurdity of the collection confused the eye and mind, producing a hallucinatory succession of double, triple and multiple images superimposed upon one another with the persistence and rapidity peculiar to amorous memories and the visions of semi-sleep.[16]

The statement was written long after the event, yet it begins to capture the qualities of Ernst's new methods, of which there were three. The first is a variation of collage whereby paint is added selectively to a printed image. Ernst's *Hydrometric Demonstration of Killing by Temperature* when stood alongside an inverted page from *Biblioteca Paedagogica* shows clearly how a physics apparatus now becomes two or more stacked machine-constructions with fluids, gases, tubes and flames, remotely connotative of sexual functions. As Ernst said about the process:

> It was enough at that time merely to add to these catalogue pages, by painting or drawing, thereby gently reproducing *what saw itself in me* – a colour, a pencil line, a landscape foreign to the represented objects, a desert, a sky, a geological cross-section, a floor, a single straight line marking the horizon…thus I formed into dramas my most secret desires, out of what had previously been banal pages of advertising.[17]

Another method was to take disjoint photographic images and collage them together inside a frame of evocative verbal non-sequiturs. *The Swan is Very Peaceful* is a fine example. Three elements of this small work are a swan, a plane, and a window-frame enclosing a detail from the rear section of Stephan Lochner's *The Virgin Adoring the Christ Child* (1440). Aragon, who came to own the work, says its inscription was both a commentary on the work 'but also its complement':

> It is the twenty-second time that Lohengrin leaves his mistress for the last time – we are on the upper Missouri, where the earth has extended its crust over four violins. We will never see ourselves again, we will not fight against the angels. The swan is very peaceful, he pulls forcefully on the oars to reach Leda.[18]

A third method was to take small 'found' photographs and jointly with Hans Arp or Ernst's wife Luise make photo-collages that they christened *Fantagaga* (*Fa*brication de *Ta*bleaux *Ga*sométriques *Ga*rantis). The well-known *Here everything is still floating…*, also of 1920,

above 52 Physics apparatus from *Biblioteca Paedagogica* 1914

above, right 53 **Max Ernst** *Hydrometric Demonstration of Killing by Temperature* 1920

Working on the inverted image, Ernst adds a sloping floor plane and shadows to anchor his precarious creations, as in work he had seen by De Chirico: the sense of an interior theatrical space is unavoidably evoked. Over a decade later Joan Miró would use elements from commercial printed catalogues as a way of generating Surrealist paintings [*73, 74*].

4 **Max Ernst** *The Swan is Very Peaceful...* 1920
The minuscule scale of this work (it is only 8.3 centimetres
(3¼ inches) high), as well as its humble paper components, is a
provocation to those expecting coherence and sensory fullness
in the artwork. Its melding of ancient and modern was
another scandal in the eyes of the bourgeois viewer.

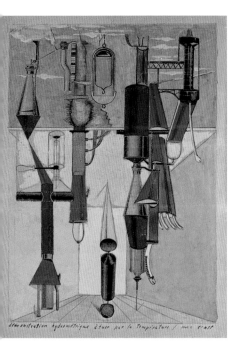

builds its mysterious atmosphere by means of a dream-like scene made out of an
anatomical drawing of a beetle (which becomes a boat) floating below a fish-skeleton in a
watery sky: its long inscription is a verbal collage one suspects to have been selected
randomly from a shelf of books:

> here everything is still floating / it is not yet 2 o'clock / no one was still thinking about
> the 2 ferdinis with their flying hams and hats (still in top form) / here the armada is
> definitely defeated for the first time/ the rainbow eater didn't know / the gut steamer
> and skeleton fish decided to take off / Fantagaga by Arp (Zurich), Max Ernst (Cologne).

In May and June 1921 these works and forty-four others by Ernst were exhibited under
Breton's auspices at the Galerie Au Sans Pareil in the avenue Kléber, Paris. A poster
announcement carried the unpunctuated announcement *dessins mécanoplastiques plasto-
plastiques peintopeintures anaplastiques anatomiques antizymiques aérographiques
antiphonaires arrosables et républicains* as Dada-names for the works on show. At the
opening night they might have appeared secondary to a series of nonsense performances
designed to irritate and amuse. Jacques Rigaud counted automobiles; Breton repeatedly lit
matches; Aragon made miaowing sounds; Soupault and Tzara played hide-and-seek; other
Dadas bellowed phrases or illicit aphorisms.[19] Such gestures lent their distinctive tone to
the works on show. Some Paris critics, notably Jacques-Emile Blanche and Pierre Deval,
responded positively to Max Ernst's visionary creations. The *Daily Mail* journalist from
London complained of a 'lobster salad' of 'faces and fishes, animals and scientific figures
and hats, all jumbled up together'.[20] Yet the ludic quality of the event has been somewhat
lost under the weight of recent art-historical scholarship which has tried to retrieve the
psychoanalytic determinants of Ernst's illicit scenes – but few, if any, of these
interpretations reflect prevailing patterns of viewing and reading at the time. As the Max
Ernst scholar Werner Spies has long maintained, it 'leads nowhere to apply psychoanalytic
methods...for [Ernst] endows his works with what is merely pseudo-psychoanalytical
effect'. Ernst's elusive pictorial situations 'should maintain the observer's imagination in a
state of permanent tension that no solution can satisfy'.[21] The more useful exercise is to
show how Ernst's collages meditate upon their relations with painting, the very artform

that Dadas (and for that matter most Surrealists) were at pains either to abolish or to redefine. For while Ernst's overpainted catalogue pages mobilize mechanical analogies for humans and humanoid beings, the smaller photo-collages (Fantagagas and others) utilize the *complete* photographic image (the fish, the aeroplane), hence opening up the possibility of displacement, compression and metaphorization (compare Höch, Klutsis, Rodchenko).

How are these processes to be understood? In Breton's catalogue essay to the Au Sans Pareil show – his first text on art – he compares photography's relation to art with that obtaining between automatic writing and traditional poetry: both photography and automatic writing, he suggests, deal a mortal blow to old modes of expression to the point where the imitation of appearances no longer applies. Nor could art somehow rejuvenate objects by paying closer attention to their material nature (another jibe at Cubism). On the contrary, we must accept objects as they are shown to us in the printed catalogue and 'distribute and group them according to whatever plan we please'. The freedom of Dada and of collage, says Breton, results from 'refusing to attach itself, even in the slightest degree, to matter: Dada regards submission to the laws of any given perspective as useless.' Then comes a statement that would take Breton far:

> It is Dada and Dada alone whose ability is the marvellous faculty of attaining two widely separate realities without departing from the realm of our experience, of bringing them together and drawing a spark from their contact; of gathering within reach of our senses abstract figures endowed with the same intensity, the same relief as other figures; and of disorienting us in our own memory by depriving us of a frame of reference.

After all, the logic of sequential experience is already violated in the cinema, says Breton, which is capable of accelerating or retarding time. Therefore Max Ernst is an artist who 'projects before our eyes the most captivating film in the world and retains the grace to smile even while illuminating our interior life most profoundly and most radiantly.'[22] 'Who knows', Breton would ask in a letter written in October 1921, 'whether we may not thus be preparing to escape one day from the principle of identity.'[23] Breton is unconcerned with the material effects of pasted paper or overpainting – merely with the fact that the image promotes disorientation in the viewer.

Yet the 'cinematic' Max Ernst is perhaps a writer's invention. To be attuned to collage as art is to see Ernst shifting Cubist painting into a new and very unfamiliar gear. First, notice the careful flatness of those gouache overpaintings; the artless perspectival systems, the bright colours, the 'frozen stage' effect whereby strange objects stand in a shallow or empty void: it is painting of a kind, but no more than a parody of Cubism's preoccupation with pictorial relationships and the relationship of forms to the frame. And who but someone in pursuit of the child-like would write captions in that careful calligraphic style? The second of Ernst's methods – suspending painting altogether in favour of montaged photographs alone – requires the displacement and reorganization of material such that the transformation of things becomes clear. And both methods require edges (of the painted plane, of the printed sheet), where the work of inversion, conversion and supplementation is registered to sight. A certain cultivated artlessness was the inevitable effect. And it was by means of these flat shapes and sharp edges that a style of painted figuration was again made possible, a style incompatible with the splintered metonyms of Cubism, one in which matter, narrative and agency are reorganized in the service of dream-like illusion, crude and naive. In fact so successful was collage in these early forms that most subsequent Surrealist painting would be based on its discoveries. Works like Ernst's own *Elephant Célèbes* (1921) or his *Oedipus Rex* (1922) are examples of how painting 'escaped' from Cubism into this second, deepened and purified post-photographic modernist world.

55 **Gerrit Rietveld** *Shroeder House, Utrecht* 1924–5
The Schroeder House carries through into three dimensions the theoretical principles of planar analysis and spatial fluidity in what amounts to a classical method of balance and proportion between the parts: the use of primary colours and black and white underpins that rational method.

Dada into Constructivism

Even though early Dada in Zurich, Berlin and Cologne was unsympathetic to Constructivist ideals, the relationship was set to change after the success of the First International Dada Fair in June and July 1920. In any case Berlin as a geographical crossroads between East and West Europe, with links to southern Europe, Austria and Italy, provided a natural forum for new international alliances after the climax of Dada. A Constructivist circle was already forming there between 1920 and 1922 out of Hausmann and Richter, Laszlo Moholy-Nagy from Budapest, Theo van Doesburg from the De Stijl group in Amsterdam, El Lissitzky, Ivan Puni, Naum Gabo and Anton Pevsner from Russia, the Austrian Hans Arp and soon Schwitters himself. Tatlin was already known. Hausmann had himself moved in the direction of the De Stijl group by the end of 1920 and the beginning of 1921: by now both Dada and *Merz* were becoming increasingly abstract and technologically oriented in their search for aesthetic equivalents of the 'new man' of post-war reconstruction. Many of the avant-garde reviews that proliferated in the period, such as *Ma* (Budapest and then Vienna, 1919–25), *Zenit* (Belgrade, 1921–6), *Dada-Jazz* (Zagreb, 1922), *Mecano* (The Hague, 1922–3) and *G* (Berlin, 1923–4) contained Dada and Constructivist statements side-by-side – and shared a commitment to collage and photomontage.[24] 1922 saw the foundation in Berlin of the magazine *Veshch/Gegenstand/ Object* by Lissitzky and Ilya Ehrenburg, in March, and the 'Erste Russische Kunstaustellung' (First Russian Exhibition) at the Van Diemen Gallery, in October. Calling for an international brotherhood of 'object' builders, *Veshch* affirmed that artists, architects, designers, writers and poets stood at the dawn of a 'constructive' effort undertaken in full cognisance of the imperatives and possibilities of the new technology. The transformation of social forms was its goal. In wider terms, a Congress of International Progressive Artists, held in Düsseldorf in May 1922, consolidated Constructivist opposition to Expressionism and early Dada with their residual and arbitrary subjectivities, while statements from the De Stijl group (van Doesburg) and *Veshch* (Lissitzky), together with Richter representing the Romanian, Swiss, Scandinavian and German groups led to the Internationale Fraktion der Konstruktivisten (International Party of Constructivists) being born.

Though important, the alliances and tensions that surrounded the birth of International Constructivism mask the more fundamental truth that collage and its offspring, photomontage, were by now accepted principles of advanced artistic and architectural practice, of graphics, advertising and fine art itself. If International Constructivism meant any single thing (it became organizationally splintered only months after Düsseldorf, at a stormy meeting of Dadaists and Constructivists in Weimar, in September) it meant a return to the use of real materials in two and three dimensions according to rational principles of design. While Russian Constructivism soon adopted a Productivist platform and moved its activities into architecture and planning as well as graphics, theatre and propaganda, in western Europe its applications were more likely to be confined in practice to domestic design and abstract art.

Selected examples of the use of collage in International Constructivism will be given here. The founding of the De Stijl group in Holland in 1917 was the earliest West European attempt to apply Cubist principles constructively to a synthesis of art, design and architecture. Theo van Doesburg, its leading advocate, emphasized that the 'new plastic art' would exclude natural forms in favour of artistic and aesthetic principles deriving from form/colour/planarity itself. Amid much rhetoric about 'purposeful organization', 'the fundamental essence of things', and 'exact artistic expression', De Stijl principles involved the 'harmony' or 'equilibrium' of elements: vertical and horizontal, large and small, broad and narrow and so on – the elements having first been distilled from each other and placed in spatial juxtaposition.[25] Examples are the interior design of apartments in Drachten by van Doesburg, which show how spatial designs could be evolved from an array of

'elements', such as four colours set out in proximity in a collage-like relation, or the remarkable axonometric drawings by Cornelius van Eesteren and van Doesburg for real or imagined buildings, comprising either black-ink lines showing load-bearing and supporting elements in a single skeletal design, or the drawings in primary colours, known as colour-constructions, which show how the primary colours can function in architecture. In 1924 van Doesburg did more of these drawings, to show the spatio-temporal aspect of architecture, which he called 'Constructions of colours in the 4th dimension of space time'.[26] Such thinking was embodied in the designs and models made by van Doesburg and van Eesteren for the Maison d'Artiste and the Maison Particulière (both 1923), or the completed (and recently restored) Schroeder House by De Stijl architect-member Gerrit Rietveld of 1924–5 [55]. As van Doesburg was to write in explanation of the new constructive method, 'Construction is setting things together in an organic and calculated manner, using real means, whereas composition…is spontaneous arrangement, in accordance with instinct and taste…'.[27] Correspondingly, the Blok group of Polish Constructivists, founded in Lódź in 1922 and whose magazine was published in Warsaw from 1924, showed an acquaintance with both Russian and International Constructivism in its emphases on 'practical' solutions to creative problems; on simplicity, economy and the relationship of the character of the created object to the material used; on 'the construction of an object according to its own principles'.[28] Wladislaw Strzemiński, who founded the Blok group, had studied in Russia and produced relief-constructions in the manner of Kliun and Puni in 1919 and 1920; the origins of his work also lie in the Cubism of Braque and Picasso. The other two editors of *Blok*, Henryk Stazewski and Mieczyslaw Szczuka – together with the Danish artist Franciska Clausen – all subscribed to the van Doesburg line that a work of art must be created by universal principles arising from material itself. All of these experiments built upon a combination of a machine aesthetic combined with the 'freedom' of material to find its own meaning, and whose point of origin was collage.[29]

In Prague in 1920, a group was formed that combined elements both of revolutionary rationalism and the subjective spirit. Devĕtsil, whose name perhaps derives from the stubborn country plant Heliotrope, stood initially for a culture of everyday life, one that celebrated egalitarianism, eroticism and play, while the group's political programme insisted that architecture, typography and graphics, the tangible public products of the new

above, left 56 **Theo van Doesburg** *Space-Time Construction II* 1924
Van Doesburg's space-time constructions do full justice to the open, asymmetrical character of the building while avoiding problems of perspectival distortion: they also embody the qualities of geometrical abstract paintings in which colour rectangles lie in all their materiality on the plane of the picture – as in a collage.

57 **Karel Teige** *Departure for Cythera* 1923–4
To Teige, the picture-poem was 'a language devoid of grammar…a word of this poetry is far from being a word of spoken language or of literary language. It is an optical symbol of reality', employing international English words and French expressions modelled on the idea of the visual sign, a 'modern pictography'.

Czech Republic, would emerge from an affiliation with Russian Constructivism. Painting, meanwhile – even such recent developments as French Cubism and Italian Futurism – would be consigned to the era of bourgeois culture and be replaced by photography, kineticism and film.

Yet Devětsil was to enter a second phase in 1922–3. Those who participated in Devětsil's 'Bazaar of Modern Art' exhibition in November 1923 demonstrated a highly eclectic mixture. The architects Bedřich Feuerstein and Jaromír Krejcar gave a polemical response to Le Corbusier and Ozenfant's programme of Purism, while the painter Josef Šíma was joined by Jindrich Štyrský, Marie Čermínová (her chosen name was Toyen), Remo (Jiří Jelínek) and Otakar Mrkvička, among others, in a loose installation-style event not entirely dissimilar from the Berlin International Dada Fair of 1920. Though no visual records survive, we know from written accounts that the Bazaar contained machine parts, film shots, collages, posters, photographs and 'modern' objects such as a tailor's dummy, ball-bearings and a life-jacket. A mirror was placed at the back of the hall bearing the message 'Visitors: Your Portrait'. Importantly, the photographer Man Ray was a guest exhibitor, represented by a series of recently published photograms known as *Les Champs Délicieux* (Delicious Fields). The collages from Devětsil's Bazaar of Modern Art have not survived and we do not know how or of what they were made.[30]

This brief description conveys how Devětsil was already softening its tone. On the one hand, it offered a lingering allegiance to proletarian art and to architectural Constructivism, 'discovered' by the young theorist Karel Teige and the Czech architects during 1922. In the words of a text published by Teige in the avant-garde magazine *Život* (Life), the revolutionary possibilities of new media could be expressed as a series of mathematical relationships, the upper term clearly replacing the lower: 'photo/painting = cinema/theatre = orchestration/piano = future photo-sculpture/sculpture'. Two aspects of this system were to become even more important later. Teige in the same text describes Man Ray's inventions as 'no longer having anything to do with photography'. Instead, they demonstrated a Constructivist approach to objects and photographic paper to which even the camera had now become irrelevant.[31] About 'photo-sculpture' we shall say more later.

The important concept that became central to Devětsil, however, had been in circulation between the poet Vítězslav Nezval and Teige in the latter half of 1923 and was published the following year, namely 'Poetism'. Nezval had joined Devětsil early in 1923 and had initially been prepared to underscore Teige's machine-enthusiasm with a series of poem-slogans extolling mechanization, America and anti-Romanticism generally.[32] Yet while Poetism aligned itself with Constructivist emphases on standardization, collectivism, and the abolition of 'art', its desire to deprofessionalize art and to merge art and life together required a definition of Poetism as:

> an art of life, an art of living and enjoying...as relativists, we are aware of the hidden irrationality overlooked by the scientific system and therefore as yet not sublimated...we are hungry for individual freedom: 'After six days of work and building the world, beauty is the seventh day of the soul'.[33]

To Teige's proletarian critics in 1923 and 1924, such a formulation was red rag to a bull: for example, the Trotsky follower Stanislav Kostka Neumann claimed that Devětsil was 'closer to circus noises than to the ascetic task of educating the proletariat'.[34] Poetism's claims were certainly contradictory: Teige claimed it to be 'nonchalant, exuberant, fantastic, playful, non-heroic and erotic', and yet 'there is not an iota of romanticism in it'. 'Constructivism is the method of all productive work'; and yet Poetism is 'the art of living in the most beautiful sense of the word, a modern Epicurianism'. No wonder then that when Teige says that Poetism 'points the way from nowhere to nowhere, revolving in a circle around a

above 58 **Man Ray** *(Paper Circle and Tongs), no. 1,* from *Les Champs Délicieux* 1922
The photograms are formed from the action on light on photographic paper, interrupted by various objects. The absence of the camera – photography without a machine – made Tzara describe Man Ray's inventions as 'photography in reverse'.

above, right 59 **Jindřich Štyrský** *Souvenir* 1924
In the picture-poem the principle of montage is used to turn photographs into film-like poems that moved through space and time and between subjectivities: travel to distant times and places became the picture-poem's central motif, with geometric abstraction its mode of organization.

magnificent fragrant park, for it is the path of life',[35] the Proletkultists were quick to accuse
Poetism of irresponsibility and nihilism.[36]

Collage in the Czech avant-garde corresponds closely to these debates around Devětsil.
Collage methods were employed in graphic design, for example in Josef Štyrský's book
cover for Nezval's *Pantomima*, 1924. Now, the new culture of Poetism would embrace
caricature, Westerns, Buffalo Bill, Chaplin, and the circus; it would 'turn life into a great
entertainment, an eccentric carnival, a harlequinade of emotions and ideas, a series of
intoxicating film sequences, a kaleidoscope'. It would draw upon 'the emancipation from
the picture frame' begun by Picasso and Braque in order to arrive at so-called 'picture-
poems' in the form of 'book illustration, photography and photomontage'[37] Devětsil's
picture-poems were made with collage and photomontage techniques by Jindrich Štyrský
and by Teige himself with the poets Nezval and Seifert between 1924 and 1926. Štyrský's
early picture-poem *Souvenir* (1924), for example, is laid out horizontally around the motif
of a cartographic panorama involving a map of the Gulf of Genoa and an assembly of
memory-images indexed to the figure of a small girl who sits on a beach among friends,
her own innocence and fascination performing as the psychological register in which the
kaleidoscope asks to be seen. 'The new poetic language is heraldry: the language of signs',
wrote Teige in the 1924 Poetism manifesto. 'It works with standards. For example: Au
Revoir! Bon Vent, Bonne Mer! Adieu! Green Light: Go! Red Light: Stop!'[38]

On one level, these small but ambitious productions can be understood as a transfer to
the visual register of the poetic theory of the linguist Roman Jakobson, since 1920 in
Prague and immediately sympathetic to Nezval, Seifert, the prose writer Vladislav Vančura,
and to Teige: these friendships had led Jakobson to membership of Devětsil as well as to
the group who formed the Prague Linguistic Circle in 1926 (Mukařovský, Havranek and
Bogatirev), to both of which he brought an intimate knowledge of pre-Revolutionary
Russia. His theory of visual semaphores, of the simultaneous metonymic sign as the mark
of poetry as opposed to prose, was exactly the register deployed by Devětsil's picture-
poems. To this emphasis on signals would soon be added the theory of film: Teige's second
picture-poem *Departure for Cythera* [57] was published at the end of his book *Film* of 1925
as a clear statement of the mutual interpenetration of the moving and static montage. Dark
and light areas and the 'fading' between them, the movement (implied by staircases)

opposite 60 **Kurt Schwitters** *Blue* 1923–6
This large work made of wooden planks and added elements
inhabits beautifully a De Stijl world of almost-primary colours
in shallow relief, while rejoicing in the rough tactility of the
wood.

below 61 **Friedrich Vordemberge-Gildewart** *Composition
No. 48: Architecture – no optical valuation* 1928
The majority of Vordemberge-Gildewart's collages are abstract
exercises relating to architecture: 'figurative' fragments are
nearly always radically dislocated from their contexts, inverted
or repeated, bringing them into humorous collision with man-
made geometrical forms.

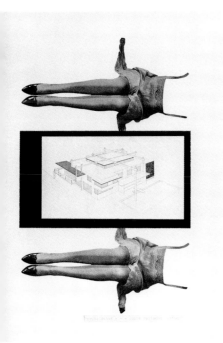

between one shot and another, the sequence from the swing-bridge to the departing steam-
boat to the sailing vessel, seen glancingly perhaps from the deck of an ocean-going vessel,
the whole being punctuated by at least two verbal 'heralds' circulating round a prominent
circular dot – such elements provide a strong impression of a flickering film record of the
mythical journey already painted by Watteau but now recast as a journey perhaps to a no
less mythical America.[39] A kind of *Gesamtkunstwerk* (total work of art) in a minor key, the
picture-poem constituted Devětsil's major attempt to reconcile lyricism and the
Constructive idea.

Though International Constructivism remained a force to be reckoned with throughout
the 1920s, some artists remained staunchly independent. Kurt Schwitters, having escaped
from Berlin Dada by 1922 or 1923, was cautious about Constructivism too. Aside from the
Hanover Merzbau, he was drawn to abstraction as a practice that abbreviated reference to
events and processes in the social world. Though his work after 1923 continues to record
elements of a private world of accumulation, of a civilization bursting with materials
rendered 'poor' by overuse, so too the picture as self-referring object – one that incarnates
the '*Merz* composite work of art' – is never far from his concerns. 'Art is a primordial
concept', Schwitters had written for the *Merz* essay of 1920; 'is it exalted as the Godhead,
inexplicable as life, indefinable and without purpose…. I know only how I make it; I know
only of my medium, of which I partake; to what end I know not.'[40] Or again: 'The picture is
a self-contained work of art', he wrote in the first issue of his magazine *Merz* in 1923; 'It
refers to nothing outside of itself. Nor can a consistent work of art refer to anything outside
of itself without loosening its ties to art…. A consistent work of art must be abstract.'[41] And
yet Schwitters succeeded in riding many horses at once. He supported Gruppe K (standing
for 'Konstruktion') when it was founded in Hanover in 1924 by Friedrich Vordemberge-
Gildewart and Hans Nitzschke. He knew Vordemberge-Gildewart's building plans and
planar constructions, as well as his occasional more figurative collage works which depart
from his customary adherence to van Doesburg and Lissitzky's practice. The present
example, for instance, with a fashion icon from which the bust and shoulders have been
cut out, and which has then been alienated by sideways placing alongside a De Stijl
architectural drawing, is an ironic comment on the widespread public resistance to
including building within the ambit of visual desire: its small type-face caption reads
'Architektur – keine optische wertung' (Architecture – no optical valuation). Meanwhile
Schwitters, the van Doesburgs and Vilmos Huszàr had toured the Netherlands together in
1923, after which the *Merz* pictures show Constructivist and De Stijl tendencies without
capitulating wholly to a rational method: the painted relief *Blue* of 1923–6 is still steeped in
the aura of old materials, and lacks the completely balanced grid beloved of De Stijl.[42] Even
though Dada as a riposte to bourgeois forms of anxiety remained a bedrock for Schwitters
until the end of his life, it is equally true that a romantic attitude to Constructivism
supported his commitment to the production of materially tactile compositions that obey
no laws other than what he persisted in calling the 'laws of art'. Schwitters would live just
long enough to see his *Merz* pictures admired in the second flush of modernism, in New
York in the later 1940s.

5

The Surrealist Years

It is no exaggeration to say that the great discoveries of the years 1919–24 in Cologne, Paris and Prague rank in importance alongside those of 1911–13 in Céret, Sorgues and Paris. For the Cubists, *papier collé* had opened onto construction, and onto design. For the Dadas, the techniques of relief assemblage, overpainting and photo-collage arrived more or less together to launch Surrealism as painting – as well as to blow apart any simple definition of 'collage' as having to do exclusively with paper and glue. Max Ernst himself, reflecting back on the period from the vantage-point of 1937, tells an apposite story. At work in 1929 preparing his punningly titled collage-novel *La Femme 100 Têtes*, an acquaintance asked him what he was doing. Collages, yes, but with what sort of glue? 'With that modest air so admired by my contemporaries', Ernst relates, 'I had to admit that in most of my collages there was no use for glue; that I am not responsible for the term *collage*; and that in my collage exhibition in Paris [at Au Sans Pareil in 1921]…only twelve justified the term *collage-découpage* out of the total of forty-seven. He recalls Aragon's words at the end of the decade, that the Au Sans Pareil exhibition had been 'perhaps the first manifestation allowing us to see the resources of thousands of entirely new artistic methods'.[1] Werner Spies has proposed more recently that the whole gamut of techniques uncovered after 1921, such as stencilling, overpainting, *frottage* ('discovered' by Ernst in 1925), the attachment of captions and the varieties of photo-collage, as well as the major part of Surrealist painting, participate in the collage method and cannot be materially or conceptually separated from it, irrespective of the use of literal paper and glue.[2]

The Tension between Matter and Text
Surrealism's association of collage methods with the plane of the verbal – hence the appearance of a tension between matter and image, matter and text – comes out of Breton's preface to the Au Sans Pareil exhibition, to appear again in a still more famous announcement. Breton's *First Manifesto of Surrealism* when it was published in 1924 made few if any references to the materials of art, to concentrate instead upon the unreliability of logic, the value of the dream, the flight from positivism, and the embrace of the absurd – 'psychic automatism in its pure state, by which one proposes to express, *verbally by means of the written word* or in any other manner, the actual functioning of thought'. Surrealism was 'exempt', as Breton put it, 'from any aesthetic or moral concern'.[3] And now Picasso's

2 Max Ernst 'Let's go. Let's dance the Tenebreuse…', page from *Rêve d'une Petite Fille qui Voulut Entrer au Carmel* 1930 Rather than fragment an object into its parts, as in Cubism, Ernst prefers to excise objects whole in the form of cheap archaizing illustrations and carefully reposition them in suggestive conjunctions – using inversion, displacement and scandalous narrative association – as here in an upper-class bedroom.

Cubist paintings and his groundbreaking *papiers collés* were claimed for Surrealism. In an essay 'Surrealism and Painting', which appeared in 1925, Breton rehearsed once more the retreat from matter:

> I mean [says Breton] a real *insulation*, thanks to which the mind, finding itself ideally withdrawn from everything, can begin to occupy itself with its own life…to the point where the words family, fatherland, society, seem to us now so many macabre jokes…so that our eyes, our precious eyes, have to reflect that which, while not existing, is yet as intense as that which does exist, and which has therefore to consist of real visual images, so as to fully compensate us for what we have left behind.

Picasso is said to have achieved in 1910 a 'sudden flush of inspiration…sometime between *Factory, Horta de Ebro* and *Portrait of Kahnweiler*', when he 'broke openly with the treacherous nature of tangible entities…and more particularly with the facile connotations of their everyday appearance'. After Picasso, Breton says, we may

> leave behind the great grey-beige scaffold paintings of 1912, the most perfect example of which is undoubtedly the fabulously elegant *Man With a Clarinet*…whose 'parallel' existence must remain a subject for endless meditation…. [It] remains tangible proof of our unwavering proposition that the mind talks stubbornly to us of a future continent, and that everyone has the power to accompany an ever more beautiful Alice into Wonderland.[4]

A second instance of Surrealism's enchantment with the textual is at the same time a sign of a change of mood within Surrealism as the 1920s came to a close. Max Ernst's collage novels are also a demonstration of the flexibility of collage methods, their adaptability to both the visual and verbal modes. Back in 1921 he had written to Tzara asking him 'If you come across any old department store catalogues, fashion magazines, old illustrations, etc., kindly make a gift of them to me…'[5] – but discovered for himself the French magazines *La Nature*, published weekly from 1873, which contained illustrated articles on discoveries and inventions, feats of engineering and medicine, and two other publications, the *Kolumbus-Eier*, published in Stuttgart for young people and illustrated with tricks and games, and *Le Magasin Pittoresque*, published in France from the 1830s. The illustrations for these magazines, made until the advent of cheap photographic printing by whole teams of wood- and steel-engravers, were not only physically small, often a few inches high or wide, but even by the early 1920s distinctly archaic in both their imagery and their tone.

Archaism as a visual métier suited the atmosphere of quaint peculiarity that Ernst was keen to establish around his new literary invention as part and parcel of his wider attack on 'painting'. Collaborating with the poet Paul Éluard on the illustrations to Éluard's poem *Répétitions* and then his *Les Malheurs des Immortels* (both 1922), Ernst renews his archaic style in three projects of the later 1920s and early 1930s, all of which are 'novels'. Aside from *La Femme 100 Têtes* (1929) he made *Rêve d'une Petite Fille qui Voulut Entrer au Carmel* (A Little Girl Dreams of Taking the Veil, 1930) [*62*] and *Une Semaine de Bonté* (A Week of Happiness, 1934), which have the distinction not merely of literary form, but of being constructed out of cheap engravings evoking the world of bourgeois entertainment, cheap horror stories, and topical illustrations of the *fin-de-siècle* and perhaps before. These collages required precision cutting and pasting, often resulting in adjacent images showing the brown and grey coloration of their original pages: while they inevitably evoked a social and commercial order undergoing sharp and irreversible decline – an era characterized by pre-First World War bourgeois respectability, decency of dress and gesture, and particular

63 **André Breton, Jacqueline Lamba, Yves Tanguy** *Cadavre exquis* 1938
This particular *cadavre exquis* employs printed magazine illustrations to result in a totemic figure (with wings) sitting authoritatively at a factory bench: his head is a compass, with leaves for ears.

64 **Pablo Picasso** *Guitar* 1926
At only ten centimetres (3¼ inches) high, this minuscule work rings yet further changes on the endlessly flexible motif of the guitar. Its sexual references now clearly paraded, it could still be read as a standing figure – or a display of virtuosity on a miniature scale.

styles of leisure and boredom. In Ernst's 'novel' of 1930 we find them set to a scandalous story about the hidden desires of a young pubescent girl, providing what Dorothea Tanning would call 'a new dimension of psychic violence to the already fraught pictures in which night and dream are…sovereign forces'.[6] In all these cases text in the form of narrative or anti-narrative supervenes upon and attempts to render out-of-date the carefully organized metonymies of Cubism. Metaphor (which Jakobson perceptively associated with prose) is their replacement.

A third symptom of the Surrealist lurch from the visual to the verbal is the game of *cadavre exquis* (exquisite corpse). It was at 54, rue du Château in Montparnasse, sometime in 1925, at a hotel run by Marcel Duhamel and with the painter Yves Tanguy and the young poet Jacques Prévert, that the children's game of Consequences was revived to such startling effect. First directed by Breton to produce verbal non-sequiturs, the game soon progressed to drawn images. The aim, to produce an analogical body, with each stage added 'blind' by successive players, paradoxically required a high degree of procedural rationality in which folds demarcated spaces for 'head', 'body', and 'legs', and where the materials were agreed beforehand and could not be varied. Breton wrote later that *cadavre exquis*, played usually in the evening, formed a natural extension of the 'absolute non-conformism and unsparing disrespect' that marked the Surrealist day, that its products 'raised anthropomorphism to its highest pitch [and] constituted the desperate negation of that futile formula of imitation of physical characteristics' to which (he felt) so much contemporary art remained enslaved.[7] Throughout the later 1920s the analogies thus concocted took extraordinary flight: they can be said to have pushed at the very limits of what an analogy or a metaphor is. *Cadavre exquis* perhaps epitomized the metaphorical drive inside Surrealism, intended to render redundant the Cubist preoccupation with 'form'. In the later 1930s, when the preoccupation with language was changing, *cadavre exquis* used photo-fragments in reference to the statuesque.

In fact even by the early 1930s Breton was changing his mind about the nature of the image. In the first issue of the magazine *Minotaure* (1933) he refers approvingly to the *bricoleur* in Picasso, the artist who (to quote Tériade) simply picked up a tube of red when he had run out of blue,[8] who allows 'the substance which is literally at hand to play the role of interpreter in determining the growth and the outcome of a work'. Picasso seems to have 'gone out of his way to seek out the perishable and the ephemeral for their own sake', Breton observes in regard to the yellowing scraps of newsprint used twenty years before. He refers to the 'amazing guitars made of shoddy strips of paper' and even countenances the possibility that Picasso had anticipated their deterioration (perhaps Breton had been talking to Gertrude Stein).[9] 'It is as if', says Breton, '…his aim had been to coax forth, to bring to terms in advance all that is precious, because ultra-real, in the process of their gradual dilapidation'. But could Breton also be referring to Picasso's 'amazing guitars' made in April and May 1926 out of string, nails, cloth, in one case a knitting-needle, which even in reproduction constitute images of unprecedented brutality and reduction? In fact there are two groups: four or so small *Guitars*, a matter of a few inches in height, in which Picasso threaded string through cardboard furnished with scraps of delicate tulle, which are schematically 'guitars' (but to my eyes evoke openings, perhaps the vagina); and two quite large works, the one reproduced here made out of an old shirt tacked onto wood, the string of which, though flat, cleverly gives the impression of a pointed spike with a shadow. Breton referred to the first group as 'extra-pictorial' outputs, not destined for public museums, works 'that will never become the object of forced admiration, or of any speculation other than the intellectual variety.'[10] You can see his point.

55 **Pablo Picasso** *Guitar* 1926
At 130 centimetres (51 inches) high the largest of Picasso's 1926 'guitars', this work even manages to evoke the ritual brutality of the bullfight through its 'wounding' spike, its tattered piece of cloth, and the near-empty arena of the bullring.

The Galerie Goemans Exhibition

For by the time of publication of *Minotaure* in 1933 – Picasso designed the first cover, as a collage – the direction of Surrealism in Paris had changed. Key moments in that process had been the opposition to Breton provided by Georges Bataille and the *Documents* group in 1929–30, and the small but very significant exhibition at the Galerie Goemans from 28 March to 12 April 1930 organized by Louis Aragon (in fact the last before that gallery closed in financial ruin). This was an exhibition devoted solely to collage, and included works by Arp, Braque, Dalí, Duchamp, Ernst, Gris, Magritte, Man Ray, Miró, Picabia, Picasso and Tanguy. Its importance to the practice and theory of modern collage is equal to that of the Au Sans Pareil show of 1921 or the Museum of Modern Art exhibition of 1948 (to which we shall come later). And the Galerie Goemans show is rightly seen as a turning point in the practice of Surrealism – away from the automatist methods of Breton's *First Manifesto* towards more deliberate and conscious ways of generating 'the marvellous'; or to have summarized an increasing tendency in that direction since about 1926. Let me repeat: Breton's early writing had emphasized *dépaysement* (disorientation) as the psychic goal of all Surrealism. Now, in a long prefatory text titled 'La peinture au défi' (The Challenge to Painting) that amounts almost to a new Surrealist manifesto, Aragon wants to talk about 'a technical consideration' that begins when Picasso and Braque used pasted elements for reasons of colour, as a critique of the palette, or as a 'quip': and he laments the lack of critical writing about an activity 'which absorbed a good part of the thought of a generation's most admired painters'. Artists who didn't use collage but who used the collage principle – Picabia and Man Ray – come in for special approval for having bypassed the hitherto normative practice of 'painting from the personality': Man Ray's rayographs, for instance, says Aragon, 'should be linked to collage [as] a philosophical operation', one that is 'beyond painting, with no real connection to photography'. Picabia's ink-blot entitled *Sainte Vièrge* (Blessed Virgin), or Duchamp's *Mona Lisa with a Moustache*, or his signed urinal of 1917, can be seen as consequences of the earliest *papiers collés* because they involve 'a negation of technique…the painter, if we can still call him that, is no longer bound to his canvas by a mysterious physical relationship analogous to procreation'. Artistic work of the new 'technical personality' is governed by impersonality, by chance, by non- or multiple-authorship, always in defiance of bourgeois 'inwardness'.

66 **Salvador Dalí** *Accommodations of Desire* 1929
The near impossibility of telling which passages are painted and which are pasted paper is of course intentional on Dalí's part – in providing the act of looking itself with a prurient obsessiveness and no little amount of difficulty. The metaphorical doubling and absences add to the anxiety enshrined in the picture itself.

At its impersonal extreme, Aragon says, collage gave rise to photomontage in Constructivist Russia (Rodchenko and Klutsis), where it had become 'a symptom of the need to signify which is characteristic of the evolving forms of thought at our current stage of human reflection' (he means the Bolshevik demand for 'content'). Aragon had himself joined the French Communist party in 1927, and by 1930 when he wrote this preface had one foot in the camp of Soviet proletarianization: he would leave Paris for Moscow in November.[11] 'Art has truly ceased to be individual' was Aragon's most cherished verdict on collage's many new-found possibilities; to which he adds a tantalizing qualification: 'even when the artist is a die-hard individual'. And lest anyone forget the full achievement of the pasted-paper revolution, Aragon reminds his readers in 1930 that Braque and Picasso had launched 'two utterly distinct categories of work'; elements pasted for 'the value of the material' and elements pasted on account of representing a whole object. Dismissing Cubist *papier collé* as really 'nothing more than pictorial work', Aragon nevertheless concedes that it opened the way for Surrealism, 'where the expressed triumphs over the manner of expression, where the object depicted plays the role of a word'. He admits that 'collage' had by now become multivalent and materially diverse, that the use of paste 'is only one characteristic, and not essential'. But he insists that the teleology implied by *papier collé* was irreversible. 'The principle of collage once admitted, painters had unknowingly passed from white to black magic. It was too late to retreat'.[12]

The other achievement of the Galerie Goemans show was to bring into sharp focus the dialectical relationship of collage and painting in the work of Dalí, Magritte, Tanguy and several others. In fact during 1929 Dalí had prepared a new body of work for a show of his own at Goemans – most of which had incorporated literally collaged elements as ways of teasing the viewer's apprehension of exactly what was being seen. They elicited the following comment from Aragon: 'He paints with a magnifying glass...the scraps of pasted-on lithograph appear painted on, while the painted areas appear to be pasted on'. Paintings such as *The Lugubrious Game, The Enigma of Desire, Illumined Pleasures* and *Man with an Unhealthy Complexion Listening to the Sound of the Sea* belong to this group: as does the very small *Accommodations of Desire* in which the lion's menacing heads are collage while the other passages have been painted in. One of the 'paper' lions has had his face cut out and dispersed to other parts of the picture – a proliferation of toothed openings that have

a directly sexual meaning. For paper is dry, the very opposite of Dalí's elsewhere liquid forms, and so effectively gives that dryness to the metaphor under construction – as well as disrupting the material unity of an already highly disturbing work.[15] Dalí acknowledged that the painting expressed his anxiety about having sex with his wife Gala ('I represented this act to myself as terribly violent and disproportionate to my physical vigour'[14]). The single work which represented Dalí in Aragon's collage show however is *The First Days of Spring* [*67*], also of 1929, in which we find a small pasted photo of the artist heightening another scene of sexual anxiety, one involving masturbation, his own childhood and the authoritarian figure of Freud, who appears on the right of the painting. Robert Desnos, who wanted to buy the painting, thought 'it was like nothing that's being done in Paris'. Dalí's biographer Ian Gibson says that the painting's combination of Freudian and personal symbols was a breakthrough and 'led directly to one of the most fruitful periods in his [Dalí's] career'.[15] Even Aragon was perplexed by Dalí's extraordinary technique. 'Is he trying to baffle the eye, and does he rejoice in the error he has caused? It's possible to think so, and yet still find no explanation for this double game'. The incoherence of Dalí's paintings is the incoherence specific to collage, Aragon says finally, and is such that to unlock their significance would be to construct something like the plot of a novel; Dalí's technique participates in an anti-pictorial spirit that is proving anathema to painters of the straightforwardly 'expressive' kind.

And so it is with Yves Tanguy, whose paintings around 1926 contained a *papier découpée* element and Magritte, about whom Max Ernst observed that his pictures are 'collages painted by hand'.[16] In fact Magritte's inventiveness with the paradoxes of overlapping or folded forms – or paper-like shapes with holes removed, or negative shapes superimposed upon other shapes – stems directly from the physical qualities of manipulated paper and to that extent mocks the collage technique while producing visual effects that are sensationally paradoxical and new. Magritte produced nearly thirty *papier collé* works between 1925 and 1927 (beginning with *Nocturne*, 1925), many of which utilized cut-out parts of a musical score (the comedy *The Girls of Gottenberg* by George Grossmith and L. E. Berman). Some of these *follow* rather than precede a related painting: and interestingly they seldom exploit the negative-image device that appeared in the paintings that were done next, such as *A Taste for the Invisible*.[17] Magritte deployed a third type of collage in the

68 **René Magritte** *A Taste for the Invisible* 1927
Magritte built upon the contemporary interest in collage by painting a variety of collage-effects, including those which make it seems as if areas have been cut out, superimposed, overlapped, repeated, stacked physically, doubled or inverted. The impression of matter as paradox is overwhelming.

69 **René Magritte** *Untitled* 1930
The scale of this work (now lost) can be gauged through the presence in it of corrugated cardboard. Among Magritte's works it is fairly untypical – but demonstrates his interests in the paradoxes of language as well as those of sight. The phrase seemingly refers to a contemporary song, the title of which translates as 'The Swallows born in Winter'.

well-known grid of surrealist artists with their eyes closed (as in dream) published in *La Révolution Surréaliste* of 15 December 1929. Yet for the Goemans show he used a fourth technique, involving stuck-on cardboard pieces in the gaps of a verbal sequence which is assumed to be 'Les Hirondelles Naissent En Hiver', a current popular song. Aragon wrote in a footnote to 'La peinture au défi', 'Is there a connection between collage and the use of writing and painting as practised by Magritte? I see no way to deny it'.[18] Then there was Picabia, who had been taunting the viewer with the redundancy of art for a whole decade, and for whom the ephemerality of collage made it the perfect technical means. Two works listed as *Le flirt* and *Très rare tableau sur la terre* were his contributions to the Goemans show. And finally Picasso, who Aragon says 'did something terribly serious' in 1926 in taking a dirty shirt and sewing it to the canvas with needle and thread [*65*]. 'He made a collage with nails sticking out of the surface'. And when people brought him old scraps for his work, he rejected them all. 'He wanted none of it, preferring instead the true waste products of human life, poor, soiled and scorned'.[19] Poverty, ephemerality, the unattributable, the dry, the anonymous: the second gist of Aragon's defence is that collage or its painted inversions could supply pictorial and philosophical sensations that no other method could. Paper with its flat, foldable materiality – its ability to conceal or obscure: such qualities were the ideological antithesis of the expressive mark. And thus the anti-individualizing 'individuality' offered by collage became a measure of its achievement: the collage-effects demand attention (Aragon is quite precise here) not by drawing attention to the painter's narcissism or his 'personality', but 'by being in absolute opposition to painting, and beyond painting. By the human possibility it represents. By substituting for a degraded art a means of expression of unknown power and range'.[20]

Joan Miró and Painting

The use of personality to conceal personality; the power of painting to go 'beyond' painting; these are also good descriptions of the strategies used between 1924 and 1933 by the Spanish painter Joan Miró, all of which depended crucially upon the use of collage-type techniques within a framework of Surrealist thought.

Miró was already reluctant to describe his works as 'paintings': writing to Michel Leiris in 1924 he refers to 'my latest X's (I don't want to say either canvas or painting)'.[21] For three years after that he produced the memorable works containing wandering lines, small metonymic signs like a hat or a breast or a star, and abrupt variations in focus, style and organization designed to tease the viewer with a sense of the multiplicity of the categories of the visual world. Crucially, there are 'paintings' from this period which play havoc with any clear distinction the viewer may try to preserve between the media and their canonical modes of address. In *Un oiseau poursuit une abeille et la baisse* of 1927 [*70*], the calligraphy of the wonderfully fanciful line of writing first of all designates its various objects by nearly touching them (the bird is the feather, the bee the dense blue smudge underneath) while the letters of the word *poursuit* unravel in 'pursuit' of the yellow path of the bee. But Miró has pulled off an interesting piece of verbal as well as visual play. 'Baisse' means 'lowers' or 'ravishes', hence literally 'A bird pursues a bee and lowers/ravishes it' (better French on Miró's part would have had it read not 'la baisse' but 'l'abaisse', suggesting to debase or humiliate). If the spelling was 'baise', the bee would be not lowered but kissed. Meanwhile, the viewer has to trace the line of flight as well as see what the words and letters say: he or she is caught half-way between reading and looking, never quite in either but always in both, thrown into categorical doubt by the collage-effect of the gap between the two.[22] Thus did Miró attempt to 'assassinate painting' – but as only a painter could.[23]

In fact Miró's position in Paris at the end of 1927 was interestingly precarious. He was selling paintings to high-profile collectors and was hard at work on a new set of works known as *Imaginary Landscapes*; but he was having doubts about the status of these works

70 **Joan Miró** *Un oiseau poursuit une abeille et la baisse*
1927
Miró's non-standard, or punning, French here disrupts the
signifying function of the elegantly painted words: it is equally
possible that his friendship with Bataille introduced him to the
concepts of 'abasement' and 'the low'.

right 71 **Joan Miró** *Spanish Dancer* 1928
Miró several times resorted to *objets trouvés* at moments
when his painting needed re-anchoring in the forms, shapes
and metaphorical possibilities of material.

in an ambience – we may call it competitive Surrealism – which viewed even the absence of 'pictorial conventions' as an insufficiently thorough revolt. Two contrasting ways of looking at his work now emerge at about this time. On the one hand some of the Spanish newspapers were proudly reporting that Miró had become a favourite among European and American collectors; and Waldemar George was praising the 'huge, bare surfaces covered with a uniform colour and scattered hieroglyphics' that placed Miró as a painter on the level of Picasso.[24] A more brutal assessment was provided by André Breton, who in February 1928 published an extended version of 'Surrealism and Painting' in which evaluations of Miró, Arp and Tanguy were now included. We would expect Breton to say that some painters suffer from petty-bourgeois smugness: it is more disarming to find him imputing to Miró the charge 'of giving himself up utterly to painting and to painting alone' – and of enjoying it too much. Breton's accusation was that Miró was following the theory of automatism, but doing so 'only summarily' and with an excess of deliberation.

Breton's comments might well have provoked Miró into making the three extraordinary works known as *Spanish Dancer* in the early part of 1928, which suddenly abandon literal painting in favour of objects stuck to a non-canvas surface. Not only do they return Miró to his national roots and perhaps to the *bricolage* manner already deployed by Picasso; they were just the kind of works of which Aragon could approve (two were included in the Goemans collage show of 1930). The work reproduced here evokes a dancing woman by the most reductive and suggestive of analogical means: her head is figured by a scrap of sandpaper nailed to the linoleum sheet, her body is another length of string at the base of which we find a draughtsman's triangle (her sex), a nail suggestively hanging above it. Meanwhile, her flailing dress is cleverly evoked by another piece of string, this time tacked to the board to help preserve its shape. A small tuft of hair is visible to the left. In his statement for the Galerie Goemans show Aragon would make his attitude to Miró clear. After berating him (as Breton had) for his one-time servitude in face of the acquisitive habits of the bourgeoisie – painting, says, Aragon, 'is becoming, soothing and flatters the man of taste who paid for it' – he abruptly affirms the contrary principle: 'Collage is poor. For a long time to come its value will be denied' – that is until monetary value is totally evacuated from art.[25] And it was with this in mind that Aragon approvingly reproduced *Spanish Dancer* alongside Picasso's large 1926 *Guitar* in the Goemans Gallery catalogue.

In the meantime there is evidence that Miró himself well understood the relevance of collage to painting, in the sense not of replacing painting but of helping invention in painting to flourish and expand. For yet another collage series was evolving during the summer of 1929 while Miró was in Montroig in Spain. Completed shortly after a series of highly elaborated *Dutch Interior* paintings following a trip to Holland in late 1928, Miró now produced an estimated 29 works by sticking coloured paper and newsprint onto another paper sheet in a manner that again rehearses the discovery that modern painting could only survive by persistently undercutting its own rules [72]. Anne Umland has recently suggested that the 1929 series comes at the moment of Miró's marriage and the conception of his first child, hence between one era of his life and another; it coincides too with Breton's drafting of the second *Manifesto* and a waning of his interest in Miró as Breton's own position became more politicized – as well as the emergence of the *Documents* group around Bataille and the discussions which eventuated in Aragon's Galerie Goemans show. Several of Miró's 1929 collages were shown directly *before* the Goemans show, at the Galerie Pierre in Paris in March 1930, and directly *after* a show of his paintings, also at the Galerie Pierre.[26] The latter may be significant: for having brought the two mediums so closely together, the rough textures of pasted paper and the appearance of improvised design in the collages (some papers crumpled as if by accident, some crudely cut or torn) must have cast the larger paintings in a new light. Indeed some of these collages are covered in a deep black tar, frequently incised with small motifs

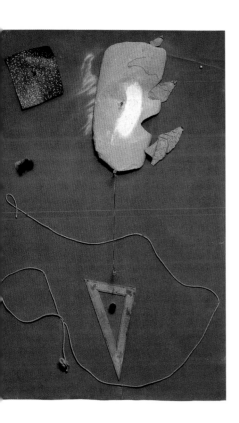

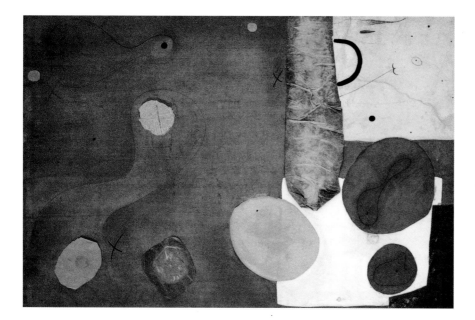

72 **Joan Miró** *Collage* 1929
Quite contrary to the *Dutch Interiors* painted the year before, the 1929 collages were seen (for example, by Carl Einstein) as attempts by Miró to counteract his own virtuosity and to return to basic, material forms; by Catalan critics (Gasch) as a reaction to French 'frivolity' and 'taste'.

looking like primeval scribblings. As Aragon would say in the text for the Goemans catalogue, 'Mineral pitch is one of Miró's favourite ingredients. It is difficult to say whether Miró's collages imitate his paintings, or whether his painting imitated in advance the effect of collage'.[27] My guess is that Miró's collages might have provided a riposte to Breton's complaint that he was too completely dedicated to 'pure' painting. Breton did not pick up the clue. Bataille did. In his review of the Galerie Pierre show in *Documents*, he seeks to emphasize how *altération* – the decay of composition into decomposition, the erosion and mutation of matter – provide the poles of modern painting's dialectic with itself. Quoting Miró's remark to Maurice Raynal that he 'wished to assassinate painting' Bataille now credits Miró with an acute consciousness of how modernist painting really works: by masochistically 'spoiling' itself constantly in a perverse but startling act of survival.[28]

And there was one further gesture that some of Miró's new admirers would have noticed and talked about. Amid the marks resembling stains, burns and glue-smudges that litter the 1929 collage works, some of the small pasted discs do not lie strictly 'on' the surface, but curl upwards slightly in betrayal of their temporary and improvised nature. Underlying Miró's *Collage* and hence not fully visible in its finished form, the complete film page from the Catalan newspaper *La Publicitat* has in fact been pasted down prior to the superimposition of the green paper to the left (that paper has over time darkened from beige): the tell-tale letters '[...]tro Goldwyn M' can just be glimpsed through the crudely torn hole. Impoverishment of materials and of execution was the main quality Miró was after here – but a wry comment at the expense of the Hollywood film industry may have been another. It seems not accidental that when Luis Buñuel and Salvador Dalí's anti-Hollywood film *L'Age d'Or* was shown for the first time in late 1930, three of Miró's 1929 collages, exhibited in the cinema foyer alongside works by Arp, Dalí, Ernst, Man Ray and Tanguy, were attacked by right-wingers protesting an infringement of public decency.[29] Fascism had reared its head in Paris. Surrealist collage had become its *provocateur*.

The final works by Miró to be considered here are a group completed in 1933, after the watershed events of 1929–30.[30] In the spring of 1933 Miró embarked upon 18 middle-sized paper collages containing elements clipped out of commercial catalogues and newspapers, each of which is then translated into a large painting in a process which loses the original clippings while preserving their approximate spatial intervals and something of their

73 **Joan Miró** *Painting* 1933

74 **Joan Miró** Preparatory collage for *Painting* 1933

At nearly three times the size of its preparatory collage, the painting has transformed machine-made forms into floating amoeba-like volumes, as if suspended in a magical ether: Miró had refreshed his painting imagination by seeding it in the world of modern manufacture. In the collage are diagrams of drainpipes, a propeller, three umbrellas, and a sideways letter 'N'

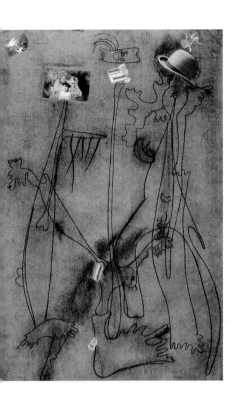

mutual incongruity.[31] Starting from a narrative-rich layout of 'real' objects within a paper rectangle, the painter denatures those objects and turns them into visual forms, but does so by stretching similarity-clues to the limit and even beyond. Who would ever associate the three painted forms at top right, for instance, with the pasted-paper umbrellas in the smaller collage? The collages themselves have occupied a controversial status. On the one hand Miró's biographer Jacques Dupin tells us that Miró never showed them 'because he does not look upon them as "works"'; but on the other hand Miró carefully preserved all of them as a form of testimony to the paintings they helped create. As to the translation process, Dupin admits that 'it is scarcely possible to describe or even to conceive of the process by which the actual metamorphosis took place'. He speculates that 'the utilitarian object or machine, in its most neutral, banal representation, enables [Miró] to interrupt the continuous elaboration of his expressive powers and to place his inner universe in the light of absolute exteriority'.[32] More precisely put, the 1933 group seems to confirm the give-and-take that Miró could exploit between commercial paper sources and paint. And they perhaps do something more – as would a more playful series of collages of 1933 and 1934 which interleave erotically cursive drawing with what Dupin calls 'old picture postcards showing bashful lovers or *femmes fatales* in the delectable bad taste of the beginning of the century'[33] – or, in a few, hats from a catalogue of his friend and adviser the hat-maker Joan Prats. Carolyn Lanchner has suggested that it was Miró's fascination with commercial catalogues and other printed ephemera that had brought him close to Bataille and the *Documents* group in 1929–30, and that Miró in his turn had seen how the journal had employed a collage editing method to stage an 'ethnographic Surrealism' of incommensurably coded images from the far larger range of human culture and artifice.[34] *Documents* had indeed been crowded with implied reorderings of high/low, exotic/familiar, archaic/contemporary – with paintings by Picasso, Hollywood movie clips, documentary photos from New Caledonia, insects and masks. Miró's photographic source material would resonate very differently a decade later in New York, among those watching the re-emergence there of abstract art. For Greenberg at that time, Miró's photographic sources would constitute a major theoretical obstacle to the otherwise considerable ambition of Miró's art.

So, indeed, would the type of Surrealist photomontage produced by the writers and literary people associated with Breton's group. Georges Hugnet deserves mention here. A friend of Breton, Tanguy and Éluard from the later 1920s, Hugnet crossed over easily between poetry and the practice of collage.[35] His volume of poetry *La Septième Face du Dé* (The Seventh Face of the Die, 1936) comprised ninety pages of *poèmes-découpages* made out of scissored magazines and newspapers arranged around photomontages exploiting chance effects and eroticism [77]. In his *Dictionnaire du Dadaisme* Hugnet would write that the main difference between photomontage and collage is that the former uses, 'not the drawings reproduced by ancient techniques such as wood engraving, illustrating diverse works and having a similarity of style, but elements borrowed from reality in the form of original photographs and magazine images...photomontage is less subject to the rules of resemblance such as lighting, scale, the personality of objects, the precision of linkage, and less prone to difficulties of minute assembly. On the contrary, the choice of elements [in montage] permits a greater freedom of expression and of format, and more adjustable and spectacular plastic development.'[36]

Surrealism in Prague: Toyen, Štyrský, Teige

Thanks largely to the missionary efforts of André Breton and Paul Éluard – as well as the newsworthy scandals of artists like Dalí, Ernst, Picasso and Miró – Surrealism spread far beyond Paris. The Czech painter Josef Šíma had been in touch with the Surrealists in Paris since moving there in 1922, and the links between his work and French and Belgian

76 **Joan Miró** *Drawing-Collage (Montroig)* 1933
Unlike the preparatory collages made for paintings, these large drawing-collages were intended for display: in them Miró bridges the gap between automatic drawing and commercial printed ephemera, including an illustration from a catalogue of stylish hats – both a Freudian dream symbol, a favourite Surrealist motif, and a nod towards Max Ernst.

COMMENT J'AI TROUVÉ LI...STONE

op 77 **Georges Hugnet** *Une Nuit* 1936
oet, bookbinder, publisher and historian of Dada and
urrealism, Hugnet worked at the centre of the movement.

bove 78 **Toyen** *Fata Morgana* 1926
eige defended Czech Artificialism against the 'literary
onceits' of the French Surrealists: the surface treatment of
oyen's paintings assures their grounding in real matter.

pposite 76 **Toyen and Jindřich Štyrský** *How I Found
ivingstone* 1925
 photograph of carved wooden children atop a wooden
iraffe surmounts an image of a Catholic boy at prayer, while
 bay tree, wax seal and circular franking mark embellish an
therwise triangular structure.

Surrealism were openly visible. Following the 'Bazaar of Modern Art' in Prague in 1923 and the early flowering of Devětsil, two of the group's members Toyen (Marie Čermínová) and Jindřich Štyrský had moved to Paris in late 1925. The flamboyant and energetic Toyen now gave up her figurative fantasies (*Paradise of the Blacks* of 1925 is the benchmark example) in favour of a cool geometry of abstract-Cubist overlaps and abutments that show a sudden awareness of the relationship between Constructivist collage and abstraction: in fact in Paris that year a certain kind of abstraction was *à la mode*. The Czech art historian Karel Srp tells of two further developments: first, that Toyen and Štyrský got to know the Paris Surrealist Georges Malkine around 1926 (like Miró at the time, Malkine was trying to put collage and painting back together); second, that Toyen and Štyrský worked on a series of book covers from 1925 to 1928 in which the partnership of collage and abstraction is at first rather conventionally exploited, then given new life in a strange design for a book called *How I Found Livingstone* (almost all the covers were done for the Odeon publishing house in Prague, but since there is no book of that title presumably it never came out). It is not quite a picture-poem: unusually for the Czech avant-garde, we see a Cubist armature supporting both picture-fragments and painted passages, the two systems punningly related in several motifs including the bay tree at the base. Evocations of travel, adventure and exploration are once more joined.[37] Toyen and Štyrský would shortly define a new manner, Artificialism, or 'the identification of painter and poet', on the basis of the textural and semantic contrasts so evolved.

Indeed, that verbal formula was the one used in the catalogue of the first exhibition of Artificialism, which opened its doors on 5 October 1926 at Studio 4, rue Barbes 51 in the centre of Surrealist Paris, anticipating a November opening in the much more public Galerie d'Art Contemporain on the boulevard Raspail. By referring to 'poetry', Toyen and Štyrský meant to propose a viable alternative both to abstract art *and* to automatist Surrealism – and to place collage at its heart. As its name implies, Artificalism appealed to rational super-consciousness: its images were seldom those of personal memory or the dream. And like other artists in Paris who turned away from automatism in the mid-1920s, Toyen and Štyrský employed the deliberate methods of stencilling and spraying through a net, as well as the careful adhesion of cardboard, feathers, apple-peel and much else. We see then how Artificialism could be claimed as the Czech contribution to Surrealism and the direct off-shoot of Poetism. Delineating common objects and sensations out of such lightly applied tactilities, the picture-surface remained a constructed, rational object even as it evoked a lyrical mood.[38] Toyen's *Fata Morgana* (Mirage) of 1926 is a case in point. The painting evokes a hallucinated scene of desert palm-trees, even though its title implies that its pictorial presences have appeared on account of physical laws. And of course they have: they are done with pastes made of sand or paint, poured or sprayed, or texturized through combing or scraping. The latter techniques, it should be said, released the painter from the use of the brush and constitute a new type of surface materiality stemming directly from the collage idea. As Srp also points out, Artificialism liked to manufacture the illusion of diverse material strata interpenetrating as if geologically. The interplay of water and earth, the sea and dry land, the desert and the well, became the origin of Toyen's later depiction of 'trickling, fluctuating living damp matter which buoyed and engulfed objects'. Before she arrived at their fluid association, 'characteristic particularly of high Artificialism and represented in all manner of swamps, marshes, pools, lakes, bays and seas, Toyen first sought to highlight the antithesis of water and earth'.[39]

We should not forget that Man Ray's rayograms were a vital source of inspiration for Artificialism's 'imprinting' techniques: he had appeared at the 1923 'Bazaar', and helped ensure that Prague was never far from Surrealist Paris, just as Paris was never far from Poetist Prague. And further connections abounded. *ReD* (*Revue Devětsil*), the magazine edited in 1927 and 1928 by Teige as a mouthpiece for the second phase of Devětsil, would be quick to pick up the visual similarities between new scientific photographs taken from the air, underwater or through a microscope, and the Artificalist vision of a world materially revealed but never quite depicted.[40] Meanwhile Artificialism itself was not publicized in the Czechoslovak Republic until Toyen and Štyrský published their 'Popular Introduction to Artificialism' in April 1927 in the Brno magazine *Fronta* (which became immediately available in Prague). In Paris, it was Philippe Soupault who enthusiastically endorsed Toyen and Štyrský's joint exhibition in Paris in December 1927–January 1928, with a text reprinted in *Paris Soir* in advance of its translation into Czech.[41]

Yet Paris and Prague now had to confront each other. Poetism had claimed universal revolutionary significance in the transformation of mankind. Early in 1928 Teige restated that the goal of Poetism was to achieve lyrical enchantment not just of the visual, but of all sensory channels working together: what he was incautious enough to call 'humanity's immeasurable thirst for lyricism' could be slaked by a single poeticism or *poiēsis* (from the Greek) constructed in full consciousness and addressed to the five senses conjointly.[42] Such poeticism would be based in Epicureanism and materialism, but transcend them. To this end, Teige's revised and expanded Poetist manifesto not only evoked Baudelaire's idea of correspondences but espoused a full range of democratically organized and contemporary mass-cultural forms: photography and typography (poetry for the eyes), radiophonic compositions of sound and noise creating sensations of space (poetry for the ears), poetry for the sense of smell, taste and touch, the physical arts of sport and dance, and even the poetry of the comic as instantiated in burlesque and popular farce. In each sensory channel collage and film montage would provide the material, Constructivism the method.

But *ReD*'s programmatics would be overtaken by events. Specifically, the Czech publication of the entire text of Breton's *Second Surrealist Manifesto* in Vítězslav Nezval's new magazine *Zvěrokruh* (Zodiac) in December 1930 began to shift the understanding of Paris Surrealism onto a new footing. With Breton now openly aligned with dialectical materialism, and with the political and social crises in Russia and Germany gathering fast, Czech artists and poets more generally saw that they had to come to terms with Surrealism as a programmatically revolutionary force. As Jennifer Mundy and others have pointed out, if hallucinatory *dépaysement* had been the mark of Surrealism in Paris, in Prague its leitmotif would be erotic fantasy.[43] Štyrský, the leader of the Czech Surrealists, published the *Erotická revue* from 1930 to 1933 in which appeared translations of Freud, writings with a sexual theme by Aragon and Éluard, and erotic illustrations by the likes of Aubrey Beardsley, Felicién Rops, and Toyen herself – though under Czech obscenity laws it could not be sold publicly, lent or distributed. Perhaps the more signal development was Štyrský's publication from 1931 of a series of six erotic books, each one published in the suggestively titled *Edition 69*. Nezval's *Sexualní nocturno* (Sexual Nocturne) was the first, illustrated by Štyrský's own photo-collages made of Victorian illustrations in which classical maidens or unimpeachable governesses are assailed by large erections, in fantasy or a dream (it is never quite certain whose fantasy it is). The second volume was a translation of the Marquis de Sade's *Justine*, illustrated by the sexually ambiguous Toyen – and the last was Štyrský's erotic reverie *Emilie Comes To Me In A Dream* (1933), with an afterword by the psychoanalyst Bohuslav Brouk, with ten of Štyrský's collages which again evoke tumescence as a waking state. Placing sexual imagery from contemporary English and German pornography against a dream-like background, they place the libido at the centre of Prague Surrealism at the expense of the revolutionary politics then being purveyed in Paris. Collage had become synonymous with the making of vulgar pornography into art.[44]

Meanwhile, the first genuinely Surrealist show in Prague, 'Poezie' (Poetry), involving Ernst, Dalí, Miró and Giacometti as well as Šíma and Štyrský, had taken place at the end of 1932, and in March 1934 the Group of Surrealists of Czechoslovakia was formed, all

top 79 **Jindřich Štyrský** *Sexual Nocturne* 1931
Štyrský here constructs an analogy between the implied thoughts of at least one of the married couple and the activities of the egg-laying locust in the diagram above.

above 80 **Jindřich Štyrský** *Untitled* (maquette for *Emilie Comes to Me in a Dream, No. 1 / Penis*) 1933
The image of the penis emerging from a natural whirlpool is the first of a group of explicitly sexual images set in dream-like spaces: the whole reverie amounting to a celebration of libido in line with Freud's concept of the 'pleasure principle' now advanced as an emancipatory programme.

Jindřich Štyrský Collage from *Portable Cabinet* 1934
~~yr~~ský used both collage and photography as a laboratory of
~~eas~~ for his painting. This series of some sixty-five collages
~~es~~ colour photography for the first time, producing vivid
~~ntrasts~~ of both colour and image.

Karel Teige *Collage No. 23* 1936
~~nange~~ of shape and texture are left visible here in order to
~~dow~~ the image with a constructed, even carved, quality.
~~ge~~ sets his creation in 'real' photographic space in order
~~convey~~ how life and libido might merge.

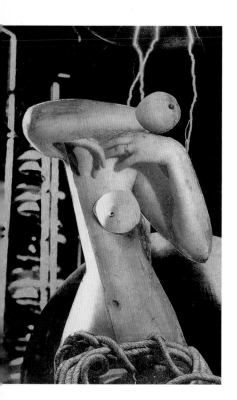

signatories to a manifesto by Nezval. No less significantly, Štyrský's series of sixty-five collages known as *Stěhovací Kabinet* (Portable Cabinet) appeared in 1934 as the most authoritative and visually disturbing Czech contribution to Surrealism to date.

But what of Teige? His contribution to the international debate on photography during the years of the Soviet First Five Year Plan had been to revert wholeheartedly to the political. Towards the end of his essay 'The Tasks of Modern Photography' (1931), and bemoaning the fact that 'modernistic' art photography (Renger-Patzsch the culprit) 'is slowly withering into a sick *l'art-pour-l'artisme'*, he recommends Soviet-style worker-photography as practised by Boris Ignatovich, Georgii Zelma, and Arkadii Shaiket, figures who were 'beginning to use the camera to address documentary tasks': or those workers in photomontage such as Klutsis, Rodchenko and Heartfield who were turning photography into 'a successful tool of political, cultural or industrial propaganda...a means and a weapon of revolutionary struggle'.[45] And yet in the aftermath of the 'Poezie' exhibition of 1932, the formation of the Group of Surrealists of Czechoslovakia in 1934 and the missionary visit to Prague by Breton and Éluard in 1935,[46] we find the ever-changeable Teige defining a photo-collage technique of his own in a series of some 374 small works made between the end of 1935 and his untimely death in 1951.

Unlike Štyrský's *Portable Cabinet*, one is struck by how consistently they take a background setting and libidinize its spaces with female flesh. Did Teige know Henry Moore's sculptures of the later 1920s and early 30s and the scandals they were causing? No doubt Teige's photo-collages inhabit a wider Surrealist preoccupation with anti-monuments that he had probably absorbed from such sources as *Documents*, the paintings of De Chirico and Dalí, or Breton's own interest in the literary and military monuments of Paris, as expressed in his novel *Nadja*. Some of them liberally quote other photographers such as Blossfeldt or Brassaï. But his purpose was perhaps a political one too. In a text of 1932 Teige had confidently related photo-montage to the Hegelian or Marxian dialectic: 'If early paintings and book graphics were intended as integral, homogeneous artwork', he had said,

> then montage is a new method of constructing the whole from heterogeneous parts. It is the pictorial synthesis of contradictory elements: the colourless, white or grey-black photograph, complemented with areas of colour, or the arrangement of photographs contradictory both in content and execution, provides a balance of contrasts, unexpected associations, and essential proportions.

Though written in support of the graphics of Klutsis and Lissitzky as 'an instrument of ideological propaganda, a powerful weapon and bugle heralding the Five-Year Plan' (he even suggested montages be provided for Marx's *Kapital* or Lenin's *Materialism and Empirio-Criticism)*, Teige was aware of the very different demands of Surrealist *dépaysement*; hence we find him concluding: 'We could say that the system of montage is dialectic: the synthesis of formal opposites brought to a higher level of *expressiveness* and *emotional impact'.*[47] It is a statement, after all, that neither Klutsis nor Lissitzky could have made; nor Heartfield nor Höch, who were exhibited in Prague and Brno respectively in 1934 and whose work Teige knew. Rejecting not only Štyrský's style but the very different satirical manner developed by Jiří Kroha in 1930–2 and titled *Sociologicky fragment bydlani* (The Sociological Elements of Living) [*83*], Teige is still the disciple of earlier Poetism and the idea that 'Lyricism is the crown of life: Constructivism is its basis'. Teige's new compromise between Constructivism and lyricism, then, seems to be composed of three main effects. First, there is a Bellmeresque isolation of the curvaceous parts: breast, forearm, belly. Second, they may compose an allegory of the statuesque female out of already-existing soft-porn images and other gadgets and surfaces, effectively totemizing

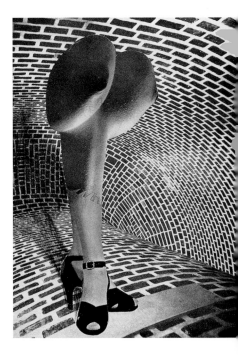

'the female', even, on occasion, as a castrating machine.[48] Yet the third and most persistent motif is one that only collage as a device could generate: the softness of bodily parts not only indexically presented but eroticized as a purely *photographic* contrast of textures: breasts against grass, breasts against landscapes or gravel or wood, inside barbed-wire, in the midst of dry leaves, or, in one case, inverted on the stalk of a neck and made into a phallic body and placed against the austere brick superstructure of Prague Castle.

Such works achieve their erotic charge through a method not attempted hitherto: the minutest visible variations in photographic colour and tone, magnified by the tell-tale curves of the paper's scissored edges. By systematically excising one grey tone and placing it against a subtly contrastive one, Teige aimed to produce an interval, a gap, which is *in itself* erotically stimulating.[49] 'It is sight', he had suggested, 'which thinks and feels'.[50] Teige's treatise 'Poem, World, Man' of 1930 had gone further in proposing a route to the desublimation of the senses: 'The optical impression provides the environment in which libidinous excitement is most frequently awakened and…which allows the sexual object to grow in beauty'.[51] This was Teige's best attempt to fuse psychoanalysis and socialism: the reactivation of Eros would 'cultivate, harmonize and socialize vital human faculties' that were vegetating or worse.[52]

And yet Teige never thought of himself as an artist, and very few of these works were shown during his life-time.[53] In any case, Surrealism in Prague was under heavy attack from the Party after 1938 (even though Teige defended the Surrealists in print while witnessing the break-up of the Czech Surrealist Group in the same year).[54] Finally, it may be relevant that only a few of Teige's montages were done before 1939: the largest number were done during the years of the war, when he had gone into 'inner exile' following the declaration of the Protektorat of Bohemia and Moravia by the Nazi invaders in that year. Some of Teige's montages might then be related to this nightmarish political see-saw suffered by his country: that, at least, is the reading offered by Teige's follower Vratislav Effenberger, who saw in the repeated fragmentation of the female body some kind of personal depressive response to the political destruction of Czechoslovakia.[55] Forced into privacy, yes; but Teige's photomontages still offer new insights into relations between the erotic body and the landscape of human thought. He ceased making them under pressure from the Stalinist police in the last few years of his life.

above, left 83 **Jiři Kroha** *The Sociological Elements of Living (Hygiene of Clothing and Underclothes)* 1930–2
'Dress and underclothes are protection against atmospheric influences' reads the message at the bottom: Kroha satirizes the slogans and images of the clothing and fashion worlds, a of them symptoms of an emerging modernity.

84 **Karel Teige** *Collage No. 358* 1948
Teige's audience would have understood the scandalous and abrupt contrast between the textures of flesh and those of a building important enough to be a national symbol: notwithstanding, most of Teige's collages were not exhibited publicly until the 1960s.

British Surrealism: Penrose, Nash, Agar

Surrealism arrived late in Britain; and was never quite the *cause célèbre* it had been in Paris. The Mayor Gallery showed Miró, Picabia, Arp and Ernst alongside the Britons John Armstrong, Paul Nash and Henry Moore in 1933, and the Zwemmer Gallery showed Dalí's paintings the following year, by which time the poet David Gascoyne was already at work on his *Short Survey of Surrealism*, to be published side-by-side with the first English translation of Breton's *What is Surrealism?* in 1935. By then, Roland Penrose, Paul Nash, Humphrey Jennings, Julian Trevelyan, Eileen Agar and John Banting had all visited France and knew Breton and some of the major Surrealist artists in that country: Gascoyne met Penrose in 1935, and along with other sympathizers worked on a plan for a major show in England. The announcement by the London group that an International Surrealist Exhibition would open at the New Burlington Galleries in June 1936 was therefore timely. Penrose wrote that he and his friends hoped to 'make clear to Londoners that there was a revelation awaiting. It could release them from the constipation of logic which conventional public-school mentality had brought upon them'.[56] The organizing committee included Breton, Éluard and Hugnet for France, E. L. T. Mesens for Belgium, and Dalí for Spain.

The event, which launched Surrealism in London, contained paintings, objects, drawings and collages. The use of collage by the British Surrealists follows the juxtapositional techniques already known from France – but with some striking differences. Herbert Read in the catalogue made the case that in Britain 'Superrealism' (exemplified by William Blake and Lewis Carroll) was the wider, romantic principle of which Paris-centred Surrealism was a modern reaffirmation. He pointed too to the appeal of folk art, children's art, urban graffiti and the 'finding' of objects in obscure places. Gone, he argued, is 'talk of form and composition, handling and handwriting' – to be replaced by the new criterion of the work of art's 'imaginative scope, its surprising incoherence, its superreality'[57] – yet another confirmation of the split between Cubist and Surrealist art. There were collages in the show by P. Norman Dawson, David Gascoyne, Humphrey Jennings, Magritte, E. L. T. Mesens, Miró, and Picasso (his *Head* of 1913 [*21*], owned by Breton). From the British contingent, Paul Nash exhibited oils, collages and objects much in line with the preoccupations of the article 'Swanage, or Seaside Surrealism' that he had published in April. Concrete seats, huge pretentious lamp standards, or quayside steps became strangely and eerily animate when photographed in a given light and from a certain angle: his photographs of the forlorn outdoor spaces of the modest British south-coast town have had the effect of determining the look and the feel of that place ever since.[58] Nash made further collages in the later summer and autumn of 1936 and modified them over the years. The only other photomontages or collages Nash made were in 1940 and 1942 in the cause of anti-German propaganda: they are considered in another chapter.

The second of the three major artists to be considered here, Penrose, who although he had contributed four paintings to the London show, developed an original use of coloured picture-postcards during a stay at Picasso's home village of Mougins in the South of France in 1937. These works, also inspired by his friendship with Max Ernst, are very different in character from his paintings (which are mostly in the spirit of Magritte). Overlapping a series of five or six postcards of the same view, clustering them together or fanning them into a curved pattern, Penrose's images seem to have something to say about the image as found: in this case, picture postcards displayed in multiples in the newsagent's rack. There are few examples of *multiplication of the same* (defying the Surrealist logic of *juxtaposition of the different*) in the whole of Surrealist art: the technology of the assembly-line is now seen as semantically relevant [*88*]. No less a couple than René Magritte and Paul Nougé wrote the earliest appreciation of Penrose's work. Defending the general practice of collage, they emphasized the futility of painting a scene when the 'thing itself' would do just as well.

5 **Paul Nash** *Swanage Surrealism* c. 1936
[H]ere Nash transfers his attention to bleached animal bones, [tr]ee roots, and naturally occurring stones found in the [b]eaches and in the local countryside, all of which, in certain [co]njunctions, would produce what Nash called 'not the [fr]eakish unlikely association of objects, so much as the *right* [a]ssociation as I feel it to be…it is only another step in the [m]ystery of relationship'.

They summarized the progress of collage in the skilful hands of Max Ernst: 'Isolating an object from a given ensemble and transporting it to another environment [they say] suddenly reveals the most amazing properties.... It must be added that the experiment is still more savoury if the image that is transferred is extracted from some "masterpiece".' Magritte and Nougé then suggest that in the unlikely event that collage could advance beyond Ernst, it would be Penrose's 'experiment' with postcards: the effect of which was to make colours out of objects (the postcard views), the exact reverse of the painter's process of making objects out of colours:

> If we take a finite number of postcards representing the Mediterranean, and enclose them in a single form, a triangle for example, then the transubstantiation operates immediately. We no longer have before our eyes the image of the sea enclosed in a geometrical contour. What appears instead is a blue triangle.... [But] there is also a dependence of the structure and the matter which is submitted to this structure, as other experiments of Roland Penrose clearly demonstrate, where the image of the shafts of columns gives place to an unknown and totally unforeseeable structure.[59]

They appear to be describing Penrose's *Real Woman* (1937), which uses the two-body format enjoyed by Max Ernst but creates winged or crawling creatures out of elements one can still read as multiple postcards. The effect is to situate the viewer precisely at the point of ambiguity between the relaxed enjoyment of garish tourist literature and its jarring transformation into a benign (or predatory) creature, far removed from the safe light of day.[60]

Yet it may have to be admitted that despite the stature of Nash and Penrose, the overall quality of British Surrealism made it 'the tail of the comet'.[61] In a country lacking an advocate as eloquent as Breton, and with an already sceptical public attitude to the visual arts, the chances of dramatic impact were never good. British Surrealists never cohered as a group, and too much of their imagery was imported from across the Channel. A succession of younger artists, nevertheless, made fine collages in a Surrealist vein. Eileen Agar, for example, had made collages as a teenager and turned to them again around 1934, beginning with one made of leaves – perhaps inspired by Picasso's cover for *Minotaure*. She made objects, decorated boxes and paintings in the Surrealist manner, and was represented by eight works at the International Surrealist Exhibition. A persistent theme of hers in the later 1930s was the merged or double-profile head, such as the delicately coloured *Head* of 1937 in which the random smudges on a sheet of wrapping paper supplant the natural features of a stone or marble bust in an act of elegant anamorphic doubling. Agar's debt to Picasso appears again in her construction *Object Lesson* (1940), by which time she was working in a canteen in London and doing little painting. In it, we see a woman's profile behind a basket-work circle, in front of which a lay-figure holds a small paint brush in the left hand, to the tip of which Agar has secured a champagne cork given to her in Mougins by Picasso, which seems to say: the brain needs champagne, perhaps Picasso's own, for creative work. Collage would continue to have a place in British Surrealism, but by the late 1940s the surreal would be rediscovered in the new consumer world – and with very different results.[62]

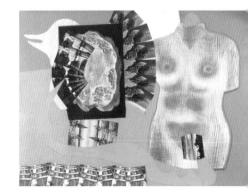

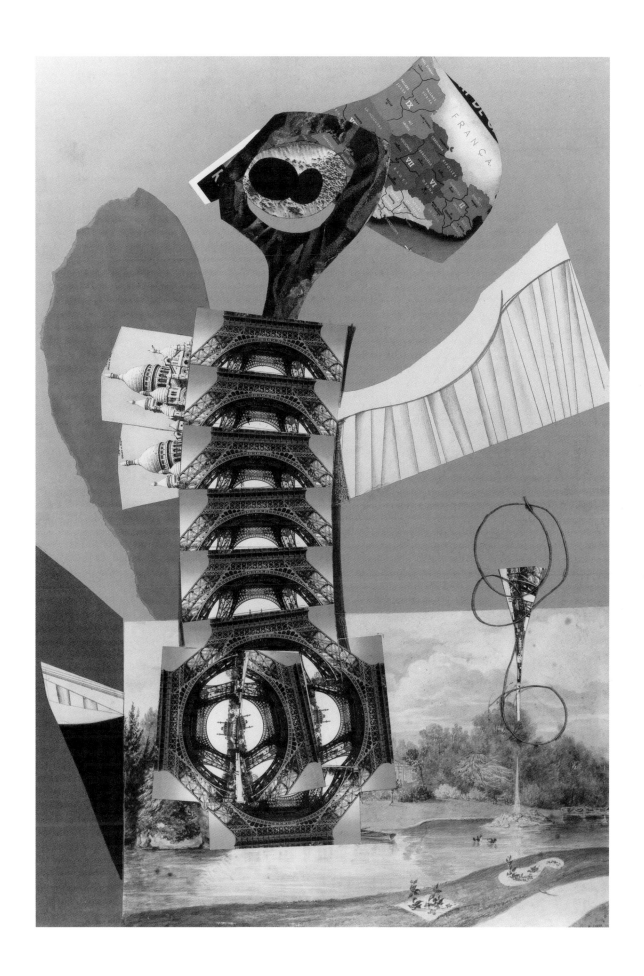

89 **El Lissitzky, Sergei Senkin and Gustav Klutsis** *The Tas[k]
of the Press is the Education of the Masses* (photofrieze at the
International Press Exhibition, Cologne) 1928
Seen by more than five million people, 'Pressa' advertised the
achievements of the Soviet state, as well as its advances in
press methods, in a new style of display involving montage,
kinetic panels, light and neon. Red triangle banners divide
the space.

6

The Political and the Personal: the 1930s

The reader can be forgiven some disorientation. What began as cut and pasted paper in the Cubist years had by around 1930 already proliferated into an army of techniques for interrogating the image, the surface, the processes of art: one suspects that no unitary definition of 'the modern' in art could embrace them all. Furthermore, the nomenclature of cut-and-paste had since Dada been thrown asunder. Surrealism especially had contested the Cubist ownership of collage in the most fundamental way possible – through an attack upon form, and upon self-reference. And in the meantime there had been many types of disciplinary wandering, away from painting, towards photography, or film, into a *rapprochement* with literature, and so on. But other changes were now afoot. For if the Cubist era was scarcely acquainted with photography, and if the post-1918 settlement saw its rapid proliferation – photographs conveying news, glamorizing foreign lands, or announcing scientific discoveries under the sea or through a microscope – then these would turn out to be merely a prelude to another revolution in the very techniques of everyday life. From the later 1920s the very context of information was beginning to change. Film was coming of age. Radio was a small child. TV was at the stage of conception. Magazine photojournalism was entering its heyday. But we are faced too with the titanic ideological clashes of the later 1920s and 1930s – the rise of state communism and fascism, and the economic crises of hyper-inflation and low employment – in which all the new media were called increasingly into the service of politics. As Walter Benjamin observed:

> Printing, having found in the book a refuge in which to lead an autonomous existence, is pitilessly dragged out into the street…. If centuries ago it began gradually to lie down, passing from the upright inscription to the manuscript resting on sloping desks before finally taking to bed in the printed book, it now begins just as slowly to rise again from the ground. The newspaper is read more in the vertical than in the horizontal plane, while film and advertisement force the printed work entirely into the dictatorial perpendicular.[1]

Large-scale Exhibitions
Montage played a vital role in the battle for hearts and minds, first in the communist world and soon afterwards in the fascist states. Lenin had been enthusiastic about photography;

90 **Gustav Klutsis** *Millions of Workers Take Part in Socialist Competition* 1927–8
Socialist 'competition' implied emulating the best working practices and production targets on behalf of socialist industry. The use of Lenin as an icon by the leading Stalin faction was a tactic employed repeatedly in the photo-posters of the First Five Year Plan.

1 Boris Klinch *Our Enemy: Churchill* 1932
The use of scissors and paste was advocated during the Five Year Plan as the proletarian and propagandistic device *par excellence*: it required virtually no training and the most ordinary materials. This image was published to mark the fifteenth anniversary of the October Revolution.

2 Aleksandr Rodchenko Page from the magazine *SSSR na stroike* (USSR In Construction) 1940
This commemorative issue dedicated to Vladimir Mayakovsky, who committed suicide under pressure from the Party in 1930, was Rodchenko's 'fact-file' method of juxtaposition to assemble a portrait of the poet – tilted diagonally.

Constructivists saw in its reality-effect an ideological tool far more powerful than easel painting. Soviet graphics of the 1920s, from book covers to commercial posters to theatre and film announcements, had followed suit. The artist-designer El Lissitzky had among his many talents a facility for photomontage in the context of the large trade exhibition. So when he was called upon to design the Soviet Pavilion at the International Press Exhibition known as 'Pressa', in Cologne in 1928, he set out with Sergei Senkin and Gustav Klutsis to present the idiom in its most spectacular form to date. The Cologne photo-frieze, at 3.8 metres (12½ feet) high and 23.5 metres (77 feet) long [89], provided a reprise of the panorama image already tried in previous international exhibitions, but did so now in the manner of a cinematic montage that implied the viewer's motion past the images, comparable to the filmic rhythms of Dziga Vertov. The frieze showed collective activities in agriculture, the workplace and the worker's club, but magnified those achievements through the command of large-scale resources which in themselves affirmed the success, the world-historical importance, of the proletarianization of the masses. Notice the cheerful figure of Lenin on the left of the vertical division, and the image of Nikolai Bukharin and a press reporter, at centre.

The period of the First Five-Year Plan in Russia and the rise of fascist politics in Italy and Germany only increased the relevance of the graphic image in the public sphere. The Proletkult (proletarian culture) movement in Russia advocated both photomontage and photography on the grounds that it was cheap, could be practised by anyone, and was visually effective, even if the results, such as the image of Churchill with an anti-USSR military squadron coming out of his head and published in *Proletarskoe foto* (Proletarian Photo), seem rather literal-minded today. On another level altogether lie the works of Senkin and Klutsis from the period of the Five Year Plan. In an impressive series of designs, Klutsis showed himself to be a master of the photomontage poster based on dynamic structure, immediacy and the collision and combination of photographic perspectives and images. A typical poster by Klutsis from the period would contain images of the masses and of industry, together with a well-known icon of Lenin exhorting the work force to ever greater efforts on behalf of heavy industry, and often to celebrate and extend its well-publicized results. In *Millions of Workers Take Part in Socialist Competition*, Klutsis forges these elements into a severe geometry of diagonals, the colour red, and the dominating 'double' of Lenin originating in a photo taken of the leader by G. P. Goldstein at a monument unveiling ceremony in 1919: most viewers of the Klutsis poster would be familiar with Lenin's salute to the assembled crowd.

Klutsis's confident virtuosity with the technique (collage proves to be readily convertible into photolithography) belies the fact that the *theory* of photomontage was a matter of constant debate in leftist circles as the 1920s came to an end. 'The photograph possesses its own possibilities for montage', Klutsis had written earlier in *LEF*, 'and they have nothing to do with composition in painting'.[2] In what she calls a 'second' phase of photomontage, Stepanova argued that Rodchenko actually renounced fragmented compositions around 1926–7 in favour of the single snapshot, 'the particular shot that will satisfy his objective' – in reaction against the very success of montage methods 'used extensively in political campaigns, from anniversary celebrations and parties right down to the decoration of offices and corners of rooms...'.[3] Meanwhile Rodchenko himself, at least in the field of portraiture, was in the late 1920s developing another method based on a loose 'fact-file' accumulation of snapshots, documents, anecdotal records, even voice recordings of the sitter, again a montage of sorts.[4] Klutsis survived these storms; and in the very different ideological atmosphere of the later years of the First Five Year Plan he abandoned the diagonal principle and showed groups of productive miners, agricultural workers or urban factory-workers as upright giants of industry. By 1931 or 1932 the mantra of 'class-equalization', which had been reflected in *Millions of Workers* in the image of teeming masses, is being replaced by a very different ideology of production superstars, technical specialists, Party leaders and other exemplars of the 'great march for socialist construction'.

It is too little realized that the generic device of montage became a propaganda weapon on the ideological right as well on as the left, though it assumed a very different look. For instance the idiom used by Lissitzky, Senkin and Klutsis at Cologne in 1928 was transformed for Mussolini's spectacular 'Mostra della Rivoluzione Fascista' (Exhibition of the Fascist Revolution) in Rome in 1932. Here, Mussolini's architect Giuseppe Terragni unapologetically steals motifs such as the hand raised in voting, or the image of the industrial machine, or huge crowds, to exhort compliant citizens to join the Fascist Party. Other large-scale photomontages followed. In Germany, the Bauhaus designer Herbert Bayer adapted Lissitzky's 'Pressa' methods first to the cause of photographic communication (clarity, mobility, variation) but then became caught up in the aestheticization of the Nazi Party through its several large-scale public displays, such as the exhibition 'Die Kamera' (1933) in Berlin, for which Bayer designed the catalogue. Many exhibitions advertising National Socialist policy between 1934 and 1937, such as 'Deutsche Volk – Deutscher Arbeit' (German People, German Work), 1934, 'Deutschland' (1936) or 'Gebt Mir Vier Jahre Zeit!' (Give Me Four Years' Time!) in 1937, all in Berlin, juxtaposed giant photographs of Hitler, marching SA troops, and applauding crowds in soberly symmetrical panels on a large scale. Other panels mounted bogus statistics relating to genetic miscegenation and the degeneracy of Jews and aliens: the photo-format was adaptable to almost any manifestation of venality or power. The entrance to 'Deutschland' for example, staged concurrently with the 1936 Berlin Olympic Games, was dominated by a large image of Hitler montaged against a crowd of his supporters from the party, the military and the Reich labour service: the whole was dominated by the expansionist slogan *Volk ohne Raum* (People Without Space). In Herbert Bayer's exhibition brochure for 'Deutschland' we find a more subtle cross between a tourist-style presentation of idyllic small-town life, rural traditions, and architectural monuments and an openly propagandistic programme for the new Germany: the whole is interspersed with images of Beethoven, Schiller, Kant and other intellectual giants. Inside is a double-page spread in which Bayer places a worker, a farmer and a soldier against a massive crowd of Nazi supporters at a rally. A caption reads: 'The Führer speaks! Millions hear him. The working population, the farming community, the military in their new freedom, are pillars of National Socialist Germany'. Ending his servitude to the Nazis, Bayer emigrated to America in 1938 and helped mobilize the anti-German war effort from the other side of the Atlantic in a series of equally large-scale photo-exhibitions for the American public, with the help of photo-techniques first used in propaganda abroad.[5]

'The dialectical problems of form': John Heartfield

John Heartfield arrived in the Soviet Union in April 1931 and stayed until early 1932. His stay coincided with a period of intense debate already taking place on the 'correct' methods of photomontage from a revolutionary perspective. Heartfield had been active in the left-wing group Rote Gruppe, from 1924, and in the Assoziation Revolutionärer Bildender Künstler Deutschlands (German Association of Revolutionary Artists, or ARBKD) from 1928. He had edited *Der Knüppel* (The Cudgel) with Grosz, had had a room set aside for his work at the 1929 'Film und Foto' exhibition in Stuttgart, had collaborated with Kurt Tucholsky on a satirical book, and in 1930 had started making images for the communist publication *Arbeiter-Illustrierte-Zeitung* or *AIZ*, which his Soviet hosts in 1931 clearly knew. Apparently free of his Dada origins, Heartfield was acquiring a reputation for political photomontage in a strikingly effective partisan style.

The debate was active in Germany too. In May 1931, just a month after Heartfield's departure for Soviet Russia, there opened the large and ambitious 'Fotomontage' exhibition

93 Anonymous photomontage before the Hall of Honour at the 'Deutschland' exhibition, Berlin, 1936
Though some elements are shared with left-wing propaganda, 'Deutschland's looming, symmetrically placed image of Hitler, flanked by bare-torsoed worker and military and Party types, constructs a leader-cult of a subtly different kind: Germany, here, is on the march.

in Berlin. Organized by Cesar Domela-Nieuwenhuis, 'Fotomontage' brought together not merely Domela and his Dutch colleagues Paul Schuitema and Piet Zwart, but Germans of the distinction of Jan Tschichold, Friedrich Vordemberge-Gildewart and Herbert Bayer, as well as former Dadas Schwitters, Hausmann and Höch, and fifteen members of the Soviet October Group including El Lissitzky, Klutsis and Rodchenko. 'Fotomontage' provided a context in which international debate about montage could be aired. The concern of several critics was the possible obsolescence of photomontage in the face of its co-option by advertising, especially the well-resourced business corporations, including the film industry. Hausmann, who gave a lecture at the exhibition, compared photomontage to the silent film – but argued against those who thought the utility of either was historically at an end. 'They lend themselves to as many possibilities as there are changes in the environment...and the environment is changing every day.... The formal means of both media need to be disciplined' was Hausmann's verdict; 'their respective realms of expression need sifting and reviewing'. The Heartfield style of lampooning, Hausmann implied, was not well poised to achieve this. He concedes that Heartfield was by that time adept at those shifts of scale, those pictorial displacements and anthropomorphisms, that made monsters out of well-known political figures or put textual matter into the wrong hands, yet Hausmann was for a 'constructive' element more in line with then current Soviet methods. Having himself left Futurist dynamics far behind, Hausmann now urged photomonteurs to recognize the 'optical element in pictorial expression':

> Photomontage in particular, with its opposing structures and dimensions (such as rough versus smooth, ariel view versus close-up, perspective versus flat plane) allows...the clearest working out of the dialectical problems of form.... The ability to weigh and balance the most violent oppositions – the dialectical form-dynamics to be found in photomontage – will assure it a long survival and an ample opportunities for development.[6]

Other cautionary voices were echoing that sentiment. The Hungarian critic Alfred Kemény (under his *nom-de-plume* Durus) warned photomonteurs of laying themselves open to being mimicked by bourgeois commercial photomontage with its appetite for selling, or of drifting away into 'artistic' montage that was out of date and not in accordance with the needs of the masses. Kemény chose as his examples a 'cubified' photo-portrait in the show (too near to Cubist painting), and a work combining old-fashioned etchings with photos (too near to Surrealism). For him the distinction was clear:

> While bourgeois photomontage uses photographed parts of reality to *falsify* social reality as a whole, disguising this very falsification of reality with the apparent *factualness* of the photographed details...(which is why the montaging of photos in bourgeois newspapers and magazines is so dangerous), revolutionary photomontage by an 'artist' (technician) of Marxist orientation brings photographic details (part of reality) into a dialectical relationship, formally and thematically: in this way it contains the actual relationships and contradictions of social reality.[7]

– an obligation most successfully discharged by the 'cliché-free' and 'ideologically irreproachable' photomontages of Oskar Nerlinger (known by his anagrammatic name Nilgreen).[8]

Against this background it is unsurprising that when Heartfield reached the Soviet Union in April 1931 his caricatural style was vigorously contested by none other than Gustav Klutsis on the behalf of the Constructivists, who favoured a mixing of photographic and linear structures in the service of visual dynamism as well as an enrichment of

Der friedfertige Raubfisch

„Ich verabscheue die kollektive Sicherheit! Ich lade die kleinen Fische einzeln ein, zweiseitige Verträge mit mir abzuschließen".

Fotomontage: John Heartfield

pictorial texture (*faktura*). The gist of Klutsis's criticism was that though Heartfield was a committed political fighter, he was still working essentially out of his satirical roots in Dada and had absorbed little from Russian Constructivism, with its revolutionary origins and tasks. In the light of the predominantly non-ironic tone of Soviet political propaganda, one can see that Heartfield's speciality, satirizing the bourgeoisie and its politicians, was perhaps never likely to gain strong acceptance in that country. In the words of the otherwise supportive Aleksei Fedorov-Davydov, 'Heartfield is much stronger in satire, in protest, in the depiction of the negative than in the depiction of the positive. We look in vain for the classical ideals of the proletariat in his works'.[9] In this statement from the later part of 1931 we can see the tell-tale signs of drastic revisions taking place within the cultural administration of the Soviet state. The left-included October Group was soon closed down and all but the most soberly instructional montages were outlawed under the dispensation of Socialist Realism, announced as a 'decision' of the Central Committee early in the following year.[10]

But the best of Heartfield's satirical work was still to come, even if this was after *AIZ* evacuated to Paris and then Prague after 1933, where its huge former circulation of some 500,000 gradually dwindled to an estimated 12,000 copies.[11] In Paris in the spring of 1935, endorsement was provided by Louis Aragon, who as a founder of the Paris group Association d'Écrivains et d'Artistes Révolutionaires (Assocation of Revolutionary Writers and Artists) had moved towards a Socialist Realist perspective by the early 1930s. In April and May 1935 Aragon helped organize an exhibition of 150 of Heartfield's anti-Nazi photomontages (most of which had already been published in *AIZ*) at the Maison de la Culture, which enabled him to claim the flowering of the Dada spirit as a new form of beauty aligned with the aspiration of the politicized working class. Aragon's catalogue text is a fine statement of the 'realism' of Heartfield's effects. By 1935 Aragon sees Dada, Surrealism and other Weimar-period movements as 'the maddened products of a society in which irreconcilable opposing forces are clashing': in contrast to which John Heartfield situates himself precisely at the point of expression of a new aesthetics, one of 'beautiful opposition'. The essential move was away from Cubist *papier collés*, 'where the thing pasted sometimes mingled with what was painted or drawn'. The new photocollages provided a verisimilitude 'borrowed from the figuration of real objects, including their photographs…the artist was playing with reality's fire'. Or as Aragon put it more concisely, the photo-fragments of Dada disruption now begin to signify: 'the social *forbidden* was quickly substituted for the poetic *forbidden*, or more precisely, under the pressure of events…these two forbiddens merged: there was poetry, but *there was no more poetry that was not also Revolution*'. Referring to the dove stuck on the bayonet in the front of the Palace of the League of Nations, or the Nazi Christmas Tree whose branches form a swastika, or the people's struggle against the hangman whose trachea is crammed with gold coins, Aragon asserts that Heartfield has 'no guide other than dialectical materialism, none but the reality of the historical process which he translates into black and white with all the rage of combat'. Based in Dada but now mobilized for more specific ends, Heartfield's technique is the true successor of centuries of painting, 'art in Lenin's sense, a weapon in the revolutionary struggle of the Proletariat'.[12]

Meanwhile in Prague, the fate of one of Heartfield's works illustrates its efficacy well. *Der friedfertige Raubfisch* (The Peaceable Fish of Prey), published in the renamed *Volks Illustrierte (VI)* in May 1937, excoriates Nazi expansionism in Central Europe by making Hermann Göring into a fish, who says 'I abhor collective security! I invite the little fishes to conclude individual bilateral pacts with me'. Heartfield, whose affiliations had meanwhile been pilloried in the 'Entartete Kunst' exhibition in Munich in June, now became further impugned in October, when the Nazi organ *Völkische Beobachter* reprinted *Der friedfertige Raubfisch* to illustrate the pernicious anti-German tendencies flourishing in Prague.

John Heartfield 'Der friedfertige Raubfisch' the Peaceable Fish of Prey), in *Volks Illustrierte* 1937 eginning from Göring's reference to 'little fish', Heartfield uilds a montage which connects word and image on several vels, notably that of the 'peaceable' predator who will suredly devour the others. The Germans invaded the udetenland the following year.

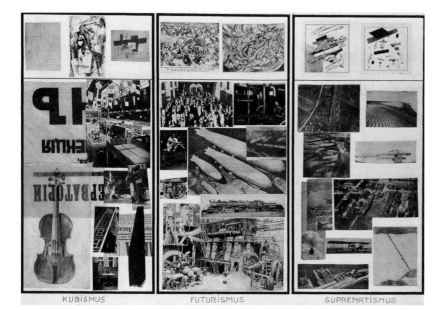

Heartfield left for London a year later and continued to make montages for *Lilliput*, *Picture Post* and *Reynolds News*. In America, and Herbert Bayer's contribution there notwithstanding, the influence of John Heartfield turns out to have been surprisingly small. The researches of Sally Stein have brought to light the fact that a certain straightforwardness marked the applications of photography in America from the early 1920s right through that and the next decade. Modernists like Paul Strand categorically rejected 'hybrid' practices that he felt impugned the absolute objectivity of the photographic surface. Photomontage, meanwhile, was treated as a European experiment: only a single photomontage can be traced in successive issues of the radical journal *New Masses*, namely Hugo Gellert's 'What's It All About?' satire on the Presidential election of 1928 – Stein is only a little unfair in calling it 'forced' and 'tentative'.[15] Even the left-leaning Photo League, though supportive of Heartfield, were hesitant to the point of publishing only a single montage, 'Workers of the World Unite', but declined to repeat the experiment. Photomontage on a truly public scale in America remained confined to the far safer codes of domestic advertising.

The Private Archive

These public stagings of the montage technique stand in marked contrast to more private uses of the medium as a form of personal or philosophical reflection. Three projects may be mentioned here: they point to a very different awareness of the photo-environment as it inflected the more private space of the teacher, the scholar and the artist respectively. In them all, we encounter ways of looking at and using photos based not upon ideology or a party programme, but upon the accumulation and comparative classification of the already given.

Already in the mid- and later 1920s doubts were being voiced in some quarters as to the relevance of the avant-gardist tactics deployed by Dada and Surrealism; notably discontinuity and defamiliarization. These doubts prompted a retreat from the loud clashes of Futurist incongruity, and a preference for a compositional format based upon the grid. In the grid, photographic unities from diverse sources could be assembled in noticeboard fashion without directly interrupting one another and without mobilizing the semantic shifts of altered scale, abbreviation or metaphor that characterized the other kind.

95 **Kasimir Malevich** Instructional panel for InKhuK (Petrograd State Institute of Painterly Culture) *c.* 1924–7
The left-to-right legibility of this panel implies Suprematism as the ultimate development, in which its aesthetic products, at the panel's top, are related to images of airplane flight and aerial photography – final freedom from gravity as man takes leave of the earth.

96 **Hugo Gellert** 'What's It All About?' in *New Masses* 1928 Amid images of corruption, war and continual unemployment Gellert places the smiling face of Republican candidate Herbert Hoover (bottom), who swept to victory following an unusually dirty election campaign in November 1928 (even though the Democratic candidate received almost one half of the popular vote).

Composition by Hugo Gellert

WHAT'S IT ALL ABOUT?

They call it a Presidential Election, but it's all a bloody farce. Pickets still go to jail, smaller nations are still oppressed, Labor is hungry, there's a new world war coming, chorus girls get Rolls-Royces, whoever succeeds Clammy Cal.

In Leningrad between 1924 and 1927, Malevich assembled several panels of pasted photo-documents as part of the twenty-two-panel instructional method at the Institute of Artistic Culture (InKhuK). Showing railway trains, inflatable airships and planes, the purpose of these panels was to demonstrate visually the evolution of art alongside its technical environment, from naturalism and Cubism to the 'higher' forms typical of Suprematism: in large measure the panels seem to be governed by visual and formal similarities thrown up by the potentialities of the photographic medium itself [*95*].[14] We saw already that for certain types of representation (the portrait) a loose collocation of data arranged noticeboard style was Rodchenko's preferred method of modernizing the easel painting [*92*]. Both the Malevich and Rodchenko projects answered to a new demand for photographic objectivity and for 'fact' that dominated Soviet photography in the later 1920s. In different ways they also imply a concept of aesthetic production no longer driven by a bourgeois author function, but by the naturally occurring simultaneity and mutual interaction of countless different permutations and arrangements of informational data, imagery and reproductive means.

It seems more than coincidental that the art historian Aby Warburg, working in a different country, was in 1928–9 constructing his private and never-finished archive known as the *Mnemosyne Atlas*. Warburg's *Atlas* comprises sixty screens on which were pinned a thousand pasted photographs, intended to constitute a kind of mnemonic or memory-system of the whole of Western humanist cultural civilization up to and including that date, but reflecting two of the central strands of Warburg's scholarly activity, namely the vicissitudes of the Olympian Gods and the role of the ancient 'pathos formulae' in post-medieval art and civilization. All the lectures and investigations on which Warburg had been engaged were to be somehow incorporated into this vast pictorial synthesis: the *Mnemosyne Atlas* contained reproductions of Late Antique reliefs, secular manuscripts, monumental frescos, postage stamps, broadsides, pictures cut out of magazines, Old Master drawings. But though the survival of ancient and pagan impulses in modernity was Warburg's overriding concern, the noticeboard method permitted countless affinities, contradictions, temporal and spatial shifts and reconnections to be established: Warburg wrote slowly and is said to have been always shuffling his index-cards – hence the photos of *Mnemosyne Atlas* were also frequently rearranged as one or another theme gained dominance in his mind.[15] In this version of the montage method, dreamlike suggestiveness and intensity arise not out of constructed meaning, but out of something more aleatory and diffuse.

Well-known literary examples of the additive montage method from the period are Walter Benjamin's *One-Way Street* (1925–6) or his later and also unfinished *Arcades Project* (1927–40, published 1982), whose governing principle was that of composed accumulation once more close to, if not literally examples of, the documentary genre. The third visual archive to be examined here, one that also seems to step aside from the disjunctive techniques of Dada, is Hannah Höch's 116-page collage-book of about 1933, which collects together photo-images of the Weimar period from illustrated magazines like *BIZ* (*Berliner Illustrierte Zeitung*), *Uhu* and *Die Dame*. Often erroneously described as a scrapbook, Höch's collage-book has an apparently very specific character – though there are no extant statements by Höch as to its origins or purpose. Surprisingly perhaps, the book seems to be constructed as a unity, unlike the more usual scrapbook principle of randomness and open-ended accumulation. Its images were drawn from a twelve-year long cache accumulated by Höch and her companion Til Brugman, then selected according to principles of visual resonance from the new photographic world: objects seen from a height, or from below, or in patterned formations (dancing or gymnastic women), giving fabulous profiles, surreal perceptions or moments of energized performance. Secondly, the book is quite precisely themed around images of the body, physical exercise or dancing,

97 Aby Warburg Panel 79 from *Mnemosyne Atlas* 1928–9
Searching for the transformations and sublimations of myth from the Classical world through to modernity, Warburg noted that: 'it is in the area of orgiastic mass seizure that one should look for the mint that stamps the expression of extreme emotional seizure on the memory.'

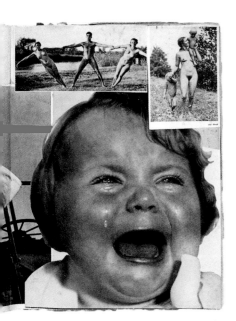

8 Hannah Höch *Sammelalbum* (page from collage book)
1933
This page from Höch's collage book contains two photographs
from one of the many naturist, dance or fitness manuals
published in the 1920s – a genre itself inflected by political
and ethical priorities and programmes.

9 Hannah Höch *Der Kleine P* 1931
This combination image in two contrasting colours of
magazine illustration is plainly that of a bawling adult-child, by
implication a ranting Nazi malcontent in full flow. The absence
of a torso magnifies the effect of the yelling mouth.

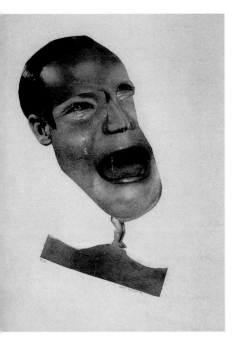

nature and childrearing, young women of Weimar culture, and African cultures: there are few references to technology, the industrial process, heavy machinery, or men. Thirdly, as a physical object it occupies a kind of middle ground between the single, exhibitable object and the flickering succession of a moving film – no doubt the reason why it has received such scant attention even in discussions of Höch's work. Turning its pages provides a series of snap-shot views that resemble a cartoon or motion picture: its reading is a one-person affair, addressed to relatively private experience as opposed to the collectivity of a show. Yet politics was never far away. For Höch's collage-book occupies the same historical moment as the rise to power of the Nazi Party and the effective end of the Weimar era. To that extent it may be seen as an act of mourning for a period of relative emancipation and of the flowering of experimental avant-gardes in art, film, music, theatre and dance.[16]

Montage as Resistance: Höch, Baumeister, Nash
Montage as a critical device of 'modern' art and literature – as opposed to its occasional use in propaganda – came inevitably under the heavy-handed censure of the National Socialists, along with abstraction, expressionism and Dada: it could never have been officially sanctioned once ideas of cultural totality in Germany gained hold. And one can see the reasons why. Several of Höch's photomontages of the period are explicitly concerned with Nazi politics or politicians – and are often tied to gender. Hence one sees in a work known as *The Strong Man* (1931) an image of male posturing as well as of the strong-man politics now threatening to impose cultural censorship in the wake of Weimar experiment. The montage puzzlingly known as *Der Kleine P* (The Small P, 1931) on the other hand, quite explicitly splices an image of a sleek male forehead and the weeping child (see the collage-book) to attribute a degree of puerility to the new political class. The German scholar Maria Makela has suggested that the title at one time was *Der Kleine Parteigenosse* (The Little Party Member), but that this was later abbreviated for reasons of security. The very fine *The Eternal Folk Dancers* of 1933 [*100*], however, explicitly references the fast-paced Bavarian folk dance repopularized by the Nazi Party – only to turn its practitioners into open-mouthed buffoons. Höch's attitude to the political decline of her day was one of quiet defiance: she knew such works could not be exhibited – even though she did exhibit several in her large exhibition in Brno in 1934. But she was increasingly vulnerable. By 1938 her former Dada colleagues Grosz and Richter were in America. Schwitters was in Norway; Hausmann in France. 'Those who were still remembered as having once been "Cultural Bolshevists" were all blacklisted by the Gestapo', Höch recalled, 'I was much too conspicuous and well-known to be safe in Friedenau, where I had lived for many years'.[17] She was being watched and possibly denounced there by zealous neighbours, and wisely moved to the small north Berlin village of Heiligensee (Reinickendorf) where she managed to escape attention for the duration.

Though Höch's works were not included in 'Entartete Kunst' (Degenerate Art), the infamous vilification of artistic modernism staged in Munich in 1937, those of the Stuttgart abstract artist Willi Baumeister were. Four of his works in the idiom (roughly) of Léger and Corbusier were included in that nefarious exhibition, and a fifth, an elegant Constructivist relief from 1920, was verbally anathematized on the last page of the 'Entartete Kunst' exhibition guide along with two other non-conformist works: Max Ernst's *Belle Jardinière* of 1923, and Johannes Molzahn's *Twins* of c. 1930.[18] The Nazis were also adepts of modernist montage when they wanted to be – as the presentation style of 'Entartete Kunst' amply demonstrated. And this was not an isolated example. The Nazi version of montage was used in the companion book to 'Entartete Kunst', Wolfgang Willrich's *Säuberung des Kunsttempels* (Cleansing of the Art Temples, 1937), where text written in opposition to works of 'degenerate' modernism is positioned close by.

opposite 100 **Hannah Höch** *The Eternal Folk Dancers* 1933
Höch represents the thigh-slapping folk-dancers as dislocated
dummies, or puppets manipulated by absent strings. Infantilist
pleasure-seekers, they are crudely constructed from ill-fitting
parts, strongly reflecting the mood of political parody more
typical of Höch's Dada years.

101 **Willi Baumeister** *Arno Breker's Der Rächer (The
Avenger) with Head drawn by Willi Baumeister* c. 1941
Breker's pseudo-Classical relief was designed to decorate
Albert Speer's planned North–South Axis in Berlin, and seems
to depict the 'revenge' of National Socialist manhood against
'impure' social elements threatening the state. In burlesquing
its genital region, Baumeister seeks to parody and marginalize
the Nazi cultural machine that had attacked him previously.

But the times were out of joint too. Not only had the Nazis paraded official National Socialist aesthetics in the nearby Haus der Kunst, but Baumeister, who visited both events, had by this time moved away from his Constructivist style to an archaic abstract idiom that tried to connect modernism with ancient cave art (these works are still critically underrated). Baumeister knew that official National Socialist aesthetics was a travesty that had to be countered. He bought the Haus der Kunst catalogue and some reproduction postcards of the second 'Grosse Deutsche Kunstaustellung' (Great German Art Exhibition) in 1938, and during the early years of the Second World War either made cut-up montages or sent some of the postcards, duly adjusted collage-fashion, to several friends.

Peter Chametzky has analysed these fragments and their recombination, and suggests that they have resisted inclusion in the *oeuvre* catalogue of Baumeister's work both because of their non-professional status and because of the authorless style that produced them; not to mention their having had an initial audience of only one, in the person of the recipient. Yet they are more interesting than that. On a reproduction of Arno Breker's *Der Rächer* (The Avenger), itself officially regarded as a pinnacle of militarized manhood in the early years of the war, Baumeister sketched a blue frame around the genital area, created a circle for the head and two lines for a mouth, and thus turned the penis into a nose: the pubic hair becomes a stylish quiff [*101*]. Breker's classical figure, designed as an image of revenge against the snake-like creatures that attack the warrior's body, thus had its ideological *gravitas* deflated by a childish gesture, as Nazi ideology and its bathetic cultural forms met their nemesis in the joke Baumeister shared with his friend.[19] This and Baumeister's other playful collages can be regarded as a form of Surrealism, perhaps, adapted to reveal the bodily and erotic impulses already present in the 'normalized' fascist body. The matching of body or face to genitals were also metaphors at the expense of the state: they constituted anamorphs that situate the viewer – any viewer – in the gap between 'serious' and 'playful', 'reality' and 'fantasy', in the Bretonian manner. Needless to say, the postcards were seized by the authorities:

> I was confronted by the Gestapo censor with my entire correspondence for the last year and a half. Thank God that Hitler in the electric chair [a collage Baumeister had made for an American newspaper] was not among the intercepted letters. I extricated myself only by explaining that they were planned for a book on colour modulation and patina.[20]

The other ideological works in the collage or montage manner from this period that show political motivation are from the British artist Paul Nash, who in 1940 tried his hand at montaging photos of flying objects laden with death about to crash into Nash's beloved landscape of southern England. The work pictured here is an effective two-part representation of a kind that Nash never repeated. All the elements of his nature-inspired Surrealism are present, now given reality by the photo-fragments that actualize the death-dealing instruments of war. Sometime in 1942 Nash made three further watercolour collages known as *Follow the Führer*, done in chalk, watercolour and newspaper on a buff paper ground. Though Nash was always at pains to emphasize that he was not a political Surrealist (rather 'a natural one'[21]) the vivid use of newspaper and painted landscape here make one regret that the British War Artists' Advisory Committee, to whom Nash unsuccessfully submitted them, did not encourage him to produce more.

102 **Paul Nash** *Dive Bomber. Parachute Trap* c. 1940
Nash's ability to personalize both man-made and natural objects is put to effective use in these rare montages relating to the threat in 1940 of invasion by dive bombers and airborne troops. The 'parachute trap' relies upon its title alone to establish its ideological force.

7

New York Conversations

While the European nations were being devastated by war, art across the Atlantic staged a renaissance of sorts. Groups of artists and intellectuals on America's West and East coasts found the opportunity to join the great enterprise of modern visual culture on their own terms. We shall look at the West Coast in due course. In New York it was Peggy Guggenheim, ironically, heiress to the Guggenheim family fortune, who first opened the conversation that would place collage at the very centre of that renaissance – that would make it, in effect, the lynch-pin around which so much practice and theory would revolve. But it would be a kind of collage practice very different in both scale and ambition from anything that had been seen in Europe hitherto.

Peggy Guggenheim and Robert Motherwell
Peggy Guggenheim came from a background uniquely attuned to the exotic possibilities of European Surrealism and life in the avant-garde. In 1922 she had married the worldly, ironic and sophisticated Laurence Vail, dubbed the 'King' of Paris Bohemia at the time:[1] he was himself a maker of Surrealist collages and *objets trouvés*, the author of several articles and plays, and a painter. It was Vail who introduced her to Venice, later the home of the Peggy Guggenheim Collection. Associations with English and French Surrealists followed in the later 1930s, notably the young Humphrey Jennings, André Breton, and Yves Tanguy, and a brief career at the Guggenheim Jeune Gallery in London in 1938–9; a city newly acquainted with Surrealism following the big international show there in 1936.[2] While in London, Marcel Duchamp had entered her circle, and through him Jean (Hans) Arp, and also Jean Cocteau, the subject of Guggenheim's first London exhibition early in 1938. Guggenheim's gallery neighbours in London's Cork Street had been the Mayor Gallery and the London Gallery, the latter owned by Roland Penrose and directed by E. L. T. Mesens. Such proximities are of course the stuff out of which modern art is made: it was Penrose who installed the 'Exhibition of Collages, Papiers-collés and Photomontages' at Guggenheim Jeune in November 1938, with works by Picasso, Arp, Max Ernst, Schwitters, Täuber-Arp, Vail and others. There was no conflict here between collage and the claims of abstraction: and the show was evidently a display-case of much that was best in Surrealist interpretations of the genre.[3] In the summer of 1941 Guggenheim, Max Ernst, the Bretons and other Surrealists sailed for New York, where Peggy's uncle Solomon had established

his Museum of Non-Objective Painting in a former car showroom on East 54 Street: the Museum would eventually become the Solomon R. Guggenheim Museum on Fifth Avenue. Peggy and Max Ernst were married in December, and the Guggenheim-Ernst home, Hale House at 440 East 51st Street, instantly became a centre of discussion for displaced European Surrealists and a fertile meeting-place between European and American artists. The following year, October 1942, Guggenheim opened her Art of This Century gallery on West 57th Street as a showcase for some of the most audacious art of this milieu.

How then was collage developed at the crossroads of American avant-gardism and émigré European Surrealism in mid-1940s New York? We should remember that American culture in the previous decade had exhibited a resistance to montage techniques – even advertising had veered towards orderly proximity, clear suggestive association, clean composition. The documentary photograph had won a certain kind of high ground.[4] Now, Peggy Guggenheim in New York was suddenly mobilizing some highly heterodox ideas about the framing and display of modern art. As the architect-designer Frederick Kiesler wrote to Guggenheim about the interiors for her new gallery, 'It is your wish that some new method be developed for exhibiting paintings, drawings, sculpture, collages and so-called objects'.[5] In Kiesler's extraordinary designs for Art of This Century, frames were to be dispensed with in a new type of Surrealist environment 'that merged architecture, art, light, sound and motion' in the Abstract Gallery, with turquoise walls, and ropes going from floor to ceiling for the attachment of works; the Surrealist Gallery had curved walls with works of art suspended from them on baseball bats, lights timed to flash on and off every few seconds, and a tape-recording of a roaring train.[6] Guggenheim's predilection for exotic and phantasmic encounters between the viewer and the art-object – an encounter in which Surrealist surprise, inconvenience and style all played their part – determined the *ambience* of the Art of This Century shows. Laurence Vail displayed collage bottles in an exhibition he shared with Joseph Cornell early in December 1942.[7] Marcel Duchamp showed his *Box-Valise*. Clearly, Art of This Century was oriented towards an aesthetics of *objets-trouvés*, assemblage and the eradication of the art–life divide.

And then, in a conversation early in 1943, Guggenheim invited the young Americans Jackson Pollock, Robert Motherwell and William Baziotes to submit works for the 'Exhibition of Collage' to be held between 16 April and 15 May. The energetic Motherwell had been the contact. He had travelled and studied in Europe, had studied art history with Meyer Schapiro at Columbia and through him had met several of the Surrealists (Duchamp, Breton, Masson, Tanguy). A biography for 1942 mentions other activities at the time: 'sees Mondrian's first one-man show (at Valentine Dudensing's gallery)'; 'makes automatic poems with the Baziotes and the Pollocks'; 'meets John Cage'; 'is included in the First Papers of Surrealism organized by Breton and Duchamp', and so on.[8] Motherwell knew the worlds of Freudian theory and Surrealist 'automatism' well, but at this stage was probably more taken with European artists involved in abstraction and the metaphorics of the figure, particularly Arp, Matisse, Miró and Picasso. Secondly, the intense Francophilism among New York liberal intellectuals following the fall of Paris, combined with a real sense of the tragedy of the Spanish Civil War and the miraculous survival of the Surrealists in New York, lent to Motherwell an awareness of the significance of his position. As Frank O'Hara summarizes it, for Motherwell at that moment, 'it had never been more clear that a modern artist stands for civilization'.[9]

But what was a modern artist? When Peggy Guggenheim invited Motherwell and his two colleagues to exhibit collages, none of the three had made anything in the medium before. Baziotes made a work called *The Drugged Balloonist* which remains an exception to the rest of his work [*106*].[10] The other two retreated to the security of Pollock's large studio to work on some pieces for the show: Motherwell remembered that Pollock 'had no particular feel for collage, but I remember being surprised at the violence of his attack on the

104 **Joseph Cornell** *Medici Slot Machine* 1942
Allegedly inspired by a chewing-gum machine on the New York subway, this is one of several Cornell boxes relating to the Medici children: here we see a painting of Piero de Medici by Sofonisba Anguissola at centre, flanked by cinematic repetitions at both left and right. Also visible are a compass and fragments of a map of Rome.

material'.[11] As well as works by Picasso, Braque, Schwitters, and George Grosz (living in New York at the time), Art of This Century's 'Exhibition of Collage' included Cornell, David Hare, Irene Rice Pereira, Ad Reinhardt, Hedda Sterne, Jimmy Ernst and (of course) Laurence Vail.[12] Though Max Ernst, the acknowledged master of the technique, had split up with Peggy Guggenheim and was about to elope to Mexico with Dorothea Tanning, he was still included in the show. Pollock's works seem to have been lost.

Motherwell, for his part, entered three collages in a medium that he found both immediate and attractive – and one that generated a range of effects of great importance to his paintings. The majority of Motherwell's collages occupy a confident easel painting format measuring some four feet high by more than two. No longer miniatures or sketches (though not yet mural-sized designs), there were few openly modernist works being done in New York at that time that had such a European look. And the process of collage involved no slow-drying oil paint. For Motherwell it could be intuitive and even 'automatic': large pieces of torn paper could be manoeuvred and re-torn at will to obtain a result, and quickly. Several collages could be completed at one go.

Even so, in the titles and the moods of his 1943 collages Motherwell seems to challenge the great Europeans on their own ground: *Joy of Living* by its title shadows something in Matisse (though its design is close to Baziotes). *Surprise and Inspiration* [*103*], titled by Peggy Guggenheim herself at a later date, contains rubbing, blurring and splotching of paint according to 'automatist' procedures; while *Pancho Villa: Dead and Alive*, which is basically a gouache painting with some collage on a cardboard base, reproduces Picasso's geometric manner of the late 1920s with its stick-like reductions of the human figure, its metaphorized ideograms and presences. A more programmatic collage like *View from a High Tower* of 1944 [*105*] evokes the mixture of height and intimacy that an aerial view provides, but projects into it a phantasized figure flying or floating or crashing – or being dispersed in the landscape below: such are the visceral sensations that are suggestively organized in the work. Motherwell's big oval-and-rectangle paintings of the next decade have their origin here, in the way that simple materials subjected to informal placing and tearing establish formats of potentially enormous scale, most often with human resonances. Yet as the artist wrote subsequently, to handle the material of collage was for him a means of *evading* representation:

> The sensation of physically operating on the world is very strong in the medium of *papier collé* or collage…. One cuts and chooses and shifts and pastes, and sometimes tears off and begins again. In any case, shaping and arranging such a relational structure obliterates the need, and often the awareness, of representation. Without reference to likenesses, it possesses feeling because all the decisions in regard to it are ultimately made on the grounds of feeling.

The statement from 1946 comes out of Motherwell's sympathy for Rimbaud and Baudelaire. 'The aesthetic is the *sine qua non* for art…the function of the aesthetic becomes that of a medium, a means for getting at the infinite background of feeling in order to condense it into an object of perception…we feel through the senses'. He talks in the same vein about 'relational structures' which the artist discovers: 'No wonder [that] the artist is constantly placing and displacing, relating and rupturing relations, for his task is to find a complex of qualities whose feeling is *just right*: veering toward the unknown and chaos, yet ordered and related in order to be apprehended'.[15] Of course, 'just rightness' as a critical standard may have recently lost much of its allure. Yet for Motherwell in 1943 collage was less an *expressive* than a *material* practice. For him, there is no personal or autobiographical relation to the pasted material of the picture. Sheet music is just calligraphy (he didn't read music). Blue Gauloises packets are just blue and packet-like (he didn't smoke Gauloises). 'For a painter as abstract as myself', he would say in retrospect, 'the collages offer a way of incorporating bits of the everyday world into pictures.... Instead of having to fuss with drawing things and re-working and changing them, you pick up objects that are in the room and simply put them in a picture – or take them out...collage is both placing and ellipsis'.[14]

At the same time, there is a strong sense in these works of a body or body-parts being there. The relational structures are not just, as Motherwell puts it, 'found in the interaction of the body-mind and the external world'; they actually echo the order of the body in material terms. 'Feelings must have a medium', he wrote at the time to explain how wrong the Surrealists were to 'do without' or 'attack' the medium – how in doing so they destroyed, inadvertently perhaps, one means of 'getting into the unknown'. For Motherwell as a modern artist, 'it is natural to rearrange or invent in order to bring about states of feeling that we like, just as a new tenant refurbishes a house'.[15] Looking back much later upon the work of the early 1940s, Motherwell recorded that 'what strikes me now is that the true subject matter of these early works is a wounded person'.[16] Unlike the much smaller works in the Art of This Century show, Motherwell from 1943 to 1947 was intent on pursuing a phenomenology of the body well ahead of most of what subsequently became known as 'expressionist' painting in New York.

Clement Greenberg's Modernism

The New York conversation about collage, once begun, was set to grow louder still. Artists, critics and museum curators alike seemed excited by the prospect that found paper materials on a variety of scales – we shall examine the extremes – could focus some central theoretical strategies of abstract art in a city already coming to terms with its new-found economic power, its entertainment and consumer industries, and its unique intellectual culture of disaffected Marxists, émigré Surrealists, and home-grown ambition. From 1947, the year Art of This Century finally closed, until nearly a decade later, collage looms large enough in the annals of the New York scene to underscore virtually every achievement of note. To take only a handful of examples: Willem de Kooning's early canvases in the *Woman* series, those of 1949–50, were composed largely with the help of collaged paper fragments. Robert Rauschenberg's early 'black' paintings of 1950–1 exploit newspaper as a ground to be both obscured and revealed by contingent matter (interestingly, Motherwell taught the young Rauschenberg at Black Mountain Collage in the summer of 1951). Jasper Johns clearly felt it to be *de rigeur* to wax over newspaper pieces in his earliest *American Flag* pictures of 1951–2. In wider cultural terms, the material plenitude of large-format painting that now erupted in New York – dripped, flung, pasted, spread, poured – by itself echoed the large material endowments of the new American city. So did paper scraps, news sheet and torn detritus. The latter signified 'plenty' – but also 'waste'. We should note too the sensibility of the 'Beat' writers and poets towards scraps of litter and 'poor' objects and materials as an antidote to a new commercial culture manically attuned to cleanliness and hygiene as standards for the consumption of goods. Torn and pasted paper then meant many things – poverty and the richness of that poverty combined.

Among the critical fraternity on the other hand the imposing question was the relation of new American art to the achievements of the European past. Some kind of measure had to be made. What was the role of the easel painting? Of decoration? Of abstraction in relation to the larger American life? Of sculpture? The critic Clement Greenberg would react badly to an exhibition of Matisse's paintings and cut-outs in New York in the spring of 1949. 'Cut-out' or *papier découpé* refers to a method Matisse had used occasionally since the early 1930s as a way of pre-composing paintings: recently, Matisse had re-launched the cut-out as a technique in its own right, in the *Jazz* suite of 1943–4, and in the *Polynesia* and

106 **William Baziotes** *The Drugged Balloonist* c. 1942–3
Baziotes here enters the miraculous world of insect wings,
feathers, leaves, the chance effects of cut paper and the
colour combinations arising from mixing together pen drawing
and printed fragments, to produce an ambitiously complex
universe of gravity-free forms.

left 105 **Robert Motherwell** *View from a High Tower* 1944
This (unusually for Motherwell) square collage evokes less a
skyscraper view than a high vantage point overlooking a forest
or park, indexed by the fragment of map, at centre left,
whose distant scale contradicts that of the cardboard and
paper patches.

107 **Henri Matisse** *Oceania, The Sky* 1946
This large work, almost four metres (13 feet) wide, is among the first in which Matisse frees his cut-out forms from the dimensions and scale of a background sheet, expanding horizontally in a frieze-like arrangement of flying, floating shapes: a degree of openness from which he would subsequently retreat.

Oceania pictures of 1946 in which dancing, music, sea-life or the sky were evoked though virtuoso carving of form. Contrasting Matisse's large new oil-paintings, which with their intense colour rhythms 'remain easel paintings in the fullest sense', Greenberg scorned the recent cut-outs for 'depending too much on the sheer quality of colour and having an elemental and static simplicity of design that makes them pieces of decoration, rather than pictures'.[17] It was a verdict that will become intelligible if we go back a couple of years and work forward. For it was none other than Joan Miró, shown at the Pierre Matisse Gallery in mid-1947, who had captured Greenberg's attention as the artist most likely to extend the achievement of pre-1925 modernist painting by Picasso, Klee and Kandinsky. Miró and Miró alone, Greenberg had said, had 'taken up the Cubist tradition where Picasso left it and added not only a positive personality but a wider demonstration of what is possible in the use of flat colour and the closed silhouette'. Greenberg startlingly refused to look at Miró's connections with Surrealism – indeed he was to claim in a short book on Miró, written in 1947 and published the following year, that Miró 'let nothing interfere with the conception he got from Cubism of painting as an irrevocably two-dimensional medium… he never made the mistake of trying to "illustrate" the strange, as the academic Surrealist painters did'.[18] As for Miró's collages, Greenberg said that in so far as they used 'photographs' (he is thinking of *Homage to Prats* and the works of 1933), 'they fall down as works of art…sacrificing as they do the abstract formal order that belongs to pictorial art to the pursuit of emotion that belongs only to raw experience'; the error of the photographs was that they 'made deep holes in [Miró's] pictures and served only to show further how little he understood the true aesthetic purpose of the new [collage] medium'.[19] Importantly, Miró was:

> a Mediterranean like Picasso…[who] adheres…to a certain quasi-sculptural conception of the picture as involving the monolithic definition of shapes, flat surfaces, smooth, compact brushwork, pure, uniform colour…. He too favours the figure as a motif, hardly ever the landscape…. It is significant that Miró's influence is prominent, along with Picasso's, in the formation of Jackson Pollock's art…

For Pollock, Greenberg confirmed, 'is the most important new painter since Miró himself'.[20]

The gulf prised open between two types of modernist art – 'flat colour and closed silhouette' on the one hand, 'deep holes' in the picture on the other – was now to play a dramatic role even at the level of the studio. I fancy Greenberg must have counselled Pollock on the uses and abuses of collage during 1947 and the following year. For it was in 1948 that Pollock started a group of smallish collage pictures that simulate at least the look and the scale of Miró's paintings – a group involving not cutting-out-and-attaching but the *excision* of one or sometimes two or three human figure-shapes. No one could deny, for example, that in *Cut Out*, perhaps the earliest of the group, or in *Untitled (Rhythmical Dance)*, there are figures of a kind: a jelly-baby-like absence in the first, and two dancers in the second, reminiscent of the silhouettes in Picasso's *Three Dancers* of 1925 (in Pollock's *Shadows No. 2* of 1948 the reference to *Three Dancers* is precise). Their elongated or star-fish bodies are of course Miró-like; yet the anatomies that read as presences in Miró are *gaps* in Pollock's work, achieved by cutting shapes out of oil-spattered paper and mounting the resulting stencil on a canvas or board. And neither work owes much to the example of Matisse. For then, in a further inversion, Pollock's cut-out humanoid segments appear in further paintings as positive motifs, where they read both as on the surface (which literally they are) as well as beneath or beyond it.[21] In this double-process, the figure first vacates and then returns to the place of its disappearance, as if to confirm that only as an unstable presence, sometimes visible and sometimes not, could 'the human' any longer figure in contemporary abstract art. And then comes the large 1949 painting *Out of the Web* [*109*] – once exhibited as *Number 7* – which has Miró-like biomorphic forms cut out of the skin of paint covering a masonite board; they read as positive brown forms dancing in an abstract field as well as 'negative' forms missing from that field: both effects are visible simultaneously. And yet those absent presences are more than just figure–ground reversals. Their effects have to do with speed: the visible surface of the masonite ground is blurred, smudged, to prevent focus from occurring. Michael Fried once claimed that those areas induce 'blind spots' or 'absences' in the visual field itself.[22] It is clear too that Pollock was being inventive here: the ghost-like forms precisely designate 'figures that aren't there'. They float and swirl, but since many of their edges mimic the dripped lines of paint already present, they seem as much *of* the surface they escape from as absent from it: the nearest one gets to the figure in *Out of the Web* is a foot-shape, or a spectral head.

Why did Pollock embark on this group of collage and *décollage* paintings at a moment when the modernist 'way forward' from Cubism and from Miró was being urgently debated in New York? One kind of explanation is that the removed parts helped relieve the oppressive energy of the all-over dripped surfaces of the paintings of 1946 and 1947, allowing them to move again and 'breathe' (Pollock surely learnt from Motherwell's example here). In terms of ambition, Pollock was able to nod an acknowledgment to the figurative modernism of European masters he needed to rival and surpass. Yet my own hypothesis is that Greenberg's obsession with the 'flatness' of pictorial art – 'flatness' as one of the self-defining qualities of modernist art – acted as the spur. And Miró was not the only guiding light. There were two further shows in 1948, one of Kurt Schwitters and the other a big show at the Museum of Modern Art, both of which Greenberg singled out for attention and no doubt spoke about to the artists he knew and met.

The Schwitters show first. It took place at the Pinacotheca Gallery in February and was Schwitters' first one-man show in the USA. As might be expected, Greenberg praised Schwitters' early work for its 'strict internal aesthetic logic', for the way its shapes 'are still more or less rectangular, the composition…built almost exclusively of rectangles on horizontal bases'. They alone, says Greenberg – and not Schwitters' later work – 'assert a superior unity and compactness of surface, texture and design', hence 'take their place among the heroic feats of twentieth-century art'.[23] Greenberg's second article on collage, published in *The Nation* in November, covered the substantial exhibition 'Collage' at the

108 **Jackson Pollock** *Cut Out* 1948–50
While the missing cut-out shape was used by Pollock to create further painting entitled *Cut-Out Figure*, the stencil we see here was not stabilized on a background until after Pollock's death. We know, however, that we was looking for an effect of something like this kind.

109 **Jackson Pollock** *Out of the Web (Number 7)* 1949
Slightly smaller that Matisse's *Oceania* [*107*], yet being grander
in scale, *Out of the Web* replays the basic brown ground and
dancing figures, but with greater turbulence. Chiming with
the drip lines in most cases, the 'cut' areas amplify the
rhythms at the same time as cutting through the thickness of
the web.

Museum of Modern Art from 22 September to 5 December 1948 and constituted perhaps
the first major attempt to theorize the collage technique since Aragon and Max Ernst in the
1930s: the show reached back beyond the Surrealists to recuperate the Cubist work of
Picasso and Braque. Curated by Margaret Miller of the Department of Painting and
Sculpture, MOMA's 'Collage' show contained 103 works by a mixture of the already well-
known and the relatively unheard-of. A press release calling it a 'Large Retrospective
Exhibition of Collages by Modern Europeans and Americans', alluded to 'the historical
importance and influence of the technique', which:

> derived originally in 1912 from analytical Cubism, but in the course of 35 years has
> developed into popular and widespread use in billboards, posters and advertisements.
> It has been used by the proponents of such divergent movements as Cubism, Dada,
> Constructivism and Surrealism. Thus the exhibition presents a miniature history of
> two main currents in twentieth-century painting: the Cubist and abstract movements
> and the fantastic tradition of Dada and Surrealism.[24]

Sociologically, reference to commercial uses of collage and montage would indeed have
been timely in late 1948 America; yet the show contained no commercial graphics, and
there was no catalogue for the show such as could justify a particular selection. The
emphasis rather was on the two traditions that collage had inspired. Margaret Miller was
quoted directly. Collage, she said:

> Played an important part in the construction of Cubist images, which display the power
> of the mind to conceive and hold several aspects of an object simultaneously. It was in
> collage, as well, that another type of mental imagery first appears, the free unregulated
> vision on the borderline of the conscious and unconscious.[25]

There were eight works by Arp, four by Braque, twelve by Ernst, four by Gris, and twenty
each by Picasso and Schwitters, the implied twin luminaries of MOMA's 'miniature history'.
The Dadaists Grosz, Hausmann, Heartfield and Baader had a mere six works between
them, including Heartfield's *The Peaceable Fish of Prey* [*94*]. Höch had a single late work.

0 Installation shot of MOMA's 'Collage' exhibition,
vember–December 1948
sible on the left wall is Picasso's large *Guitar* of 1926, made
cloth, paper, string and nails, and part of a series made in
e spring of that year [*64, 65*].

The American contribution comprised Cornell, Arthur Dove, Ronnie Elliott, William Kienbusch and Robert Motherwell (represented by *Pancho Villa, Dead and Alive*) – again a single work each except for Dove who had three. Klutsis had *Fulfilled Plans: Great Work* (1930), Lissitzky *Proun III* (1926), Miró a collage from 1933, and Penrose *Elephant Bird* [*88*]. As far as we can reconstruct it, the twelve works by Max Ernst stand out as the strongest showing of Surrealist methods (*Here Everything is Floating* and *The Swan is Very Peaceful* [*54*]), aided by single pieces from Bellmer and Dalí (*Illumined Pleasures*), and a 1928 *cadavre exquis* made collectively by Breton, Morise, Naville, Peret, Prévert, and Yves and Jeanette Tanguy.

The tone and the manner of Greenberg's short review indicates that this was to be a key statement in his account of the values of modernist art. Launched initially against a battery of journalists who had written off collage as a 'fad', or 'dated', or a 'stunt' used by lazy painters, Greenberg eulogizes the collage medium as 'the most succinct and direct single clue to the aesthetic of genuinely modern art'. Once you appreciated collage as practised by the Cubist masters, Greenberg claimed, 'one is in a position to understand what painting has been about since Manet first laid his shapes in flat'. In collage alone one could see:

> how the fictive depths of the picture were drained, and its action...brought forward and identified with the immediate, physical surface of the canvas, board or paper. By pasting a piece of newspaper lettering to the canvas one called attention to the physical reality of the work of art and made that reality the same as the art.... Painting was no longer a matter of fictive projection or description, and the picture became indissolubly one with the pigment, the texture, and the flat surface that constituted it as an object...the central premises of painting since Manet, and a great source of its virtues, has been its progressive surrender to, its increasing acknowledgement of, the physical nature of the medium...[26]

Several features can be noted. The most obvious is how little Greenberg found himself able to enjoy the *frisson* of popular culture; how poorly he understood the workings of the sign, or the relationship of pasted paper to the surrounding culture. Neither emphasis was compatible with what he had described in 'The Prospects of American Painting and

Sculpture' the previous October as 'the development of a bland, large, balanced, Apollonian art…in which an intense detachment informs all'.[27] And it was this detachment that enabled him to see a Cubist collage by Picasso or Braque in a radically anti-illusionistic way: 'the Cubists always emphasised the identity of the picture as a flat and more or less abstract pattern rather than as a representation'. Greenberg felt that Juan Gris in such a perspective triumphed when aiming at representation and when keeping the surface decoration under control. The best of Gris's four works according to this standard, namely *The Breakfast* and *The Packet of Coffee* [*18*], both of 1914, succeed only because he does not muddle the two aims. To choose between them is preferable to ambiguity: 'With one's eyes focused primarily on the flat surface pattern…one finds the picture disorganised and congested, but when one shifts focus and views it as a conventional picture it springs instantly into perfection'.[28] It was not the first time that Gris had been used as a foil.

For Greenberg the logic of the surface pattern had a further consequence, in relation to modernist sculpture. The discovery of collage in 1912 by Picasso and Braque, Greenberg believed, had involved the lifting of extraneous elements above the surface and bringing that part of the picture physically closer to the eye, as in bas-relief. By this means three-dimensionality was no longer an effect of illusion, but of literal volume:

> the picture had now attained to the full and declared three-dimensionality we automatically attribute to the notion "object", and painting was being transformed, in the course of a strictly coherent process with a logic all its own, into a new kind of sculpture. Thus we see that without collage there would have been no Pevsner, Gonzales, or Giacometti, no Calder or David Smith.[29]

The new sculpture – Greenberg would lay out the full case for saying so in *Partisan Review* the following summer – asserts even more strenuously than painting the claim to provide an 'ordering of experience' in the modern world. Sculpture (like painting) also took its cue from Cubism and now undergoes nothing short of a 'transformation, or revolution'. Starting from Picasso and Braque's collages, which 'thrust forms outward from the picture plane instead of drawing them back into the recessions of illusionary space', it followed the bas-relief style of Picasso, Arp and Schwitters to detach itself from the picture plane completely in Gonzales and David Smith, alongside a generation of younger Americans including David Hare, Herbert Ferber, Seymour Lipton and Burgoyne Diller. It is a 'new, pictorial wealth of forms…as palpable and independent and present as the houses we live in and the furniture we use'. Beginning in collage, the new sculpture is 'perhaps the most important manifestation of the visual arts since Cubist painting'.[30]

The third major emphasis in Greenberg's account of collage concerns the uses of montage techniques in commercial and mass culture. Greenberg is plain: collage was 'taken up' by people outside the Cubist movement and applied to contexts 'many of them popular and few of them with any real relation to the aesthetic of Cubism'.[31] The exclusion applied immediately to the Dadaists and Surrealists. By Greenberg's lights, the latter groups saw in collage

> only a means of achieving strange and surprising effects by juxtaposing incongruous images. The result was not works of art – even in Miró's case – but montages, truly stunts: rectangles littered with small pictures connected by no aesthetic necessity, rectangles that do not delight the eye and whose value is wholly exhausted in literary shock effects that have by now become unspeakably stale.[32]

Greenberg had been enough of a Marxist – he was the author of 'Avant-Garde and Kitsch' after all – to believe that late 1940s America was seeing the definition of a new model consumer under the aegis of public relations techniques given over first to the psychological penetration and then the wholesale subordination of the masses. Encouragement to 'hate' communism in the later 1940s was official too. And yet his account of 'genuinely modern art' is now beginning to mobilize a conformist language and a conformist perceptual psychology in which modern art's 'surrender' to the physical qualities of its medium in effect rehearses – it seldom resists – the surrender of the masses to their commercial fate. On the other hand, Greenberg repeats again and again that the Surrealists' 'surrender' to the demands of their unconscious limited and diffused their art. For him, Surrealism's flirtation with popular culture was already a step too far.

Krasner/Pollock

The conversation about collage in New York has one further episode that takes us into a very different era. Greenberg, for his part, would write about collage again, and at greater length, as his influential voice began to be listened to and even obeyed.[33] Pollock, for his, remained uncertain about the implications of his smaller *découpé* works of 1948: we can deduce this from the fact that none of them left his studio until after his death. Perhaps Pollock felt he had reached a spacious and grand enough format in *Out of the Web* to accommodate excised dancing shapes when they were not quite figures (ghosts, I called them) but that he just did not know how to proceed when the presence was too-human, as they were in the single-figure *Cut Out* or the Miró-like *Untitled (Rhythmical Dance)*. The art historian T. J. Clark has studied the problem: he speculates about the smaller works that they were a way of allowing abstraction to signify the 'impurity' of the figure that abstraction in modernist painting was at that moment trying hard to supplant. 'The problem…was to find a way of reconciling that second coming of the figure with the work to annihilate likeness being done at the same time. The figure, if it was to appear at all, would have to do so *out of* or *against* that [abstract] work, as the strict contrary of it – the negation of the negation'.[34] The qualification we need to enter is that *Cut Out* turns out not to have been completed by Pollock at all. Studio photos show it unfinished in 1950, and still not resolved by the time of Pollock's death in 1956. Almost certainly Pollock's widow Lee Krasner finished it by finding a piece of canvas-board on which to glue the stencil-like shape. In fact, shortly before Pollock's death, and apparently in response to the several conversations about *papier collé* and *papier decoupé* that were animating New York, Krasner began her own paintings in which she boldly mangled several of Pollock's oil-on-paper works to produce collage paintings of her own.

The background to this benevolent act of 'completion' is inevitably complicated by Krasner's relationship to Pollock. And she was a painter with her own career; hence this was no ordinary act of tidying up of a work left unfinished at her husband's death ('"Waste not, want not", there's a little of that in me', Krasner would nevertheless say later[35]). In fact, just as Pollock himself had had difficulties with the coagulating density of the all-over surface and had taken a knife to portions of it, apparently to open it out and let space and air back in, it turns out that Krasner had her own adventure with collage soon afterwards, that is between 1951 and 1955. We must remember that the two painters worked alongside each other and continually saw each other's work. In Krasner's case however the position is roughly this. First, she had a show at Betty Parsons in October 1951, a matter of weeks before Pollock's own first one-man show there, in which she exhibited fourteen paintings in a startlingly new manner. Against the grain of her tumbling, confident abstractions of the later 1940s, the Parsons pictures were suddenly classical and calm, comprising rectilinear units spread across the canvas in a manner recalling Klee or perhaps Kupka (assuming she knew the latter artist's work). And the show was a modest critical success in more or less these terms: even though we shall find evidence for thinking that Krasner soon became disenchanted with the work.[36]

In point of fact Krasner *shared* the Betty Parsons Gallery in October 1951 with another collagist, Ann Ryan, and it may well be that Ryan's small, closely-worked abstractions after Schwitters – Ryan had seen the Schwitters show at the Pinacotheca in February 1948 – had impressed Krasner with their sensuous physical qualities. The poet John Ashbery was later to draw a nice distinction when he said that for Ryan, '*matière* is far more important than for Schwitters. One is aware of his lovely found objects as elements of composition: they have renounced their thingness in favour of the *Ding an sich* of the whole'. American art often seemed 'formless and lacking in intellectual justification to Europeans' because '[Americans] are trying to sort out the meaning of what is visual or audible, and in doing so we have to get into something which temporarily looks chaotic'. He says that American art is sometimes 'brutal but not cruel'.[37] It is a nice point; and conceivably Krasner recognized even in Ryan's extremely small works how a certain brutality was compatible both with femininity and with abstract art. At any rate some hiatus occurred after Krasner's 1951 show. It seems significant that there are *no* Krasner works dated 1952 in the Landau *catalogue raisonnée*.

What happened, then, both to Krasner's confidence and to her art? In 1953 she turns back to turbulent rhythmic abstraction, but with the difference that she now uses old drawings, both her own and Pollock's, cut or torn or sometimes both, and bits of discarded canvas – and then pastes them on to a stretched canvas support within a framework of painted motifs. Not only are Krasner's new collage paintings exceptional in re-using her own and her husband's work. The vehemence and the brutality are back. Krasner explains:

> My studio was hung with a series of black and white drawings I had done. I hated them and started to pull them off the wall and tear them and throw them on the floor…. Then another morning I walked in and saw a lot of things there that began to interest me. I began picking up torn pieces of my own drawings and re-glueing them. Then I started cutting up some of my oil paintings. I got something going there and I start pulling out a lot of raw canvas and slashing it as well.[38]

Self-excavation seems to be the issue, for Krasner's *objets trouvés* are now her own. One group produced with Howell paper uses strips of torn-up drawings and canvas pasted on masonite board in close-knit predominantly vertical bands, jostling with each other like the buildings of Manhattan (one work of 1953 is called *The City*): Krasner and Pollock both learned about Howell paper from the 1951 Ann Ryan show. In a further group of collage paintings from 1955, Krasner worked directly on top of geometric canvases from the 1951 Parsons show,[39] another gesture of self-appraisal in which oil-painted paper and sometimes burlap are pasted on in large, rough areas in rushing, vertical foliate sweeps and curves. Shown at the Stable Gallery in September–October 1955, they evoked a variety of precedents, including the Matisse pieces seen at Pierre Matisse Gallery in 1949 or his subsequent *Memories of Oceania*, 1952–3, as well as the new *Spanish Elegy* paintings of Robert Motherwell. But what did Krasner's studio *bricolage* signify? For *Bald Eagle*, also of 1955 but significantly not shown at Stable, Krasner takes some old drawings of Pollock, cuts them along the dribbled ink lines to form 'edges' (Pollock had cut along the dribble lines in his paintings too) and disposes the resulting pieces hectically in all-over rhythms of startling elegance and brutality. The title of this work comes from the fragment of a Pollock drawing, visible at dead-centre, which has a beak-like shape and an 'eye', and which might be read as a kind of bestiary reworking of Pollock himself.

Krasner's turn to the collage idiom in the years prior to 1955 represents the kind of breakthrough all too rare in an artist's career. Greenberg thought the Stable show 'one of the great events of the decade'[40] (even if he valued it primarily for what he thought Pollock could learn from it). The British critic Bryan Robertson later described Krasner's collages

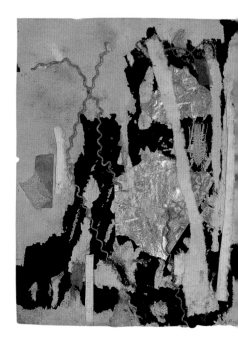

111 **Ann Ryan** *Untitled (No. 234)* 1948–54
Operating on a scale of only a few centimetres, Ryan 'knew how to speak the secret language of around-the-house and could say beautiful and startling things in it…'. (Ashbery)

opposite 113 **Lee Krasner** *Bald Eagle* 1955
In this majestic work of almost two metres (6½ feet) in height Krasner affixes fragments of a Pollock drawing and some canvas strips to another canvas, building on the promise of large-scale American abstraction to recirculate parts of the painter's environment in an all-over expressive way.

112 **Lee Krasner** *The City* 1953
Simulating the violence and energy of the city, Krasner's large collage paintings also respond to the precedent of Matisse's cut-out style with a bravura display of torn edges, agitated spatial rhythms and rushing lines of force.

as 'some of the peaks of her massive achievement...among the most original, energetic and radiant works of my lifetime'.[41] Yet Krasner's unique approach to authorship raises some vexatious questions. Given that her plundering of Pollock's studio rubbish is more than tidy reuse, it might be read as an effort to define a contemporary artistic 'voice' with some already existing pieces of conversation from the past: Pollock with his audience, Krasner with hers. It seems that at least two impulses are in play. In magnifying the focus and making the viewer feel 'up close' to the shapes and details of her work, Krasner moves away from Pollock, while in those collages that include bits of Pollock's drawings the rhythms are more like his own. The art historian Anne Wagner has done most to probe the interplay of registers and authorial voices that animated Krasner's project. She proposes that the artist's 'self' in this process of creative recycling involves a form of fiction paradoxically indispensable to the task of autobiography. Emphatically in the collage work, Wagner says, Krasner's painter self 'becomes speakable only by being treated as Other – torn up and redeployed, as if in tacit recognition that the artist's self is always already assembled and constructed out of another language' – both hers and Pollock's.[42] Bryan Robertson described both the 1953–5 works and another series of collages begun in 1976 as giving out 'the illusion of buried references, exhumed and reformed, of an artist's personal history disrupted and pulled together again at another altitude and in a fresh light'.[43]

Yet it may be that by 1955 or so the eruption of interest in collage launched by Peggy Guggenheim back in 1943 had run its course – that tearing, *bricolage* and recycling were now about to chart different kinds of artistic ordering. The young Allan Kaprow, for instance, had exhibited constructions and assemblages alongside paintings at his early Hansa Gallery show in 1952, explaining that he had been 'casting around for a way to include all the levels of meaning that I intended'. Out of that experience came what he called 'a kind of action-collage technique', seemingly stimulated by the scale and gesture of Pollock rather than by his figurative concerns:

> These action-collages, unlike my constructions, were done as rapidly as possible by grasping up great hunks of varied matter: tinfoil, straw, canvas, photos, newspaper etc. I also cut up pictures which I had made previously.... The straw, tinfoil, occasionally food, whatever it was, each of these had, increasingly, a meaning that was better embodied in the various non-painterly materials than in paint. Their placement in the ritual of my own rapid action was an acting-out of the dramas of tin soldiers, stories, and musical structures that I once had tried to embody in paint...[44]

Out of these static works there soon emerged a more environmental art. Kaprow observes, 'I introduced flashing lights and thicker hunks of matter. These parts projected farther and farther from the wall and into the room.' Soon he introduced ringing buzzers, bells, sheets of plastic, tasks for the audience to perform – to make the visitor part of the event and render the phenomenal space of the gallery irrelevant. Kaprow's claim in 1958 that this method of working was truly 'the legacy of Jackson Pollock' marked the start of the movement known as Happenings.[45] Once more, collage was the motivating technique.

114 **Allan Kaprow** *Caged Pheasant No. 2* 1956 Kaprow's action-collages quickly developed into whole environments, and to 'performances' with (and within) these environments – a type of avant-garde art also explored by Jim Dine and Claes Oldenburg. Kaprow explains that a Happening is 'something rather spontaneous that just happens to happen'.

8

California Collage

For almost a decade following the end of the Second World War, artists on America's West Coast had little exposure to the great experiments of European modern art, and little contact with the New York art world and its critical debates. Even before the war, few ideas were circulating in Los Angeles and San Francisco art circles beyond certain principles from French and Belgian Surrealism, and what could be seen of European modernist works from reproductions in books and magazines. There were few galleries, and little ambition for a distinctive Californian contribution to specifically modernist art. On the other hand Louise and Walter Ahrensburg's collection of European avant-garde art (which included a significant Duchamp group) was there to be seen, and Mexican muralists of the quality of Diego Rivera, José Orozco and David Siqueiros taught at both the California School of Fine Arts in San Francisco and the Chouinard Institute in Los Angeles. In San Francisco a poetry revival led by Kenneth Rexroth showed evidence that California culture could become as rich and varied as any in the 'old world'. Aware of the limitations of its geographical isolation yet mindful too of its freedom from suffocating precedents, Californian art was well placed after 1945 to evolve attitudes and practices all its own. And here again we encounter collage as the guiding principle of most if not all of the new art of the period. On the one hand the enthusiasm of some artists for poetry and jazz provided technical and emotional models that could be shared. On the other hand the absence of regulatory boundaries between 'painting' and 'sculpture' enabled several Californians to evolve a hybrid that no nation outside America would ever master so well: that of assemblage.

Beginnings of Assemblage: Spohn and Berman
In San Francisco much of the post-war experimental activity in the arts emanated from the California School of Fine Arts, situated in the North Beach area and led from 1945 by the energetic and far-sighted Douglas MacAgy, formerly of the San Francisco Museum of Art. Already his wife Jermayne had been active in organizing exhibitions in the city, and by the late 1940s San Francisco had seen exhibitions of Pollock, Rothko, Motherwell, Gorky and Clyfford Still. The passage in 1944 of the GI Bill of Rights gave opportunities to thousands of war veterans to take up places on college courses, and by common consent this generation, the first of whom entered college in 1945, were highly motivated, intellectually

15 **Jess (Burgess Collins)** *Paranoiac Portrait of Robert Creeley* 1955
'Coming of age in the forties, in the chaos of the Second World War, one felt the kinds of coherence that might have been fact of other time and place were no longer possible', wrote Creeley later. His collage portrait by Jess invokes the surrealist universe of Max Ernst, as well as the anamorphic surprises of Hieronymous Bosch and Arcimboldo.

curious, and already mature enough to take emotional and technical risks. The result was that the ethos at the California School of Fine Arts under MacAgy's directorship was adventurous and eclectic, one in which the distinction between staff and students tended to dissolve, akin to 'a community of monks, all praying, but each in his own way', to cite the reminiscences of the artist Elmer Bischoff, a member of the faculty.¹ What Bischoff elsewhere refers to as the 'religious character' of the encounter between the GI Bill generation and their art – and other observers seemed to agree – made two aesthetic positions especially attractive. One was Abstract Expressionism under the tutelage of painters like Still, Hassel Smith and Richard Diebenkorn, even though neither Still nor Smith had any time for the Cubist-inspired art of French modernism: expressionists such as Munch or Soutine were more to their taste. The second position was the anarchic attitude to objects and their interrelations adopted by the older but no less influential figure of Clay Spohn. Spohn, born in 1898 and a student of Fernand Léger in Paris in the 1920s, had been a stalwart of the California WPA programme in the 1930s, after which a more Dada side to his talent emerged. In 1941 he made a mixed-media piece inspired by the fall of Paris: a life-size fly painted on the back plane of a box, to which a fly-swatter was attached via a spring mechanism, for manipulation by the viewer. The exhortation contained in the title of *Wake Up and Live* was intended to jolt Spohn's audience to recognition of the fate of a Europe threatened by fascism – unfortunately the piece is now lost. And then a series of 'war machines'; gouaches painted in the wake of the bombing of Pearl Harbour (1941), which have the menacing quality of real objects, but of a totally invented kind. In 1949 Spohn's philosophical 'prankism' (as he called it) produced a 'happening' in the form of a multi-part assemblage, staged at the California School of Fine Arts where he was by now a teacher of abstract art. Known as the 'Museum of Unknown and Little Known Objects', its forty-two separate objects were constructed out of scrap metal and other cast-off materials which Spohn discovered in trash cans and on garbage dumps. The idea was to illustrate a vague philosophical dictum which said that the Unknown is indefinable because its definition makes it Known, even though the Unknown underlies everything in the form of categoryless matter apprehended by intuition and feeling. One imagines that garbage exemplified the Unknown very well. As Spohn himself recalled:

> I would pick up little pieces of cast-off parts of machinery and then get some wire and a piece of metal and put it all together and make an object of it. One had a little watch attached to it that I found: it was called 'Starter for a Rat Race'; another was 'A Hat Tree for a Neighbourly Garden'…I gathered up a lot of stuff from the brush of the vacuum cleaner, stuff from the carpet, and called it 'Bedroom Fluff'.²

The relative absence of modern artistic traditions in California meant that Spohn's objects had few philosophical or aesthetic links with the attempts by European Dadas to 'destroy' art. On the contrary, Spohn's intention was to demonstrate how all objects inhabit a cycle of rising and falling value – an idea of some force in a culture already mired in rapidly changing patterns of consumption and obsolescence. Secondly, the absence of a normative artistic taste in remote California, combined with the absence of a market for new art, seems to have prompted the artist to endorse such values as spontaneity and independence of choice. Added to which, as Hassell Smith pointed out, the world of jazz was already supplying terms like *improvisation, virtuoso, self-assertion,* and *naivety* for use in the visual arts. Meanwhile Los Angeles after 1945 was a changed city. As the full horror of the European holocaust dawned, and as America faced the consequences of her intervention at Hiroshima, Los Angeles looked upon itself as a sprawling melting-pot of nations and cultures, including the Jewish community with its Kabbalistic traditions,

116 **Clay Spohn** *Precious Objects* 1949
Planned as a 'happening' for the San Francisco Art Association's annual costume ball, Spohn's 'Museum' was designed to prompt party-goers to look at waste as interesting in its own right. The dejecta assembled in this rare survival from the 'Museum' exemplify Spohn's idea that 'all things, even man-made things, having once been things of nature…must again, sometimes, return to nature'. Some objects were stolen, some were given away.

17 **Wallace Berman** *Veritas Panel* c. 1952–6
features having significance within Berman's home-grown
philosophy are the leather straps which fasten the stone in the
shape of a cross, and a smaller door at the top, behind which
the viewer encountered a mirror, providing an image of the
self. Jewish mysticism and an intense private life are here
combined with currents already moving in the wider culture.

a large African-American community who had migrated to Los Angeles during the war
in search of jobs (and which spawned the thriving jazz scene), original Spanish-speaking
Angelenos, and the Hollywood entertainment community, already steeped in *noir*
fiction and elements of the Surrealist *mise-en-scène*. Here too, for a time, were Man Ray,
Bertolt Brecht, Arnold Schönberg and Thomas Mann, as well as L. Ron Hubbard and
Aleister Crowley.[3]

In the experimental visual arts, values of improvization and independence were
common in the two cities. Yet in Los Angeles as well as in San Francisco a further precept
governed the emergence of assemblage, in that the artist would typically seek, not public
approbation, but (at best) the approval of a local audience or even a handful of like-minded
friends. Years before the completion of Simon Rodia's famous *Watts Towers* in 1954,
perhaps the best known work of public assemblage in the state, a 'community' aesthetics
can be detected in the work of Wallace Berman, an artist who only later would become
widely known. On his discharge from the US Navy in 1946, the twenty-year-old Berman
enrolled at the Chouinard Institute in Los Angeles but soon dropped out in favour of
playing pool and listening to jazz. The next year Berman switched from part-time artwork
and graphics projects to the making of objects having a quasi-religious significance in the
assemblage manner. The first of these was *Homage to Herman Hesse*, a wooden
construction made out of scraps brought home from his job at the Salem Furniture Factory
in East Los Angeles. For the next six years he worked at a group of assemblages
embodying private religious meanings revolving around his relationship with his wife. The
so-called *Veritas Panel*, begun in 1952 and completed in 1956, takes the form of an upright
board on which are collaged a series of knobs and dowels, a flat stone, a photograph of his
wife with two messages scrawled across (*Veritas Certior Exstat* = The Truth is Certainly
Revealed, and *Ea Concipiti* = She Has Conceived, or, She Draws Things Together), a variety
of Hebrew hieroglyphs and an image of swimmers reaching up towards the light. Two
hinged doors, one bearing '12' (the number of Apostles and the magic number of the
zodiac), provide alternative positions of 'revelation' and 'closure' for a piece that stands flat
against the wall in the manner of a shrine or a devotional altar. Before its first exhibition in
1957, this and other assemblages would be displayed at home to those who knew Berman
and his wife. One friend recalled:

> People would just come [to the Bermans' home] and he wouldn't put on a show or
> entertain. They came happily and sat down and left four hours later: you'd listen to
> some music and you'd smoke some pot and look at things. What I enjoyed was not the
> conversation but the things we looked at...there were evenings where there was not
> much talk.[4]

It is easy to imagine how both Stuart Perkoff and the poet Robert Alexander's informal
collage works fitted into this intense, private, self-enclosed milieu with its multiple
crossovers between poetry, art and jazz. Alexander, a good friend of Berman's since 1945
and publisher and seller of literary magazines, was a lynch-pin of what was soon to
become known as 'Beat' writing and art in the Lost Angeles area, and whose backroom
hand press was responsible for much of the publicity for those involved.

The San Francisco Scene: Duncan, Jess, Hedrick and Herms
In San Francisco, a very different collage aesthetic emerged at around the same time in a
relationship between the artist Jess (Burgess Collins) and the poet Robert Duncan. Duncan
had since 1940 been a leader of the San Francisco poetry revival, and had written a brave
defence of homosexuality at a time when such discussions were both risky and rare.[5] By
1950 Duncan had met Jess, a trained atomic chemist turned artist who had studied under

Spohn, Hassel Smith, Still and Bischoff at the California School of Fine Arts: the poet and painter set up a thoroughly non-bohemian *ménage* together and began a creative partnership based on mining a rich vein of metaphor and allegory that would last for some thirty years. There was a small exhibition of assemblage called 'Common Art Accumulation' at a North Beach bar known as 'The Place' in 1951 – which presumably everybody saw. Jess himself worked in several series having a basis in collage sensibility. After a group of abstract paintings from 1949–52, he produced 'Paste-Ups', 'Assemblies', 'Translations' and 'Salvages': the common thread running through each is the act of taking *objets trouvés* – old photographs in the case of 'Translations', thrift-shop paintings in the case of 'Salvages' – and reconstituting them as new works. Jess's first Paste-Ups however (he always used this term in preference to 'collage') were directly inspired by his and Duncan's conversations on the importance of disjunction, surprise and transformation in the generation of the revelatory image. A work known as *The Mouse's Tale* of 1951–4 assembles fragments from body-building magazines on one side, set off by colourful clowns down the left, to constitute a single crouching figure in some sort of parody of masculine gym culture. Jess's attitude to these mass-media fragments was plain:

> [Robert Duncan and I] often talked about the element of surprise and disjunction in forming an image. When I am pasting up, I am moving images around constantly, surprising myself with new meanings…*Mouse's Tale* was constructed of male nudes with the idea of showing innocent beauty as opposed to macho body-building. It was a beginning for me to see how I could reuse the recurrent images that would jump out at me, for fantasy or mythological reasons, from all these marvellous and seemingly innocent publications.[6]

Jess emphasized that for this and other early collages, *Life* magazine 'was a gold mine of imagery for me…I really could not paint well enough at the time to create images as fantastic – in all senses of the word – as were available in *Life* magazine'.[7] An enthusiasm for Max Ernst's collage novels of the late 1920s and early 1930s followed. Then, in December 1953, Jess with Robert Duncan and Harry Jacobus set up the King Ubu Gallery at 3119 Fillmore Street, San Francisco, as a showplace for avant-garde poetry readings, performances and exhibitions. It closed a year later, but not before Jess himself had shown a series of junk assemblages under the title 'Necro Facts'. There was also a small number of collage poems: *Feature F* of 1953 creates a visual–verbal composition out of scissored texts, the majority of which begin and end with a single, isolated letter. Normal conventions of reading are destroyed. Jess at this time was reversing everything given him by the culture, mischievously ambiguating anything that smacked of normative manners or received speech. The nonsensically titled *Goddess Because Is Is Falling Asleep* of the following year is a pictorial collage of images from fashionable American life bordered with verbal cut-outs evoking the pretentious polite speech of society gossip, glossy advertising, and magazine journalism. In that year, 1954, Jess began his celebrated *Tricky Cad* collages [*120*] – again melding verbal and visual incongruities, this time by rearranging the words and phrases of a Dick Tracy cartoon and changing the order of the pictures to produce sheer surreal inconsequentiality out of a national cartoon icon. 'For me', recalled Jess, 'the *Tricky Cad* paste-ups were fun. Many, as I recall, were done at the kitchen table, and certainly not with the idea of a historical statement about collage'.[8] A sure hint of Jess's knowledge of international collage is to be found nevertheless in the highly surrealist *Paranoiac Portrait of Robert Creeley* of 1955 [*115*]. Here the poet Creeley appears as in Dalíesque mode as a hallucination of interlocking patterns that are visibly something other: field-systems seen from the air, clouds, mountains and photo-textures that cannot be identified. Reworking the austere geometry of Picasso's *Portrait of*

opposite 119 **Jess (Burgess Collins)** *The Mouse's Tale* 1951–4
'With so much on the table and in my not-so-organized files…the stories or images that can be created and pulled through time seem endless. Everything has to fit, not only in terms of form but also in its mythic, spiritual or psychological presence' (Jess). The mouse's 'tale', visible lower left, gives a humorous twist to a gathering of clowns.

118 **Jess (Burgess Collins)** *Feature F* 1953
The semantic dislocations so frequently explored by Jess evoke Cubist collage word-play as well as anticipating the 'concrete' poetry movement shortly to emerge. They rehearse on the plane of the text something of Jess's discoveries with images during these early years.

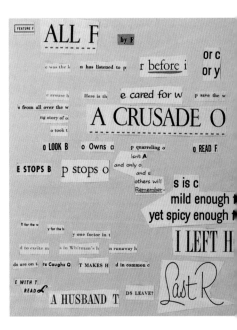

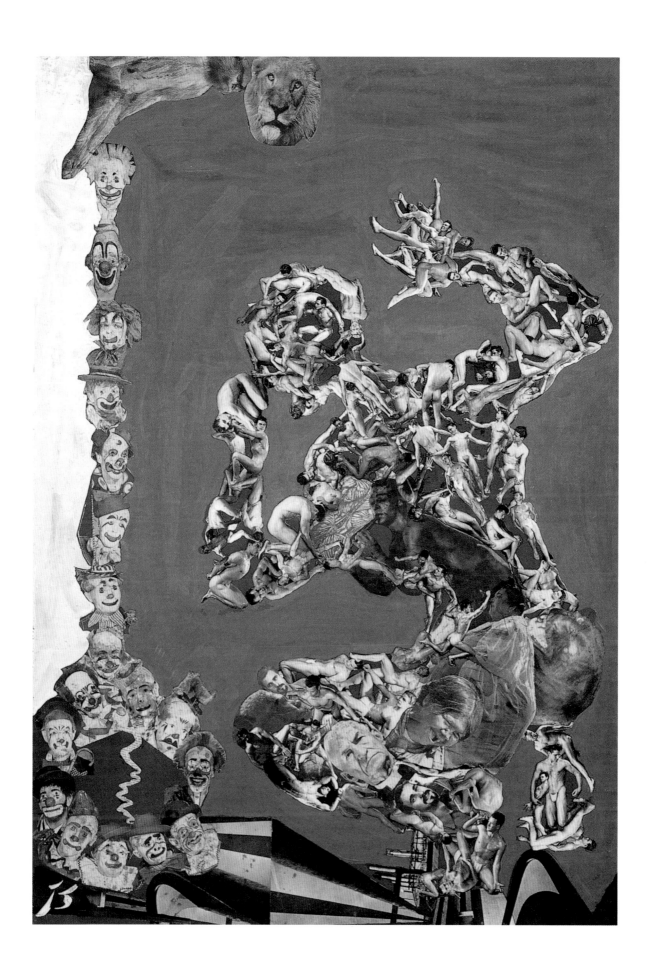

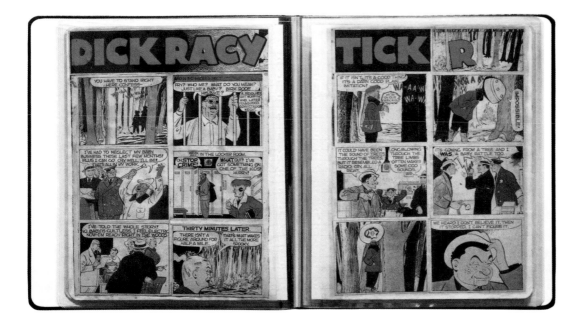

120 **Jess (Burgess Collins)** *Tricky Cad, Case I* 1954
Jess's use of popular imagery has prompted comparisons with
Pop art, but the artist has claimed 'I wasn't really aware of Pc
art and to this day I don't really feel any kinship with that
movement.' On the contrary, his rearrangements of the
speech-patterns of the famous detective and his absurd
antagonists such as Flyface and B. O. Plenty – themselves
parodies of American stereotypes – result in narratives which
are subversively nonsensical.

Kahnweiler, Jess finds his poet friend as he was in the second year at Black Mountain
College: Creeley wrote subsequently that his life there in 1954–5 had in personal terms
been epochal. Coming of age after the war,

> there seemed no logic that could bring together all the violent disparities of that
> experience…the picture of the world that might previously have served [the arts] had
> to be reformed…. Once the containment of a Newtonian imagination of the universe
> had been forced to yield to one proposing life as continuous, atomistic, and without
> relief, then discretions in the first situation were not only inappropriate but
> increasingly grotesque. There was no *place*, finally, from which to propose an
> objectively ordered reality.

By the time of Jess's portrait, Creeley had found the milieu he had been looking for,
one in which American painters were moving towards 'a manifest directly of the *energy*
inherent in materials, literally, and their physical manipulation in the act of painting…
material was instantly crucial again'.[9] Creeley confirmed to me that the *Portrait* 'is fact of
the very real *sturm und drang* of that time'.[10] Jess has also spoken of how he often pinned
the collage pieces until their mutual interactions made a weave, as in a complex tapestry,
until after some shuffling back and forth each area finds its proper composition. Jess, I
think, enjoyed using pasted paper in just such a process-oriented, aleatory way.

It must nevertheless be clear from these examples that the style evolved by Duncan and
Jess – scholarly, intellectual, romantic – was different in kind from the rumbustious,
homespun mysticism emerging simultaneously from the avant-gardist movement known
as 'Beat'. The term had been in circulation since a November 1952 *New York Times
Magazine* article by John Clellan Holmes explained that 'This is the beat generation…it
involves a sort of nakedness of mind, and, ultimately of soul, a feeling of being reduced to a
bedrock of consciousness'.[11] For Allen Ginsburg and Jack Kerouac, the two writers
routinely associated with the term, 'Beat' also signified 'beatific', the mystical perspective of
one who was defenceless and defeated before the world. As Ginsburg put it: 'The point of
Beat is that you get beat down to a certain nakedness where you actually are able to see
the world in a visionary way'.[12] The term regularly occurs in Kerouac's second novel

On The Road, written on a continuous 120-foot roll of paper in a three-week Benzedrine-driven typing stint in New York in April 1951, before being published after several revisions in 1957. The book famously relates a series of hitch-hiking journeys back and forth across the country that came to stand for a set of spiritual quests through the nether regions of a rapidly changing and massively heterodox American cultural landscape. By the time Ginsburg read his epic poem *Howl* at the 6 Gallery in San Francisco on 13 October 1955 (the gallery having taken over the automobile repair shop on Fillmore Street that was once the King Ubu Gallery) in his chanting, rhythmic, intoxicated style it was clear that 'Beat' was an attitude of mystic fervour rooted in poverty, drugs and the deep seriousness of a new bohemian life – a life premised on the enchantment of the unnoticed: an attitude to 'finding' and 'experience' with which collage practice in the visual arts had many contemporary and historical affinities.

The cross-overs between collage, assemblage, poetry, writing and film were many and fertile.[13] The painter Wally Hedrick, having attended the California School of Fine Arts on discharge from war service in Korea (another GI Bill beneficiary), was not only prominent in San Francisco's North Beach arts community but a director of the 6 Gallery from its opening in 1954 through to 1957. He was also a jazz musician. Art for Hedrick was a form of social protest, and alongside some expressionistic paintings protesting injustice and American global imperialism his main works of the mid-1950s were 'objects' collaged together out of broken radio and television sets, washing machine parts and other junk-yard scraps, frequently covered with thickly impastoed paint and gesso. A 1955 work called *Xmas Tree*, built out of two radios, two phonographs, flashing lights, electric fans, and a saw motor, all controlled by timers (one phonograph rigged up to play 'I Hate to See Christmas Come Around'), accidentally tangled a woman's fur coat at the San Francisco Museum of Art's annual Christmas Party in 1958 and gave her an electric shock – a mark of success in Hedrick's eyes: 'I wasn't making it as an art thing. I was more interested in making a "thing", and if it attacked people – well, I guess I knew it was going to attack because I laid the trap'.[14] Hedrick's wife Jay DeFeo was also primarily a painter who had made several photo-collages from the mid-1950s and like Hedrick himself was soon beginning to attract attention further afield. Her photo-collage *Blossom* of 1956 [*122*] with its spiralling limbs made out of female body-parts (an answer to *The Mouse's Tale*?) seems to have set the tone for a mandala-like painting of huge proportions called *The Rose* that obsessed her from 1958 to 1966 and that effectively prevented her from doing any significant work until the 1970s.[15] Notwithstanding, both Hedrick and DeFeo were selected for the Museum of Modern Art's important '16 Americans' show of 1958 alongside the more cosmopolitan Johns, Rauschenberg, Stella, Kelly and Nevelson. In true Beat style the Californian duo gave away the air tickets provided for them and did not attend the opening, believing that to do so would compromise their 'independence'.

A further sign of the carefully cultivated provincialism of Beat art and assemblage – Beat poetry and prose travelled more readily – lies in the fact that none of the California artists (except perhaps Jess) seem ever to have heard of, let alone seen, works by Schwitters, Höch, Heartfield or Picasso in the genre they were now practising. The French Surrealists were available, and Max Ernst was becoming known in California in the 1940s and 1950s (Man Ray lived in Los Angeles from 1941 to 1952).[16] Though selectively acquainted with Cubist art, by no means all of those who would become associated with Beat would have necessarily paid attention to the anthology *The Dada Painters and Poets*, edited by Robert Motherwell and published in 1951. And as with every bohemian milieu, its flowering was relatively brief. By the time the art historian Walter Hopps and the painter Ed Kienholz opened the Ferus Gallery at 736A La Cienega Boulevard in 1957, the charisma of artists and poets like Wallace Berman, Robert Alexander, George Herms and Stuart Perkoff in Los Angeles was probably at its height. By this time, Berman had collected around him a group

121 **Wally Hedrick** *Xmas Tree* 1955
Refusing to attend the exhibition, Hedrick allegedly set a timer so that the sculpture would suddenly begin to flash its lights, honking its horns and playing its records: such declarations of rebellion against the conventions of artistic display gave him a counter-cultural status outside the spaces of the museum and beyond the comprehension of collectors.

of like-minded artists, poets and writers who were heavily into Kabbalistic mysticism, peyote rituals, marijuana, personal gifting and domestic creativity, and had published the first issue of a small-format journal *Semina*, in which poems, photographs and drawings would be assembled loose-leaf and circulated within this community but not far beyond. *Semina* itself helped to define this community around values of personal integrity, sensory derangement, intimacy and freedom from oppressive social norms, always stimulated by a drug-induced search for the transpersonal and the divine.[17] When Berman was invited to exhibit a decade's worth of assemblage art at Ferus in June 1957, the latent conflict between his milieu and normative society became clear. The Los Angeles Vice Squad raided the show and charged Berman with 'displaying lewd and pornographic matter' – the police found a drawing of a copulating couple by the poet Cameron and Berman was found guilty and ordered to pay a $150 fine. Angry and depressed, Berman and his family left Los Angeles for San Francisco. Alexander and Herms were soon to follow. The poet and jazz player Herms, while preparing to move north to Berkeley, gathered some found materials and placed them on the foundations of some demolished houses. Called 'The Secret Exhibition', it was both unannounced, unreviewed and unvisited except by the cognisant few. An era in Los Angeles assemblage had come to a close.

'Beat' Constructivism: Bruce Conner and Ed Kienholz

The Berman incident was the first of several to focus the challenge rendered to 'straight' American society by the art of the Beat fraternities and their lifestyle of drugs, sensory adventure and alienation from consumption and work. Though television was already widespread in California, the world of glamour magazines and films would be more likely to engage the attention of the Beat collagists and assemblagists on the West Coast. The early works of Bruce Conner, who arrived in San Francisco in 1957 (coincidentally the year of Vance Packard's *The Hidden Persuaders* and of Roland Barthes's *Mythologies*) demonstrate how collage could not only replicate the sensory overload of the glamour industry, but also use it critically against itself when presented as a display of graphic and pictorial imagery from a multiplicity of sources. *UNTITLED* is a two-sided work which occupied Conner from 1954 to 1961: The 'front' bears elegantly fused pieces of cardboard and wooden scraps, reminiscent of Schwitters but on a far grander scale. On the back, which was not originally meant to be seen except by those handling the work, Conner's critique operates largely by accumulation: erotic pin-ups are collaged against historical paintings of women, interspersed with medical diagrams of the body, stage frolics, victims of war or torture, pages from *Good Housekeeping* and *Parents' Magazine*, an 'Ez for Prez' (Ezra Pound for President) sticker of 1956, an image of Marcel Duchamp, and a photograph of James Joyce prominent in the upper right – to only begin an impossible description. By the time of its eventual completion Conner had attached a letter ordering him to attend an Armed Forces Medical Examination, and in the centre, a prominent sign stating 'Warning: You Are In Great Danger', which speaks ironically to the viewer of the risks of enjoying pornographic imagery (still officially illegal) while seeming to address that culture censoriously on the perils of its own double-standards [*171*]. But the explicit programme of a work like the rear of *UNTITLED* should never be overstated. Like contemporary collage in Europe by Eduardo Paolozzi in Britain or Jean-Jacques Lebel in France (discussed in Chapter 11), Conner's work accumulates quantities of unrelated imagery whose very randomness induces an out-of-focus awareness that pulls precisely against the communication of 'content'. The selection is both throwaway, a reduction to 'junk' status, while at the same time a crafted composition having all the personal investment of a private noticeboard. The viewer is caught cleverly between alienation and inclusion – or has somehow to reconcile his or her position between the two.

A friend of the poet Michael McClure since his high-school days, Conner had arrived in

123 **Bruce Conner** *UNTITLED* (front view) 1954–61
Standing at over 1.6 metres (5½ feet) high, *UNTITLED* is one of the largest Beat assemblages ever made – though Conner did not like the term and attempted to evade art-world categorization throughout a prolific career, including film editing and an artistically fertile friendship with Dennis Hopper. See ill. 171 for the back view.

opposite 122 **Jay DeFeo** *Blossom* 1956
Like the very large painting *The Rose*, but more successfully, this collage organizes itself around a radiating centre; unlike it, it unfolds larger forms out of smaller ones like a flower, hence launching an analogy with the natural world.

San Francisco already deeply immersed in collage aesthetics in several media. Through the film-maker Stan Brakhage he gained an introduction to Larry Jordan, who himself worked with Joseph Cornell and had used stop-animation to make his own collage films. Conner decided to start an experimental film society with Jordan, and in 1958 completed his first work in the genre, a 12-minute black-and-white film self-reflexively called *A Movie*, composed of existing scraps of film *cliché* edited inventively against themselves in a manner radically unlike the classical Eisensteinian 'montage of attractions'. A much later Bruce Conner film, the thirteen-and-a-half-minute black-and-white *Marilyn Times Five* of 1968–73, operates not just on time but on the material look and substance of film itself, registering diverse juxtapositions and simultaneities deconstructively through repetition, inversion, jumps, and Conner's distinctive editing style. Conner has spoken of the 'pseudo-criminality' of 'stealing' already-formed film fragments on sale in local 16mm stores; has likened that 'stealing' to using already tried techniques and languages in painting, to building *on* the past *with* the past.[18] But in tandem with the films, Conner proved himself a pioneer of assemblage in a manner that went beyond the mystical orientation of the already overused term 'Beat'. His playful tactic was to found in 1958 the so-called Rat Bastard Protective Association as a focus for discussions, meetings, and parties (the term allegedly derives from the slang 'rat bastard' that Michael McClure picked up in the gym, from the Scavenger's Protective Association as the San Francisco garbage men called themselves, and perhaps from a desire for association with the nineteenth-century Pre-Raphaelite Brotherhood).[19] Artist-members such as Joan Brown, Carlos Villa, Jay DeFeo, Wally Hedrick and Wallace Berman were entitled to place the initials 'RBP' on their work and were urged to think of themselves as 'rat bastards'. Occasionally the term entered the work. The very title of Conner's *RATBASTARD* of 1958 seems to confirm that the Beat work of art is the illegitimate offspring of 'normal' artistic work, broken and dishevelled albeit still occupying the format and demeanour of an easel painting from the great tradition.

Conner's work stands out from the majority of West Coast assemblage in being compressed and concise enough to challenge East Coast and European assemblage on its own terms. Even though signs of distress and redundancy became the hallmarks of his other three-dimensional work of the period, Conner seems to have understood, in a way that Berman and other California assemblagists did not, that a kind of shallow flatness, the kind that any object must possess if it is to present itself as an image rather than a material entity, was a condition still inhabiting the artwork in the degree to which it was capable of being viewed as 'modern'. Brute three-dimensional things belonged elsewhere. Meanwhile the majority of Conner's object-assemblages, like those of the Los Angeles painter Ed Kienholz, seem to understand that a single viewpoint (or narrow range of angles) is certainly to be preferred. Spattering them with paint or distressing them with uniformly sprinkled liquids or cuttings was one way (perhaps the most effective) to that end.

Such a distinction seems important. Indeed, a gulf of understanding threatens to open up here between the homespun inventiveness of West Coast collage and assemblage, and the more abstract discussions then taking place in New York. For it was in 1958 that Clement Greenberg published the most demanding account of collage so far. It was the burden of his 'The Pasted-Paper Revolution' to explain to readers of *Art News* how the skilful steps Picasso and Braque had taken back in 1911 and 1912 prevented the surface emphases of pasted paper from reducing to 'mere' decorativeness; how painted letters and numbers first stopped the eye at the picture plane, which then became 'pushed into illusioned depth' by the presence of pasted-paper; how real and imaginary picture-planes shuttle back and forth against each other; how flatness permeates illusion and vice-versa; and finally how the demise of shading in Synthetic Cubism had given rise to the replacement of depicted depth first by 'optical' depth, and then by the beginnings of constructed sculpture, the true beacon of modernist art.[20]

124 **Bruce Conner** *RATBASTARD* 1958
Doubling as a thing to be carried as well as looked at pictorially, the face of the work is veiled in a suggestively erot nylon, Conner's assemblage material of choice. The presence of the photocopy at the top – a new medium in the 1950s – anticipates the combine style of Rauschenberg a decade later.

West Coast artists remote from the circuits of East Coast criticism struck their own kind of bargain with ideas of pictorial structure.[21] West Coast assemblage reflected how the radical newness being offered by America to the world at the time (its highways, kitchens, and spacecraft) needed returning to it in the form of destruction, wreckage and poverty. The junk shops and junkyards were bulging as Victorian property was demolished and modernist buildings rose. Some of Conner's assemblages of the period, like *SPIDER LADY* of 1959, torture the viewer with lacy underwear, torn nylon and an ambience of cob-webbed junk chaos, maintaining all the while the discipline of a shallow box-like space organized in rectilinear parts. Other Conner assemblages refer to current issues of concern: *CHILD*, of 1959 is a response to the long-drawn-out Caryl Chessman indictment on trumped-up charges of child kidnapping, while *BLACK DAHLIA* of 1960 displays erotic allurement in the form of nylon and boa feathers, and nails, to evoke a horrific Los Angeles murder of the 1940s. In such works Conner once more divides the viewer's attention between attraction and repulsion, identification and withdrawal, enticing the viewer with promises that turn distinctly sour. In the early 1960s Conner moved to Mexico in pursuit of a culture already replete with bizarre conjunctions of religion, domesticity and faltering mechanization, and effectively gave up making assemblages of his own in 1964.[22]

Beat and 'Ratbastard' artworks of the period both contributed to a far deeper stream of disquiet at post-war America's cultural and social contradictions. They were everywhere, and gathering pace. On the one hand Explorer I, the first US satellite (1958), a futile space race with the USSR, and a consumer boom at home propelled by the rapid spread of TV; on the other, the continuing social exclusion of African-Americans and minorities, the consolidation of American democracy at home, and the national paranoia about Communism leading to the Bay of Pigs invasion (1961) and the first US interventions in Vietnam. It was a loss of innocence registered with disillusionment and anger by artists such as the Los Angeles painter Ed Kienholz, who first moved into constructed objects around the watershed year of 1957 and whose *John Doe* assemblage of 1959 presents an armless upright manikin on a baby stroller to insinuate with extreme bitterness the infantilism of the average American male. True to the work's pictorial posture, smatterings of paint drip down over the manikin's stupefied expression, while attached to the stroller is a riddle which asks to be read: 'Why is John Doe like a piano? Because he is square, upright and grand'. For the title of his 1960 work *The Psycho-Vendetta Case*, again dealing with the Chessman execution, Kienholz again refers back to the police witch-hunt during the Sacco and Vanzetti case of the 1920s when two Italian immigrants were executed in retribution for their anarchist politics. Begun in anger, California's important contribution to Pop art collage was under way.[23]

5 **Ed Kienholz** *John Doe* 1959
The following year, 1960, Kienholz completed two works in a similar vein, *Jane Doe*, a severed head amid wedding regalia on a table, and *Boy, Son of John Doe*, who is mounted on a toy car surrounded by beer cans, a cigarette pack and a book on impotence.

9

Later Surrealism

The story of collage tells us that the real tension within modern art of the post-war period was between the procedural licences of Surrealism (chance, and the strangeness of the image) and the formal inheritance of Cubism (surface articulation, material construction, even abstraction). The last two chapters have been spent in America; for this one we return to Europe.

Post-War Paris: Jacques Prévert and Co.
Second-generation Parisian Surrealism has never received its due – yet in collage alone its achievements were remarkable. After 1945 André Breton's presence in Paris alongside the younger Surrealist poets and painters remained important, even as new agendas (notably existentialism) were being formed. An eager participant in *cadavre exquis* in the 1920s, the poet Jacques Prévert finally took to making collages in 1943 and is responsible for several hundred small works of astonishing narrative diversity. A catalogue from a recent Paris exhibition records the following themes and categories within his work: angels, beasts, celebrities, Christ, clowns, decapitations, devils, doubles, children, machines, masks, monsters, musicians, fish, penitents, saints, monkeys, statues, and religious virgins.[1]
The list is already indicative of Prévert's penchant for scandalous corruptions of Catholic religious imagery, of medieval piety, of mendicant orders and of other scenes. Prévert is generally merciless with dignitaries and historical notables, and with the suppression of libidinous fantasy in religious or bourgeois thought: we see him turn men and women into grotesque animals, and render heads and bodies deformed, fantastic or obscene – as is his corruption of Girodet's portrait of Napoleon. It is less easy to describe the critical context into which Prévert's work was judged at the time, and to which it appeals now. As one of France's best film scriptwriters of the post-war period, Prévert did not need collage in order to cultivate a larger career in the fine arts; rather he used it to flex his thinking about the strangeness of the theatrical *mis-en-scène* or to supercharge dramatic effect. Most of Prévert's material was obtained in Paris flea-markets or on the Quais of the River Seine, which in turn implies that the contemporary world is almost entirely missing from his *oeuvre* – as are the debates of the world of avant-garde art. This *was* Prévert's context, and one he enjoyed with his old friend Picasso. They flattered each other endlessly. Prévert made several 'portraits' of Picasso as a modern genius, in return for which Picasso paid his

friend compliments in the form of a paradox ('You can't paint or draw, but you are a painter'[2]) in recognition of Prévert's mastery of his colourful, fantastic world. Yet collage had become a minor genre in Paris by the time of Prévert's most active years of the later 1940s to the 1970s, and his hallucinatory collage scenes existed in defiant opposition to the wider aesthetic debates of the day. By their miniature scale alone were they beyond the discussion about mural-scale abstract art, yet neither did they comport with the alternative world of international Fluxus with its appetite for the ephemeral and the anarchic.

Prévert's younger contemporary Max Bucaille had made collages from the 1930s, often as accompaniments to poems or verbal collages, and in the post-war period crafted images of sudden or violent interruption of otherwise quiet scenes in the life of the wealthy bourgeois – like Ernst before him he favoured the archaic wood and steel engravings of the previous two centuries. In *Explosion in the Museum* of 1947, he shows the walls of the art museum rent asunder as a young girl tumbles from an air balloon into the gallery space, an event which the enraptured viewers of art do not even see. It is a late nineteenth-century world of billiard rooms and salons, Dion-Bouton automobiles and new electric comforts, that Bucaille exposes to hiatus, to shock, and to the bizarre demands of reality that lie beyond (or within) the real. In another collage of 1947, the innocent Alice in the underwater scene seems scarcely to recognize the watery environment that we viewers can clearly see. Around 1950 Bucaille made a group of unique object-collages that have seldom been exhibited: they exploit the uncanny effects obtainable from placing a mirror at a ninety degree angle to a collage so as to create a symmetrical image – evoking an animal of some unknown species, or tempting the viewer to 'read' strange phantasms into images known to not literally contain them. Dalí's anamorphic or paranoiac visions must be one source for Bucaille's experiments, which Philippe Soupault in 1950 greeted with the words: 'Our contemporaries still do not understand the importance, the power, of what can only be called a process: in my opinion collage corresponds to one of our most urgent needs: you know I refer to the marvellous'.[5]

Mention should also be made here of Gaston Chaissac, who participated in the melting-pot of post-war Paris, but at a distance. The apparently aimless Chaissac first arrived in Paris in 1937, but was urged to paint and draw by Otto Freundlich and his artist partner Jeannine Klosnick-Kloss with whom he shared a house. Through Raymond Queneau and

above, left 127 **Max Bucaille** *Explosion in the Museum* 1947
Like the director of a play or a film, Bucaille 'takes his props and his actors where he finds them – he chooses but does not create them – and then stages quite unbelievable enchantments'. (Jean Laude)

128 **Max Bucaille** *Alice in the Land of Fish and Daisies* 194[7]
Bucaille conspires with his viewers to show them events and qualities of which the characters in his scenes seem blithely unaware.

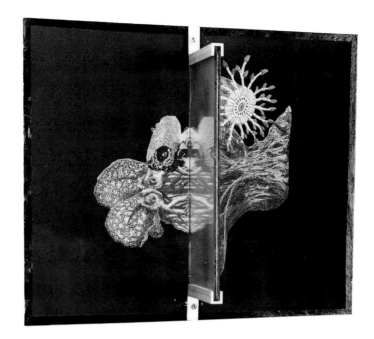

Jean Paulhan he was soon in correspondence with Jean Dubuffet, and by 1947 Chaissac's work was on display in Paris at the Galerie de l'Arc en Ciel and at the much-followed Galerie René Drouin, centre of Dubuffet's self-styled 'Art Brut' movement, where Chaissac's intuitively made sculptures in wood, painted stones and improvised constructions fitted the mood perfectly. Chaissac's intuitive *bricolage* aesthetic (he likened himself to a 'Picasso in clogs') led him to paint old cans and farmyard junk, farm implements and walls: It comes as no surprise then that even when he adopted the more cultivated art of collage, he was often described as an 'outsider' figure.[4] Yet that description is too simple. Chaissac like the Surrealists was absorbed by children's art and by the art of untrained people like himself (he was also claimed as a 'proletarian painter' in the revolutionary mould by the young critic Michel Ragon).[5] He also knew of the use of wallpaper by Picasso and the Cubists, to whose formal language it seems he was highly responsive. Yet at the same time he remained aware of his 'demi-naif' status, and sometimes worried about it. 'I used to accentuate my clumsiness', Chaissac once confessed revealingly, 'as I'd realised that the worse my drawing was, the less it had the look of an apprentice draughtsman about it... besides, to break with my origins would have been very bad manners'.[6] Chaissac's collages occupied him from 1955 to around the time of the death through ill-health in 1964.

Surrealism in the Independent Group: Paolozzi and Henderson

Surrealist collage flowered in post-war Britain among a generation who came to see how the existing tension between high art and mass culture could not survive the onslaught of American goods and services; who developed a conviction that the old hierarchies of the fine arts were no longer valid. They were a generation born in the 1920s who had been young combatants in the Second World War or else too young to be combatants at all. The critic Lawrence Alloway said of his contemporaries that they

> were born too late to be adopted into the system of taste that gave aesthetic certainty to our parents and teachers...we grew up with the mass media. Unlike our parents and teachers we did not experience the impact of the movies, the radio, the illustrated magazines. The mass media were established as a natural environment by the time we could see them.

Alloway went on: 'As I saw the works of art that Roger Fry and Herbert Read had written about, I found the works remained obstinately outside the systems to which they had been consigned. Significant form, design, vision, order, composition etc I saw as high level abstractions, floating above the pictures like ill-fitting haloes'. He relates how his first critical attempts to hold the experiences of 'fine' and 'popular' art together were a failure:

> My [earliest] strategy was the Surrealist one of looking for hidden meanings to unify John Wayne and Bronzino, Joan Crawford and René Magritte. But one day my patient Mr Goldwyn got up and walked away, and as his couch cooled I knew a chapter had closed. A trap for the consumer looking for a unifying but tolerant aesthetic is the alignment of top and bottom without the middle.

Alloway's eventual way out of the dilemma lay in the idea that both art and the common culture are 'part of a field of general communication' in which 'many levels and types of messages are transmitted to many types of audience along a multitude of channels'.[7] The implication was that no distinction could be drawn between the 'high' and 'popular' arts; that they coexisted in the field of consumption. And that consumption itself – perception, apprehension, desire, cognition, identification, ownership – formed a fascinating new field of study.

That new field of study came into focus around the year 1952, when Richard Hamilton, Nigel Henderson, Eduardo and Freda Paolozzi, William Turnbull, Victor Pasmore, Toni del Renzio, John McHale and Alison and Peter Smithson (along with Alloway) first came together as 'The Young Group' at the Institute of Contemporary Arts (ICA) in London – soon to be known as 'The Independent Group'. Alison Smithson described herself and her colleagues as:

> the lost generation: that is, the generation immediately ahead of us were coming back from the war, back to their lives before the war. There was just no room, there was too great a backlog in all walks of life for any of us to be let in and we were all just the people queuing up; and while we were queuing we talked together, and that was the only common ground, the fact that we were all queuing to get into life, as it were.[8]

What they mainly talked about was culture – the new technological and consumer culture that was already visible in the magazines, on the radio, in the shops (or some of them). United by a dislike of what the later recruit Reyner Banham would call 'the marble shadow of Sir Herbert Read's Abstract-Left-Freudian aesthetics',[9] the group called for lectures on Photography, Mannerism, Existentialism, Decadence, one by A. J. Ayer on Logical Positivism, and one on the design for Coventry Cathedral,[10] topics that spoke of a desire for an aesthetics of complexity, heterogeneity and inclusiveness. One modernist aesthetic was about to be supplanted by another.

Surrealism and certain elements of Dada would now assume some unfamiliar forms. Not only did members of the group know that photography as collage had already infected the fine arts in Dada and pre-war photomontage, they also saw the uses to which technical photography was now being put in microscopy, radiography, aerial photography, medicine, rocket and space flight, design, even the reproductive technologies applied to the fine arts. And it was the *enfant terrible* of this group, Eduardo Paolozzi, who in April 1952 delivered an epidiascope lecture consisting of photographic fragments, pop-culture clippings and his own collages made from illustrated magazines. The lecture was itself a collage of sorts: chaotic, unarticulated, attended only by a handful – who must have sat bemused as Paolozzi projected a mish-mash of technical, mechanical, soft-porn and advertising images in a new fusion of erotics and technology that would come to dominate his thinking for years to come. The name Paolozzi gave to the lecture was *Bunk!*

Paolozzi had by this time been active in collage-making for at least seven years. Born in Scotland of Italian parents, hence multi-lingual in street Scots, Italian and English, he already had 'outsider' status in British culture. As a child he had accumulated printed cigarette cards and the like from his parents' shop; had possessed few toys,[11] and drew obsessively in a disarmingly naïve idiom. In adult life his rich fantasy life has given him independence from the trends of his time. Even in successful middle age he is described as 'never giving to friends the feeling that they really knew him'; always preferring to leave the party early and work alone.[12] He seldom smiles.

Paolozzi's earliest known collages date from his first days at (or in escape from) the Slade School of Art in London just after the war. He had been compiling scrapbooks of mass-culture images from about the age of 10 before becoming fired by the work of Schwitters which he saw in E. L. T. Mesens' London Gallery late in 1945 or early in 1946, and by the work of Picasso, Ernst and Arp at Zwemmer's Gallery and at Roland Penrose's house. It was at this time that Paolozzi started his own meccano-morphic collages deriving from 'medical and greasy motor manuals, and broken museum books on sculpture'.[13] During Paolozzi's time in Surrealist Paris, from mid-1947 to 1949, his friend the slightly older Nigel Henderson frequently came to stay.[14] The two artists met Giacometti and Braque. Paolozzi visited the collections of Mary Reynolds, who showed him a room Marcel Duchamp had papered over with pages from *National Geographic* magazine, and Tristan Tzara, who showed him early Picasso collages and Max Ernst's *Chinese Nightingale* collage of 1920.[15] He also visited Arp, who showed him *After Torn Papers*. In Paris, Paolozzi was able to assimilate the writings of Raymond Roussel, whose elaborate use of homonyms in works like *Impressions d'Afrique*, *Locus Solus* and *La Poussière de Soleils* provided a model of literary collage based on verbal and semantic analogies, wordplay and unconscious 'resemblance'.[16] He met Ellsworth Kelly, John Cage and the painter Charlie Marks; and came into contact with a wealth of American magazines, including *Astounding Science Fiction*, *View*, *Collier's*, and *Saturday Evening Post* that arrived with other American artists studying in Paris courtesy of the GI Bill. Further forages in second-hand bookshops in London and Paris uncovered the sources for what Paolozzi would later refer to as:

> this magic process of picture-making – of introducing strange fellows to each other in a hostile landscape or placing objects amongst the rubble of a bombed church without recourse to a standard drawing and painting practice…of strange weddings between marooned boats on ancient plazas or bizarre flying machines trapped in city halls.[17]

Paolozzi's early private scrapbooks, many of them now in the Krazy Kat Arkive in London, demonstrate his enthusiasm for letting the 'outside world' of sci-fi magazines, food and health advertisements, comics and magazine illustration enter and contaminate the 'pure' traditions and practices of fine art.[18] The so-called *Yale Iron* scrapbook of 1948–53 has images juxtaposed to bring out the startling effects both of the new colour photo-printing and the shiny optimism of later 1940s USA as delivered through its popular magazines; magazines that Paolozzi was to call 'a catalogue of an exotic society, bountiful and generous, where the selling of tinned pears was transformed into multi-coloured dreams, where sensuality and virility combined to form…an art more subtle and fulfilling than the orthodox choice of the Tate Gallery or the Royal Academy'.[19] *Yale Iron* as a whole is obsessed with the graphic representation of children, food, mothers – some fathers – basically America's stereotypical nuclear family at the time of the hydrogen bomb and the diplomatic and cultural 'war' against the USSR. Its shiny non-sequiturs – a new car jammed up against the hyperboles of advertising language, or the concatenation of

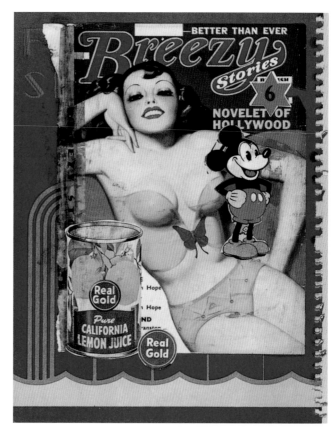

135 **Nigel Henderson** From Bethnal Green Series 1948–52
...top! Here For American Comics' reads the sign below this
...owded shop window – which is replete with the latest
...pies of *Photoplay*, *Crime Patrol*, *Super Boy* and books for
...le 'To Adults Only': a blend of novel pastimes and illicit
...easures unavailable during the austerities of war.

...oposite, left to right (top and bottom)

31 **Eduardo Paolozzi** Page from *Yale Iron* scrapbook
1948–53

32 **Eduardo Paolozzi** *Real Gold* 1950

33 **Eduardo Paolozzi** *Take-Off* 1950

34 **Eduardo Paolozzi** Page from *Telephone Receiver*
...rapbook 1947–53

...mong the master works [I saw at the London Gallery] were
...ollages by Schwitters. These were a revelation, as were the
...productions of Max Ernst. It was this that hardened my
...esolve to go to Paris…'. Paolozzi elsewhere speaks of the
...xhilarating brew' of possible combinations in collage. 'To
...nally harness this set of free spirits is like an act of betrayal,
...nprisoning these individuals, condemning them to a life of
...ozen violence'.

domesticity, sex and warfare in one image of childhood innocence, seduction, washing powder and bombers – show us the artist's successive attempts to manufacture the effects of radical irony and dislocation out of already familiar images from the culture.[20]

Once back in London, Paolozzi took a close interest in Henderson's own anthropological photographs taken in London's Bethnal Green – photographs which tell us much about how Henderson and perhaps the two of them looked at the exotic tribal semantics of shopfronts, magazine covers, pin-ups, and cut-price goods. Reprising Brassaï's photos of Parisian wall graffiti, or Walker Evans's or Atget's pursuit of vernacular themes, as well as reflecting Mass Observation thinking, Henderson's photographs present their flat interlocked consumer surfaces in a manner comparable to a scrap-book page: scenes of dereliction intercut with glimpses of sci-fi, detective and pin-up magazines in a ready-made aesthetic to which Paolozzi was already well attuned. In 1949, responding in turn to Paolozzi's example, Henderson began his quadripartite *Collage Screen* (two parts were complete by 1960) which brought together primitive masks, images of Charles Atlas, pin-ups, figures with artificial limbs, and reproductions of Old Master paintings.[21]

Meanwhile Paolozzi's private scrapbooks were in part rehearsals for 'finished' works. The dominating irony of the well-known *Evadne in Green Dimension* (1952) for example comprises Charles Atlas in leopard-skin swimsuit holding aloft a new Cadillac, a diagram of the erect male member with a pin-up in the scrotum forming the secondary joke. 'I could never achieve a body like yours, it would take years', says the feeble wimp pictured in the original *Sketch* advertisement. 'Bunk!' retorts Charles Atlas in a phrase that lends a title to the series and the lecture, 'you can have a body like mine in seven days'.[22] Increasingly, robotic men and stereotypical women appear in these parodies as an expression of real cultural anxieties about new American goods and their insertion into a depressing but still hopeful British post-war world. On the other hand, the more austere bipartite *Take-Off* (1950) hovers between the informal scrapbook page and the finished work: its daring proximity of tough male activity with soft female glamour is both an amusing visual fact as well as a clever, because simple, mix.

Indeed *Take-Off*'s more noticeboard organization marks a somewhat different vein of Paolozzi's imagery in which there are no interruptions, pastings-over or colliding areas. The majority of the images of the scrapbook *Telephone Receiver* [*134*], also begun around

136 Double-page image from *Lilliput* 1938
Lilliput's photographic pairings came close to political
Surrealism in a popular vein. Other conjunctions might include
Lord Hailsham with W. C. Fields, the Chancellor of the
Exchequer and a Hungarian peasant, the Lord Privy Seal and a
smiling goat.

PLANET NEWS   LONDON PLANET NEWS   LONDON

"I DEFY HIM TO TOUCH ME"   "WE DEFY THEM TO TOUCH US"
Skittish Foal   *Sir Oswald Mosley*

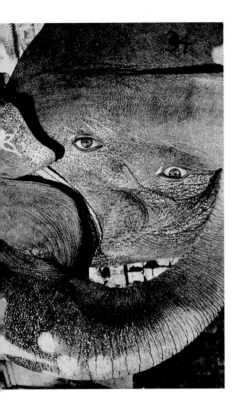

37 **Eduardo Paolozzi** Page from *Psychological Atlas* 1949
The dominant mood of *Psychological Atlas* is one of
constraint, of a dysfunctional nightmare world of men reified
as machines, of machines crushing or inhibiting men, of
strange animal creatures. Of such ghoulish visions, Paolozzi
said that they reflected 'a true state, both autobiographic and
dynamic'.

1947 and finished around 1953, are right way up, side by side, and black and white: a disciplined grid now operates as the principle of organization. Jazz players, film and TV stars, business diagrams and monsters, androids and underwear, fighter planes and oversize tyres: one has the impression of a new accumulation of image-types not intended to relate to each other, unless accidentally. One thing next to another, perhaps. For Paolozzi had come to know and admire books such as Amedée Ozenfant's *Foundations of Modern Art* (1928), Lewis Mumford's *The Condition of Man* (1944), and Siegfried Giedion's *Mechanisation Takes Command* (1945),[23] in which he saw historically or culturally remote images meet each other often with apparent indifference. Perhaps it was more entertainingly done in a magazine like *Lilliput*, in wide circulation in late 1930s Britain, in which what the observer saw were not single photographs, but difference itself – the strangeness to be found in visually similar but unlike pairs. But for Paolozzi, by contrast, contiguity *without similarity* was the new principle – suggesting fascination at the sheer range of representational types, photographic angles, magnifications and pictorial conventions that a trawl through the daily and weekly magazines could uncover. Yet if *Telephone Receiver* is an additive, accumulative work, it is also a kind of glossolalia, a speaking in tongues whose aim is to undo or evade sense-making by pure enthusiasm alone. In this book above all Paolozzi seems to have been reaching beyond or beneath sense, where meaning wasn't.[24]

Only one of Paolozzi's scrapbooks fails to live up to the generalizations made so far. *Psychological Atlas* (completed in 1949 and one of the earliest) is uniquely over-crowded and too small, and contains hallucinatory visions such as a car marooned in a field, or a robot at the scene of a grave-robbery. There are pages containing a yeti in the back of a freight aircraft; a fashion model, a biplane, and a watch interior floating incongruously on a picture of a river delta taken from *Picture Post*. There is a seal on dry land with Charles Atlas. Remarkably and frighteningly, another page contains an elephant turned on its side and supplied with eyes and teeth to make an unspeakable monster. It is about this most anguished and personal of scrapbooks that Paolozzi seems to be speaking when he affirms that only in collage

> can improbable events can be frozen into peculiar assemblies by manipulation: time and space can be drawn together into new spatial strategy…figures from a Turkish landscape trapped by cruelty may be released and find themselves perplexed and frightened in a French nursery flanked by a mechanical sphinx…the Rathaus in Zurich dwarfed by a frog represents not only poetic ambiguity but a personal hypothesis.

He adds: 'The word "collage" is inadequate as a description because the concept should include "damage", "erase", "deface", "transform" etc, all parts of a metaphor for the creative act itself'.[25]

The Non-Aristotelians: John McHale

The humanoid head and upper body was an image of particular interest both for Paolozzi and for other Independent Group members: notably John McHale. McHale made his first *Transistors* collages in 1953 [*138*], in which (unlike the equivalent image in paint) the additive process of collage-making provides a strong formal analogy with the sequential processing of electronic impulses; in which the viewer's perceptual process is also analogized as a part-by-part information-processing operation on a par with the given subject-matter of the work. Several were shown in an important ICA exhibition organized by Alloway in late 1954 (designed by McHale) entitled 'Collages and Objects'. This was a collection of over eighty works which attempted to give a history of collage by dividing the

genre into groups: first, a display of 'poor' material as it appears in the *papiers collés* of Picasso, Braque and Gris; second, the Surrealist revolt against form by Max Ernst, Duchamp, Arp, Dalí, Magritte, Miró and Penrose; third, the urban subject-matter of Schwitters, Dubuffet, Austin Cooper, Paolozzi and Henderson; and fourth, the 'abstract' or 'painterly' collages of Pasmore, Anthony Hill, Kit Barker, John Piper, John Forrester and William Turnbull (objects were limited to Max Ernst's 1919 version of *Fruit of a Long Experience* [*48*], Duchamp's *Belle Haleine*, Magritte's *The Future of Statues*, a poem-object by Breton and Paolozzi's *Psychological Atlas* and two collage-books by McHale). The purpose of 'Collages and Objects' was to announce the inclusiveness of Independent Group attitudes to hybridity and to mass culture, and in so doing to establish continuity with selected aspects of Herbert Read's Surrealism.[26] McHale also participated in the second series of Independent Group lectures of 1955 – he convened them with Lawrence Alloway – on the relation of the popular to the fine arts. McHale himself spoke on Hamilton, Advertising, and 'Dadaists as Non-Aristotelians', the very title of which implied that Dada artists had surmounted the logic of the law of non-contradiction: the clear message was that non-Aristotelians were enthusiastic to embrace contraries, disliked hierarchies and were averse to binaries, particularly the subject–object distinction and the distinction between perceiver and perceived. McHale then went on a Fellowship to Yale University to study colour theory and industrial materials with Josef Albers, and returned in the summer of 1956 with a trunk of very un-Albers-like material comprising 'the first Elvis Presley records to land on these shores…protectively interleaved with copies of MAD magazine',[27] a tranche of architecture and design magazines and a cornucopia of printed commercial ephemera. As Alloway would write later the following year: 'The point about the Dada attitude, which we can see clearer than at any time before, is its indifference to strict, exclusive categorised thinking. Instead of setting up an absolute standard of performance Dada is sceptical and permissive.'[28]

For McHale as for others, the contents of the Yale trunk were seminal. Opening the cargo to his colleagues at the ICA released a new spirit of urgency and interest in American popular culture and arguably spelt the beginning of the end of the fertile 'first phase' of engagement with the European landscape of consumption. Even before his return to England, McHale had completed the first of his *Head* collages, in which a new type of

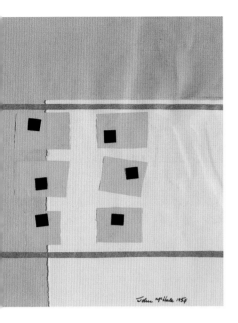

39 **John McHale** *Machine-Made America I* 1956–7
McHale's consumer consisted of symbols of the food he reads
bout and eats. His body is peeled like an anatomical chart as
the artist were looking for a swallowed pin… The outside
nd inside of the consumer are equally available for
spection.' (Alloway)

mecano-morphic totem figure had emerged from the interplay of torn paper and painted marks. Early works such as *Carburettor Head* (1955) provide the crudest mechanical analogy for the human, with engine parts for eyes, a circuit diagram for a face, a turbine for a neck, and a carburettor protruding from the forehead; the image of an ill-assembled robot already ruined by the very technology that made him. Now in possession of the new American material, McHale could extend his range. There was just time to organize his 'fun house' pavilion with Richard Hamilton and John Voelcker at the 'This is Tomorrow' exhibition at the Whitechapel Art Gallery in London in August and September 1956. McHale then showed eleven new collage heads at the ICA in November and December 1956. Made from garishly coloured images from the Yale trunk as well as from European magazines, these works intensified their radical differences from Ernst's methods, and from Picasso's. Now inverting coloured elements so that imagery disappears into texture, McHale synthesizes those textures into a single lumbering cyborg of uncertain appetites and capacities. They are men – and not just men, but managers, politicians, the organizers-rendered-primitive of the brave new world of atomic bombs and supermarket shopping, of 'communications' and TV. Alloway was again the writer: 'The details of the collages, viewed close, refer back to their original status, but from a distance the individual images are subsumed by an impression of fertile waste…of lavish ambiguity'. Calling attention to the 'brilliant colours of the ever-improving print process, the haze of competing messages as you turn a magazine's pages', Alloway also spoke of 'collages slowly assembled out of images which reveal the new scale of resemblance and strangeness created by modern photography'.[29] We should notice that the mechanical robot, familiar from pre-war science fiction as an efficient, sometimes benign machine, was transformed in the form McHale now gave it. What now appeared was the very parody of a self-declaring technical civilization, making use of its high-gloss surfaces, its glowing colours and its irrational shifts of scale. Furthermore, these oversize person-machines are internally as well as externally exposed: sensing and digesting machines whose mechanical subjectivity has been exposed to the general view. Indeed food was a central topic. And yet the viewer's position is challenged too. As with the earlier *Transistor* series, his or her consumption of visual data finds its counterpart in the tearing, cutting and assembling of urban and commercial fragments. In the very process of looking, therefore, the viewer meets head-on the reality of modern rhetorics of information-processing, and by implication the redundancy of the old Aristotelian contraries of inside–outside, mind versus body, objective perception versus subjective state. As McHale would write in his later and much-anthologized essay 'The Plastic Parthenon', 'as the apparatus of cultural diffusion becomes increasingly technological, its "products" become less viewable as discrete, individual events, rather more as related elements in a contextual flow'.[30]

Collage into Sculpture: Paolozzi

Paolozzi applied comparable images after 1956 to the making of figure sculpture. Beginning in that year, his method was to collect small-gauge toy cars and machine-parts and press them into clay, then to bend the impressed clay into shapes suitable for wax moulds, out of which bronze collage-like surfaces would emerge. We have Paolozzi's notes from a 1958 lecture at the ICA, delivered in what *The Times* (whose reporter was present) described as 'a break-neck pace, against a quick-changing background of slides of his figures as well as of photographs of crashed cars and aircraft, men with mechanised arms, and other odds and ends which he had carefully cut out of newspapers'.[31] These notes (as published) are a textual collage which re-enact on the plane of the verbal the sorts of incongruities and recombinations that their author manipulates in the studio. They spin through concrete poems, photographs, sketches and handwritten notes with category-destroying abandon: a *bricolage* of the urban with the ancient, the adult with the naïve, the

140 **Eduardo Paolozzi** *Jason II* 1957
'Certain quasi-geometric shapes *intrude* up fierce projections resembling…geological phenomena. The marriage of mixed elements. The design sheet as a broken fragment or as part of a *construction* (figure)'. (Paolozzi)

mechanical and the human, scribbles and Zen prose. There are collaged robots aplenty. Paolozzi's sometimes unfelicitous language dwells insistently on science-fiction and robotics, but also upon ancient scripts, sunken cities, fantastic weapons and primitive fetishes. He adverts repeatedly to the idea that a reflection of that jumbled universe is to be found in the world of the toy – a doubling of adult enthusiasms in the world of the child that strikes him as on the one hand a scientific miracle ('modern polythene toys, due to the combination of plastic injection methods and steel dies, have a microscopic precision impossible to the handcraftsman of the past'), but on the other, the perfect analogy for the adult world of dystopic mechanistic control of all our thoughts and behaviour ('giant machines with automatic brains are at this moment stamping out blanks and precision objects, components for the other brains which will govern other machines'[32]). Then, under the heading of 'Metamorphosis of Rubbish' comes a poem-list of both adult and toy fragments which 'are used in my work, that is to say, pressed into a slab of clay in different formations':

> Dismembered lock
> Toy frog
> Rubber dragon
> Toy camera
> Assorted wheels and electrical parts
> Clock parts
> Broken comb
> Bent fork
> Various unidentified found objects
> Parts of a radio
> Old RAF bomb sight
> Shaped pieces of wood
> Natural objects such as pieces of bark
> Gramophone parts
> Model automobiles
> Reject die castings from factory tip sites
> CAR WRECKING YARDS AS HUNTING GROUNDS

Eventually we see Paolozzi narrowing to what he calls 'my preoccupation or obsession with metamorphosis of the figure'; the end-result of which is 'a parade of politicised robots gone criminal'. He seems already to know that his collaged and sculpted 'robots' (he made eight of them between 1956 and 1958) are being registered as brutal, powerful, and mysterious. Describing *Jason I* of 1956 (the work sold in the USA) and *Jason II*, now in Edinburgh, Paolozzi ends the published notes by reverting to prose:

> My occupation can be described as the ERECTION OF HOLLOW GODS with the head like an eye, the centre part like a retina…a base containing the title, date or author in landscape letters. The legs as decentred columns or towers, the torso like a tornado struck down, a hillside or the slums of Calcutta. A bronze framework containing symbols resembling bent mechanisms. An automata [sic] totally exposed, with ciphers.

Private collage had produced public sculptures. Paolozzi's looming anti-heroes had come successfully to stand for the fears and anxieties of an epoch.

141 **François Dufrêne** *L'Inconnue* 1961
Dufrêne wrote of how he fell into 'ecstasy' at the first sight of
the transfer effect visible on the undersides of posters and
sheet-signs ruined by the weather; and how he then
remounted them without alteration, as a Duchampian
readymade, but paradoxically in the format of abstract art.

10

The Critique of Cities

In the decade and a half after 1945 the new lifestyles and technical possibilities of the consumption culture adorned magazines and printed material everywhere in a period of reviving prosperity. But whereas the Independent Group in Britain responded largely to the printed page, their contemporaries in Rome, Paris and beyond took their cue from the large-scale advertising hoardings that increasingly dominated public space. Entertainment and political posters, especially – and later commercial advertising – covered wall surfaces so spectacularly as to make them the most appealing visual data of their time. Mayakovsky had exhorted the post-Revolutionary Russian avant-garde to 'take the streets as our palette and the squares as our brushes'. The Paris Surrealists had expressed a desire to 'poetize' the walls of the city and render them the site of the marvellous. Now *décollage*, or tearing down, came into its own. It is a historical irony that with the end of a destructive war in Europe, destruction of the image now became relevant to making art.

Collage and décollage *in Rome*
We begin in a city struggling to rid itself of the memory of fascism: Rome after 1945 was divided artistically between the claims of figurative realism, à la Renato Guttuso, and those of the Nuovo Secessione artists such as Renato Birolli and Emilio Vedova, who looked for a modern, autonomous practice based on Cubism. Both groups were bound up in fierce theoretical disputes within the PCI (Italian Communist Party). Yet not perhaps until the rise to power of the Christian Democrats in 1948 and the landmark Venice Biennale of that year did the Italian cities provide fertile conditions for an avant-garde art of international significance. Thereafter, at least three relatively new directions can be identified which bore upon the articulation and disruption of the material surface in art. In one, Lucio Fontana created his first *Buchi* (holes) pictures in 1949 as a means of marking the bare canvas with paradoxical absences – excised holes – created with a knife. Fontana's *Buchi* perform a kind of negative collage with the canvas itself (Pollock's work of 1948–9 might be compared). In the second, Alberto Burri's abstract paintings using tar (*Catrami*), mould (*Muffe*), and other materials date from about 1948 and were exhibited within the Origine group in Rome in 1949: they shortly anticipate his works covered with abrasions, tears, rags and patches sewn together, the earliest of which date from 1950.[1] Burri had trained as a medical doctor before leaping into art: his works belong to a collage aesthetic in so far as

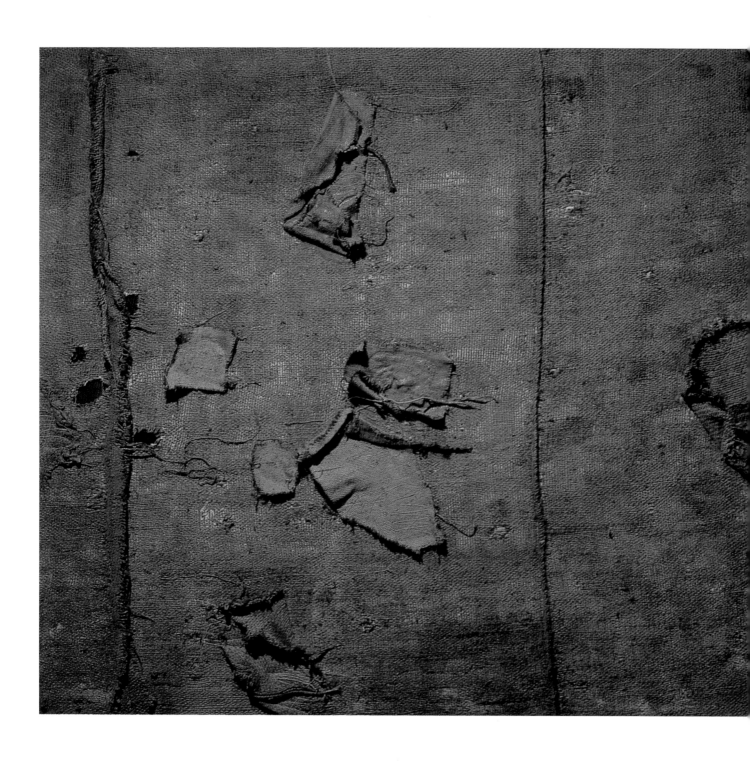

142 **Alberto Burri** *Sacco* 1952
Burri, in common with Fontana, adopted a position outside
familiar or ideological structures: in the words of the Origine
group statement, his origin was to begin 'from truth
contained within ourselves, located here in rough materials
damaged in a struggle for survival.'

they assert ruined or distressed material itself as a surface. Burri always refused to associate concepts with his project. Yet his works could often be referred to an Italian tradition of art. He wants, says one critic in an apposite phrase, 'to resort to the *furor* [sic] of Tintoretto and the passion of Bernini to confront the weight, the interweavings, the heat and burden of the image'.[2]

Very different from both Fontana and Burri was the Calabrian born Domenichino (Mimmo) Rotella. From 1945 until 1951 Rotella was a painter of figurative and abstract styles; he was also a competent jazz drummer and the founder of a type of phonetic poetry he called *epistaltici* (the word has only a suggestive meaning) which he performed enthusiastically in public after the example of Russolo's Futurist sound machines. It was not until returning to Rome after a year in the United States at the end of 1952 that Rotella gave up painting: 'I was not satisfied', he later tells us, 'since I knew that all of the problems had already been solved before me, by Mondrian, [Jules] Herbin, [Fritz] Glarner, and by the Constructivists'. Rotella turned instead towards the material texture of the city of Rome and specifically its layered entertainment posters and its crumbling wall surfaces near his studio in the Piazza del Popolo. Venturing out to 'raid' these surfaces of their fragments seemed enough: here seemed a ready-made pretext for a gesture of protest against what Rotella was to call 'the grey of houses, sky, faces, roads, dust, feelings, all the great grey things' of his childhood in the Italian south, '...to tear posters down from the wall was the sole compensation, the only means of protest against a society that had lost its appetite for change and transformation'.[3] Made first in 1953 and exhibited in 1954, Rotella's new *décollages* (also called *affiches lacérées*) required taking down scraps of already torn advertising poster, sticking them on canvas and sometimes cutting or tearing them again to form textures of contingency and incoherence. Both sensual and critical, the *affiches lacérées* occupied the format of large-scale easel painting in a manner at once beguiling and apocalyptic. The early *Un Poco in Su* of 1954, for example, presents an image of degraded, even violent beauty. 'If I had the strength of Samson', said Rotella in another statement, 'I could have stuck down the entire Piazza di Spania, with its tender autumn tints upon the sunset-reddened squares of the Gianicolo'. But displays of ready-made abstract colour were not his only concern. 'What would the earth be like after the Apocalypse?', he also asks. 'Perhaps a cool, smooth marble surface, veined with sinuous canals, like the cracks in the desert floor. *Collage* offers a yellowish patina to this geography of decay; but it is [also] the patina of hope'. Furthermore, the controlled anonymity of *décollage* technique secured a new model of artistic agency for Rotella at a time when the metaphysics of individualism was being re-examined throughout the European avant-garde. Unpredictable effects in *décollage* occur 'just as if a trumpet, a drum and a saxophone were playing by themselves', Rotella said. ' I am simply holding the instruments. Instead, I strip the posters down, firstly from the walls and then from the surface of the work itself. What a thrill, what fantasy, what strange things happen, clashing and accumulating between the first and last layer! "Originality" is reactionary now'.[4]

Décollage *in Paris: Hains and Villeglé*

Despite an expanding web of exhibitions and publications devoted to new trends in Italian and international art (the 1948 Venice Biennale was one showcase, underpinned by Peggy Guggenheim's enthusiasms newly on display nearby, and in 1950 an exhibition 'Art Italien Contemporain' held in Amsterdam and Brussels) the most experimental Italian art was not at this stage widely known either in Paris or New York.[5] In both those cities, nevertheless, a parallel concern for the interplay between degraded public surfaces and the bright icons of commercial modernity was emerging. French art at the time was dominated by the moody, highly individualized abstract paintings of Soulages and De Stael on the one side, and the small-scale Surrealism of the drug-inspired work of Wols or Michaux on the other. Both

43 Mimmo Rotella *Un Poco in Su* 1954
'When he rips a poster, Rotella is captured by a sense of the grandeur of his gesture. For him, it is the only conceivable way to appropriate an aspect of the real in all its objective and sociological totality. Within the lacerated poster, no doubt, here is complete sociological reality, the commerce of the world.' (Pierre Restany)

were opposed to a third tendency, namely left-wing *engagé* painting in figurative realist styles by André Fougeron and Boris Taslitzky. It was against this diverse background, yet aligned with none of the previous three camps, that Raymond Hains and Jacques de la Mahé Villeglé, both born in 1926 and both Bretons (from Saint-Brieuc and Quimper respectively) proposed a *décollage* of the city's streets and dilapidated advertising hoardings. As early as February 1949 they 'discovered' their first long frieze of torn and lacerated posters, which they dismounted from their hoardings and transferred with minimal adjustment to canvas, at once shifting the scene of artistic agency from the privacy of the studio to the public arena of the street, as well as reviving the philosophy of the 'ready-made' in its most colourful and obtrusive form. From its emergent letter-combinations they titled this frieze *Ach Alma Manetro.*

Ach Alma Manetro inaugurates several advances upon the most important pre-war collages, those of Picasso and Braque's Cubism, of Dada, and of Ernst and Arp's Surrealism. Aside from its literal incorporation of the very scale and order of the fragmented street hoardings of the post-war city, whose inducements to travel, entertainment or political affiliation stood suspended between bold assertion and rapid decay, *Ach Alma Manetro* – a near-meaningless configuration of syllables – instantiates a new kind of formal dismantling of the artwork and a new kind of attitude to time. As Benjamin Buchloh has pointed out, close attention to the surface of the work reveals that the lacerations performed upon the urban billboard surface (as well as the lacerations already there) are more insistently fragmenting and destabilizing than many or even most of the Surrealists' random, dream-like images. And second, that those very lacerations activate and temporalize the multiple collage fragments in a manner far exceeding the modest cutting and gluing processes of Cubist collage, processes aimed not at a temporal but a spatial evocation of forms.[6] We may add that the much larger scale of the new *affiches lacérées* instantly related this temporalization to the expansive manipulative gestures of the whole physical body, an ambitious extension of previous collage practices involving merely scissors, knife and glue.

What is less clear is how far dismemberment within these early *affiches lacérées* does go. Buchloh claims that the collapse of meaning operates even at the level of the word which, unlike the carefully excised or punned fragments of Cubist collage, here disintegrates

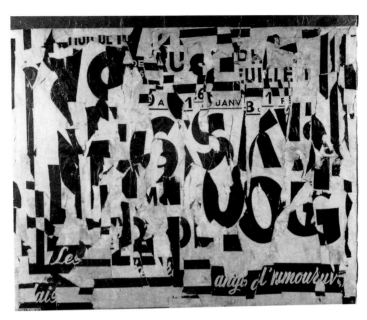

44 **Raymond Hains and Jacques de la Villeglé** *Ach Alma Manetro* 1949
At over 2.5 metres (8 feet) wide, this elegant work occupies the format of a Classical frieze, but from a modern city (Paris) whose verbal texture is ruined, abstract. Villeglé also saw his *décollages* against the backdrop of Duchamp, Ernst, Arp, Schwitters, even Leonardo.

45 **Jacques de la Villeglé** *L'Humour Jaune* 1953
Describing the appearance of 'lacerated letters' Villeglé proposed that 'typographic characters are so intermingled with a swarm of other typographic characters as to introduce us to the domain of *the elusive*.'

phonetically, lexically and semantically right down to the level of the syllable and the alphabetic letter: he asserts the 'total disintegration of internal pictorial relationships and the almost complete erasure of the phonetic, semantic and lexical dimension of written signs...it is within *décollage* that the total erosion of even the smallest semantic units is accomplished'.[7] Another route to describing the same effect is to register how, both in *Ach Alma Manetro* as in Villeglé's other *affiches lacérées* of the early and mid-1950s, it is first and foremost linguistic decay that is on view. The viewer sees a surface whose successive and inconsistently overlapping layers of meaning have been gradually effaced by laceration, not to zero, but to an affirmation that language is being forced to take a new form. Here, language survives as depletion, stuttering and ruin: the work's title resonates inefficiently with *Bach* (the family of musicians), *Alma Marceau* (the station at the junction of Avenue du Président Wilson and Avenue Marcel Marceau), and with *Metro*, to suggest a range of geographies, histories and technologies to which the temporalization of the image's manufacture somehow corresponds. It is much in this sense that Villeglé (when working alone) aligns himself as much with high art as with 'low' forms of ready-made urban and prison-wall graffiti, powerful photographs of which had already been published before the war by Brassaï and by Camus's friend the writer Benjamin Calet.[8] Villeglé saw himself positioned between and beyond all simple affiliations:

> The artist is one who, at the cross-roads of the world and turning to the winds, is the point of coincidence between art and the profane, the law-governed and the secular, the individual and the collective. As Lautréamont said: 'Art is made by all and not by one'...poster-tearing thus oscillates between intellectual culture and collective life, between savagery and civilization, between cross-breeding and internationalisation.[9]

At the same time, in a typology written later for his ten-volume *catalogue raisonnée*, Villeglé lists his artistic forbears in exclusively high-cultural terms: his list includes Picasso, Dada, Surrealism, Apollinaire's 'Windows' poem of 1912, Joyce's epiphanies, Céline, Monet's *Waterlilies*, Van Gogh, Lautréamont, and so on: avant-garde traditions which in practice he is as prepared to invoke as to violate.[10] Hains, for his part, when working alone, exploited a similar range of chance effects in the *affiches lacérées* manner, aimed at a semantic meltdown capable of standing alongside not only the lacerations of Villeglé, but the 'unreadable poems' of Camille Bryen belonging to the movement known as Lettrisme, and even the fundamental realignment of language and the unconscious being proposed at the same time by the psychoanalyst Jacques Lacan.[11]

The involvement of Raymond Hains with the theory and practice of the lacerated visual work is best understood through his early involvement (once more with Villeglé) in photography and film. Hains had exhibited a set of 'hypnagogic' photographs at Paris's avant-garde Collette Allendy Gallery in 1948, the same year that he met Bryen and Wols, the latter of whom had himself photographed decaying poster hoardings in the later 1930s. These hypnagogic photographs, objects photographed through fluted glass, had presented the world of things in a jumbled, repeated and fragmented manner which constituted a small-scale revolt against painting at a time of perceived faltering in the momentum of Paris Surrealism. As with Rotella in Rome at the same time, painting, like language itself, was by sections of the Parisian avant-garde regarded as deeply problematized by its inability to 'deal with' destruction and war. Both convictions led Hains first to attend to poster-hoardings, then to the implosion of signification itself, in a series of photographs visually transforming a phonetic poem by Camille Bryen. Bryen's small-format book *Hépérile* was photographed, again through fluted glass, and the results displayed at Collette Allendy in 1953, accompanied by a text by Bryen entitled *Hépérile Éclaté*: 'We are saturated with messages, lectures, humanism. Welcome to the fresh air of illegibility, unintelligibility, openness.... Hains and Villeglé are the two Christopher Columbuses of the "ultra-letter"...*Hépérile Éclaté* is the first *poème à dé-lire*' – referring to the delirium of escape from semantic wholeness, the rational order of the word. Hains and Villeglé claimed in the preface to *Hépérile Éclaté* that

> we didn't discover the ultra-letters, rather we discovered ourselves in them.... Writing didn't wait for our intervention before exploding – they were already there in nature. We took panels of fluted glass which robbed writing of its original meaning. By analogy, it was possible to explode the speech of every human mouth into these ultra-words.... *Hépérile Éclaté* was our excuse.[12]

By 1953 or so Hains was friendly with Guy Debord, Yves Klein and other former members of the Surrealist-inclined Lettriste movement that had in 1952 become the Internationale Lettriste and would become the Internationale Situationiste a few years after. Hains's torn-poster 'paintings', meanwhile, attend more closely in these years than Rotella's to the political sign-systems (election posters, graffiti, etc) that appeared in Paris streets in an abused and barely legible form – resulting in works such as *Paix en Algérie* (Peace in Algeria) of 1956, first shown in a shared exhibition with Villeglé at Collette Allendy in 1957 in an exhibition given added resonance by its title, 'Loi du 29 Juillet 1881', referring to an old law regulating the display of posters in France, now made ironic by the invitation extended to the gallery-going public to look at what Villeglé called 'lyricism without permission'.[13] *Paix en Algérie* also formed part of another Hains exhibition with a provocative title 'La France Déchirée' (France Torn Asunder) of 1961. Whether torn by circumstance or by the artist's own intervention (as in an 'assisted' ready-made), such ostensibly politicized *décollages* are in fact subtly suspended just *outside* direct engagement in political language, and *outside* the debate about painting and engagement already mentioned. Villeglé would later explain that he and Hains were fired to produce *affiches lacérées* by the example of the self-proclaimed chief of Berlin Dada, Johannes Baader, who in addition to the *Plastic-Dada-Dio-Drama* [50] is supposed to have collated vast amounts of daily ephemera, including posters, in a 'Manual', since lost; and secondly that they already admired Schwitters and had read about both him and Baader in Motherwell's book

146   Raymond Hains *Paix en Algérie* 1956
The scrawled appeal for 'peace' reflects France's current conflicts with her North African colony – but also the constantly degrading quality of political messages in the public space.

147   Robert Rauschenberg *Untitled (Mona Lisa)* c. 1952
In a series of small collages made from his North African journey, Rauschenberg rehearses the grid format which accommodates while elevating the marks of difference: printed texts, architectural illustration, European artworks, and the texture of paper itself.

8 Robert Rauschenberg *Untitled (Matt black paint with ?ville Citizen)* c. 1952
?ntaining layers of black paint as well as tones of grey and
?k brown over newspaper, this tall (1.8 metres, 6 feet) work
?nals Rauschenberg's early fascination for layering and for
?fts of scale, as well as relationships between 'popular' and
?gh' art materials.

of 1951.[14] German Dada was therefore their context. Now, Hains and Villeglé were discovering a new painting aesthetic based on torn and glued paper, compatible with the found visual forms of the city yet bound up with the degeneration of verbal signification to mere visual 'noise' within the fabric of the post-war urban space. Here was a forensic analysis of the condition of viewing and understanding within the 'society of the spectacle' (as Guy Debord would later call it) that the European nations were inexorably becoming.

The Mood in New York: Rauschenberg

Something equivalent had been taking place in New York. The young Robert Rauschenberg had spent most of 1948 in Paris courtesy of the GI Bill of Rights, before returning to North Carolina to enrol at Black Mountain College under Bauhaus master Josef Albers in the fall. Rauschenberg's attraction to collage in the years 1949 to 1954 has scarcely been studied; but it remains crucial to a generation of artists who were instinctively resistant to the abstract painting academy and the often doctrinaire modernism that surrounded it critically. Certainly the mood among younger artists at Black Mountain was one of hostility to the 'modernist' painting clique. Albers's Bauhaus methods, especially those of his *Werklehre* course, suggested his students play close attention, not simply to paint but to the inherent qualities of all kinds of materials, where necessary used 'in combination'.[15] What first motivated Rauschenberg's very dark oil and newsprint works of 1951–2 remains unclear; but here was a collage idiom which could at least absorb materials and subjects from the information-rich public sphere – one newly dominated by the commercial revival of early 1950s America – while at the same time remaining visibly 'art'. Additionally, Rauschenberg's experience of working with John Cage on the latter's *Theatre Piece No. 1* at Black Mountain in the summer of 1952, an event in which several performances were delivered simultaneously (dance by Merce Cunningham, a lecture by Cage, poetry by M. C. Richards and Charles Olsen, piano-playing by David Tudor, and hand-winding a record player by Rauschenberg), set an adventurous precedent for the ontologically heterogeneous mixing of performance, language and sound.

Then everything moves at once in Rauschenberg's work. His photographs of the late 1940s, already positioning objects and surfaces as flat arrangements of forms, now become suddenly object-rich, multivalent, and spatially complex. In the course of a stay in Rome – as it happens near Rotella's Piazza di Spania – then on a journey to North Africa in the winter of 1952–3 in the company of the painter Cy Twombly, and seemingly in thrall to the special sensibilities of that artist's work, Rauschenberg sticks together collages on shirtboards from Italian laundries, using newspaper scraps, old engravings, and an eclectic array of graphic fragments from the North African cities they visited. Acquaintance with Rome's 'Informalist' controversies – he did not yet know of Rotella's contemporaneous work – gave Rauschenberg a further sense of how advanced practice in art required, not a univocal aesthetic register but a rich and often surprising inclusiveness in regard to objects, images and forms, the sensibility above all of the *bricoleur*. The immediate result was a set of box-like 'constructions' for a March 1953 exhibition in Rome (the same month that Rauschenberg first met Alberto Burri, to whom he gave one of these 'healing fetishes') that for the first time extended *bricolage* from paper scraps to objects themselves [*149*]. A statement Rauschenberg wrote for the exhibition tells us that:

> the material was chosen for either of two reasons: the richness of their past: like bone, hair, faded cloth and photo: broken fixtures, feathers, sticks, rocks, string and rope; or for their vivid abstract reality: like mirrors, bells, watch-parts, bugs, fringe, pearls, glasses, and shells...the actual boxes ranged in contrast from a Victorian change-purse to Baroque crystal cases to the discard pile of any street. The full inside view of a box may look like a photographic still life before the picture has been taken.... You may

develop your own direct creation of the viewer assisted by the costumed
provocativeness and literal sensuality of the objects.[16]

Already Rauschenberg is proving adept at moving between two dimensions and three, even
erasing the distinction between them. He had discovered how to contain contingent
meanings within a low-relief structure: a device that would become essential to all his
subsequent work.

For notice how Rauschenberg's new Italian photographs of the period capture, not the
full depth of photographic reality, but its tendency to arrange itself as crushed or flattened
or folded matter, pressed up against the plane of vision or lying close behind it, just like
objects in a shallow box. In Venice in 1952, an image taken through several reflective glass
surfaces trebles or quadruples the objects assembled therein. In a second photo, an
overcoated man stands writing in a notebook next to the display of a Roman *occhialeria*
(spectacles vendor), a dirty carpet passing across the foreground like a flat pilaster under
the scene. In a third, a flotilla of gondolas animates a surface through its rhythms and
tonalities alone. We are getting used to the fact that the data that catches Rauschenberg's
attention is incongruous, abstract, planar, its mood suffused by the melancholy of the
broken or the heavily or regularly used. It is often marked, as a recent commentator says,
by a predilection for the out-of-date:

> It is as if Rauschenberg's clock froze at a particular moment in our history, the
> moment when mass consumer culture, not yet matured, still met with the passive but
> obdurate resistance of past (obsolete) forms of economic exchange and semiotic
> communication.[17]

Collectively, too, the Italian photos bring to the fore an often-noticed indifference to
'content' which pervades Rauschenberg's work. In a fourth photo, taken in Rome in 1953,
Rauschenberg addresses a torn wall poster announcing *Stalin e morto* (Stalin is dead),
which acts less as a witness to the politics of Italian communism as to the pockmarks and
erasures of an ancient stone surface and with the remnants of other posters long since
washed away in the Italian rain, in short, the remotely registered 'facts' of general
material decay. We feel ourselves to be in the presence of a melancholy of indifference,
of political and social neutrality, of a superior interest in the effects of chance that links
Rauschenberg to very early Dada and provides yet another benchmark for the mood of his
subsequent work.

Which is to say that, after Rauschenberg's Italian journey, the resources were in place
for the first 'combine paintings', made back in New York in the summer of 1954. By this
time Rauschenberg lived and worked in the trading district of the lower East Side, an area
whose material culture of signs, garbage and rapid exchange could hardly have been better
prepared for the attentions of a gathering Beat sensibility attuned to the emotional and
spiritual enchantments of the 'low'. (I believe too that that same Beat sensibility echoed the
Cherokee Indian culture of Rauschenberg's maternal grandmother, for whom
happenstance and *bricolage* had the status virtually of traditions[18]). Hence the combine
paintings *Charlene* and *Collection* (both of 1954) eschew painted canvas in favour of the
bulletin-board appearance of upright wooden panels evocative of old doors or improvised
surfaces on which, to use a phrase of Leo Steinberg's penned some years later, 'objects are
scattered, on which data is entered, on which information may be received, printed,
impressed – whether coherently or in confusion'. *Collection* in particular, which at over
two metres (six feet) high constitutes a parody of heroic American abstraction, draws into
itself paper, fabric, newsprint, printed reproductions, wood, metal and mirror-surfaces in
addition to paint dripped *à la* Pollock [*152*], its informal rectangular grid loosely giving

149 **Robert Rauschenberg** *Untitled (Scatole Personali)*
c. 1952
This 'personal' box, with lid painted white inside, contains dir
protruding pins, a photograph with a magnifying glass, and a
fragment of mica: it is a little less than eight centimetres
(three inches) in length.

150 **Robert Rauschenberg** *Venice Canal* 1952
Framed as a series of syncopated rhythms presented by the gondolas' bows, the photograph also organizes two shafts of bright reflection in the water below – 'boxed' in the manner of the *scatole* of the same year.

structure to a kind of surface, to which, in Steinberg's felicitous words:

> anything reachable-thinkable would adhere. It had to be whatever a billboard or dashboard is, and everything a projection screen is.... It seems at times that Rauschenberg's work surface stands for the mind itself – dump, reservoir, switching center, abundant with concrete references freely associated as in an internal monologue...Rauschenberg's picture plane is for the consciousness immersed in the brain of the city.[19]

Paris: the later 1950s

On an international stage, collage became the *lingua franca* of young artists in the 1950s who saw it as a method of confronting and reflecting the new conditions of city life: the glamour of goods, and of course the fetishism of 'news' itself. By his own testimony, the young artist Wolf Vostell was on his first visit to Paris in September 1954 when his attention was drawn to a newspaper headline at a kiosk in the rue de Buci, where a newsvendor was calling out 'Peu après son décollage une Super-Constellation tombe et s'engloutit dans la rivière Shannon' (shortly after take-off, a Super-Constellation fell and sank in the River Shannon). Vostell, from Leverkusen in Germany, associated the peacetime disaster with an event from his childhood, when in 1940 he had witnessed bombs and aircraft falling from the sky 'like flocks of birds'.[20] Consulting the Langensheid dictionary for a rendition of the French *décollage*, Vostell found:

> *dé-coll/age*: loosen, unglue, start, ascend from the ground (aeroplane), separate, go away, die [pej. form of *abkratzen*, literally 'scrape off']

an etymology linking technological destruction, decay and death, but also suggesting a method for renovating the hallowed collage techniques of the pre-war avant-garde. With or without knowledge of the Parisian *affichistes*,[21] Vostell was struck by the contrast between physical destruction in his own country and the lacerated wall-surfaces of post-war commercial Paris:

I was struck by the contrast between the physical destruction of post-war Germany, and Paris – at least on the outside, an intact city. The contrast was uncanny [*unheimlich*]: though there were no physical ruins, there were more ruined posters than readable ones in every Paris street and Metro…. I established an immediate analogy between the pulverised aeroplane and the torn posters…and henceforward I pursued ambivalence and iconographical complexity – two phenomena in our environment that were not being addressed by *tachisme* – within the event-happening.[22]

Also at that time Vostell discovered Georges Hugnet's 1932–4 essay 'The Dada Spirit in Painting' in Robert Motherwell's *The Dada Painters and Poets*, in one part of which Hugnet relates the 1920 Dada exhibition in Cologne featuring Max Ernst, Baargeld and Arp.[23] Henceforward Vostell's production was to be allied pre-eminently with Dada, especially its assault on the 'given' of the urban spectacle. In his earliest *dé-coll/age* works (he insisted on preserving the dictionary hyphen and stroke) Vostell launched a method more overtly violent than that of the French *affichistes*, scraping or obliterating whatever remnants could be negotiated on the street. A *dé-coll/age* series of 1957–60 was produced by burning as well as tearing, for example the *Club du K.C.* of 1958, whose fierce abrasions evoke the shattered war-time German cities of Vostell's early memories. An earlier work of this series, the *Hommage à Cassandre* of 1957, refers to Vostell's teacher at the atèlier Joubert, A. M. Cassandre, whose book *Le Théâtre est dans la rue* (Theatre is in the street) appears in the work embellished with a series of discoloured, burnt and otherwise defaced images.

The next year, 1958, the same project was staged as a real-time street 'action' having collective as well as individual significance. For *Tour de Vanves: Le Théâtre est dans la rue*, Vostell issued instructions to passers-by and invited guests (several of them artists) to walk through the rue de la Tour de Vanves in Paris declaiming aloud the textual fragments of any visible *affiches*, reading both up and down, left to right and diagonally, and producing gestures and postures to suit.[24] 'Read at the top of your voice the texts and fragments…. Continue until a group of 100 readers has formed…. Do not synchronise your reading…. Go on tearing to reveal new texts and new fragments of images' were typical of Vostell's instructions. Other elements of *Tour de Vanves* required participants to gather up remnants

151 **Wolf Vostell** *Club du K. C.* 1958
'I resolved to take possession of what I saw and experienced, as well as incidents and processes in the work, for I knew how to reinvent the art of the time, using my interests in destruction, ruination and waste.' (Vostell)

152 **Robert Rauschenberg** *Collection* 1954

e most of the artist's early combines, done in the studio on
lton Street, *Collection* is dominated by the colour red: its
ry title is descriptive of the method by which diverse types of
atter meet and coexist on a single tripartite surface, 'in the
p between art and life'. (Rauschenberg)

of an automobile accident and place them at a street junction 'until traffic becomes impossible' (this was never performed) and to record the acoustic effects of *dé-coll/age* activity in a manner that owes much to Vostell's friendship with the radical experimental composer Karl-Heinz Stockhausen. '*Dé-coll/age* music equals Anti-Music', said Vostell in the *Tour de Vanves* manifesto; 'a large municipal mechanical digger with an iron ball smashes juke-boxes, radios and other metal objects. Another digger picks up a load of metal and lets it drop in a heap'.[25] Clearly intended to complicate and reconcile the elements of art and life, Vostell's *dé-coll/age* methodology would henceforward spawn provocative happenings, participatory theatre, and mixed-media events that made him a natural collaborator for George Maciunas when he came from New York to Wiesbaden to establish his first International Fluxus Festival in 1962.

Meanwhile, and elsewhere in Paris, the meeting between Hains and Villeglé and the poet and artist François Dufrêne in 1955 had been important in binding the Parisian *affichiste* tendency with a third distinctive member. Yet by Dufrêne's own testimony he remained 'totally indifferent' to the *affiches lacérées* by Hains and Villeglé until their October 1957 exhibition at Collette Allendy, on which occasion, so he said, he had the intuition that their work might after all be a form of literature.[26] From then on Dufrêne began his own versions of *dos* (back), *dessous* (underneath) and *envers* (wrong side) poster-collages. In retrospect this development seems also to signal Dufrêne's final disenchantment with avant-gardism in its standard revolutionary guise – for 1957 was the year in which Debord and others merged the Internationale Lettriste with another short-lived splinter group, the International Movement for an Imaginist Bauhaus, to create the Internationale Situationiste, a formation which Dufrêne's sceptical temperament found distinctly unappealing. Dufrêne's *décollages* of the later 1950s remained wedded to an essentially literary conception of the semantic variability, ambiguity and potential for humour within the lexeme or alphabetic unit. As he put it somewhat later,

> Letters were to suffer a double objective alteration, that of a partial *decalcomania* [transfer] and that of an inverted order, to which can be added the most subjective irrationality of aesthetics – nothing other than designifed signs, empty of intellectual life, pure marks of non-publicity recuperated from the base metal of politics and transformed into poetic gold.[27]

Naturally, Dufrêne's scepticism about politics was not shared by Guy Debord and the remaining members of the Internationale Situationiste, for whom methods deriving from a rather different collage aesthetics now became crucial. Debord had himself produced collages of loosely arranged cut-ups of text and cartoon, overlaid with ink connections – as had other SI members such as Ralph Rumney in London – as a visual expression (indeed a demonstration) of the *dérive* or wandering journey through the spaces of the city, which they saw as a way of revolutionizing the consumption routines of everyday life through abitrariness and above all through a kind of revolutionary play. For Debord the 'society of the spectacle' (the title of his book of 1967) was continuous with the legacies of imperialism and colonialism and in dire need of revolutionary opposition. Hence Debord's collages showed disdain for all formal niceties in their relentless drive to overturn (*détourne*) every aspect of spectacular visual pleasure, to re-frame and re-route familiar paths and actions. They were published together with the prolific Danish avant-gardist Asger Jorn under the title *Mémoires* in 1959 [*181*]. Also in 1959, Jorn, a colleague of Debord in the SI, showed his extraordinary *Modifications* at the Galerie Rive Gauche in May: they are themselves a kind of collage performed by defacing old flea-market paintings with paint, in a manner intended precisely to sublate what to him was a false opposition, one famously codified by Clement Greenberg in 1939 and still in evidence within modernist

 Asger Jorn *Le canard inquiétant* 1959
modern, collectors, museums. If you have old paintings,
not despair. Retain your memories but *détourn* them so
that they correspond with your era. Why reject the old if one
can modernise with a few strokes of the brush?' (Jorn)

Raymond Hains *Palissade des emplacements réservés*,
the Biennale de Paris 1959
Palissade takes to a kind of limit the idea of the urban
readymade, one that Hains offered as an alternative to the
'created' works of Villeglé and Dufrêne and one that
functioned as the largest demonstration to that date of
monde comme tableau.

theory, between high art and mass culture, between 'avant-garde' and kitsch.[28] Equally, Jorn's *Modifications* were intended not merely to corrupt and deface the sacred surfaces of 'high' art however cheaply obtained, but magically to transform them into libidinously charged, living things out of whose bizarre conjunctions something vital and strange might again grow. Mutilation *was* creation, for Jorn. His Rive Gauche exhibition was framed by a text presented in two versions. In the first, 'Intended for the General Public: Reads Effortlessly', he proclaims in manifesto fashion: 'Painting is over. You might as well finish it off. *Détourne*. Long live painting'. In the second, 'Intended For Connoisseurs: Requires Limited Attention', he likens *détourned* painting to a sacrifice: 'I want to rejuvenate European culture', he says; 'and so I begin with the sacrifice of art'. Bad painting, or kitsch, the despised underbelly of popular art and taste, is to be shamelessly paraded in a perverse union with the 'primitive':

> Those forest lakes on coloured paper, hanging in gilded frames in thousands of apartments, are among the most profound artistic experiences…. In this exhibition I erect a monument in honour of bad painting…. It is painting sacrificed. This sort of offering can be done gently the way doctors do it when they kill their patients with new medicines that they want to try out. It can also be done in barbaric fashion, in public and with pomp. This is what I like.

Jorn ends his mock-serious attack: 'I solemnly tip my hat and let the blood of my victims flow while intoning Baudelaire's hymn to beauty'.[29] Jorn's show, strategically timed to coincide with the large 'Jackson Pollock and the New American Painting' exhibition at the Musée d'Art Moderne de la Ville de Paris (one of the first incursions into the European art circuit of abstract expressionist art) was surely intended to stake out a position that would be perceived as neutralizing the 'official' American avant-garde with the cruellest iconoclastic gesture.[30]

The year 1959 was indeed a kind of *annus mirabilis* of avant-gardist experiment in Paris; but also one of significant change in the conditions of visibility of the avant-garde itself. American art, like American consumer products, was sweeping through Europe with an intensity never seen before. The corollary was that large international exhibitions now came increasingly to dominate the public discussion of art, while trans-national competitiveness became a significant factor in how exhibitions were curated, presented and controlled. Paris, as the embodiment of 'modern' sensibility in Europe, suddenly had an aggressive new competitor in New York. An early symptom of the change, the first Biennale de Paris, held in October 1959, showed the École de Paris alongside a range of international work. And it would not be an exaggeration to say that collage was the terrain of maximum tension and novelty: a large work by Raymond Hains, his *Palissade des emplacements réservés*, took the Biennale by storm and constituted the first major exposure to an international public of the vitality of Paris's new *collage-décollage* aesthetics. At three metres by seven (10 feet by 23), the size of a mural-scale abstract painting such as Pollock's *One* of 1950, Hains's *Palissade* comprised the twenty-seven wooden planks of an extant building site wall, covered with posters illegally attached, together with the lacerations made by anonymous passers-by or construction-site employees, or by the addition of incongruous notices [*154*]. The *Palissade* was otherwise untouched by the artist's hand; on the ceiling of the same gallery was hung a work by Dufrêne entitled *Crawl-Crawl*. Though exhibited in the special 'Groupe des Informels' section of the Biennale, Hains's *Palissade* was in fact one of the great scandals of post-war French art. The Biennale organizers were threatened by other artists with the withdrawal of their work. Insults were hurled in the street. And yet the context of the work is significant. Large-scale French paintings by Paul Rebeyrolle and Georges Mathieu, as well as by Pollock and the Americans, had recently upped the stakes in a widely visible international contest for artistic supremacy – a mill to which Hains's virtually ready-made *Palissade* must have offered further grist. Added to all of which, three new combine works by Robert Rauschenberg, namely *Talisman* (1958), *Forge* (1959) and *Photography* (1959), were his first before a French public and simultaneously signalled a new direction away from abstract expressionism in New York.[31] My judgment is that the exhibition of Hains alongside Rauschenberg, as well as the presence in the Biennale of *Stabilisateur méta-matic no 15* (1959), Jean Tinguely's vast auto-destructive machine which also vividly captured the public attention, precipitated a decisive change in the status of collage as an avant-garde medium. Henceforward collage would need to review its relationship to the public space, remain alive to the fast-changing conditions of international exhibitions of new art, and come to terms somehow with the place occupied by dissenting artistic experiment within an increasingly spectacular culture.

London: The Moment of 'Pop'

The later 1950s in London provided further opportunities and challenges for experimental collage practice. The Independent Group's lecture of April 1955, 'Dadaists as Non-Aristotelians', had pointed up the connection between the overstepping of categorial boundaries and the end of 'art' with great precision: at least some of that diversity, plus an apocalyptic tone, was carried over into the Group's contributions the next year to an exhibition in East London. Futuristically and a touch fearsomely titled 'This is Tomorrow', the exhibition required converting the Whitechapel Art Gallery's interior into twelve discrete but interlocking cave-like spaces, now quite explicitly addressing the continuum of architecture, art and design by techniques of juxtaposition, inclusiveness and almost limitless heterogeneity.[32] Said critic Lawrence Alloway in one of 'This is Tomorrow's three introductory statements, Mondrian, the Bauhaus and Le Corbusier all needed recuperating and re-utilizing for a new generation, and the principles of that recuperation were to be non-specialized, transient, impure, provisional, expendable, multi-channel, simultaneous, and even antagonistic towards each other. 'This is Tomorrow' would be designed as an antidote to purity, the golden section, and clear iconography. In Alloway's characteristically astute description, it would effectively be a lesson in spectatorship, one in which the visitor 'is exposed to space effects, play with signs, a wide range of materials and structures,

155 **Robert Rauschenberg** *Talisman* 1958
'These are the feelings Rauschenberg gives us: love, wonder, laughter, heroism…fear, sorrow, anger, disgust, tranquility. Perhaps after all there is no message… As the lady said, "Well, if it isn't art, then I like it".' (John Cage)

which…make of art and architecture a many-channelled activity, as factual and as far from ideal standards as the street outside'.[33] Alloway's percipient idea was that the new spectator would not be able to rely upon the 'learned responses' called up by a picture in a frame, a single house in a street, or a univocal text upon a page, but would have to take on responsibility for flexible and mutually inconsistent interpretations of contrasting messages consisting of both text, object and image amounting to something like a 'new contract' for the aesthetic exchanges which were to come.

Within the multi-part 'This is Tomorrow' the McHale-Hamilton-Voelcker pavilion (known as Group Two) erected flickering optical panels (deriving from the Bauhaus), a five-metre (sixteen-foot) high image of Robbie the Robot, Marilyn Monroe holding her skirt down in the scene from *The Seven Year Itch*, Duchampian roto-reliefs, a jukebox, and much more – it was the only room that referred to Hollywood mass culture and it was the wittiest and perhaps the visually most compelling of the set. Hamilton's recognition of the fascination effect exerted by the glamorized mass-media image marked a real change of sensibility in England at that time (albeit one that owed everything to Paolozzi). As a maquette for 'This is Tomorrow's poster Hamilton made a small paper collage some 12.5 centimetres (five inches) square, titled *Just What Is It That Makes Today's Homes So Different, So Appealing?*, which itself constructs an architectural space no less internally incongruous than the various cave-like pavilions on show. Seemingly a parody of current advertising rhetoric and interior design, this virtually miniature work looks back to an April 1956 *Picture Post* feature entitled 'Are We Enjoying Too Much of Tomorrow Today?' that had taken an askance look at the easy availability of hire-purchase consumer credit schemes in which fridges, furniture, new lampshades, the TV in the corner, even the glamorized body – could all be purchased by instalments, with minimal down payment.[34] Yet Hamilton's small collage organizes its imagery with particular aesthetic acumen. There is some kind of play on the theme of the body beautiful (though the half-dressed woman looks off-balance and too small). There is a typical Hamilton self-reference in the tin labelled 'Ham' placed on the coffee table. And there is a mood of general distrust of glossy consumer blandishments in a world of expanded technical possibilities: a second TV channel with commercial advertising and American programmes had been introduced in Britain in September 1955, and the magazines were overflowing with images of those same goods and services that

156 'Are We Enjoying Too Much of Tomorrow Today?' in *Picture Post* 1956
'Hire Purchase is a social safety valve amid rising material plenty; a potent stimulus of the mass-consumption needed f mass-production; a diversion of depreciating pounds from frivolous indulgence to useful durables.' (Picture Post)

7 **Richard Hamilton** *Just What Is It That Makes Today's
...mes So Different, So Appealing?* 1956
...e space of this small collage is neither clearly interior nor
...terior: the 'ceiling' is a space-age view of the earth, while
...e 'carpet' is a distant photograph of people on a beach.
...me of the imagery is from McHale's collection from the USA.

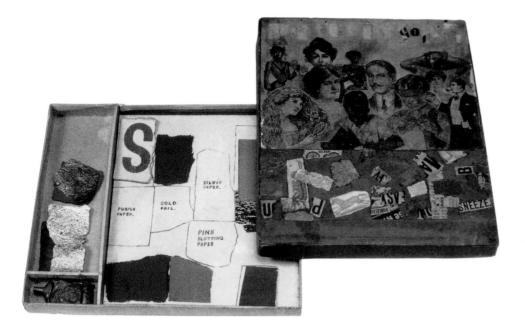

158 **Peter Blake** *Make Your Own Collage* c. 1955
This small box cleverly occupies the boundary between a 'real'
kit for collage making and a collage-object in its own right.
The provisional quality of the half-made collage inside is an
effect much enjoyed by artists of Blake's generation.

suggested to Prime Minister Harold Macmillan that 'most of our people have never had it
so good'.[35] And yet Hamilton's *Just What Is It?* is not obviously a parody of this consumer
world – rather a comment-free list of its major effects. We know (what visitors to 'This is
Tomorrow' did not) that Hamilton had previously written down a list of categories as a
kind of plan for the work: 'Man, Woman, Humanity, History, Food, Newspapers, Cinema,
TV, Telephone, Comics (picture information), Words (textual information), Tape Recording
(aural information), Cars, Domestic Appliances, Space' – taking care to specify that the
final image should be 'tabular as well as pictorial'.[36] Hamilton's wife and Magda Cordell
had then spent several days clipping out magazine images under each heading. And hence
the inserted elements of the finished work do not occupy a coherent narrative space but
appear as if taken from a list, looking as if they could have landed in the collage in any
order or arrangement. It is this very contingency that makes *Just What Is It?* not just (or
even) a critique of consumption, but rather the reflection of an information environment in
which types of data (words and sound, pictures and text, science and commerce, near and
far, true and false) crowd in upon the hapless consumer as so many channels, in which the
categories of 'real' and 'inauthentic' are now thrown into drastic relativity. The Independent
Group's attack on Aristotelian categories implied that the distinction between celebration
and critique was now in confusion too.

The fact that the lollipop/phallus given to the strong man is embellished with the word
'Pop' is often taken to show that Hamilton's *Just What Is It?* marks the beginning of 'Pop'
art. But the term 'Pop' had been used by Lawrence Alloway in an Independent Group
discussion in 1954,[37] and my guess is that it would have been in conversational circulation
ever since. Hamilton tried to define the term more precisely in the aftermath of 'This Is
Tomorrow'. Writing to Alison and Peter Smithson in January 1957, he suggested that 'Pop
Art' is 'Popular (designed for a mass audience), Transient (short-term solution),
Expendable (easily forgotten), Low Cost, Mass Produced, Young (aimed at youth), Witty,
Sexy, Gimmicky, Glamorous, Big Business'; another list, but one that seems to refer to the
effects rather than the products of consumer culture directly. For Alloway himself the term
'Pop' denoted the raw material of advertising, sci-fi graphics, popular music and cinema –
not art as such. Hamilton at this stage seems genuinely uncertain. He adds tellingly: 'I am
not yet sure about the "sincerity" of Pop Art', suggesting an attitude of Duchampian

Pauline Boty *Untitled (with pink lace and curls of hair)*
1960–2
Boty frequently rehearses the world of dislocated social identities found in Max Ernst's collage novels, as well as Hannah Höch's parodic treatment of feminine glamour.

disengagement somewhere between 'liking' and 'disliking' but not firmly identified with either. 'Pseudo-sincerity' he proposed as a term of more general validity.[38]

This folding of popular culture into 'art' through collaging of previously unrelated consumer categories – ironically or not – was in mid- to late 1950s Britain a cultural process of some complexity and originality. Among painters, it held a special appeal for the young Peter Blake, who arrived at London's Royal College of Art in 1953 from a working-class background and with an interest in graphics and typography. Around 1955 he heard about collage from a student friend (Richard Smith) whose relatives had known Schwitters and Hausmann: 'it was a revelation', said Blake,[39] after which irony began to dominate Blake's work and infiltrate Pop art as a whole. Blake's *Make Your Own Collage* of about 1955 introduced many of the artist's subsequent interests: corner-shop culture and Victorian illustration (both recycled with a mixture of cynicism and endearment), popular graphics, childhood and play. In fact, strategies of irony, artful mimicry and attention to popular graphics soon became the signature method of a whole group of playfully disaffected students, notably David Hockney, Allen Jones, Peter Phillips and Pauline Boty (later, Patrick Caulfield) at the Royal College of Art. In this company Boty was a 'natural' collagist: she made vast wall collages assembled from art reproductions, contemporary music icons, advertising and pornography (all *mélangés*) and she produced some fine small works on the theme of feminine stereotyping, travel, and the lure of the exotic. Elsewhere too, such as in Liverpool, art school students John Lennon and Adrian Henri, shortly to prosper in the fields of music and poetry respectively, cut their teeth making collage works out of mass-media fragments in a celebratory but distinctly non-Aristotelian vein. London would soon join other cities internationally in a brief period of fascinated indulgence in the new consumer world that was being born. The moment of 'Pop' had arrived.

160 **Daniel Spoerri** *Le Lieu de repos de la famille Delbeck*
1960
'A kind of information, a provocation, directing the eye
towards regions that it does not generally notice, that is
all…and art, what is that?' (Spoerri)

11

Collage in the Counter-culture: the 1960s

The early years of the 1960s marked a crisis for collage-based practice in Paris, London, New York and elsewhere. In Paris, Hains together with Tinguely, Yves Klein, Daniel Spoerri, Arman, Villeglé and Dufrêne formed themselves in October 1960 into the group Nouveau Réalisme, also the title of a manifesto written by Pierre Restany in April the previous year. In it, Restany not only intoned the avant-gardist mantra that 'painting is dead', but insisted that 'the passionate adventure of the real perceived in itself' – what he called 'sociological reality' – would replace the kind of conceptual or imaginative transcription which defines a painting. Restany claimed that 'sociology comes to the assistance of consciousness and of chance, whether this be at the level of choice or the tearing up of posters, of the allure of an object, of the household rubbish or the scraps of the dining room, of the unleashing of mechanical susceptibility'[1] – suggesting in effect that the processes and commodities of the capitalist city are to be made over into the stuff of art. Yet for anyone wedded to the belief that the cornucopia of consumption by itself contained the key to the revitalization of modernist art – or that collage techniques in their existing forms would survive – cultural changes were already afoot that would test those convictions severely. In this and the final chapter we shall see both why and how.

Vernacular Glances: Paris, London and New York
Very shortly after Nouveau Réalisme was born in Paris, signs of a loss of vitality began to appear. There were, it is true, several impulses wrapped inside the Nouveau Réalisme platform. The additive, accumulative methods enshrined in Arman's boxes and vitrines around 1960 may be described as collage by extension: in effect he organizes categories of the 'real' into relief-like pictures indebted simultaneously and ingeniously both to Cubism (the shallow space) and to Dada (a hint of the absurd). No less firmly wedded to the arrest of the real was the Romanian-born Daniel Spoerri. He had been a concrete poet with affiliations to Lettrism before making his first 'trap' or 'snare' pictures around 1958. In these, he fixes the chance arrangement of mobile domestic situations, especially meals, and then tips them through 90 degrees to transform a quotidian surface into a pictorial thing (a guiding principle of most collage). 'What am I doing?' Spoerri asks himself: 'Gluing together situations that have happened accidentally so that they stay together permanently'. He speaks provocatively of the 'optical lesson' taught when the observer is

confronted with 'situations and areas of life that are little noticed…in other words, the formal and expressive precision of chance at any given moment' – adding perversely: 'I hate stagnations. I hate fixations. I like the contrast provoked by fixating objects…. Please don't think of the trap pictures as art'.[2] Spoerri was soon making snare pictures 'to the mathematical power of 2' – meaning that the tools for fixing objects were themselves included in the work. In 1959 followed his *détrompe l'oeil* pieces in which a junk-store picture is augmented with some metaphoric or humorous object that profanes the original (and indeed the entire concept of representational art). In one early *détrompe l'oeil* piece a shower faucet hangs provocatively over a sentimental picture of a valley stream. In a second, an old portrait of the inventor of aspirin has a white object stuck upon his mouth. Any yet even though 'snare' and *détrompe l'oeil* marked Spoerri as perhaps the most disrespectful of the Nouveaux Réalistes and the guardian of its Dada inheritances (he described himself as 'the arrogant and obedient servant of chance'), that posture would soon have to confront the danger that art itself might appear spectacular in an over-active consumer world.

A second point of vulnerability was that, in the six or seven years since the appearance of the first *affiches lacérées* in Rome and Paris, the very nature and quality of public urban space (and hence the relation of avant-garde collage to both that public space and the private domain), had shifted decisively and perhaps irreversibly: the consumer revolution had taken hold, and the public space of the city was becoming something like a backdrop for the ever more regimented private spaces of the home. For example, 1960 was the year in which Mimmo Rotella began to introduce into his work images of spectacular human individuals (film stars especially) derived from the torn remains of high-colour Italian film posters generated in the Cinecittà film industry headquarters just outside Rome [*163*] (the films of Rossellini, Visconti, Fellini, as well as American imports from Paramount and Twentieth Century Fox dubbed into Italian for a new trans-continental public). It is often said that Rotella's interest in Cinecittà glamour and excitement signals important cultural differences between Rome's entertainment hoardings and the political posters which adorned Paris: but the distinction cannot be sharp. Moreover the 'adjusted' nature of these images (just as a painter might adjust a composition on canvas) is clear from the more-than-circumstantial tears, revelations and obscurings visible in their surfaces. But a new challenge was making the critical work of *décollage* more difficult. Not only Rotella but also Villeglé and especially Hains would now have to adjust their sights to the gradual evacuation of public space by the rise of TV. As Benjamin Buchloh has it, the *flâneur* figure who could once 'botanize' pleasurably on the asphalt of the big city would now acquire the poetic dimension of an almost extinct species as he or she was progressively ousted by waves of haunted tourists:

> The formerly public spaces of the big cities became increasingly rationalized: either planned to serve as organised spaces of traffic flow in areas of urban labour and production: or designed to allow crowd control in areas restricted for organized mass consumption (malls); or, again, instrumentalized as axes for rapid transportation between these spaces and the correlative suburban dormitories.[3]

It was not to be a simple task. Not only was public space being electronically transformed, but new discourses in the international art system were now threatening to banalize the critical purchase of avant-garde art, or at the very least to challenge the efficacy of its subversive power. Indeed, the growth of international artistic competition – the Paris Biennale was initiated in 1959 chiefly as a French response to Venice and Kassel – meant that hereafter any avant-garde grouping would become immediately vulnerable to the very conditions, not of its private or sub-cultural reputations, but of its own public

opposite, above 161 **Peter Blake** *Got a Girl* 1960–1
Above the painted panels we see photos of Fabian, Frankie Avalon, Ricky Nelson, Bobby Rydell and Elvis (twice). At top left is a record by The Four Preps group entitled *Got A Girl*, about the frustrations of teenage love.

opposite 162 **Gwyther Irwin** *Letter Rain* 1959
At nearly two metres (six feet) high, this very large collage collects evidence of distressed urban signage, but merges that experience with an image of pollution or 'atomic rain' falling from the sky.

success. In London, the moment of mass-media collage was declining almost as soon as it was born. Peter Blake, to take one example, might switch at will between painted illusions of collage elements (as in *On The Balcony* of 1955–7) to actual collage fixings in works like *Saucy Girls from Montmartre* (1956), *Girlie Door* (1959) or *Got a Girl* (1960–1).[4] But the larger argument is that collage methods collapsed into something like banality as soon as they became publicly fashionable in London, around 1960 or 1961; the precise point of collapse can be reconstructed with some accuracy. The beginning may be traced to the year 1959, when Lawrence Alloway organized the '3 Collagists' exhibition at the ICA. Alongside works by John McHale and E. L. T. Mesens, the show included the young artist Gwyther Irwin, who ran the gauntlet of the Metropolitan Police to collect street posters that were then shredded into smaller pieces for large collage works approaching the size and scale seen in the 'New American Painting' exhibition at the Tate Gallery in the same year.[5] On this evidence alone, collage was now entering the arena of large-format painting, to rival it aesthetically as well as to absorb its myth-making and subjectivity along the way. By the same token, large works made of collage tended to suffer devaluation thereafter in comparison to more marketable oil paintings; which is to say that a process familiar from earlier phases of modernist art became repeated with a vengeance in the publicity-hungry days of 'Pop'. Pauline Boty, to take another example, married the left-wing literary agent Clive Goodwin in 1963 and immediately produced a series of 'political' paintings in which collage-like composition contained easily recognizable symbols of power and pleasure amidst selected icons of commercial modernity. She also produced deconstructions of wealth and glamour in works such as *It's A Man's World II* of 1965–6, in painted, not collage form. Here, Boty reaches for legitimate fine art status in works which a truly collage aesthetic could have delivered in very different terms.

By 1960 or 1961 TV was on the rise in Britain: adverts for American products were being beamed at an unsuspecting population by means of techniques of persuasion largely perceived as American. Not only was TV from the beginning explicitly montage-based and more graphically sensational than feature film (as such it became a source for young artists), but TV as an informational medium did much to glamorize London 'Pop' artists and in the process immediately rendered their work innocuous. Ken Russell's BBC TV film *Pop Goes The Easel* of March 1962 had something like this effect: among other things it

LA STORIA DI UNA DELLE DONNE
PRESENT
MO DA
CON LE
SCENE INEDITE
DEL SUO FILM INC
MARiLYN

64 Richard Hamilton *Interior II* 1964
...gns of contemporaneity are present in the shiny Eames 'La
...onda' chair (reconstructed in relief), in the images of Larry
...vers's studio in the space behind, and in the TV-screen image
... JFK's assassination in November 1963. The immobile Patricia
...night lends mystery to the thoroughly ambiguous scene.

63 Mimmo Rotella *Marilyn* 1962
...Thanks to Rotella the lacerated Cinecittà has become an open
...ty...its personalities and characters no longer mystified, freed
...om their mythological position, they once again start to live,
...o come forward to meet us.' (Pierre Restany)

showed the heavily collaged studio and bedroom walls of Boty, Boshier, Phillips and Blake (in one respect not unlike Malraux's *Musée Imaginaire*) and in so doing inspired a thousand teenage bedrooms. And the printed media were instrumental too. Just a month before, Peter Blake and others had been 'profiled' by John Russell in the newly launched *Sunday Times Colour Magazine* – this was the mass-media christening of 'Pop'. By February 1963, Pop Art, film culture, fashion and advertising had become merged into the effervescent social whirl of 'swinging' London, and its music, fashion and style. By such a process was a potentially satirical and critically parodic style launched upon a mass public, while in the same moment becoming absorbed into a market mechanism far removed from the agency of the critical avant-garde.[6]

Perhaps only Eduardo Paolozzi and Richard Hamilton, significantly both Independent Group members, remained aloof from this fashion-driven ambience. Though Paolozzi was attracted to shiny sculptural work in the early 1960s, he kept faith with collage aesthetics through the compilation of books like the extraordinary *Salmon Pink Scrapbook* of around 1960, in which we find him mining a seam of machine-parts, industrial installations, and scientific components, superimposed upon a sober art-historical text about Camden Town artists from an art encyclopaedia. The image of the robot survives, but most of Paolozzi's clippings are of exotic technicalities made into illustrations for popular instruction – insulators at a Zilwaukee sub-station, Edison accumulators, gearboxes. Meanwhile the names of artists (William Scott, Graham Sutherland) peek modestly out from under these exotica as if to suggest that older art had become eclipsed by the wonders of this fabulous technical universe.[7]

Richard Hamilton too remained relatively detached from the commercial fizz. His small *Interior Study (a)* of 1964 is a collage rehearsal for two larger paintings, and preserves the marks of physical facture that the larger and 'finished' work erases. As in the miniature *Just What Is It?*, Hamilton constructs an interior scene: in fact it begins with a publicity still from the 1948 film *Shockproof* (Patricia Knight and Cornel Wilde, directed by Douglas Sirk) in which a table disguises the body that Knight has just killed. The collage reproduced here (one of three) he has described as 'ominous, provocative, ambiguous; with the lingering residues of decorative style that any inhabited space collects. A confrontation with which the spectator is familiar yet not at ease' [*168*].[8] Hamilton then transcribed the subtle spatial effects of the collage into new materials such as cellulose and actual relief for the paintings themselves. And yet – with an Yves Klein monochrome leaning against the wall in the far room, and with the dead body replaced by a lurid coloured carpet, on the right – they are less paintings than essays in radically heterodox styles of depiction in which multiple clues to narrative end up as ambiguity, diversion and even abstraction [*164*]. Handcrafted paper collage lives on in Hamilton's work at least until 1965 (*My Marilyn* of that year is made out of oil paint slapped on photographic sheets, on panel) as the basis of paintings of remarkably juxtaposed materials. But a new technical universe was now in view.

Elsewhere, an early sign of the museum's newfound ability to package avant-garde agendas to a wide international public (a public that would henceforward need recharacterizing in its relation to the commodity and the city spectacle) was the exhibition 'The Art of Assemblage', curated by William Seitz for the Museum of Modern Art in New York in 1961. Travelling to Dallas and San Francisco (it did not reach Europe), 'The Art of Assemblage' both widened and severely narrowed the meanings of collage as a radical technique. Widened, in that it sought to subsume collage within the inclusive category of *assembled* art, ranging from Braque, Picasso and Schwitters, right through to Cornell, Kienholz, Tinguely, Martial Raysse, even David Smith, John Chamberlain, César and Richard Stankiewicz; but narrowed, in side-stepping any treatment either of Matissean paper cut-outs or of photomontage. Simon Rodia's *Watts Towers* (1921–54) were held up as 'masterpieces', while *découpée* works by Sophie Täuber-Arp and Sonia Delaunay (indeed all Dada *Klebebilder*) were excluded. Seitz associated the latter with 'trick photography' of the nineteenth century and claimed that Dadas used the concept of assembly *ironically* for 'collages of photographs and other illustrative material'. Simultaneously, Seitz confined application of the terms 'collage' and *papier collé* to the pasted-paper works of Picasso, Braque and Gris between 1912 and 1914, adopting Dubuffet's 1953 use of the term 'assemblage' to cover every kind of two- and three-dimensional construction, now adapted to function 'as a generic concept that would include all [sic] forms of composite art and modes of juxtaposition.'[9]

165 'The Art of Assemblage', 1961, MOMA, New York. Installation view
This section, controversially devoted to Marcel Duchamp, shows his *Fountain* (1917), *Tu'M* (1918), *Bottlerack* (1914), *Fresh Widow* (1920) and *Bicycle Wheel* (1913).

Moreover careful attention to 'The Art of Assemblage' reveals a clear line of demarcation between American experience and European: even the elevation to superior status of American attitudes to happenstance and urban ruin. Such an emphasis was to be found in the discussion of junk – a new *American* vernacular repertoire that already included, in Seitz's words:

> beat Zen and hot rods, mescaline experiences and faded flowers, photographic bumps and grinds, the *poubelle*, juke boxes, and hydrogen explosions…the images of charred bodies that keep Hiroshima and Nagasaki before our eyes; the confrontation of democratic platitudes with the Negro's disenfranchisement; the travesty of the Chessman trial…[even] the peeling *décollage* on abandoned billboards in the blighted neighbourhoods of Chicago or Jersey City, accented by the singing colours and clean edges of emblems intended to sell cigarettes and beer, or the rubble of fallen New York tenements piled between walls patterned in flowered pinks and blues [that] can take on an intense beauty *more poignant* than that of the lacerated posters and graffiti that cover the old walls of Rome and Paris.[10]

Now, within the portals of the powerful Museum of Modern Art, the Europeans Spoerri, Hains, Dufrêne, Villeglé and Rotella were being competitively juxtaposed with new works by Americans against the backdrop of substantial sections devoted to the ostensible progenitors of assemblage, Duchamp, Schwitters and Man Ray. And language was being realigned too: the English-American word 'assemblage' would hereafter replace and extend

166 Jean-Jacques Lebel *Parfum Grève Générale* 1960
1958 Lebel and others on the French political left called for
general strike to support the National Liberation Front in
Algeria: in this work we find references not only to the
Algerian war, but also to the clash between emancipated
libido and authoritarian politics.

167 Enrico Baj *Lady* 1963
With Piero Manzoni and Yves Klein, Baj enjoyed links with the
Parisian Nouveau Réalisme, took part in MOMA's 'Art of
Assemblage', and pioneered a variety of Surrealism with found
materials that was consistent in being 'against style'.

the French words *assemblage* and *collage* as designations for a whole gamut of avant-garde mannerisms and techniques centred on composite material juxtaposition. It is in this sense that 'The Art of Assemblage' might be read as a turning point – after which any politicized avant-garde driven by the disjunctive methods of collage, and under any name, would have to find dissemination techniques far away from the historicizing display spaces of the international museum of art.

Younger European artists drawn to collage methods would encounter many other challenges. Back in Paris, a young teenager with a well-connected father was sowing seeds of anarchist revolt to rival the early action-collages and happenings of Allan Kaprow in New York. In 1948 Jean-Jacques Lebel (son of Robert Lebel, biographer of Duchamp) had written to André Breton from a reformatory where he was incarcerated for stealing cars: the twelve-year old received a reply that emboldened him to launch a career as a Surrealist painter and soon as a collagist. Early in this trajectory in the early 1950s he had by chance encountered Guy Debord (he intervened to prevent Lebel getting beaten up in a street fight) and through him met Situationists, Lettrists, other Surrealists and indeed anyone who was anyone in Paris's politicized intellectual community, and particularly those who vigorously opposed the Algerian war. Collage immediately served an anarchist sensibility indifferent to questions of form or niceties of theory: the work reproduced here happens to coincide with Lebel's dismissal from the Surrealist group, still under Breton's imperious guidance, that by this time claimed to stand against anarchy and individual revolt in the name of a collective moral programme.[11] The hallmark of Lebel's work became a kind of crude admixture of provocative sloganizing (the main inscription here reads 'General Strike Perfume: A Pleasant Smell'), sexually provocative images, and violence.

The situation of the Italian Enrico Baj around 1960–2 illustrates another kind of difficulty well. Baj had already founded the Nuclear Movement with Sergio Dangelo in 1951 and (with Asger Jorn) the International Movement for an Imaginist Bauhaus in 1953, before launching into his own heterodox style of figure painting with collage around 1955, using for his *Mountain* series a sedimentation of enamel paint in a water emulsion, which formed encrusted shapes that could then sit eerily amid kitschy scenes from ready-made pictures. Baj called this collaged material 'heavy water'; the purpose was to 'interrupt' a complacent scene with ugly excrecences floating in the air and seemingly threatening invasion [*169*]. The *Mountain* series was succeeded by *Generals* and *Portraits*, 1959–61, and *Furniture* from 1960–2. They attracted the attention of Breton, forever willing to read Surrealism into the latest art: he wrote vividly of the Père Ubu qualities of Baj's monsters and of the 'invasion' of our domestic existence perpetrated by his unsettling images.[12] For example, Baj in the *Portraits* constructs a bridge between the fabulous luxury of the noble court and the brocades, ribbons, fabrics and trimmings of the modern Parisian department store. That he knew and worked with the format of the *cadavre exquis* is not to be doubted, but one might think that the fantastic jumps and inversions of the Surrealist pastime are now largely missing from Baj's fundamentally analogical procedure: a language of mischievous equivalences in which the bourgeois is parodied through a use of its own material surfaces. The *Generals* open on to a more dangerous and persistent theme in Baj's subsequent work: the caricature of repressive military types as brutal and indiscriminate (both from fascist armies and the police). The critical difficulty with Baj's methods however was two-fold. First, his implausible association of all geometric art and most Bauhaus aesthetics with 'repression'; and second, his attempt to inject humour into art in a period of acknowledged breakdown of the codes of 'serious' avant-gardist work. Of course, the friends of kitsch are happy on this unstable ground. Baj eagerly embraced the newer forms of collaged eclecticism in the even more febrile and market-obsessed period of the 1980s.

The changes imminent in Robert Rauschenberg's work around 1960 are more symptomatic still. *Talisman* of 1958 [*155*], exhibited in 'The Art of Assemblage' in the

168 **Richard Hamilton** *Interior Study (a)* 1964
In this collage sketch, Hamilton takes a sepia photograph of
the drawing room of the elderly Mme Rouart (Berthe Morisot's
daughter); he adds a 'modern' woman from a washing
machine ad, and a TV showing a game of soccer. The curtain,
left, turns the viewer into a kind of voyeur.

opposite 169 **Enrico Baj** *Vetra Body* 1959
At the time of the 'heavy water' collages, Baj was associating
with Fontana, Hausmann and Farfa in the production of
'collective' works. In 1960 he was to participate in the making
of a 'Grand Tableaux Antifasciste Collectif' with Lebel, Erró
and others in Milan.

company of Villeglé's *Boulevard Poissonnière* of 1957, Rotella's *Before or After* of 1961, Dufrêne's *J* of 1961 and Hains's *De Gaulle comptez sur vous, aidez-le*, also of 1961, mounts pasted paper, wood, lettering, an image of a jam-jar and news photos in a loosely structured grid, but seems to offer no single focus, no 'theme'; instead, and like Rauschenberg's other combines, it emits a dispersed relational energy vaguely evocative of the disorder of everyday urban perception subtly different in character from Parisian or Roman *affichisme*. In pronounced contrast to the dissonance and destruction of the Europeans, Rauschenberg's transparent inattention to 'issues' and 'content' – his management precisely of their degradation and incoherence – was emerging as the most important critical problem of his project. *Canyon* of 1959, also in the 1961 New York show, added cardboard, paint splodges, a stuffed eagle and a feather pillow. It too seemed to concretize no specific area of thinking or feeling; yet in failing to do so encapsulated a way of seeing that was apprehended as somehow new. It is possible of course that Rauschenberg's pronounced dyslexia has helped, not hindered, the dissociative happenstance effects of which his works are full.[15] But it was probably not until the poet and writer Brian O'Doherty recognized the paradoxical power of Rauschenberg's *non-*commitment, his withdrawal from the assertoric mode, that the relevance and timeliness of his method became finally clear. What Rauschenberg presented in the later 1950s, wrote O'Doherty later, was:

> not just a recognition of images, but a recognition of a familiar state of feeling that had to do with 'informational overload', a part of daily life everyone more or less learns to ignore…. The images were like deadlines that just happened to be around, the casual information of the man who scans the paper, gathers fragments of news on television and radio, flips through an art book now and then. Public issues, this art seemed to say, are too complicated to understand or to take positions on…. Rauschenberg tolerated, indeed welcomed, whatever accidents interfered with his work, and like a good host tried to make them at home.

Which is to say that Rauschenberg's refusal to manipulate specific images, his 'failure' to align himself politically, lent itself to the agenda of thinking and reflective looking itself. Watching the artist select old photo-engraving plates one day at the *New York Times*, it was clear to O'Doherty that *non-specificity* was in his mind: that incidents residing easily in their event-categories were those that caught his attention. Rauschenberg showed no interest in the specific occasion depicted by a given image, choosing non-specific images to be put in non-specific relationships:

> His art encouraged what could be called the city-dweller's scan…. [His] early work as a window designer of Fifth Avenue Stores…could not be more consistent with his [artistic] aims of provoking perception, of jogging attention and measuring its decay… a Rauschenberg [of that period] was an unsettling and marvellous glimpse of lapsing histories, half-chewed processes, sputtering feedback from nutty dissociations, all contained in the crowded arc of one rapid perception…Rauschenberg had introduced into the museum and its high-art ambience not just the vernacular object but something much more important: the *vernacular glance*.[14]

Rauschenberg's achievement stands nevertheless alongside other features of the contemporary American avant-garde. We saw earlier how, coming out of a Beat sensibility and by no means unaware of the West Coast contribution to the junk aesthetic, a generation of New York-based artists were in the later 1950s extending their activities into events based on randomness, the accumulation of detritus, and performed actions. In 1959

Allan Kaprow published a script entitled 'Something to Take Place: A Happening'. Itself full of collage-like discontinuities, that script served as the structure for the *18 Happenings in 6 Parts* which Kaprow performed at the Reuben Gallery in New York in the fall, having made it clear to his small audience that 'as one of the seventy-five persons present, you will become part of the Happenings – you will simultaneously experience them.' Throughout, a roughly textured collage aesthetic predominated: from the invitation card consisting of a plastic envelope filled with collaged bits of paper, photographs, painted fragments and cut-outs, to the scenario of the event itself, one wall of which (in Kaprow's own words) was 'a collage of vibrating patches of red black silver yellow and white cloth torn and shredded pasted in as great an ordered disorder as possible edges hang free – All over this sea of confusion will be scrawled broken words in all sizes and colours such as HEY! HI! RAH! HOO! BARROOM! YAY! BARROOM! BOO! OH! HO! WHOOM! AH! – readable sometimes and sometimes not.'[15] Aware of the tumult caused by this and other happenings by Red Grooms, Robert Whitman and Claes Oldenburg, the British-Canadian painter Brion Gysin had suggested to his writer friend William Burroughs that 'writing is fifty years behind painting' – that montage techniques derived from Dada and Surrealism should be applied to the written word. According to the possibly apocryphal story, Gysin while staying at the so-called 'Beat' hotel in the rue Git-le-Coeur in Paris accidentally cut through some pages of the *Herald Tribune*, but then rearranged the pieces to form startling new orderings of verbal texture: Burroughs, already practised in verbal montage from his soon-to-appear *The Naked Lunch* (1959), took Gysin's lesson to heart. His cut-up and fold-in novels such as *The Soft Machine* (1961) would exploit that fertile technique to the full.[16]

There is some sort of irony then in the fact that at the very historical moment when avant-garde writing was learning to mimic collage techniques of the visual arts, the visual arts themselves would now abandon those techniques as no longer up-to-date. Indeed, as the Cuban missile crisis unfolded in the spring and summer of 1962 – to result in a terrifying *dénouement* in the autumn that is a watershed of another kind – visual artists attuned to new image technologies were ready to make a dramatic 'break' with collage methods of manufacture (one that would have no obvious counterpart in the literary arts). In this and the following year, both the French *affiches lacérées* and American 'combine' methods underwent a profound and seemingly irreversible change. For 1962 was the year in which photo-silk-screen methods first invaded the studio, both in Europe and the USA. Originally put to wide use in printing lengths of cloth for fashion, silk-screen methods needed only the addition of photo-sensitive emulsion before ready-made media images could be transferred quickly onto canvas.

This sudden change – vitally important to the subsequent career of collage in the West – can be understood in two simultaneous ways. In the first, the abrupt disappearance of the ready-made fragment can be read as the end-point of the long tradition started around 1908, in which material reality was imported into the illusionistic surface, comprehensively to undo the representational language of at least four centuries. In the second, the adoption of photo-silk-screen methods was almost certainly intended to enlarge the possibilities of collage-like juxtaposition by means of new orderings of scale, orientation and above all registration that the squeezing of paint through photographic mesh could deliver. To look at Rauschenberg's early black-and-white silk-screen paintings of 1962–4 for example is to witness the exuberance born of a new technical repertoire of smudging, overlapping, inverting and recolouration that photo-silk-screen so readily provides. In Andy Warhol's case it needed only a celebrity tragedy in the form of Marilyn Monroe's suicide in August 1962 to impel him to adopt the silk-screen image in a way that is now often seen as a form of memory-trace, real and quickly degenerating, from the fast-moving celebrity world. In point of fact Warhol's careful *mis*-registrations and *mis*-colorations stem directly from the collage-like quality of the silk-screen process. His *Race*

Riot and *Electric Chair* images would shortly follow.[17] The adoption of photo-silk-screen technique is comparable superficially to the moment around 1914 when Picasso and Braque began reinventing the *effects* of collage in paint itself. Equally, both 1914 and 1962 may be understood as moments of falling-away from radically disruptive modernism towards a market-friendly postmodernism, the latter as a kind of parody of the former. The cardinal feature of 1962 of course is that the collagist's source materials are not simulated wood-grain or stencilled commercial lettering, but photographs themselves, treated on the one hand as a material thing, on the other as a disembodied image.

It is probably right to insist with Gregory Ulmer that 'by the 1960s the collage revolution seemed to have run its course' – at the very least that the whole culture was shifting to a photographic mode.[18] Other artists were swept up in the technical change. By 1962, the date of the deteriorated film imagery of his *Marilyn Monroe (Marilyn Idolo)*, or *Marilyn Monroe II*, made for his first New York exhibition at the Smolin Gallery in 1963, Wolf Vostell too was on the brink of photo-silk-screen methods as well as a concerted move into performance (for example *You*, staged in New York in 1964). Rotella for his part resorted after 1963 to an epidiascope, from which he projected a *mélange* of historical and media images straight onto an already emulsified canvas: he called the results *mec-art* (mechanical art).[19] Rauschenberg had visited Warhol's studio in September 1962 and saw how the process worked: within weeks he was silk-screening his own images from *National Geographic, Life, Esquire, Boxing and Wrestling* (his 10-metre (32-foot) long silk-screen painting *Barge*, 1962, was among the first results) and would only occasionally revert to *objets trouvés* thereafter. Besides, after a large sculpture show in Amsterdam in September 1962 he claimed he was 'really sick of sculpture: nothing appealed to me more when I got back than the gentility of a beautifully stretched piece of canvas'.[20] Meanwhile, French and Italian *affichisme* did not decline all of a sudden. The specifically Lettrist evaluation of language as constantly degraded, always corrupted and unstable, was expressed in an awkwardly-scaled work by Dufrêne, the punningly-titled twelve-panel work of poster-undersides *Mot-Nu-Mental* of 1964, whose importance, wrote the Paris correspondent of *Art International* Annette Michelson, 'far exceeds that of the visual pun; it constitutes, rather, that definitive synthesis of Lettrisme and *affichisme* for which, through twenty years of post-liberation *ennui*, we have been breathlessly waiting'.[21] And yet this wholesale switch from collage or *décollage* elements to the mechanical methods of photo-silk-screen and photo-emulsion painting was more than just technical. At the least, it signalled the beginning of the end of a long phase of avant-garde activity embedded within a material culture based on printed magazines and street-hoardings for the advertising of services and goods. After about 1964, the meanings of collage would never be the same.

West Coast Endings: Conner, Herms and Hopper

The situation of West Coast America in the early 1960s can be directly compared. Both Bruce Conner and his friend Dennis Hopper were producing collages and assemblages on the crest of the Beat sensation in the very late 1950s when an interesting change of sensibility occurred. On the reverse of his large private work *UNTITLED* [*123*] Conner had been sticking labels and photos. Now, they suddenly seemed to him worth displaying: the year was 1960. 'I'd seen paintings in the museum that had stamps or seals from certain collections or exhibitions' Conner recollected about the first mass-media images he had stuck to *UNTITLED's* reverse [*171*]:

> All those pin-ups and pictures were basically things you don't see behind the art-work... I started feeling that there was this whole world of communication that was happening on the backs of paintings and artworks that nobody was paying any attention to, and I decided that was an area I was going to work in.[22]

Wolf Vostell *Marilyn Monroe II* 1963

TV sets are mounted behind this large canvas covered
deteriorated paper images of the recently dead film star:
work presents (in the artist's words) a 'chaos of visual
sciousness and acoustic environment'.

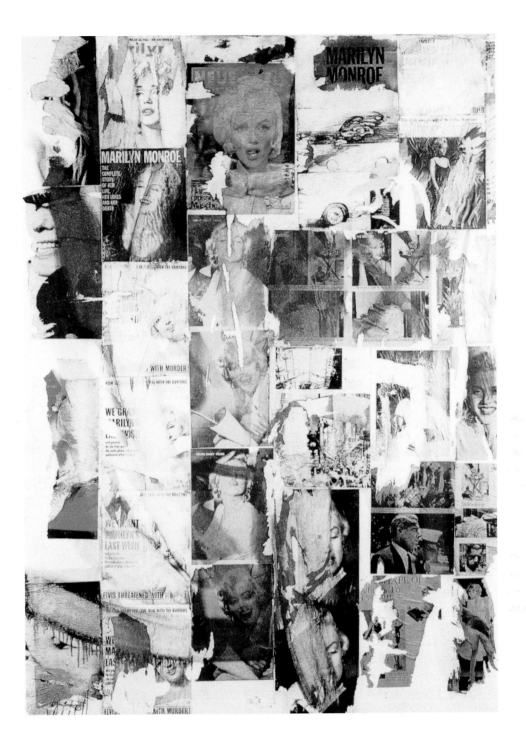

Wallace Berman's friend the poet George Herms had also begun to sense a semantic shift in the way signs and urban graphics were coming to be regarded. From 1960 Herms's collages/assemblages constituted a sort of votive offering to the fairly recently damaged or fallen-out-of-use. On a verbal level the melt-down of coherence was aimed, as he put it, at a desire to stave off meanings 'accepted and fixed by society'.[23] Collage for Herms did just what jazz music did: 'the musician takes part of a melody from one song, part of a melody from another song, and puts them over these chord changes and makes a musical collage'.[24] *Saturn Collage* of 1960, for example – which is a relief of shallow depth – shows early recognition of the peculiar aura of signage, as well as signifying directly the necessity for a 'detour' of the familiar, one in which the names of some things collide with the substance of others. One has the impression from both works that modernity in the form of graphics and advertising imagery was about to assert itself as image – and in so doing to suffuse the culture with the hitherto unrecognized glamour of advertising, celebrity and fame.

But Conner was as eclectic as he was prescient in his use of collage in film, engraving and the *métier* of junk. A series of flat engraving collages produced around 1961 points to a philosophically more complex attitude to authorship. He was known at the time to have been amused by the occurrence in most telephone books of several Bruce Conners; indeed the linkage of authorial identity with aesthetic achievement he viewed (in common with Marcel Duchamp) with grave suspicion. His first plan therefore was to exhibit twenty-six of his collages (stylistically they derive from Max Ernst) as the work of his friend the actor and artist Dennis Hopper. In the series, weird dancers with insect heads cavort, or mountaineers get lost on impossible journeys. In the plate reproduced here, biological diagrams cluster with archaic machines, a fish tank, and a large winged bird, in a crowded, hallucinatory space of the mind [*172*]. Yet Conner could not persuade his gallerist to connive in the joke, and the works were not exhibited for another decade, by which time questions of conceptual reframing and/or simulation were once again current.[25] Meanwhile, Hopper, who had been an Abstract Expressionist-type painter in the 1950s, gave up painting after his studio and all but two of his works were destroyed in the notorious Bel Air fire of 6 November 1962 [*174*] and in the company of Roy Lichtenstein, James Rosenquist, and his new friend Andy Warhol took part in the 'return to reality' involved in turning attention to billboards, commercial images, road signs and – in Warhol's case – the use of silk-screen forms. Hopper himself started making photographic assemblages, a practice that he continues today.[26] Conner gave up making assemblages in 1964 after constructing *LOOKING GLASS* [*173*] in which the pin-ups in the lower section appear scarred, torn, stapled and pinned, while above the shelf one finds more lingerie, frills and boudoir material, not in a condition of erotic newness but distressed, jumbled and over-used. It seems that by that time Conner's original attraction to assemblage he considered to be no longer viable. The shiny surfaces of the commercial environment were suddenly exciting. The junk aesthetic had had its day.

Jiří Kolář and the Prague School

A few exceptions prove the rule. Our thesis of a historical rupture in collage aesthetics is on the face of it sundered by the work of a figure the utterance of whose very name resembles the word 'collage': the Czech poet and visual artist Jiří Kolář. During Kolář's activities with Group 42 in Prague from 1942 to 1948 we see him reverting to poetry after an early attachment to Surrealism; but switching back to collage in 1949 when he embellishes his own poetry with representations of the city, or with reproductions of famous works of art. It is then, in the early years of Communist rule in Czechoslovakia, that Kolář embarks on a lengthy experiment with the image, first of all and to great effect

1 **Bruce Conner** *UNTITLED* (back view) 1954–61 ough not originally intended as 'art', Conner's spare-time cumulation of pin-ups, Old Master reproductions, tickets d labels now became aesthetically relevant, as avant-garde nsibility became attuned to commercial culture around 60. See ill. 123 for the front view.

posite 172 **Bruce Conner** FROM THE DENNIS HOPPER
E-MAN SHOW c. 1961
e of seven collages made from wood engravings and
strative material, at the centre of which a large winged bird
hanges glances with a bearded, hatted figure.

3 **Bruce Conner** LOOKING GLASS 1964
e pervasive aura of distress and damage in this work was by
54 threatened by new erotic blandishments from the
nsumer world. Overcrowding seems to mark the last phase
the 'junk' aesthetic.

in the series of *rapportages* and *confrontages* of 1951 and 1952 which stand comparison with the other great scrapbooks of the period, those of Eduardo Paolozzi in Britain. Now, Kolář's methods stage a revolt against Surrealist methods of *dépaysement*, of convulsive beauty. Inspired by a conversation with his friend Zdeněk Urbánek, Kolář mounts images classically on a page, anecdotally – that is, without hair-raising *frisson* or scandalous *bizarrerie*, but with a restrained suggestion of a hidden relation between them. 'He [Urbánek] showed us how two reproductions juxtaposed without any artificial intervention can create a new anecdote, and how these two images, when simply placed next to each other, begin to establish a dialogue and to communicate.... We were considering the necessity of replacing the so-called Surrealist collage. It must have been in 1950 or 1951'.[27] In another on-going series called *chiasmages*, from around 1951, Kolář took pages of text in an unfamiliar language, cut them up into small pieces, and from them created patterned grids that look innocent from a distance, but more and more mysterious the closer we come.

It was not until the end of the 1950s however that Kolář embarked on the vast experiment with the divided image for which he has become justly celebrated since. In a curious historical parallel, it was in the years of French Lettrisme that Kolář's unique experiment with the verbal image began, first as a 'cut-up' technique applied to given items of printed matter ranging from labels, recipes, mathematical formulae, and texts on medicine and astrology: such poems were collectively called 'Instructions for Use' and immediately endeared Kolář to concrete poetry movements further west. 'From the beginning', Kolář has said, 'my concern was to find the interfaces between the fine arts and literature. All previous attempts in this direction seemed inadequate, and above all *not consistent*.'[28] Imprisoned for most of 1953 and officially debarred from publishing until 1964, he nevertheless created from 1961–2 entire series of sign-poems, number-poems, puzzle-poems, and eventually 'silent' poems composed of hyphens, question-marks, commas and other resources of the typewriter (some were dedicated to the memory of Malevich). Soon came object-poems, or things subjected to essentially literary structures such as repetition, rhyming, or inter-leaving, or books themselves which are ruined, torn or glued, as if evading the censor of his poetry by craftily switching into another medium. 'Someday', said Kolář, 'it will become possible to make poetry out of anything at all.'[29]

That statement seems to me to distinguish Kolář's experiments with cut-and-pasted imagery from the traditions of West European and American modern art. For at the very historical moment when West European modernists were embracing photo-enlargement techniques such as silk-screen in order to enlarge the resources of their art, Kolář set out to create a lexicon of his own. In *prollage* (another invented term) he takes two or more images, and having cut them into identical width strips reassembles them in sequence: *prollage* stretches images lengthways, giving a behind-bars appearance that is also a simultaneity-effect whose purpose is to tease the mind and the eye. A variation known as *rollage* (from 1964) meant cutting several copies of the same image into strips and then mounting them in staggered sequence, creating a dazzling 'optical' effect not unlike Op Art in the West [*176*]. 'My head was bursting when I realized the possibilities which opened up for me when ı put together the first two reproductions for the first time. I was permeable and so was the whole world; a non-illusionistic space could be created...'.[30] Nevertheless, Kolář's position in Communist Czechoslovakia placed him at one remove from ideas and techniques further west. A second suspicion is that Kolář from the beginning was operating with verbal and not visual structures. '*Rollage* has enabled me to see the world in at least two dimensions', he has said; 'the stratifications made me realise just how many unknown layers make up life and just how many unknown deposits exist within each of us.'[31]

In fact, following his one-person show at the Klub VU Mánes in Prague in 1962, Kolář was taken up by the international circuit and has exhibited worldwide ever since. My point

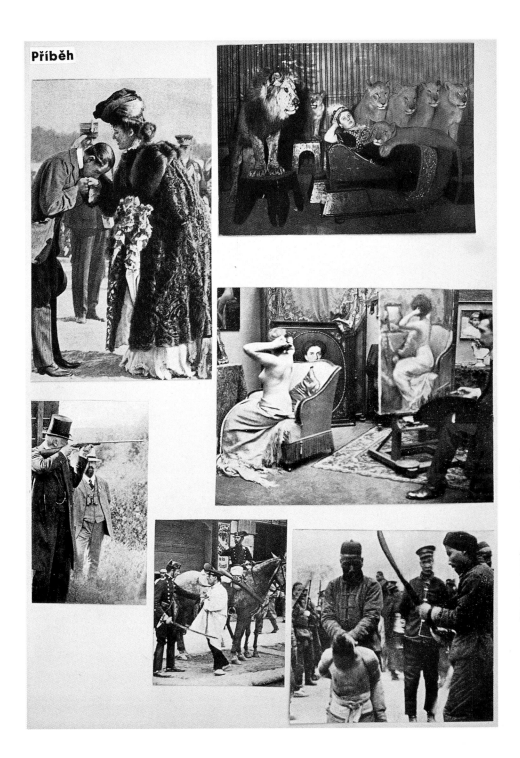

e of two paintings that survived the Bel Air fire, this work
eals Hopper's affinity with assemblage as well as 'the return
reality': 'being an Abstract Expressionist, I could just attack
anvas like an actor could attack a role.' After 1961, Hopper
ned to photography and film directing.

5 **Jiři Kolář** _Story_ 1952

this _confrontage_, Kolář positions images of similar activities
ut with different protagonists – close to one another. In the
ist's own words, 'it's a confrontation of gestures, activities
d events seized by the camera lens or the painter's brush'.

176 **Jiři Kolář** *Baudelaire (Les Fleurs Du Mal) Series* 1972
Kolář here interleaves two of Etienne Carjat's photographs of
the author of *Les Fleurs du Mal*, with one of them inverted.
The artist has said that 'contradictory states are the driving
force of every endeavour. Nothing is born without both inner
and external contradiction.'

is that the origins of Kolář's collage lie in the struggles of a censored poet to be heard, even though his reputation has been created largely within the visual arts. But a poet of sorts he has remained. Not trained as an artist, he has seldom invented a line or cut a silhouette that was not already given in the image in front of him – this too confirms his status as a writer for whom 'poetry' resides in images that resemble, dissemble, repeat or inhabit each other, and perhaps never more so than in the recent series known as *intercollage* which exploits the Magritte-effect of silhouetting one reality into (or through, or against) another: many *intercollages* enjoy a joke at the expense of Old Master and modernist paintings, even if their humour may be slight [*177*]. True to his writer's mission, Kolář compiled a *Dictionary of Methods*, published in Paris in 1986, in which he articulates all the other techniques of his invention such as *ventillage, crumplage, kinetic collage*, and which underline further still his affinity to conceptual classification, lexicography, systematization, seriality: not only an implacably anti-Romantic attitude to the image, but one attuned to the linguistic as such. 'The world attacks us directly', he has said, 'tears us apart through the experience of the most incredible events, and assembles and reassembles us again. Collage is the most appropriate medium to illustrate this reality.'[32]

To this literary achievement must be added the example of the polymathic Adolf Hoffmeister. The youngest founding member of Devětsil in 1920, Hoffmeister was successively a painter, caricaturist, stage designer, critic and diplomat. He took part in Czech Surrealism in the 1930s and gradually introduced collage into his brilliant caricatural style (there are fine renditions of Pasternak, Aragon, Huxley and others from these years). First guided by his admiration for Max Ernst's collage novels, Hoffmeister turned against the archaism of Ernst's materials and what he saw as the morbidity of his fantastic images when he returned to collage-making in the 1960s – to deploy now a humourous and detached attitude having much in common with the British Monty Python designers [*178*]. In this example (which shows his enthusiasm for the international reach of Pop art) Hoffmeister's caricatural impulse submits the artistic category of landscape to the eroticizing process of photography in a new commercial age.

Inspired by Kolář and Hoffmeister, Prague has remained to this day the foremost centre of collage practice in Europe, easily living up the Breton's description of it as 'one of those sites which electively attract poetic thought, always more or less adrift in space.'[33] Breton's compliment cuts both ways, of course. A substantial group of artists born in the later 1920s or early 1930s, hence coming of age as Czechoslovakia emerged from Communism in the later 1960s, adopted collage as the natural, inevitable technique of any worthwhile avant-garde. The work of Jan Kotik, Věra Janoušková, Adriena Šimofová, Ladislav Novák, Karel Trinkewitz, Jaroslav Vožniak and others performed a destabilizing role in the visual, typographic and material culture of those worrisome years. Take the work of Ivo Medek, who in his ominous *A Phone* of 1968 seems to evoke party functionaries spying from the tops of school desks on a private conversation: secrecy is the theme [*179*]. The Arp-like collages of Radoslav Kratina on the other hand have no difficulty reasserting the values of 'art' by means of distressed material fragments whose holes and worn edges evoke the beauty of poor material in a sensuous yet still painterly way, but without the stigma of paint itself. A younger generation, including Jiří Hůla, Pavla Aubrechtová, Oldřich Hamera, Roman Havlík and others stands as further evidence of a tradition of collage-making in that city which persists in spite of the crises enveloping the medium further west. The extraordinary animated films of Jan Svankmayer testify that the genre has withstood even the predations of digital technique.[34]

posite 177 **Jiři Kolář** *Cow Having Eaten Up Canaletto*
58
hile cutting out the silhouettes, it occurred to be that I
uld put the cut-outs over another photograph or
roduction. *Intercollage*...recalls the world reflected in show
es, windows of trains, buses and streetcards, the world
ected on the surfaces of rivers and puddles.' (Kolář)

8 **Adolf Hoffmeister** *Landscape of the Photographers*
56
ffmeister left occupied Czechoslovakia for the USA in 1939,
d became Czech Ambassador for France in the 1940s, later
ching animated film at the School of Applied Arts in
gue. This even later collage shows Hoffmeister exploiting
hionable contrast between glossy soft-porn images and late
th-century illustration.

The Spirit of Play: Architectural Collage

The urban scene had figured in collage and photomontage both in Dada and in 1920s visionary exercises like those of Paul Citroën – as well as in artists as diverse as Podsadecki, Lissitzky and the somewhat later André Verlon. It is perhaps only in Schwitters' wanderings to collect garbage in the gutters and on the pavements of Hanover that we get glimpses of a different aesthetic, one governed by the need to rearrange city experiences in accordance with the artist's intuitions about the likely locations of the most numerous and resonant scraps. Yet the full spirit of play in architectural and urban thinking did not really gain hold in twentieth-century culture until the crisis of the post-Second World War. Johan Huizinga's great 1938 book *Homo Ludens: A Study of the Play Element in Culture*, translated into English in 1949, became a source for many of the activities and concepts of the Internationale Situationiste, especially in relation to urban experience in the age of commodity spectacle and particularly the Situationist concept of the *dérive*. Though Debord himself preferred to see his experiments against the background of Romanticism, even stretching back to the age of chivalry with its tradition of long voyages undertaken in a spirit of discovery, Huizinga's emphasis on the 'serious' dimensions of play enters the Situationist revision of the city in the form of the famous graffiti incitement *Ne travaillez jamais* (Never work) which the Situationist journal referred to as the 'minimum program' of the movement in 1953. The historian of Situationism, Libero Andreotti, points out that the same proscription animates the entire production of the 1959 book *Mémoires* which Debord composed with the radical Danish painter and thinker Asger Jorn.[35] Itself a leading exemplification of the Situationist idea of 'collective play', the book comprised literary fragments and excised sections of the map of Paris freely dispersed over, under or among lines and blotches of colour loosely dripped by Jorn. Some pages are like disordered maps: one fantasizing Paris as 'une ville flottante' (a floating city) and another suggesting 'C'est un jeu de la vie et du milieu' (It's a game of life and milieu), into which sections of the boulevard Bourdon and the Luxembourg gardens are cut as if pieces from a Cubist collage. Another page might intercut an ancient battle scene, an image of a sea-battle in Rio, and a map-fragment of the Contrescarpe region of Paris that the Lettrists celebrated for its 'suitability for play and forgetting' [*181*].[36] Here the word-fragments propose 'On balaierait le vieux monde' (We would wipe away the old world), 'On n'entre pas seul dans l'histoire, comme le chevalier entre seul en lice' (One doesn't enter history alone, as the horseman enters the lists alone), 'Rien ne s'arrête pour nous…nous brûlons de désir de trouver (nothing ever stops with us…we burn with a desire to find). Finding, in play-behaviour, converts as naturally in the Situationist city as it does in childhood into erotic desire: hence the new Situationist re-mappings become *The Naked City* and *Discourse on Love's Passion*, to cite two other psychogeographical journeys.

Indeed, collage and desire are closely related in the architectural imagination – which is partly why we see a correspondence between Debord and Jorn's work on cities and the early urbanist theories of Alison and Peter Smithson in London. Alison Smithson has made it clear that her and Peter Smithson's attitude to the new American imagery of the 1950s had been sharply distinguishable from that of Paolozzi. She had looked at *Ladies Home Journal* and *The Companion* as an evacuated schoolgirl in war-time Edinburgh – even as she bought ice-cream at the Paolozzis' – but she and her husband had oriented themselves to Europe rather than the USA. Their critique of European modernism was directed towards experience of an ever more mobile society in the grip of new image technologies such as scientific and magazine photography – informed by an 'as-found' understanding of the social and physical realities of the working city, an understanding in turn indebted to Nigel Henderson's anthropological photography in Bethnal Green [*135*]. 'The "as found" was a new seeing of the ordinary, an openness as to how prosaic "things" could re-energise our inventive activity', they wrote; 'In a society that had nothing, you reached for

180 **Alison and Peter Smithson** *Golden Lane Housing, View along a Deck* 1952

[Pa]sting cut-out photographic figures onto a pristine [ar]chitectural drawing, the Smithsons imagine new forms of [v]ernacular texture in the modernist city: in the foreground are [M]arilyn Monroe and the American baseball star Joe DiMaggio [a]s models of the classless new citizen.

[O]pposite 179 **Ivo Medek** *A Phone* 1968
[T]he artist writes that 'the collage was inspired by the feeling [of] the period, well understood by George Orwell, of a Big [Br]other watching… It was originally named *Telephone Call to [Ea]st Berlin*.'

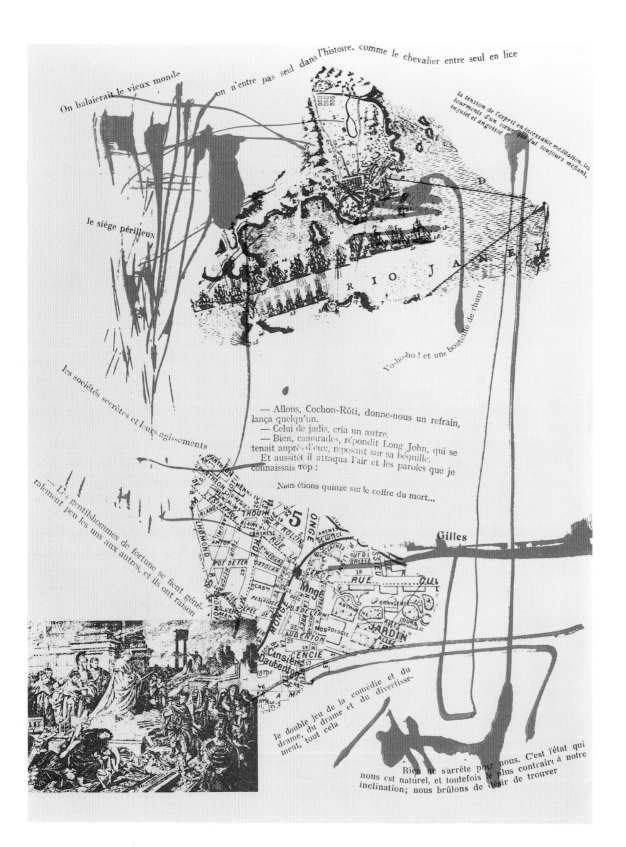

On balaierait le vieux monde

on n'entre pas seul dans l'histoire, comme le chevalier entre seul en lice

la tension de l'esprit en incessante méditation, les tourments d'un cœur inquiet et angoissé qui fut toujours méfiant,

le siège périlleux

R I O J A N E I

Yo-ho-ho ! et une bouteille de rhum !

les sociétés secrètes et leurs agissements

— Allons, Cochon-Rôti, donne-nous un refrain, lança quelqu'un.
— Celui de jadis, cria un autre.
— Bien, camarades, répondit Long John, qui se tenait auprès d'eux, reposant sur sa béquille.
Et aussitôt il attaqua l'air et les paroles que je connaissais trop :

Nous étions quinze sur le coffre du mort...

Les gentilshommes de fortune se fient généralement peu les uns aux autres, et ils ont raison

Gilles

le double jeu de la comédie et du drame, du drame et du divertissement, tout cela

Rien ne s'arrête pour nous. C'est l'état qui nous est naturel, et toutefois le plus contraire à notre inclination ; nous brûlons de désir de trouver

what there was…'.[37] The Smithsons' entry for the Golden Lane housing competition of 1952 gives an initial sense of this 'as-found' architectural aesthetic in two-dimensional form: its implied critique of the purity of modern architecture is conveyed in the polysemous imagery and the human inhabitation of the architect's imagined forms. Their 1953 ICA exhibition 'Parallel of Life and Art', organized with Independent Group members Paolozzi and Henderson, was another expression of the quartet's explorations of the non-Aristotelian attitude to the urban image in its new diversity. Admiring the technical virtuosity of the magazine-ad of the early 1950s, the Smithsons remarked elsewhere that 'we could not ignore the fact that one of the traditional functions of fine art, the definition of what is fine and desirable for the ruling class and therefore what is desired by all society, had at that moment [the early 1950s] been taken over by the "ad-man".'[38]

The surge of energy generated by 'Pop' art was also conducive to a type of urban imagination that collage techniques could serve uniquely well. That at least is the evidence of Rem Koolhaas and Hans Hollein's architectural imaginings from the mid-1960s onwards. The dominant mood of 'emancipation' lent to their projects a suggestive bravura in tune with those experimental times. In fact, a plethora of groups and individuals took to photographic collage as a means of imagining real or fantastic architectural and urban schemes as the 1960s unfolded, among them Superstudio (Italy), Walter Pichler (Austria), Raimund Abraham (Germany), Venturi and Scott Brown (USA), and Richard Buckminster Fuller (USA). Yet the play credentials of collage were perhaps nowhere so effectively used as by the most futuristic architectural group of the early 1960s, Archigram (whose name, as in *telegram, aerogramme* implies the urgency of communication as much as a design practice). According to one of its founders, Peter Cook, Archigram originated in late 1960 in conversations and meetings which aimed 'to criticize projects, to concoct letters to the press, to combine to make competition projects, and generally prop one another up against the boredom of working in London architectural offices'. Peter Cook, David Greene, Warren Chalk, Mike Webb, Ron Herron and Dennis Crompton were all recent graduates, and all were devoted to perpetuating the polemic and enthusiasm of architecture school in the face of what they described as 'the general sterility of the scene'.[39] Based loosely upon ideas of expendability, impermanence, *bricolage* and a fascination with new materials and technology, collage was Archigram's natural means of expression and the vehicle for their

most cherished principles of experimentation. Projects such as Warren Chalk's *Capsule* (1964) or his *Gasket Housing* (1965) demonstrated ideas of standardization, interchangeability and 'servicing' by a central core of utilities. Peter Cook's *Plug-In City* (from 1962) lent itself to ideas of mega-structure, transformation, gregariousness, collectivity. David Greene's *Living Pod* (1965) visualized individual life-styles based on mobility, curiosity and nomadism rather than traditional Western permanence and 'security'. With due apologies to Le Corbusier's 'a house is a machine for living in', Greene proposed instead that 'the house is an appliance for carrying with you. The city is a machine for plugging into…. It is likely that under the impact of the second machine age the need for a house (in the form of permanent static container) as part of man's psychological make-up will disappear'.[40]

Though collage and montage were the natural visual idioms of most Archigram members, the visualizations of Ron Herron surpass the majority in sheer dexterity and imaginative freedom. The son of an East London docker and the most politically 'left' of the group, Herron's design contributions to Archigram took the form of the graphically vivid image in which existing structures could be seen to be extended by unfamiliar additions such as funnels, tubes, canopies, towers, cranes and other high-tech gadgets which complicate and hence humanize an environment already determined by routines, hierarchies and constraints. In the early *Walking City* collages of 1963 and 1964, Herron visualized New York as suddenly animated by large living pods capable of communication and movement: the image comprises a low-quality documentary photo of the East River superimposed by drawn and photocopied additions reminiscent of a sci-fi fantasy, and like the fantastic architecture of the Russian Constructivists, clearly not intended to be built. 'The Walking City', Herron wrote, 'a world capital, consists of a series of giant vehicles, each housing elements that collectively made up a metropolis. The vehicles roam the globe forming and reforming. Moscow, a desert, New York Harbour, a pacific atoll and the Thames Estuary, any place and every place, a world capital of total probability'.[41] In a series of *Tuned Suburb* collages from the revolutionary spring of 1968, Herron visualizes the reanimation of a familiar environment by the insertion of pods, plug-in structures, and service pipes. 'The tuning-up is shown as being achieved by the juxtaposition of old with new so as to provide the possibility and potential gradual change…they make a "now"

183 **Ron Herron** *Archigram: Walking City on the Ocean* 1966
Drawing on sources as diverse as Dada, the Smithsons, and 'This is Tomorrow' (1956), Heron helped articulate Archigram philosophy of 'tune up, clip on, plug in', to enable entire cities to migrate and communicate – a utopian vision implying the collapse of national boundaries and independence of the natural environment.

Ron Herron *Archigram: Tuned Suburb* (detail) 1968
[Herr]on was also attuned to Beat sensibility, Los Angeles and
[Rob]ert Venturi's maxim that 'Main Street is almost right': the
[tun]ed' suburb becomes a location of experiment and play.

possible'.[42] Indeterminacy, metamorphosis, and what Archigram as a whole elsewhere called 'emancipation' were the watchwords of a new theory of urban pleasure.

And yet Archigram lay itself open to the complaint that its love affair with new technology was an end in itself that reached for 'emancipation' at the cost of enforcing solipsistic privacy, even (according to Archigram critics) of producing alienation. It is certainly regrettable that Herron, in common with other Archigram members, allowed himself to be drawn away from ideals of community and collectivity towards what the social critic Raymond Williams was to call 'mobile privatization' or the sealing of individual consciousness inside an envelope of contemporary technical communications channels: thus in his so-called *Manzak* collages of 1969 stylish individuals are pictured as the proud possessors of a personalized robot called an 'Electronic Tomato' that supercharges the subject's functionality in the capitalist city. 'It has on-board logic, optical range-finder, TV camera, and magic eye bump-detectors.... Direct your business operations, do the shopping, hunt and fish, or just enjoy electronic instamatic voyeurism, from the comfort of your own home'.[43] At their more reflective, Herron's later collage projects demonstrated the redundancy of architectural terminology based on urban hierarchy (library, club, cinema, university, office) and offered the radical possibility of endless migration, interchangeability and metamorphosis of each and every category and function. 'On the brink of the seventies', Warren Chalk would soon write,

> a whole new era can be seen to be opening up. Man has jumped up and down on the moon and in the streets. Students have laid down at Woodstock and Hyde Park and on campus. Some, unfortunately for the last time. Among all the conflicting ideas, none seems more important at this time than creating a humane environment...to which the ordering individual can reconcile himself without the intolerable effort and stress of his own mental and physical adaptation.

Yet a series of doubts already haunted such utopian hopes: doubts which conjured up images of ecological disaster, of communication breakdown, of informational excess. The date is 1972. The electronic utopia of the early 1960s threatens a backlash. The speed of the last few minutes 'no longer thrills'.[44]

185 **John Stezaker** *The Voyeur* 1979
At least for the male viewer, screen identification becomes problematic once the figure is removed; meanwhile the outline of the dark silhouette frames the woman's face in what may almost be seen as a Picassean style.

12

Collage after Collage

To speak of the crisis of collage-based aesthetics since the 1960s is to speak of many things. The new technical processes – photo-silk-screen, then photo-litho, followed by real-time video, computer graphics and more recently digitalization – have provided resources with which almost everyone is now familiar. Some readers will already have decided that the whole of Western culture has found its new velocities in image techniques borrowed from the fine arts – collage and its near relative montage, of course, being two. And it is substantially true that collage-*effects* (too often mannerisms) have passed effortlessly into the wider culture, to appear as sub-cultural magazine graphics, film montage, and much more: recent post-punk 'zines' such as *Zimmerframepileup* and *Ego*, available only by mail or in alternative bookshops, have creatively filched the techniques of earlier Dada to wild and perhaps useful effect. A further recognition is that 'collage' has gradually become generic to the fine arts right across the spectrum of media, from painting to performance, photography, film, installation and beyond; especially installation, where the artist now conventionally deploys jumps and ruptures to surprise or disorientate the adventurous viewer.[1] Yet to race to the further conclusion that modernist collage has melted all the barriers between the fine arts and the wider culture, that an epistemic 'break' has thrown asunder all models of historical knowledge, is to travel too quickly too far. The survival of collage since the 1960s is a story that may now unfold.

Late Flowerings
It is really no paradox that the discoveries of earlier modernism, especially the juxtapositional styles of Dada and Surrealism and the rational graphics style of Constructivism, inspired a number of projects during the 1960s and 1970s which sought to extend, rather than supersede, the discoveries of that earlier past. Hannah Höch made collages from the later 1950s through to the late 1970s which are no less incisive or beautiful than her works as a Dada pioneer. Shredding fragments of colour magazines (notably *Life International*) to the point often of unrecognizability, Höch now recombined them astutely in the manner of *art informel*, often building in a single figurative fragment which comments upon feminine glamour and the fantasies mobilized by the female gaze. That her intention is still parodic – but less aggressively so – is suggested by the way in which she frequently reverts to imagery used in the 1920s in which eyes, legs, lips, and

distortions of scale make for provocative sexual scenes. It is worth noting *en passant* that the large Robert Rauschenberg show at the Amerikahaus in Berlin in 1965 proved important to younger as well as older German artists. Höch, who saw the show, makes a diary entry at that time: 'Huge collages à la DADA'. She was to write in her 1968 notebook, apparently with approval, that 'collage has spread throughout the world to become the medium for the most subtle of creations...our little sheets from long ago have brought a powerful following'. Referring to Rauschenberg's large new photo-silk-screen works, she says that 'Giant printing machines produce proofs several meters long...the colour photo released endlessly fascinating material, without any boundaries'.[2]

The Rauschenberg show was in West Berlin, and not easily visited. In East Germany a significant number of artists who survived the Nazi period clung to modernist techniques of collage, montage and abstraction against the pull of Eastern-bloc aesthetics in favour of figurative realism. A husband-and-wife team of some stature but little reputation was Herbert Behrens-Hangeler and Dorothea Behrens, both resident in East Berlin after 1945 and to that extent sealed off from progressive ideals of later modernist art. Herbert had been a member of the Novembergruppe from 1921–33, had been close to Baumeister, Gies, Schlemmer, Kandinsky and those branded *entartet* in 1937, and was a painter and collagist of a modernist sort after 1945. Perhaps the more remarkable achievement belongs to Dorothea Behrens, without artistic training and apparently without any conscious engagement with 'modern art'. Her works in cut-and-paste magazine fragments from the mid-1960s have an elegance and suggestiveness that renders astonishing her claim never to have visited an exhibition or spoken to an artist other than her husband. 'It was Christmas nineteen sixty-five', she told me recently. 'Behrens-Hangeler [as she always referred to him] was working at the Weissensee art school in Berlin, and was making some cards for some friends. He asked me to help cut out the shapes and stick them down. When he saw how well I could do it, he told me I should do more. That was the beginning. I did one thousand and eighty-five, before my hands got too bad'.[3] The imagery Behrens managed to generate is biomorphic and mysterious – sometimes land- or sea-scape, according to whether the forms are predominantly straight (hard) or curved (soft): it is a later-Surrealist world of discovery, achieved through the beguiling colour-textures of commercial magazine printing submitted to marvellous formal control. It is difficult to

186 Hannah Höch *On With The Party* 1965
After a foray into abstraction in the 1950s, Höch here reintroduces an awkward Picassean female into a festive scene. The often garish and sometimes faded cheap printing colours of *Life International* became a hallmark of Höch's later work.

opposite **187 Dorothea Behrens** *VIII / 70 / 94* 1994
It took Behrens three hours, on average, to construct a single work at her kitchen table. 'I would arrange everything, then stick them all at once, without changing. Then I flattened them with a pile of books. Never changed anything,' she once said.

believe that Behrens had never seen the work of Hannah Höch or the earlier Berlin Dadas: she must rank among the best unacknowledged collagists of her day.

For a second severely undervalued artist for whom Berlin Dada was fundamental, we need look no further than Romare Bearden from New York. In every way the antithesis of Dorothea Behrens, Bearden had studied at the Art Students' League with George Grosz in 1936–7 and during the depression had created biting magazine cartoons protesting against white supremacism, poverty and unemployment among African-Americans, for the magazines *Baltimore Afro-American*, *Collier's* and *Life*. After a career as an abstract painter in post-war New York, Bearden quite abruptly switched to collage around 1964 in the context of the so-called Spiral Group, convened at Bearden's Canal Street Studio to articulate the position of the African-American artist in relation to the burgeoning civil rights movement. What is fascinating about his case is the relationship between his apparent move to a socially 'engaged' position, and a set of deeper convictions about the formal values of visual art, or more precisely the coming together of the two.

Bearden's efforts to synthesize these two generally distinct identities grew from an early project of the Spiral Group, to create a collaborative work expressive of their radical social beliefs. In practice that enterprise proved unworkable – and Bearden went ahead alone to produce five or six small photomontages, no larger than the size of a sheet of writing paper, which afterwards were enlarged by Photostat to three by four feet, then enlarged again to as much as six by eight feet. Some of the middle-sized versions – twenty-four were exhibited at Cordier and Ekstrom in October 1964 – contain painted passages and went by the name 'Projections'. They maintain an exceptionally intelligent balance between 'content' and 'design', for to attend successfully to *The Street* or *The Dove* is to become aware that in advance of any overt narrative of African-American customs or behaviour – though individual faces do add up to a kind of collectivity – is a pervasive sense of flat constructive organization whose principle is that of the inner rectangle echoing the format of the picture. Bearden tells us that it was out of the study of Dutch interiors by De Hooch and Vermeer that came 'an understanding of the way these painters controlled their big shapes', after which he turned to the Cubism of Picasso, Braque and Léger to learn the lessons of modernist structure: 'Nevertheless I find that for me the Cubism of these masters leads to an overcrowding of pictorial space…. In fact, such exceptions as the collage

188 **Romare Bearden** *The Dove* 1964
'I think a quality of artificiality must be retained in the work of art, since the reality of art is not to be confused with that of the outer world. Art, it must be remembered, is artifice…the primary function of which is to add to our conception of reality.' (Bearden)

drawings of Picasso', Bearden says, 'in which emptier areas are emphasised, only point up what is otherwise typical'. The small brick-like units of Bearden's *The Dove*, then, are intended to be read as part of a larger structure – what he calls 'maximum multiplicity, without the surface fragmentation which I object to in the early Cubist paintings'. 'My aim', Bearden explained, 'is not to paint about the Negro in America in terms of propaganda; rather to reveal through pictorial complexities the richness of a life I know'.[4]

That last statement could have been uttered in self-description by another New York artist, Lee Krasner. Certainly both artists used the pictorial complexities licensed by the use of pasted paper for broadly similar formal ends. But the deployment of collage as an exploration of Krasner's perceived self-identity goes further. The appropriation of drawings and paintings from her personal past which had begun in the 1950s [*112, 113*] was both more and less than the familiar tactic of the readymade: twenty years on, it became a highly individual encounter with things already familiar but now 'seen' very differently. Krasner described these recyclings as 'a form of clarification...I'm going back on myself'; 'I'd like to think it's also a form of growth'.[5] In a series of collages from 1976, exhibited in a solo exhibition (her first) at the Pace Gallery in 1977, we see Krasner reaching further back still, to a series of drawings done between 1937 and 1940 while a student of Hans Hofmann. Discovering the drawings after a long interval, Krasner said that they 'surprised me...and set me to thinking about what it was I was feeling at the time I made them; in what ways I as an artist differed now from then'. Here too the body reasserts itself as somehow the correlate of the materially cut and assembled thing that collage unapologetically is. The drawings from the Hofmann studio were 'mostly nudes of a studio model'; but the way that subject-matter was now treated 'would be truths contained in my own body, an organism as much a part of nature and reality as plants, animals, the sea, or the stones beneath us'.[6] Collectively known as *Eleven Ways to Use the Words to See*, these new works were surprisingly titled each with a grammatical verb-category indicating a possible way the re-viewing process might occur. For example the *Imperative* form is the command 'see'. This collage-painting incorporates a vividly coloured oil sketch sliced up with a set of smudged life-class drawings from almost forty years before [*189*]. *Imperfect Subjunctive* 'denotes an action going on, but not completed, and very dependent on other possibilities. The subjunctive, which we don't really use in English, is the mood of doubt, uncertainty, feeling, will or desire...rarely a hard fact'. In *Past Conditional*, the sliced drawings go straight onto unprimed canvas, and the verb form is 'You might have seen'. Of this work Krasner said that it 'describes a pause, a hesitation in which I am asking myself, is there a precedent which must be fulfilled? What kind of bargain am I trying to strike? Am I being induced by habit to follow a stimulus other than a natural, spontaneous spur to action?'[7]

The titling of these works was the more surprising given Krasner's description of herself as an 'almost completely non-verbal type'[8] – though friends described her conversation as sparkling, acerbic and idiosyncratic. A slightly later series of collages known collectively as *Solstice* (1981) illustrates the oblique but highly original thinking behind her paper expressions. The solstice, Krasner explains, 'means a turning point, a culmination...it is the furthest limit, a crisis. It marks an interval of time between two appearances'. And she gleefully quotes two very different statements which seemed relevant to this work, from John Donne ('A Christian hath no solstice...where he may stand still and go no further' – though Krasner wants to substitute 'artist' for 'Christian'), and Ralph Waldo Emerson ('There is in every constitution a certain solstice.'). Then Krasner adds: 'And I thought – that's also me, I am my own solstice'. Her collages, she says finally, diverge from Cubism, from Surrealism, from Schwitters, from Ann Ryan. 'My collages have to do with time and change'.[9]

The 'expressive' treatment of collage in New York stands in interesting contrast to more impersonal uses of pasted paper back on European soil. In Germany, the mammoth

189 **Lee Krasner** *Imperative* 1976
The imperative 'see' attached to this work – the first in a serie
based on the conjugation of the verb 'to see' – signified
Krasner's need not just to examine old drawings, but 'a
peremptory desire to change them, a command, as it were, t
make them new.' (Krasner)

90 **Gerhard Richter** *Atlas: Panel 8* 1962–6
ichter's accumulative methods in *Atlas* subject the terms of
olitical photomontage and documentary alike to a profound
cepticism: attending instead to forms of collective memory
nd amnesia articulated by the photograph itself.

archive started by Gerhard Richter in 1961 and known simply as *Atlas* (its compilation continues to the present day) counts as a late-modernist version of those projects of the 1920s and early 1930s which include Malevich's pedagogic panels for InKhuK, Warburg's *Mnemosyne Atlas*, and Höch's 1933 collage-book [*95, 97, 98*]. Richter's accumulating *Atlas* (the name evokes the geographical, astronomical and medical treatises of old) is significant for the manner in which it deals with mass-culture imagery in post-war Germany neither as play, nor as celebration, nor as connotative displacement or recombination, as in the classical avant-garde. On the contrary, the over six hundred sheets making up Richter's *Atlas* make none of collage's traditional radical moves. The first fifteen sheets, all done between 1961 and 1963, display family photographs, landscapes, photojournalistic images of celebrated or notorious persons (many from *Stern* or *Bunte Illustrierte*) organized grid-like as on a noticeboard. Yet though the open-ended nature of Richter's archive renders it impossible to summarize and may not even belong to the category 'art' (Richter transcribed a number of the images from *Atlas* into paintings in the period 1964–7), the arrangement of images seems to have its own significance. Unlike the Warburg or Höch projects of the period of impending fascism, when the entire project of humanist historical memory was threatened with extinction, and when humanist subjectivity desperately sought other forms of relatedness to events, Richter's post-war archive accumulates images without comment and without narrative significance: its style of additive display is what Benjamin Buchloh has called 'anomic', that is, alienated by repetition, indifference and near-meaningless excess.[10]

Further to the east, the epistemic 'break' referred to earlier took a form specific to the culture of the USSR; arising in the context of a gradual erosion of confidence in Soviet Communism after the death of Stalin in 1953, and of a generational divide that grew in tandem with the piecemeal exposure of his crimes in the decades to follow. For Russian artists born (unlike Bearden and Krasner) in the 1930s and trained in the academic manner in the late Stalin period, a widening awareness of the bankruptcy of official Soviet 'realism' combined with an increased understanding of modernist art in what was still confusingly called 'the West' placed them in a unique position in the late 1960s and 1970s to engage in many varieties of cultural dissent. A circle of friendship between Erik Bulatov, Oleg Vasiliev and Ilya Kabakov proved especially fertile ground. The classically trained

sculptor Gennady Gushchin, who was part of this circle by 1970, made a sudden switch into photo-collage in his impressive series (still unpublished and seldom exhibited) known as *The Alternative Museum*. Gushchin's formula was simple and effective for the underground circles in which he now moved: take a high-quality colour reproduction of an iconic Soviet or Russian painting (easy to obtain from art books or posters) and transform its pictorial meanings by the addition of images from elsewhere, carefully chosen for their compatibility with the light-source, scale and tonality of the original. In his early *Tragic Romance* (1970), Gushchin took a print of Isaak Brodskii's popular and widely reproduced painting *Lenin at Smolnyi* (1930) and placed inside it a figure of a guitar-playing peasant from a painting by the minor nineteenth-century genre painter Vladimir Perov. Mixing pre-Soviet with Soviet visual culture, Gushchin now has a member of the peasant class serenading the leader of the Bolshevik Party at a moment of crisis in the latter's dealings with the countryside. And Gushchin's example has been followed by countless other *monteurs* in the aftermath of the collapse of the Communist bloc – not least on account of the cheapness of the materials involved. The younger Aleksandr Zossimov takes a 1950s painting of Moscow's Bolshoi Square and dominates it by the figure of the briefcase-carrying 'biznesman', a new figure in the Russian townscape in the 1980s and still a figure of suspicion today. The even younger Maria Serebriakova more recently made a series of extremely fine adaptations of 'found' photographic views, using a few deft strokes of white paint to transform buildings into pieces of furniture, specifically tables or chests which now stood (absurdly) raised on legs above the ground they once occupied: a resonant metaphor of cultural change accomplished with a minimum of means.[11]

Political Montage: the 1970s
In the West, the practice of modern – and especially abstract – art came directly into conflict with those types of photomontage that explicitly addressed the political: 'political' here meaning tendentiously political, the politics of a tendency or a group. Modern art and its theory, for practitioners of the latter, became synonymous with elitism, isolationism, hermeticism and self-serving ambiguity. Throughout the decade following the social revolutions of 1968 it could be said that the two types of work became irretrievably estranged.

191 **Gennady Gushchin** *Tragic Romance* 1970
By plundering fine reproductions of iconic works by the likes of Repin, Shishkin, Aivazovsky and Mukhina, Gushchin corrupts both their original meanings as well as their contemporary political uses, turning approved ideology into burlesque.

92 **Aleksandr Zossimov** *Gulliver* 1987
Photographic painting evolved in the USSR partly because of
its mass-reproducibility, but in doing so played directly into the
hands of photomonteurs with more satirical purposes in view.

Ambitious artists are always migrating out of 'art' towards something else: a better version of art, a more collective vision, a wider public, greater accessibility, and so on. And that is how it was for the British photomonteur Peter Kennard, who recollects that 'the orthodoxy of modernism [in the late 1960s] was that modern art was a bus driven by Cézanne, with Matisse as the conductor and Jackson Pollock as the drunken passenger. Clement Greenberg was the inspector whose eye you tried to avoid as he came up the aisle in case you'd got the wrong ticket'. The alternative was to get a different bus. As Kennard recalls, 'Against the odds, and to find a way to relate my growing political commitment to my art, I got on the "wrong" bus and found the driver was John Heartfield'. 'His work', Kennard says with some authority (he was there) 'was distinctly off-limits in England at this time'.[12] Yet by the early 1970s wave upon wave of social crises, from housing to education, from price inflation to industrial strife, called out for images that carried clear messages and made the modern art establishment look shabby and venal – which in many respects it was. As exhibitions of political montage started to circulate, and as Walter Benjamin's essays on Brecht and Heartfield were published for the first time in English translation, launching a critical vocabulary which explained how 'montage interrupts the context into which it is inserted',[13] a disaffected younger generation enthusiastically jumped off the modernist bus. Kennard's work was taken up with alacrity by CND and other causes. Correspondingly, the German artist Klaus Staeck adopted the poster-format to advertise the rights of immigrant workers, to oppose the CDU in the German elections of 1972, and to press for rent reforms in Dürer's home town of Nuremburg in 1971. In the latter, an image of Dürer's aged and emaciated mother carried a question: 'Would you rent a room to this woman?' One anti-CDU poster bore the ironic reflection: 'The rich must get richer. So vote CDU'. As Staeck has explained many times (and not only in the art press) his work is meant to be *without* aura and cannot be identified with the hand-crafted product from which a poster begins. He claims that while for Heartfield the montage method had been pictorial, for him the tension is to be found almost entirely in the textual overlay: scaled up and multiplied by offset printing, the results have a flatness which is that of the declarative text. 'I took advertising and flipped it around', says Staeck:

> That's how text came in…. The trigger is a particular political situation…a slogan occurs to me, and then I work on it until every word is right. Then I consider does one add a picture, which intensifies the irritation effect, or does the typography selected produce a dialectical picture character on its own? … What distinguishes me from Heartfield is a no-art look, the text-picture montage, the working method, and action.[14]

Symptomatically, the spring 1976 issue of *Studio International* in which Staeck's interview appeared collocated a spectrum of artists' organizations working with trades unions, revolutionary theorists, and models of how art could work for 'society', interspersed with revivals of Soviet formalism, factography, and the theory of the commune. That same moment saw a crisis of confidence of modernist architecture and planning, both of which were seen as dependent upon even more fundamental modernist aesthetics in painting and sculpture. The message was stark: painters had better lay down their brushes for the sake of community-based photography and video. There just seemed to be nowhere else to go.[15]

Indeed, every moment of the 1970s seemed transitional: a sequence of pressure-points being applied to 'modernist' art and theory in the face of intractable social and welfare crises throughout the West. Depending upon where you stood and what you read, the possibilities for a revolutionary popular culture based on montage seemed real and profound. Situationist literature was translated into English first in 1970;[16] its theory of *détournement* insisted that artifacts and texts which had become 'frozen solid in a hierarchic array' undergo 'an all-embracing re-entry into play' such as to invent 'a new

193 **Klaus Staeck** *Nostalgie ist noch lange kein Grund CDU zu wählen* (Nostalgia is hardly a reason for voting CDU) 1973 Beneath the sarcastic message we see a group of former CDU and CSU politicians: (left to right) Ludwig Erhard, Rainer Barzel, Kurt Georg Kiesinger and Franz-Josef Strauß.

kind of social speech' beyond the stale oppositions between art and everyday life.[17] Little else was needed to trigger the anarchic music/graphic style launched by Malcolm McLaren, known as 'punk'. Amid the meltdown of the UK economy in 1976, McLaren's group the Sex Pistols careered onto London's music scene with a vitriolic attack on the suburban values which made up their own social background. To the graphic artist of the group, Jamie Reid, collage and montage were obvious resources: for the Pistols' 'God Save the Queen' hit single of 1977, already a scandalous intervention in the year of the Queen's Jubilee celebrations, Reid took a Cecil Beaton photograph of Her Majesty and alienated it by fixing a safety pin through the nose and attaching two swastikas for the eyes, before finding it rejected by the Sex Pistols' record company A&M Records. In common with the group's lyrics, Reid's graphic style, inspired over the longer historical interval by Dada, in fact contained imagery of the ultra-right as much as the ultra-left, and threw into open contradiction a series of secure ideological divisions between the tactics of anarchism, fascism, and sheer youthful disaffection.

The question of women, both as authors and subjects of the political montage, received an unquestioned hike in prominence in the aftermath of Reid's photographic attack on the British monarchy. Feminism was already firmly on the cultural agenda by 1970, but it took an artist like Gee Vaucher to articulate its values from the perspective of the punk-inspired left. A member of the avant-garde performance group EXIT from 1968 to 1972 – whose members included Penny Rimbaud (real name Jeremy Ratter) and Steve Ignorant, shortly to form the anarcho-punk band CRASS – Vaucher first of all earned money from a commercial graphics job in New York before launching an intermittent anarchist broadsheet *International Anthem* ('a nihilist newspaper for the living', in the words of its masthead), which she illustrated with gouache drawings exquisitely reproducing the 'look' of collage, as well as actual collages themselves. The majority of the latter cleverly construct interior scenes evoking domestic hypocrisy, war, and the sheer banality of life amidst the disappointed hopes of late 1970s Britain. The second of the three *International Anthem* broadsheets that made it into publication was subtitled *Domestic Violence*, and like so many of Vaucher's images the scene is one of 'normality' gone crazily awry: in this case, wealthy consumers floating in domestic comfort who end up looking like zombies, their 'morality' signalled by a crucifix above the bed and a child dressed as an obedient nun [*194*]. 'Art' is indexed by catalogues on the table, one of which is seemingly devoted to the work of the French abstract artist Simon Hantaï.[18]

Yet by the end of the 1970s punk was becoming dispersed as a cultural force in both London and the provinces by an abrupt political lurch back to market economics under Prime Minister Margaret Thatcher, elected in 1979: which made more urgent still the contradictions of gender and commerce in the late-capitalist city. Linder Sterling, the former lead singer with the avant-garde Manchester punk band Ludus (she once sang at the legendary Haçienda Club covered in pigs' entrails and wearing a large black dildo) had a brief engagement with collage compositions in 1977–9 after reading Germain Greer's *The Female Eunuch*. The dozen or so photo-collages Sterling made in these years are all about this world of fetishized female bodies, the male look, and the determining role of machinery in the production of desire [*195*]. We get references to masturbation, food, consumption, and the objectification of sex – all located in easy suburban homes in which these conflicts bore most intensively upon women themselves. With the brief shooting-star of punk now in eclipse, overtly political graphics also made a brief return after 1979 with a series of anti-Thatcher images of some timeliness and force. During the first four years of her first parliament, she was pictured being viciously scythed by a hammer and sickle (David King, 1980), as the 'new' Queen Victoria calling for a return to hard work, duty and self-reliance (Peter Kennard, 1983), and as stealing the purse out of a shopper's basket (Cath Tate, 1982) [*194*], widely reproduced on posters, T-shirts, mugs and calendars.

95 **Linder Sterling** *Untitled Photomontage* 1977
'I had two piles of magazines, trashy men's stuff and trashy women's stuff...I was fascinated by the fact that as a woman I was supposed to be in both these worlds.' (Sterling)

opposite 194 **Gee Vaucher** *International Anthem 2 – Domestic Violence* 1979
Vaucher adapted her anarchic style to the covers of CRASS singles and LPs, where we see scenes of piety, social collapse, high culture and the Western consumer cycle, all interwoven.

96 **Cath Tate** *Prevent Street Crime* 1982
The title is a slogan devised by the London Metropolitan Police warning the public against street crime – at the same time as investment in inner-city infrastructure was being cut by Mrs Thatcher's government.

PREVENT STREET CRIME

Post-modernist Collage

The reader may be forgiven for thinking that such cases stray too far from the use of pasted materials in the drama of late modernist art. They may be right; yet my reading of the situation is that with the rapid seepage of montage techniques into popular graphics, fashion and comedy during the 1970s, an imperative was created to rethink the values and techniques of collage aesthetics within fine art itself. And indeed we find that alongside the swing to the political right at the start of the Reagan–Thatcher period came a market-led turn back to the production of good-sized and confidently made paintings and sculptures: but with the important difference that the definition of a *former* modernism was now becoming a significant preoccupation among theoretically aware painters, sculptors, photographic artists and critics. It is a shift of theoretical perspective that may be symbolized by the interval between two critical texts. The first, Peter Bürger's *Thëorie der Avant-Garde* of 1974, had confidently reached the conclusion that 'montage' (of which collage was for Bürger one important part) and 'avant-garde' were virtually synonymous term; that modern art derived its subversive and self-critical tendencies by jarring one context against another, by mixing contrary representational codes in order to corrupt or desublimate one or the other or both.[19] By the time of the book's translation into English a decade later, the American critic Fredric Jameson had begun to theorize a new category known as 'post-modernism' in terms which made Bürger's analysis look alarmingly out-of-date. In a talk at the Whitney Museum in the autumn of 1982, subsequently published as 'Post-Modernism and Consumer Society', Jameson located the break between high modernism and its post-modernist afterglow at the moment when high modernism and its aesthetics became established in the university curriculum, after which they were 'felt to be academic by a whole generation of poets, painters and musicians':

> Not only are Picasso and Joyce no longer weird and repulsive, they have become classics and look rather realistic to us. Meanwhile, there is very little in either the form or the content of contemporary art that contemporary society finds intolerable and scandalous. The most offensive form of this art – punk rock, say, or what is called sexually explicit material – are all taken in stride by society…. This means that even if contemporary art has all the same formal features as the older modernism, it has shifted its position fundamentally within our culture.[20]

In place of the 'underground' status enjoyed by modernism, post-modernism (he suggested) thrives on pastiche, parody, intertextuality, and the sudden onset of historical amnesia with respect to even the most recent social and political events. Jameson's position quite clearly implied that montage and collage could no longer command respect as the avant-garde's most audacious and flexible tool.

Post-modernism seemed to throw everything into doubt. Walter Benjamin had defended Brecht's epic theatre in his 'Author as Producer' essay on the basis that its structure obeyed the laws of 'the principle of interruption'; that montage in epic theatre allowed the play 'not to reproduce conditions, rather to disclose, to uncover them'.[21] Likewise the Marxist critic John Berger had defended Peter Kennard's political montages on the basis that they contribute to 'making the invisible visible…in disclosing what is being both deliberately and unconsciously hidden'.[22] Yet for most post-modernists the project of 'exposing the real' could no longer be sustained in the absence of a concept of 'the real' independent of language itself. The collapse of the former into the latter – with all its consequences – was just the case argued by Jean-François Lyotard's post-modernist 'report on knowledge' published in French in 1979 and in English translation in 1984. Contemporary existence, argued Lyotard in *The Postmodern Condition*, is characterized by a sort of constantly self-parodying consumer experience in which dislocation lies at the very core. In the age of consumer capitalism 'one listens to reggae, watches a Western, eats McDonalds food for lunch and local cuisine for dinner, wears Paris perfume in Tokyo and "retro" clothes in Hong Kong'. Capitalism in its later, post-industrial stages, de-realizes familiar objects, social roles and institutions, Lyotard says, to such a degree 'that so-called realistic representations can no longer evoke reality except as nostalgia or mockery'.[23] In a culture where eclecticism is the norm, in which reality has become a collage of logically and materially incompatible texts, it would seem to follow that collage *inside* the artwork would be reduced to merely mimicking the general cultural condition to which it now itself belonged.

The migration into the visual arts of literary critics and philosophers during this phase of enthusiasm for 'post-modernism' had a further effect in regard to older modernist assumptions about the author function – the artist or writer as a centred and organizing intelligence of the work. To expose the critical defects of this ancient humanist assumption was often claimed as the prime effect of painting projects by the New York painters David Salle and Julian Schnabel, or by the very different Sigmar Polke from Germany, in which a collage-like mixture of materials, images and styles produced mildly pleasant sensations of multiplicity, overlap, or sheer unorganized excess. For a while, high-profile artists across the international spectrum could be seen producing paintings in which quotation became elevated to the status of a principle. For example a typical painting by Salle in those years might comprise all or any of: a reproduction old-master painting, an unconventional pornographic image, fruit, cartoon characters, and patterns, many of them inverted. Style would jump abruptly from one image to the next: unrelatedness and ambiguity were systemic. Yet 'quotation' was hardly the word for Salle's method, given that quotation normally requires a background context of utterance against which to be recognized at all. On the contrary, Salle has been at pains to affirm that *nothing* is asserted by the elements in his paintings – except unrelatedness itself. Polke, to take perhaps the most celebrated case of an authorless artist working out of collage, produced during the 1970s some works of dazzling waywardness on surfaces as diverse as velvet, linoleum and leopard-skin as well as canvas before drifting off into playful mysticism as the 1980s wore on.[24]

The other brand of theory that came to bear heavily on the fine arts at the moment of post-modernism concerned film, and the aesthetics of the photograph. For artists already convinced that painting was a bankrupt tradition, the still or moving photo-image came to possess special phenomenological meanings in relation to the spectator as an active and gendered subject. If the question for the French film theorist Christian Metz was the nature of film spectatorship – its 'scopic regime' – in the light of Jacques Lacan's psychoanalytical framework of Symbolic, Imaginary, and Mirror Identification, then for the British feminist critic Laura Mulvey the question was the nature of pleasure in the scopophilic drive: more precisely the gendering of that pleasure vis-à-vis the interests and values of women. Both analyses were published in the journal *Screen* in 1975. Metz's 'The Imaginary Signifier' summarizes one of its arguments thus:

in order to understand the film (at all), I must perceive the photographed object as absent, its photograph as present, and the presence of this absence as signifying. The Imaginary of the cinema presupposes the Symbolic, for the spectator must first of all have known the primordial mirror. But as the latter instituted the ego very largely in the Imaginary, the second mirror of the screen, a symbolic apparatus, itself in turn depends upon reflection and lack.[25]

while Laura Mulvey's 'Visual Pleasure and Narrative Cinema' argued that:

the defining male gaze projects its phantasy on to the female figure who is styled

opposite, above 197 **David Salle** *Dusting Powders* 1986
'My work has absolutely nothing to do with popular culture. Not only does it have nothing to do with popular culture in any kind of didactic, deliberate way, it simply doesn't have popular culture on its mind.' (Salle)

198 **John Stezaker** *The Bridge I* 1981
In a series of film-still collages, Stezaker uses arches, bridges, entrances and other voids to camouflage the already artificial on-screen presences, meanwhile dramatizing them as literal absences.

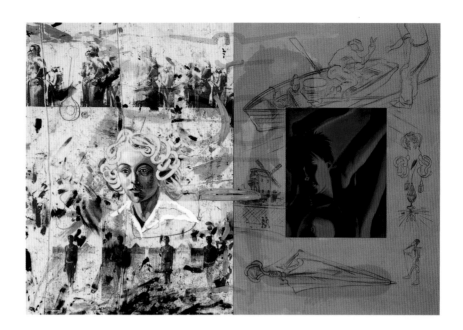

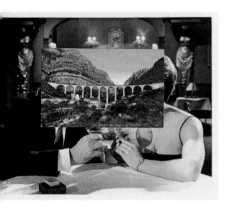

accordingly. In their traditional exhibitionist role women are simultaneously looked at and displayed, with their appearance coded for strong visual and erotic impact so that they can be said to connote *to-be-looked-at-ness*

About close-ups of bodily fragments such as legs (Dietrich) or face (Garbo), Mulvey suggests that they 'destroy Renaissance space, the illusion of depth demanded by the narrative; they give flatness, the quality of a cut-out or icon rather than verisimilitude, to the screen'.[26]

Such reflections were enough to mobilize a host of photographic exercises based upon the new analysis of the look and of the scopic drive(s); and nowhere more effectively than in the work of the most prolific European collagist of the last three decades, the London artist John Stezaker. In *The Voyeur* (1979) [*185*], large enough in format to present the characters at exactly life-size, we see these spectatorial paradoxes literalized through the physical excision of the male protagonist from the film still itself. Reduced in this way to occupancy of a static frame, the power of the male 'look' becomes if anything heightened by its literal absence from the image, or rather its replacement by the blank silhouette. In a further series based on stills from B-movies, we see Stezaker playing once more with the occlusion of the intra-filmic look, the on-screen interaction that normally mobilizes the film narrative and demands our various identifications. In placing a tacky tourist post-card of the Gorges du Loup over a moment of kitschy B-movie romance, Stezaker interrupts the action with a built structure (the viaduct) that renders bizarre the heads of the protagonists, and does so by recalling Max Ernst or the early Picabia. But he does something more, for he casts in image form the metaphor that the philosopher Max Black used to describe metaphor itself: 'a bridge between two worlds'.[27] In other *découpées* or collaged images Stezaker pays further respects to Magritte and Kolář's virtuosity with negative images, or to those varieties of Surrealism motivated by paranoid hallucination as the condition of the photograph *per se*.

Digital Structure

We come finally to the transfer of cut-and-paste methodologies from the studio to the computer screen. As long ago as the later 1960s and early 1970s researchers in California found ways of dividing the screen into extremely small pixels (short for 'picture elements') and associating each one with the computer's memory. When Stanford University researchers Douglas Englebart and Ivan Sutherland then invented the hand-held mouse, capable of isolating and dragging a given group of digitally defined pixels from one location in data-space to another, extraordinary new possibilities for image-processing were suddenly born. Opportunistically developed by Xerox and Apple Macintosh, those discoveries led rapidly to the now ubiquitous 'desktop' display with layered 'windows', providing electronic image-manipulation processes beyond our forefathers' wildest dreams.[28]

Has the Internet made collage more or less important as an instrument of contemporary aesthetic work? The arguments seem to diverge in puzzling and intriguing ways. On the one hand, my impression is that the French term 'collage' remains applicable only to those artworks prepared by literally cutting and pasting image-fragments, usually photographs, implying a *bricolage* attitude having much in common with older modernist projects by Picasso, Schwitters, Rauschenberg or Paolozzi. After all, we still resist describing as 'collage' a work that does not recombine actual physical surfaces by hand, eye and glue. On the other hand, pixels are in some sense obviously physical too, and it is absurd to deny that combinatory artworks made by computer manipulation can achieve an order of appearance very close to that of modernist collage. The evidence is that computer collage will proliferate just as long as 'cut' and 'paste' remain virtual instructions on virtual desktops, which artists can use to open virtual windows onto virtual image-data from any and every source. By this argument, computer collage is among the most persuasive (certainly the most ubiquitous) characters in the afterlife of modern art. The really difficult question is whether that afterlife marks the 'end' of modernist art, or a vivid new identity.

It can be both, presumably – and contemporary artists show a keen awareness of the paradox so generated (the reaction of painters to the birth of photography might be compared). It should be remembered that up until the end of the 1980s few visual artists had access to expensive computing equipment and several would have shunned it even if they were offered it. The sensational milieu around Damien Hirst in London in the 1980s and 1990s was reared on the radical effects of modernist collage: his early works come directly out of Schwitters (and with no apologies to the Hanover master). Sarah Lucas too has refused the materiality of the computer in her disrespectful collages of tabloid journalism, popular headlines, or sexual joking. Her early and scandalous *Soup* (1989) is made up of photographs of penis tips that collectively look like eyes, hence playing on the rich tradition of Surrealist experiment involving the displacement and repetition of body-parts, and the erotic mysteries of the gaze.

By that time, the first crude computer manipulations were already well under way. The earliest known commercial instance of a digitally altered photograph was the February 1982 cover of *National Geographic*, which had erased the distance between two Egyptian pyramids in order to make them appear more like clustered Alpine peaks: its significance lay in the break it seemed to announce with the *Geographic*'s reputation as a leading publisher of high-quality documentary images from exotic parts of the globe.[29] Soon after, the New York artist Nancy Burson was 'condensing' images of national leaders (Reagan, Brezhnev, Thatcher, Mitterand, Deng) or screen beauties (Hepburn, Kelly, Loren and Monroe) to produce composite faces that combined traces of them all, yet corresponded to none.[30] Their significance lay in the fact that the photograph as hard visual evidence now seemed compromised. Lacking negatives recording the imprint of light on photo-sensitive paper, how could the photographic print any longer be checked for its correspondence to 'the real'?

It took a set of new works by Austrian artist Valie Export to suggest how computers could create collage-effects without the need literally to cut photographs or paste their

opposite 200 **Valie Export** *Untitled, 12.4* 1989
In a radical feminist manifesto written in 1972, Export had urged that 'women must make use of all media as a means social struggle and social progress in order to free culture of male values.'

199 **Sarah Lucas** *Soup* 1989
Lucas's images and references are taken from tabloid newspapers and cheap magazines: 'I don't take pornograph as my subject, I take the acceptable stuff available at 25p: common currency rather than the deviant or the marginal.'

paper surfaces together. Export's 1989 computer-mixtures of architecture and anatomy show – in her words – 'female bodies in a duel with objects and architecture and sometimes with text: shoulders and arms are coded as skyscrapers, from cheeks stairs grow…the human face is made strange through an urban code'. In a continuation of her earlier performance works, Export says that self-representation and social representation qualify each other in images which show 'the trace of reality's menace, and the strength of its utopia.'[31] The effect is one of Baroque visual complexity transcending the style-language of later modernism as well as welcoming, rather than refusing, the new materiality of screen, mouse and pixel.

Already by the 1990s it was apparent that for many artists digitalization would become just another resource to be used alongside other techniques for manipulating and combining images. It comes as no surprise to find the octogenarian Robert Rauschenberg now combining digital scanning, re-photography, degrading by water spray and screen printing as sequential processes – of early twenty-first-century art. Referring to computer methods more obliquely, painters like Chris Finlay have carefully mimicked the distinctive colours of the digital palette and the graphic limitations of current imaging software, in paintings that examine the 'look' of digital imagery on a grand and imposing scale. Yet another kind of modernist temporalization is to be found in the acrylic-on-canvas paintings by the New York artist Joseph Nechvatal, whose 'computer-robotic assisted' paintings, acrylic on canvas, intermix flower or fruit ornaments with body-imagery (frequently sexual) into what might be termed a virally created collage – at the least, a hybrid between the biological and the technical, the viral and the actual: 'viractual' is the artist's chosen term. 'For me,' he writes, 'the hermaphroditic sign serves as an emblem of the variance that characterizes virtualism…where hierarchies are put into crisis by the digital, the hermaphrodite become the harbinger of new creative territories by flickering between static boundaries.'[32] His works are created, in the words of a recent account, 'by means of a virus-like program that performs a degradation and transformation of the image. After digitally composing and manipulating image elements, most notably through the transformations induced by the virus, [Nechvatal] transfers his files over the Internet to a remote computer-driven robot painting machine, which executes the painting.'[33]

An interest in doubling and hybrdity is also to be found in John Stezaker's recent works that employ a single, usually vertical cut that dissects a static image in two. In a series based on the naked human body, whose original photographs come from Edwardian magazines on posture, Stezaker splices male and female halves together to form an almost-unitary body that then generates perceptual and psychological confusion of a particular kind. Whereas high quality black-and-white photography has given the bodies in question a lustre and beauty entirely man-made, the artist's pictorial displacement triggers multiple questions about the binary structure of vision and about its epistemic objects: two eyes, two genders, two halves that (pictorially) deconstruct each other. The original paper collages are then enlarged digitally so as to restore the human scale.[34] Such examples point to the survival of the modernist impulse to borrow, plunder and rework on the level of the image the technical resources of the culture at large. Another kind of digitally produced collage requires a greater leap of faith: it requires us to abandon the cut, or the slice, or the edge, and reconcile ourselves to a fast-growing distance from the Cubist experiment where our story began. 'Morphing' of the image by applying algorithmic displacements to the tone, colour, shape and definition of a given pixel set is a tool not of modernist discontinuity but of illusion: we are familiar in the cinema with Tom Hanks (as the antihero *Forrest Gump*) shaking hands with JFK, or Keanu Reeves (Neo in *Matrix Reloaded*) wiping out three-hundred Agents without his sunglasses or hairstyle being disturbed.

In the static visual arts a technically similar kind of illusion was first produced in the early 1990s and has proliferated since. In the new photo-works of the German artist Kris

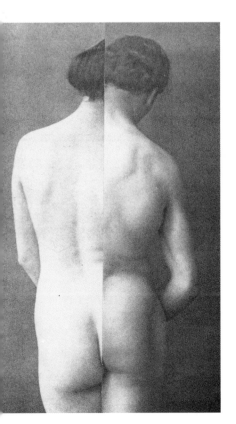

above 201 **John Stezaker** *Fall I* 1992
The puzzled eye attempts to restore both halves of the dissected images, only to confront the paradox of the impossibility of the task – in cognition's own peculiar 'fall'.

Scholz – for example in his *Corina* (2001) – we see a digitally adjusted photo of a woman posed in a Renaissance three-quarter length seated posture, against a background of a blurred landscape. Scholz, who is from the Düsseldorf photography school of Bernd Becher, here places speed and stability in perplexing (because impossible) conjunction, as in collage: in practice the sitter has been carefully excised using an electronic light-table in which her digitalized image is displayed.[35] And digitalized collage-effects are enjoying prominence across the globe. Works such as Taiwanese artist Chieh-Jen Chen's *Rebirth I* (2000), in which diseased citizens lie abandoned in a public subway or hospital corridor suggest whole populations alienated from the very technologies that were invented to sustain them. Given Chen's background as a performance artist in the period of Taiwanese martial law, his daring photo-pieces are nothing other than metaphors of disability and stagnation in a time of torture and political repression. The appearance of a dystopian scene struggles against the viewer's awareness that the entire work is in fact artificially staged and digitally processed. *Refusing* to suspend disbelief may become an attitude necessary to the comprehension of a digital image as art.

The relation to modernist art is stretched still further when we come to work made entirely in data-space and intended to be viewed not in a gallery, but on a screen. Here, operations such as on-screen 'mapping' raise interesting questions about the very territory that is being charted – as well as the medium in which this new cartography is being carried out. One feature of the new 'maps' is the movement of data as it layers, coalesces and self-modifies in a more or less ceaseless flow. In the digital world, says a recent expert, 'the spaces that are being mapped can range from computer networks and the Internet itself, as one vast communication territory, to a specific database and data set, or the process of networked communication',[36] allowing the digital artist to transcend the conventional ways that information is organized and allowing the user to experience the Internet in new and potentially radical ways. Given the new languages of the computer age, it is not surprising that projects such as the British group I/O/D's *WebStalker*, Andruid Kerne's *Collage Machine*, or Mark Napier's *Riot* all reach for terminology that refers back to familiar operations in the visual field. The latter project, for example, is a cross-content Web browser that blends different websites, for example those of CNN, the BBC, and Microsoft, and by collapsing domains and web-pages offers an experience of the Internet relatively free of institutional boundaries and corporate control.

Does *Riot* belong to modern art, or somewhere beyond it? While its first split-second appearance is on-screen, its printed reproduction at the end of this book suggests similarities with collage of a far older kind. In the end, such works point both backwards and forwards. Whereas cut-and-pasted paper in the Cubist revolution of a century ago corresponds to the paper-rich environment of advertisements and newsprint of that time, computer-generated collages of the recent past have absorbed the newest technology while keeping alive the paradoxes of vision and representation – the cognitive cord that binds the viewer to the world and the world to the viewer – upon which modernism in the visual arts has always been based. In the arc that stretches from the 1960s to the twenty-first century, the critical and formal conditions of collage may have changed utterly. The challenge presented by the digital age is whether collage in any of its older senses of displacement and rupture will find other ways of continuity, but by other means.

202 **Kris Scholz** *Corina* 2001
Placing his sitters in front of landscapes of which they are no visibly aware, Scholz recalls the paintings of Piero della Francesca – and of a longer European tradition – by photographic means.

203 **Mark Napier** *Riot* 2001
The flickering noticeboard of the screen is always in motion, never still – a collage effect in which words and images ceaselessly shift and flow.

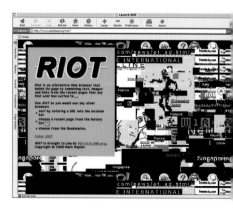

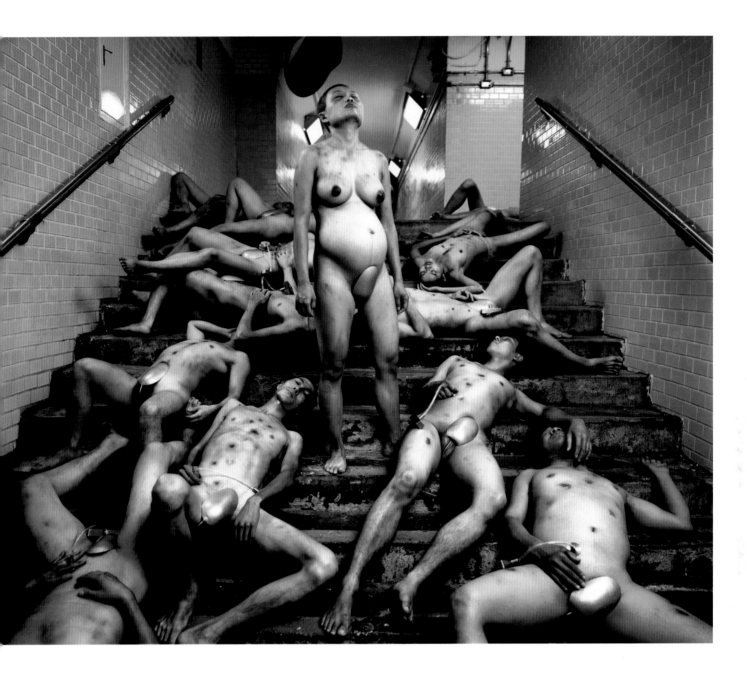

04 **Chieh-Jen Chen** *Rebirth I* 2000

l of Chen's works show the body in conditions of extremity
r duress. Reflecting the dissolution and reconstruction of his
ountry in recent years, his digitalized colour images function
powerful social metaphors during a time of rapid change.

NOTES

References for quotes in captions follow main notes for each chapter, by illustration number.

Introduction pp. 7–9

1 G. Apollinaire, 'Picasso et les papiers collés', *Montjoie*, Paris, 14 March 1913. From Breunig (ed.), *Apollinaire on Art: Essays and Reviews 1902–18*, New York, 1972; reprinted in G. Schiff (ed.), *Picasso in Perspective*, Prentice-Hall, 1976, p. 50.
2 See successively *Larousse: Grand Dictionnaire Universèl du XIX Siècle*, *Larousse Du XX Siècle*, Paris, 1929, up to *Grand Larousse Encyclopédique en 10 Volumes*, Paris, 1960.
3 J. Golding, *Cubism: A History and an Analysis 1910–1914*, London, 1959, p. 106.
4 Apollinaire, 'Picasso et les papiers collés', in G. Schiff (ed.), *Picasso in Perspective*, Prentice Hall, 1976, pp. 50–2.

Chapter 1: Inventing Collage pp. 11–23

1 Stein, *Picasso*, p. 26.
2 Gilot and Lake, *Life with Picasso*, p. 76.
3 Assumed in much of the literature to date from October 1911, Richardson argues convincingly that it dates from the spring. See Rubin, *Picasso and Braque*, p. 24 and n. 35, p. 56; and Richardson's correction, *A Life of Picasso*, pp. 190–2.
4 Richardson, *Georges Braque*, p. 26.
5 Picasso to Braque, 25 July 1911; J. Cousins, 'Documentary Chronology', pp. 375–6; Richardson, *A Life of Picasso*, pp. 183–4.
6 Richardson, *Life of Picasso*, p. 187.
7 The work is titled *Cubist Still-Life: Apple*, in Baldassari, *Picasso*, p. 61, fig. 65.
8 See Richardson, *Life of Picasso*, chs 14, 15.
9 Picasso, letter to Kahnweiler, 12 June 1912; Monod-Fontaine, *Daniel Henry Kahnweiler*, p. 110, Richardson, *A Life of Picasso*, p. 225.
10 Rubin, *Picasso in MOMA*, pp. 72, 206.
11 Daix, *Dictionnaire Picasso*, p. 130.
12 Picasso to Kahnweiler, 12 June 1912; Cousins, 'Documentary Chronology', pp. 394–5; Richardson, *A Life of Picasso*, pp. 236–7.
13 Gilot and Lake, *Life with Picasso*, pp. 76–7; Richardson, *A Life of Picasso*, pp. 245–6.
14 Vallier, 'Braque; La Peinture et Nous', p. 14.
15 This also proves to a characteristic of avant-garde subcultures throughout the century. See D. Hebdige, *Sub-Culture: The Meaning of Style*, London, 1979.
16 Braque was also experimenting with 'paper sculptures' in the summer of 1912, on the evidence of his letter to Kahnweiler of 24 August; see J. Cousins, 'Documentary Chronology', p. 410; Richardson, *A Life of Picasso*, p. 252. But they were used to solve pictorial problems, and were all destroyed.
17 Braque to André Verdier; Rubin, *Pioneering Cubism*, p. 40; Richardson, *A Life of Picasso*, p. 249.
18 Daix also reports 'He was continuously aware of the possibility of cutting an image up or pasting something on top of it ... [he] would often tear up a drawing and then, if it was fixable, glue it back together'; P. Daix, in 'Discussion' in Rubin, *Picasso and Braque: A Symposium*, pp. 76–7.
19 Picasso to Braque, 9 October 1912; Cousins, 'Documentary Chronology', p. 407; Richardson, *A Life of Picasso*, p. 250; reproduced in Monod-Fontaine, *Daniel-Henry Kahnweiler*, 1982, fig. 5, p. 40.
20 Poggi, *In Defiance of Painting*, p. 137.
21 Duncan Grant to Clive Bell, 26 Feb 1914; in R. Shone, *Bloomsbury Portraits*, London, 1993, p. 130; Richardson, *Life of Picasso*, p. 250.
22 On this kind of visual duplication, see Krauss, *The Picasso Papers*, pp. 159–71.
23 Leighten, *Re-Ordering the Universe*, p. 128.
24 Stein, *Picasso*, p. 26.
25 Cottington, *Cubism in the Shadow of War*, p. 140.
26 Weiss, *The Popular Culture of Modern Art*, p. 36.
27 Stein says that 'later [Picasso] used to say quite often, paper lasts quite as well as paint and after all if it all ages together, why not' (Stein, *Picasso*, p. 22).
28 Severini, *Tutta la vita di un pitore*, I, pp. 174–5; Poggi, *In Defiance of Painting*, p. 171.
29 For Greenberg, see chapter 7, below. For J. T. Soby, see the catalogue *Juan Gris*, p. 35.
17 Picasso to Pierre Daix, reported in Daix, 'The chronology of proto-Cubism', in Rubin (ed.), *Picasso and Braque*, pp. 74-6

Chapter 2: Paths to Construction pp. 25–35

1 Y. Tugendhold, 'French Pictures in the Shchukin collection', *Apollon*, no. 1, St Petersburg, 1914; in McCully (ed.), *A Picasso Anthology*, p. 109.
2 Salmon, *L'Air de la Butte*, p. 82; J. Richardson, *A Life of Picasso*, II, New York, 1996, p. 256.
3 R. Krauss, in *The Picasso Papers*, London and New York, 1998, extends this semiotic analysis to the entirety of Picasso's production; see especially chapter 2, 'the Circulation of the Sign', pp. 25–88.
4 The suggestion is not fanciful. Picasso anticipated the subsequent life of these works with uncharacteristic pessimism: 'no one will see the picture, they will see the legend of the picture ... it makes no difference if the picture lasts or does not last'; see G. Stein, *Picasso*, Paris, 1938, p. 27.
5 I am indebted here to A. Baldassari, *Picasso: Working on Paper*, particularly pp. 74, 104–5.
6 The question is Elizabeth Cowling's; see her 'The fine art of cutting: Picasso's *papiers collés* and constructions in 1912–14', *Apollo*, vol. 142, no. 405, November 1995.
7 The group as a whole seems to devolve from attempts to portray Frank Burty Haviland: see in particular *Zervos*, XXVIII, nos 176, 216, 272 and 284, in addition to the Edinburgh collage reproducted here. The sequence has been recently published (though not as a group) in *Picasso, Dessins et papiers collés*, pp. 162, 209, 193, 211.
8 See Chapter 5 of Paulhan, *La Peinture Cubiste*, pp. 109–34, and Picasso's acknowledgment of Paulhan's idea, in 'Discussion', in W. Rubin, *Picasso and Braque: A Symposium*, MOMA, New York, 1992, p. 76.
9 R. Krauss, 'Re-Presenting Picasso', *Art in America*, Dec. 1980, p. 96; and *The Picasso Papers*, London and New York, 1998, ch. 2.
10 Kahnweiler, preface to *Sculptures of Picasso*.
11 Y.-A. Bois, 'Kahnweiler's Lesson', in *Painting as Model*, Cambridge (Mass.) and London, 1990. This quotation, p. 74.
12 To Picasso's contention that the constructions were neither painting nor sculpture, just a 'guitar', André Salmon wrote 'And that's it. The watertight barriers have been breached. Now we are delivered from Painting and Sculpture, themselves already liberated from the imbecile tyranny of genres. It's neither one thing nor the other. It's nothing. It's the guitar ... Art will at last be fused with life, now that we have at last ceased to make life fuse with art'. *La Jeune Sculpture Française*; J. Richardson, *A Life of Picasso*, vol. 2, New York, 1996, p. 254; Cowling and Golding, *Picasso: Sculptor/Painter*, p. 57.
13 N. Berdyaev, 'Picasso', in *Sofya*, no. 8, Moscow, 1914, pp. 57–8, 61–2; translation by P. S. Falla in McCully (ed.), *A Picasso Anthology*, pp. 111, 112.
14 Markov, *Manifesty i programmy*; in Janacek, *The Look of Russian Literature*, pp. 3, 87.
15 A section of Stapanian's translation runs: 'A conjurer/ hidden by clock-faces of a tower/ pulls rails/ from the maw of a tram/ We are conquered!/ Bathtubs/ Showers/ An elevator/ The bodice of a soul is unfastened/ ...' (lines 21–9).
16 The others are *Composition with Mona Lisa* (State Russian Museum, St Petersburg), *Reservist of the First Division* (MOMA, New York), *Englishman in Moscow* and *Aviator* (both Stedelijk, Amsterdam), all from 1914: the first of which employs collage.
17 According to Anna Leporskaya, as related to Andrei Nakov. See Nakov, *Kazimir Malevich*, p. 163.
18 'The First Pictorial/Painterly Relief Exhibition', 10–14 May 1914, in Tatlin's studio at Ostozhenka, p. 37.
19 V. Shklovsky, 'On *faktura* and counter-reliefs', *Zhizn isskustvo*, 20 October 1920; in Zhadova, *Tatlin*, pp. 341–2.
20 Shklovsky, *Sentimental Journey*, which reprises Sterne's anti-novel of the same title. Jean Cocteau would shortly defend Surrealist practices of poetry in terms that are practically identical to Shklovsky's – and he was certainly not familiar with Opoyaz. See J. Cocteau, 'Le Secret Professionel', in *Le Rappel a l'Ordre*, Paris, 1926.
21 V. Shklovsky, 'On *faktura* and counter-reliefs' [1920], in Zhadova, *Tatlin*, p. 342; also Erlich, *Russian Formalism*, p. 177.
22 R. Jakobson, 'The Path Towards Poetics', in Jakobson and Pomorska, *Dialogues*, p. 8.
23 ibid., p. 9.
24 K. Malevich, letter to Matiushin, 1916, in K. Pomorska, 'Afterword', in Jakobson and Pomorska, *Dialogues*, pp. 172–3.
25 To be more exact, it was the interplay between the visual and the verbal in Futurism that answered to Jakobson's tendency to think about language structurally. See R. Jakobson, 'Futurism' [1919], in *Selected Writings*, III, pp. 717–22
26 Khlebnikov would write of his own epic poem-drama *Zangesi* (produced by Tatlin in 1923) that it was less a narrative than a 'meta-story', one constructed out of 'autonomous fragments, each with its own God, its own faith, and its own status.... The unit of construction, the building block of the meta-story', wrote Khlebnikov, 'is itself a story.... It resembles a statue made of many-coloured blocks of different natures...carved out of the polychromatic blocks of the word, or different constructions'. See Khlebnikov, Introduction to *Zangesi* [1922], quoted in K. Pomorska, 'Afterword', in Jakobson and Pomorska, *Dialogues*, pp. 170–1.
27 R. Jakobson, 'Memoirs', in Jakobson and Pomorska, *Dialogues*, pp. 28–9. For Rubens, see the catalogue *Rubens: Drawing On Italy*.
28 Rodchenko, 'To the Artist-Proletarians', 11 April 1918, in Noever (ed.), *Rodchenko, Stepanova*, p. 118.
29 A. Rodchenko and V. Stepanova, 'From the Manifesto of the Suprematists and Non-Objectivists' [1919], written for *Nonobjective Art and Suprematism*, in Noever (ed.), *Rodchenko, Stepanova*, p. 122; 'Programme of the Working Group of Constructivists of InKhuK (known as the Productivist Manifesto), 1 April 1921, in Khan-Magomedov, *Rodchenko*, p. 290.
30 Stepanova, 'Notes from the Diary on the Preparation and Management of the 10th and 19th State Exhibitions', in Noever (ed.), *Rodchenko, Stepanova*, pp. 124–5.
31 V. Stepanova, 'From the Manifesto of the Suprematists and Non-Objectivists', in Noever (ed.), *Rodchenko, Stepanova*, p. 161; Janacek, *Look of Russian Literature*, p. 118.
32 A. Rodchenko, 'Line', in Noever (ed.), *Rodchenko, Stepanova*, p. 135.
33 'Programme of the Working Group of Constructivists of InKhuK' (also known as the Productivist Manifesto), 1 April 1921; versions given in Elliott (ed.) *Alexander Rodchenko*, p. 130, and Khan-Magomedov, *Rodchenko*, pp. 290–1.
34 At least according to Brik, *Erinnerungen an Majakowski*, p. 82.
35 The first part of the poem was published in *LEF*, no. 1, March 1923; a good fascisimile edition is V. Mayakovsky, *It*, Ars Nicholai, Berlin, 1994. The poetic implications of *lesenka* technique and Mayakovsky's debt to Bely are analysed in Janacek, *The Look of Russian Literature*, pp. 219–36.
36 According to Lodder, *Russian Constructivism*, pp. 186–8, and n. 44, p. 296.
37 The conflict between the antagonistic parts of Revolutionary Russian culture is a theme of my *Art and Literature under the Bolsheviks*.
38 I use both the translation of 'Fotomontazh', *LEF*, 4, 1924, given in Lodder, *Russian Constructivism*, pp. 186–7; and Phillips (ed.), *Photography in the Modern Era*, pp. 211–12
25 I. Kliun, 'Primitives of the 20th Century' (1915), in J. Bowlt (ed), *Russian Art of the Avant-Garde: Theory and Criticism 1902–1934*, 1976, pp. 137–8
27 Stepanova, 'Notes from the diary on the preparation and management of the 10th and 19th state exhibitions', p. 124

Chapter 3: Dada Dialectics pp. 37–49

1 Ball, *Flight out of Time*, p. 42.
2 T. Tzara, 'Zurich Chronicle 1915–1919', from Huelsenbeck (ed.), *The Dada Almanac*, pp. 18–21.
3 R. Jakobson, 'Dada' [1921], in *My Futurist Years*, New York, 1997, pp. 169, 172.
4 The multi-font version of H. Ball, 'Karawane' [Caravan], 1917, from Huelsenbeck's *Dada Almanach* [1920], is given in Huelsenbeck, *Dada Almanach* (pres. by H. Green), p. 61. Ball read it alou in the Waag Guild House, Zurich, 14 July 1916, wearing a shaman's costume.
5 H. Arp, *Moderne Wandteppiche, Stickereien, Malereien, Zeichnunges: Hans Arp, Adya von Rees-Dutilh, Otto van Rees*, exh. cat., Galerie Tanner, Zurich, 1915; in Arp, *Arp 1886–1966*, p. 285.
6 T. Tzara, 'Zurich Chronicle 1915–1919', in Motherwell (ed.), *Dada Painters and Poets* p. 235.
7 H. Arp, 'Dadaland', in Jean (ed.), *Arp on Arp*, p. 232.
8 Richter, *Dada: Art and Anti-Art*, p. 51.
9 G. Hugnet, 'The Dada Spirit in Painting', 1932 and 1934, in Motherwell (ed.), *Dada Painters and Poets*, p. 134.
10 H. Arp, 'Dadaland', in Jean (ed.), *Arp on Arp*, p. 232.
11 H. Arp, 'And So the Circle is Closed', in Jean (ed.), *Arp on Arp*, p. 245.
12 R. Huelsenbeck, 'First Dada Lecture in Germany' [1918], in Huelsenbeck (ed.), *Th Dada Almanac*, p. 113.
13 R. Hausmann, 'Synthetisches Cino der Malerei' [1918], in Riha (ed.), *Dada Berlin*, pp. 30–2.
14 R. Huelsenbeck, 'En Avant Dada', in Motherwell (ed.), *Dada Painters and Poets*, pp. 28, 29.
15 Richter, *Dada: Art and Arti-Art*, p. 116.
16 Grosz, cited in Richter, 'Photomontage', in *Dada: Art and Anti-Art*, p. 117.
17 Richter, *Dada: Art and Anti-Art*, p. 118.
18 R. Hausmann, 'New Painting and Photomontage' [1958], in Lippard (ed.), *Dadas on Art*, pp. 61–2.
19 Höch confirms that the official photographers of the Prussian army regiments pasted photos on to oleolithographed mounts showing uniforms, barracks, etc. 'Interview with Hanna Höch by Eduard Roditi', in Lippard, *Dada on Art*, p. 73.
20 Richter, *Dada: Art and Anti-Art*, p. 117.
21 See R. A. Sobieszek, 'Composite Imagery and the Origins of Photomontage, Part I', *Artforum*, New York, September 1978: Barbara Jones's introduction to Ouelette's *Fantasy Postcards*; or E. Milman, 'Photomontage, the Event, and Historicism in Foster (ed.), *"Event" Art and Art Events*.
22 W. Herzfelde, 'Zur Einführung', in Burchar *Erste Internationale Dada-Messe*, p. 2.
23 Burchard, *Erste Internationale Dada-Messe*
24 K. Schwitters, *Merz 4*, 1923, p. 48; Schwitters, *Literarisches Werk*, p. 148; Elderfield, *Kurt Schwitters*, p. 67.
25 K. Schwitters, 'Katalog' [1927], in Schwitters, *Literarisches Werk*, p. 76; Elderfield, *Kurt Schwitters*, p. 19.
26 K. Schwitters, 'Kurt Schwitters' [1930], in Schwitters, *Literarisches Werk*, p. 335; Elderfield, *Kurt Schwitters*, p. 12.
27 In barely decipherable letters lower down we read 'Unter diesen Gesichtspunkten sir die meisten letzten Streiks...' – 'From these points of view, most of the recent strikes are...'.
28 R. Cardinal, 'The Case of Kurt Schwitters', in Cardinal and Elsner (eds), *The Cultures c Collecting*, p. 73.
29 Schwitters' own account is to be found in *Sturmbilderbuch* [1920], in Schwitters, *Das Literarisches Werk*, pp. 82–4.
30 Baudelaire, 'The Painter of Modern Life' [1863], in R. Mayne (ed.), *The Painter of Modern Life*, London, 1964, p. 13.
31 Huelsenbeck, 'First Dada Manifesto', 12 April 1918, in Huelsenbeck, *Dada Almanac* (pres. M. Green), pp. 44–9.
32 This has not prevented the former term reappearing in titles such as Dietrich, *The Collages of Kurt Schwitters*.
33 K. Schwitters, 'Die Merzmalerei', *Der Sturm* July 1919, Berlin. Elderfield has argued tha the first collages (*Merzzeichnungen*) and assemblages (*Merzbilder*) can be traced to the Der Sturm idea of making poetry 'through the rapid juxtapositions and unfettered free associations of individual

word-units and short phrases which first affect the reader as units of evocative sound,' an emphasis, once more, on *speed*. As Schwitters said, '*Merzmalerei* aims at direct expression by shortening the interval between the intuition and realisation of the work of art'. (Schwitters, 'Die Merzmalerei' [1919]). Or as he wrote in a major anti-Huelsenbeck statement the following year, 'In poetry, words and sentences ... are torn from their former context, dissociated [*entformelt*] and brought into a new artistic context ... As word is played off against word in poetry, in Merz, factor is played off against factor, material against material' (Schwitters, 'Merz' [1920], in Motherwell (ed.), *Dada Painters and Poets*, p. 64). But then: 'I play off sense against nonsense. I prefer nonsense but that is a purely personal matter. I feel sorry for nonsense, because up to now it has so seldom been artistically molded. That is why I love nonsense' (ibid., p. 60). See Elderfield, *Kurt Schwitters*, p. 36.

4 According to Schwitters' son; see Dietrich, *Collages of Kurt Schwitters*, pp. 213, n 23.

5 On Schwitters' pasting methods, see Steinitz, *Kurt Schwitters*, as well as G. Noland, 'William Dole', *Art International*, vol. 23, no. 5, Summer, 1979, pp. 96, 112.

5 Some interest in semantic play can be observed among the incomplete word-fragments, hints of letters, jumbled fonts, and registers of scale. In the small work of 1919–20 called *Mai 191* one can read references to electrical- and metal-workers' strikes around the time of the government attack on the Bavarian Soviet: it is one of a handful of works that take the poster or placard format with its declarative type as providing a palimpsest of social disturbance.

7 K. Schwitters, 'Merz' [1920], in Motherwell (ed.), *Dada Painters and Poets*, pp. 62, 65.

8 From a review in *Berlin Börsen-Courier*, 13 April 1918; reported in C. Thater-Schultz (ed.), *Hannah Höch: Eine Lebenscollage*, vol. I: *1889–1920*, Berlin, 1989, pp. 367–8.

9 'Interview with Hannah Höch by Eduard Roditi' [1959], in Lippard (ed.), *Dadas on Art*, pp. 71–2.

0 This is Höch, 'Die stickende Frau' [The embroiding woman], in *Stickerei-und-Spitzen-Rundschau*, 20, 1–2, Oct.–Nov 1919. See the chronology by K. Makholm in *Photomontages of Hanna Höch*, pp. 185ff.

1 The dolls, now in the Berlinische Galerie, are illustrated in ibid., p. 66.

2 See 'The Dada Years' with notes by M. Makela, in ibid., this quote from p. 27, on which appears reproductions of all the original constituent sources of *Dada Rundschau*. For *Cut with the Kitchen Knife*, see G. D. Dech, *Schnitt mit dem Küchenmesser...*, Münster, 1981.

3 It was destroyed by Allied bombing in 1944.

4 Schwitters, 'Merz', in *Literarisches Werk*, p. 76

hapter 4: Legacies of the Dada Mind p. 51–65

Lomas, *The Haunted Self*.

Max Ernst to John Russell, cited in Camfield, *Max Ernst*, p. 35, n. 32.

Franz Baltz, letter to Werner Spies, 4 May 1920; cited by Spies, *Max Ernst*, p. 40.

Ernst, 'Art and Ability', *Volksgrund*, 30 October 1912; Spies, *Max Ernst*, p. 288.

Ernst, 'At the Obernier Museum', *Volksmund*, 11 December 1912; Spies, *Max Ernst*, p. 288.

For an attempted decoding of this group in terms of war and Eros, see L. Drerenthal, 'Max Ernst: Trois Tableaux d'amitie', *Les Cahiers du Musée National d'Art Moderne*, Paris, Spring 1990.

Ernst, *Ecritures*, p. 25; Camfield, *Max Ernst*, p. 41.

For further information on the *Bulletin D* show see Camfield, *Max Ernst*, p. 59 and n. 15, p. 333.

Baader's description is 'Germany's Greatness and Decline, or the Fantastic Life Story of Superdada', in R. Huelsenbeck (ed.), *The Dada Almanac* [Berlin 1920] (pres. M. Green), London, 1993, pp. 97–102.

0 G. Hugnet, 'The Dada Spirit in Painting', in Motherwell (ed.), *Dada Painters and Poets*, pp. 159–61.

1 Unsigned review, 'Der letzte Schrei', *Kölnische Volkszeiting*, 11 May 1920; Camfield, *Max Ernst*, p. 71.

12 This and a simlar group of works was shown (despite Ernst's hostility to Berlin) in the First International Dada Fair in June 1920.

13 Ernst, *Ecritures*, p. 42; Camfield, *Max Ernst*, p. 74.

14 From T. Tzara, 'Dada Manifesto 1918', *Dada 3*, 1918; in Tzara, *Seven Dada Manifestos and Lampisteries*, pp. 3–13.

15 Benjamin, *One-Way Street*, pp. 61–2.

16 Ernst, 'Au dela de la peinture', *Cahiers d'Art* (special Max Ernst issue), 1937. I have used the translations by Lippard (*Surrealists on Art*, pp. 118–40), and that of Tanning (*Max Ernst*, pp. 3–19), with my own.

17 Again I merge the Lippard and Tanning translations, with my own; from Ernst, 'Au dela de la peinture', *Cahiers d'Art*, 1937.

18 See L. Aragon, 'Max Ernst, Peintre des illusions', in *Ecrits sur l'art moderne*, Paris, 1981, p. 14; Camfield, *Max Ernst*, n. 100, p. 341.

19 Camfield, *Max Ernst*, p. 96.

20 Adamowicz, *Surrealist Collage in Text and Image*, p. 76.

21 W. Spies, *The Return of La Belle Jardinière, Max Ernst 1950–1970*, New York, 1971, pp. 42, 46.

22 Breton, Introduction to the Au Sans Pareil show, in Camfield, *Max Ernst*, p. 97.

23 'I sometimes maintain that we owe a brand of art to him that corresponds to the new conception of things advanced by Einstein', André Breton to André Derain, 3 October 1921, Spies, *Max Ernst*, p. 67.

24 D. Ades, 'Dada-Constructivism', in *Dada-Constructivism: The Janus Face of the Twenties*, exh. cat., Annely Juda Fine Art, 1984, pp. 33–5.

25 These phrases are from van Doesburg, *Principles of Neo-Plastic Art*, drafted in 1915 and published in Holland, 1919; from C. Harrison and P. Wood (eds), *Art in Theory 1900–2000: An Anthology of Changing Ideas* (new edn), London, 2002, pp. 281–4.

26 Van Doesburg had made Dada collages under the alter ego of I. K. Bonset in 1921.

27 T. van Doesburg, 'Beeldende Constructie-leer. Eerste deel: de Kleur', unpublished MS 1924–6, p. 12; cited in E. van Straaten, *Theo van Doesburg: Constructor of the New Life*, Kroller-Müller Museum, Otterlo, 1994, p. 46.

28 Editorial, 'What Constructivism Is', *Blok*, nos 6–7, 1924; in S. Bann (ed.), *The Tradition of Constructivism*, London, 1974, p. 106.

29 Szczuka and Clausen were both pioneers of photo-collage in their respective countries. For Szczuka's montages, see A. Stern, *Europa: A Poem* (illustrations and layout by Szczuka) [1929], London, 1962.

30 For an account, see K. Srp, 'Karel Teige in the Twenties', in Dluhosch and Švácha (eds), *Karel Teige*, p. 45.

31 Teige, 'Foto Kino Film', *Život*, no. 2, 1922–3, pp. 153–69; Srp in Dluhosch and Švácha (eds), *Karel Teige*, n. 19, p. 44.

32 See Nezval, 'Abeceda', *Disk*, no. 1, December 1923, pp. 3–4.

33 K. Teige, 'Poetism', originally published in *Host* 3, nos 9/10 July 1924, pp. 197–204; translated by A. Büchler, in Dluhosch and Švácha (eds), *Karel Teige*, pp. 66–7.

34 S. K. Neumann, 'Disk', *Proletkult*, vol. 3, no. 36, 5 December 1923, in *Stati a projevy* VI, 1922–9, Prague, 1976, pp. 224–6; cited in Levinger's 'Rejection and Acceptance of Teige', p. 114.

35 Teige, 'Poetism' in Dluhosch and Švácha (eds), *Karel Teige*, pp, 68, 69.

36 For example J. Kopta, 'Proletarian Art and Poetism' [Umeni proletarske a poetismum], *Přerod*, II, 15 August 1924, in Levinger, 'Rejection and Acceptance of Teige', p. 114.

37 Teige, 'Poetism' in Dluhosch and Švácha (eds), *Karel Teige*, pp. 68, 69. He would later add cooking, gardening and sport: See Teige, a second manifesto, 'Poetism', *ReD*, I, no. 9, June 1928; Levinger, 'Rejection and Acceptance of Teige', p. 115.

38 Teige, 'Poetism', in Dluhosch and Švácha (eds), *Karel Teige*, p. 69.

39 Teige and Seifert's experimental film librettoes *Mr Odysseus and Various Reports* of 1924 and *The Port* (Přístav) of 1925 build upon the romance associated with the railways, factories and bars, arrival and departure, and travel to new lands. Watteau's *Departure for Cythera* (1717) is in the Louvre, Paris, and was seen by Teige on his visit there in 1922, as well as being already symbolic within the ranks of the French and Czech avant-gardes. It is referred to again in Breton, *Nadja*, 1929, p. 108.

40 K. Schwitters, 'Merz' (1920), in Motherwell (ed.), *Dada Painters and Poets*, p. 59.

41 K. Schwitters, 'Holland Dada' [1923], in *Das Literarishces Werk*, vol. 5, pp. 133, 134; Elderfield, *Kurt Schwitters*, p. 88.

42 Schwitters' unwillingness to adopt what might appear to be mechanical principles of construction can also be seen in the beautiful *elika* collage of *c*. 1925: a work whose forms fall slowly from a grid-like pillar on the left towards more formless modes of organisation in the centre. Their clean, crisp edges and more visible figure-ground relationships betray (at the most) a cautious attraction to Constructivism.

57 K. Teige, 'Poetry for five senses' (1925), cited by S. Czekalski, 'The Postcards from Utopia', *Umění*, XLIII, 1995, p. 42

58 T. Tzara, in *Man Ray: Les Champs Délicieux*, Paris, 1922

Chapter 5: The Surrealist Years pp. 67–85

1 M. Ernst, 'Au dela de la peinture', in L. Lippard (ed.), *Surrealists on Art*, Princeton, 1970, p. 127; the Aragon passage is from 'La Peinture au défi'.

2 W. Spies, *Max Ernst: Collages*, pp. 113–15.

3 Breton, *First Manifesto of Surrealism*, from Breton, *Manifestos of Surrealism*; C. Harrison and P. Wood (eds), *Art in Theory 1900–2000: An Anthology of Changing Ideas* (new edn), London, 2002, p. 452. My emphasis.

4 Breton, 'Surrealism and Painting', from *Surrealism and Painting*, pp. 4–6. My emphasis.

5 Max Ernst, letter to Tzara, Oct. 1921; in W. Spies, *Max Ernst: Collages*, London, 1991, p. 272.

6 D. Tanning, in the translator's note to *Rêve d'Une Petite Fille Qui Voulait Entrer au Carmel*, New York, 1982, p. 5. On Ernst's archaism, see H. Foster, *Compulsive Beauty*, Cambridge (Mass.), 1995, pp. 174–82.

7 Breton, 'The exquisite corpse: its exultation' [1948], in Breton, *Surrealism and Painting*, pp. 288–90.

8 E. Tériade, 'Talking with Picasso. A few thoughts and reflections about the painter and the man', *L'Intransigéant*, Paris, 15 June 1932.

9 See again Chapter 1, n. 27, above.

10 A.Breton, 'Picasso dans son element', in *Minotaure*, 1–2, June 1933, translated in Breton, *Surrealism and Painting*, p. 109.

11 Both Lissitzky's *Tribune*, and a page from Rodchenko's *Pro Eto* series ('One More Cup of Tea') are illustrated in the Galerie Goemans catalogue, though not exhibited. The former, at any rate, looks forward to Aragon's defection from Surrealism, and his long and problematic flirtation with Politburo aesthetics in Russia throughout the 1930s.

12 L. Aragon, 'La Peinture au défi'. I have usesd the good translation in Hulten (ed.), *The Surrealists Look at Art*, pp. 47–72. This last quotation, pp. 54–5.

13 This speculation on the dry–liquid antithesis as an alternation in Dali's account of the feminine finds further support in another small collage made in 1929. A photograph of a work known as *Nu Féminine*, published in *Cahier de Belgique*, no. 4, April 1930 (the original is now lost) makes clear it was made of a real piece of bark that casts an undulating shadow-presence to its left.

14 See Gibson, *The Shameful Life of Salvador Dali*, p. 231.

15 ibid., pp. 207–8.

16 M. Ernst, *Oeuvres de 1919 à 1936*, Paris, 1937, p. 42.

17 The *papier collés* are cat. nos 1599–1628 in Sylvester (ed.), *René Magritte*.

18 Aragon, 'La Peinture au défi', p. 68.

19 ibid., pp. 68–9.

20 Aragon pointedly refuses to believe those who traced collage to mass-culture, to the 'hoaxes, caricaturists and forgers' of previous centuries. He prefers to cite the name of Tzara's friend Jacques Vaché, who 'in 1916 made collages with scraps of cloth on postcards, editions of twelve which he sold for two francs each' – Aragon admits their location was unknown (ibid., p. 60).

21 Miró, letter to Leiris 10 Aug 1924, in *Selected Writings and Interviews* (ed. M. Rowell), London, 1992, pp. 86–7.

22 The effect has been called 'anamorphic' and compared to Breton's 'interval between sleeping and waking', by Katharine Conley, in 'Anamorphic Love: The Surrealist Poetry of Desire', in Mundy (ed.), *Surrealism: Desire Unbound*, pp. 101–24.

23 Miró's often-quoted desire to 'assasinate painting' in fact comes from the statement to Maurice Raynal, and published in Raynal's *Anthologie de la Peinture en France de 1906 à Nos Jours*, Paris, 1927.

24 This was in response to Miró's May 1928 exhibition at Galerie Georges Bernheim, Paris. The reviews just cited were in *Amic de les arts*, Barcelona, and by Waldemar George, in *Presse*, Paris, 16 May 1928; cited by Lanchner, *Joan Miró*, pp. 48–9.

25 Aragon, 'La Peinture au défi', p. 61.

26 The dates of the two Galerie Pierre shows are 7–14 March and 15–22 March respectively. See A. Umland, 'Joan Miro's *Collage* of Summer 1929: "La Peinture au défi"?', in Elderfield (ed.), *Essays on Assemblage*, pp. 42–77. This quote, p. 48.

27 Aragon, 'La Peinture au défi', p. 69.

28 G. Bataille, 'Joan Miró: Peintures Récentes', *Documents*, no. 7, 1930. The wider reach of Bataille's interest in modern painting's masochism is discussed in R. Krauss, 'Michel, Bataille et moi', in *October*, 68, Spring 1994, pp. 3–20, and Fer, *On Abstract Art*.

29 I am again indebted to Umland, this time from p. 52, and n. 52, p. 73. See the account of the raid by the two groups in Gibson, p. 270.

30 In fact there are two very beautiful relief-objects from 1930 and a group of little assemblage-objects from 1931, all of them attempts to launch new vocabularies of making and of being seen. See Lanchner, *Joan Miró*, cat. nos 91–3, 95–7.

31 Lanchner, *Joan Miró*, cat. nos 106–9 inclusive: the process has been discussed in Dupin, *Joan Miro: Life and Work*, pp. 252–5; Rubin, *Miro in the Collection of MOMA*, pp. 58–60.

32 He is writing in the present tense: Dupin, *Joan Miró: Life and Work*, pp. 252, 253.

33 ibid., p. 255.

34 The term is James Clifford's; see his 'On Ethnographic Surrealism', in *The Predicament of Culture: Twentieth Century Ethnography, Literature and Art*, chap. 4.

35 Hugnet was to become one of Surrealism's major historians (contributing essays to both the New York and London Surrealist shows of 1936). See also his *Pleins det Déliés*; *Dictionnaire du Dadaisme*; *L'Aventure Dada* (intro. by Tzara), Paris, 1957.

36 Hugnet, *Dictionnaire du Dadaisme*, p. 244.

37 See Srp, *Toyen*, pp. 34–46. Malkine's solo exhbtion was at the Galerie Surréaliste, Paris, January 1927.

38 Karel Teige would himself defend Artificialism in 1928 in the context of chastising the French Surrealists for leaping beyond consciousness for the sake of merely 'literary' conceits – that most damaging of accusations. See K. Teige, 'Ultra fialovéobrazy čili artificielismus' [Ultraviolet paintings or artificialism], *ReD*, I, Prague, 1927–8, pp. 315–17, and also 'Abstraktivismus, nadrealismus, artificielismus' [Abstraction, Surrealism, Artificialism], *Kmen*, 2, Prague, 1928, pp. 12–13; cited by Bydžovska, 'The Avant-Garde Ideal of Poiēsis: Poetism and Artificialism During the Late 1920s', in Dluhosch and Švácha (eds), *Karel Teige*, pp. 52, 54.

39 Srp, *Toyen*, p. 53.

40 See Bydžovska, in Dluhosch and Švácha (eds), *Karel Teige*, p. 59.

41 In *ReD* I, 1927–8, no. 6, March 1928, pp. 217–18; see also the statement by Štyrský and Toyen, 'Artificialism', in *ReD*, I, 1927/8, pp. 28–9.

42 The quoted phrase is from Teige, 'Manifest Poetismu' [Poetist Manifesto], *ReD*, I,

1927–8, no. 9, p. 325. I am indebted here to Bydžovska, 'The Avant-Garde Ideal of Poiēsis', in Dluhosch and Švácha (eds), *Karel Teige*, in which this citation appears).

43 J. Mundy, 'Surrealism in Prague', in Mundy (ed.), *Surrealism: Desire Unbound*, p. 239.

44 *Emilie Comes To Me In A Dream* was reissued in translation by the Ubu Gallery, New York, 1993.

45 K. Teige, 'The Tasks of Modern Photography' [1931], in C. Phillips (ed.), *Photography in the Modern Era: European Documents and Critical Writings 1913–1940*, New York, 1989, pp. 319, 321.

46 Their visit was the occasion of Breton's lecture 'The Surrealist situation of the Object', in Hulten (ed.), *The Surrealists Look at Art*, pp. 159–87.

47 K.Teige, 'O fotomontáži', *Žijeme*, no. 6, October 1932, pp. 173–5. My emphases. In Srp, 'The reality of desire: Karel Teige and Collage', in *Karel Teige*, pp. 6–7.

48 In a montage called *No. 129* of 1940, the left-hand figure shows a sharp metal hinge where the softness of the breasts should be, while the right-hand figure is a graphically aggressive *vagina dentata* on four legs, sitting menacingly on top of what seems to be a bread-basket.

49 Teige looks forward to a feature of desire that Roland Barthes would later spot in the readerly relation to the text: the *frisson* generated by the gap, by discontinuity, by the interval *per se*. See Barthes, 'The Third Meaning' in *Image-Music-Text*, London, 1977.

50 K. Teige, *Film*, Prague, 1925, p. 112; Srp, 'The Reality of desire', in *Karel Teige*, p. 6.

51 K. Teige, 'Basen, svet, clovek', *Zverokruh*, I, November 1930, pp. 9–15; Srp, 'The Reality of desire', in *Karel Teige*, pp. 8, 26.

52 ibid., p. 26.

53 Apart from work for book-covers, the only collages to be shown were in 'Le Surréalisme en 1947' in Paris. A larger number were then brought to light during the political 'thaw' of the 1960s, first in 'Karel Teige: surrealisticke koláže', Grafický Kabinet domu umění, Brno, 1966, and Gallerie Vincent Kramář, Prague, 1966: a few were reproduced in *Opus International*, 19/20, November 1980, and in *Cahiers du Musee National d'Art Moderne*, no. 10, Paris, 1982. See Císarová, 'Surrealism and Functionalism'.

54 Teige published *Surrealism proti proudu* [Surrealism against the current], Prague, 1938. Nezval lost his nerve and placed his poetry at the service of the Party. See Císarová, 'Surrealism and Functionalism', p. 81.

55 V. Effenberger et al., *Výbor z díla*, 3 vols, Prague, 1966 ff; Císařová, 'Surrealism and Functionalism'. Those were also the years of Teige's research for a major theoretical text given the working title *The Phenomenology of Modern Art* (this was never published). Hew also gave collages to members of the Ra group: Puchmertl, Lorenc, Istler, Zykmund.

56 Penrose, *Scrapbook*, p. 245.

57 H. Read, 'Introduction', *The International Surrealist Exhibition*, p. 13.

58 Nash had written of Swanage as a place 'of such extreme ugliness architecturally that its inhabitants instinctively look out to sea'. Nash, 'Swanage, Or Seaside Surrealism', *Architectural Review*, April 1936; reprinted in Nash, *Outline*, pp. 323–7; these quotations, pp. 234, 237.

59 R. Magritte and P. Nougé, 'Colour – colours: Or An Experiment by Roland Penrose', first published in *London Bulletin*, no. 17, 15 June 1939, pp. 9–12; reprinted in *Roland Penrose, Lee Miller*, pp. 65–6.

60 It should be recorded that Penrose acquired from André Breton Picasso's triangular pasted-paper *Head* (1913) [DR 595] in the same year that he began his own collages. Clearly Penrose, who would become one of Picasso's best biographers, found the work sealed an affinity between him and his (by that time) legendary subject.

61 See Rémy, *Surrealism in Britain*.

62 The poet David Gascoyne made derivative collages, in his case after Max Ernst. The slightly younger Conroy Maddox published an important statement on 'The Object in Surrealism' in the *London Bulletin* in 1940 (illustrating Agar's *Object Lesson* for good measure). Maddox's post-war collages contain a conventional binary structure which generate a single, animating contradiction; but he lacked the obsessive search for the bizarre achieved by (say) Max Ernst or Dalí.

85 P. Nash, 'Swanage, Or Seaside Surrealism', *Architectural Review*, April 1936

88 R. Magritte and P. Nougé, 'Colour-colours: Or An Experiment by Roland Penrose'

Chapter 6: The Political and the Personal
pp. 87–101

1 Benjamin, *One-Way Street*, p. 62.

2 G. Klutsis, 'Fotomontazh', *LEF*, 4, 1924, pp. 43–4.

3 V. Stepanova, 'Fotomontage' [1928], not published until *Fotografie*, Prague, 3, 1973, pp. 18–19; in Phillips (ed.), *Photography in the Modern Era*, pp. 235–6.

4 A. Rodchenko, 'Against the Synthetic Portrait, for the Monumental Snapshot', *Novyi Lef*, 4, 1928; Phillips (ed.), *Photography in the Modern Era*, pp. 238–42.

5 These included 'Road to Victory' (organized by Edward Steichen and designed by Bayer), Museum of Modern Art, New York, 1942.

6 R. Hausmann, 'Fotomontage', in *a bis z*, Cologne, May 1931; in Phillips (ed.), *Photography in the Modern Era*, pp. 179, 180.

7 A. Kemény (durus), 'Fotomontage, Fotogram', *Der Arbeiter-Fotograf*, 5, no. 7, 1931; in Phillips (ed.), *Photography in the Modern Era*, pp. 182–5; this citation pp. 183–4.

8 See O. Nerlinger, 'Die Zeitgemässen – Eine Kunstlergruppe', in *Alice Nerlinger-Lex: Oskar Nerlinger*, Catalogue, Hanover, 1982

9 A. Fedorov-Davydov, 'Kämpferische Kunst: John Heartfield, ein proletarischer Künstler', *Brigada khudozhnikov*, 1, 1932; from the detailed account given in H. Gassner, 'Heartfield's Moscow Apprenticeship 1931–1932', in Pachnicke and Honnef (eds), *John Heartfield*, pp. 256–90; this quotation from pp. 273–4.

10 The tortuous route to this 'decision' can be traced in my *Art and Literature Under the Bolsheviks*, vol. 2, London, 1992.

11 See *Asthetik und Kommunikation*, no. 10, January 1973; cited by D. Evans,'John Heartfield', in his *John Heartfield: AIZ/VI 1930–38*, to which I am indebted.

12 L. Aragon, 'John Heartfield et la beauté révolutionnaire', *Commune*, no. 20, April 1935; in Phillips (ed.), *Photography in the Modern Era*, pp. 62–5. In fact this was not Lenin's position in reality, but only according to Socialist Realist theory.

13 See S. Stein's '"Good Fences make Good Neighbours": American Resistance to Photomontage Between the Wars', in Teitelbaum (ed.), *Montage in Modern Life*, p. 135. The Photo-League's 'Workers of the World Unite!' is reproduced in M. Lincoln Schuster (ed.), *Eyes On the World: A Photographic Record of History-In-The-Making*, New York, 1935, pp. 24–5.

14 The charts were devised by members of the so-called Formal Theoretical Department in InKhuK, headed by Malevich but including Vera Ermolaeva, A. Yudin, Anna Leporskaya, and Konstantin Rozhdestvensky. They are in the collection of Stedelijk Musum Amsterdam (17 panels) and the Museum of Modern Art, New York (5 panels).

15 See Gombrich, *Aby Warburg*, pp. 283 ff. For the pagan and the modern in Warburg, see C. Schoell-Glass, '"Series Issues": the last-numbered plates of Warburg's picture atlas Mnemosyne', in R. Woodfield (ed.), *Art History as Cultural History: Warburg's Projects*, Amsterdam, 2001, pp. 183–208. The panels are in the collection of the Warburg Institute, London.

16 Höch and her circle were close devotees of the Marxist Ernst Bloch, who in his theoretical writing advocated a montage aesthetics to achieve an 'illuminated' perception of how a humane, utopian society might be imagined: Bloch's chosen word was *Staunen*, meaning 'intended to startle us in mysterious and mystical ways; wonderment, astonishment': it applies to Höch's collage-book as well as to her collages of the period. The most complete account of the book, now in the Berlinische Galerie, is Lavin, *Cut With the Kitchen Knife*.

17 H. Höch, as cited in 'Interview with Hannah Höch', in E. Roditi, *Dialogues: Conversations with European Artists at Mid-Century*, San Francisco, 1990.

18 To these illustrations was attached a passage from the Expressionist magazine *Die Aktion* for 1915: 'We act as if we were painters, poets or whatever, but what we are is simply and ecstatically impudent. In our impudence we take the world for a ride and train snobs to lick our boots, *parce que c'est notre plaisir*' – it comes from a frenzied manifesto by A[nton?] Undo and no doubt served to underline why Nazi culture could not have embraced Expressionism as a German national style.

19 See P. Chametzky, 'Marginal Comments, Oppositional Work: Willi Baumeister's confrontation with Nazi Art', from Chametzky, *Willi Baumeister*, pp. 251ff.

20 See Lehmann-Haupt, *Art Under a Dictatorship*, p. 87.

21 P. Nash, 'Swanage, Or Seaside Surrealism', *Architectural Review*, April 1936; P. Nash, *Outline*, London, 1944, p. 233.

97 Warburg, 'Introduction to Mnemosyne Atlas', Warburg Archive No. 102.1.1, 6

Chapter 7: New York Conversations
pp. 103–17

1 Guggenheim, *Out of this Century*, p. 27.

2 Guggenheim's London gallery was titled mischievously to evoke the name 'Bernhein-Jeune' from Paris, while also giving the misleading impression that Peggy was daughter of Solomon.

3 The catalogue is reproduced in Rudenstine (ed.), *Peggy Guggenheim Collection*, p. 754.

4 The exceptions prove the rule: collage techniques were tried by Stuart Davis, Arthur Dove, Charles Demuth (see the latter's *I Saw The Figure 5*, 1928), and in prose technique by J. Dos Passos, *Manhattan Transfer* (1925). For photomontage in America see again S. Stein, '"Good fences make good neighbours": American Resistance to Photomontage between the wars', in Teitelbaum (ed.), *Montage in Modern Life*.

5 The architect F. J. Kiesler to PG, 7 March 1942, in Rudenstine, *Peggy Guggenheim Collection*, p. 763, cited in Vail, *Peggy Guggenheim*, p. 55.

6 Phillips, *Frederick Kiesler*, p. 114.

7 C. Greenberg, 'Review of a Joint Exhibition of Joseph Cornell and Laurence Vail', *The Nation*, 26 December 1942. Greenberg ended: 'An infinite prospect lies ahead. Vail could put his collage around an equestrian statue ... Cornell could construct landscapes ten feet square inside his boxes. I am in dead earnest'. O'Brian (ed.), *Clement Greenberg*, vol. III, p. 132.

8 'Chronology', in *Robert Motherwell* (1965 exh. cat.), p. 74.

9 F. O'Hara, 'Introduction', in *Robert Motherwell* (1965 exh. cat.), p. 10.

10 The first work Baziotes ever sold, according to its first owner Mrs Saidie A. May.

11 Potter, *To a Violent Grave*, p. 71. According to another piece of Motherwell testimony, 'Pollock became more and more tense and vehement, as he tore up papers, pasted them down, even burned their edges, splashed paint over everything, quite literally like somebody in a state of trance', in H. Wescher, *Collage*, 1968, pp. 299–300.

12 Other names were Herbert Bayer, Cornell, Calder, Suzy Frelinghysen, Gris, Picabia, George L. K. Morris, Henri Laurens, Boris Margo, A. E. Gallatin, Mina Loy, Arp, Miró, Reinhardt, Gerry Kamarowski, Balcolm Greene, Jacqueline Lamba, Bolotowsky, Benno, Barbara Reis, Andre Racz, Suzy Hare, David Hare and Duchamp. See Rudenstine, *The Peggy Guggenheim Collection*, p. 774.

13 R. Motherwell, 'Beyond the Aesthetic', *Design*, April 1946; reprinted in *Robert Motherwell* (1965), p. 37.

14 J. Flam, 'With Robert Motherwell', *Robert Motherwell* (1965), p. 16.

15 Motherwell, 'Beyond the Aesthetic', in *Robert Motherwell* (1965), pp. 38, 37.

16 See *Robert Motherwell* (text by H. H. Arnason), New York, 1977, p. 98.

17 The *Jazz* cut-outs were conceived as desigr for stencil prints (*pouchoirs*) to be looked a in book form: they were published by Tériade in 1949. For Greenberg's reaction t the show 'Paintings, Papiers Coupés, Drawings 1945–8', at the Pierre Matisse Gallery, February 1949, see 'Review of An Exhibition of Henri Matisse', *The Nation*, 5 March 1949, O'Brian (ed.), *Clement Greenberg*, vol. II, p. 293.

18 Greenberg, *Joan Miró*, p. 26.

19 ibid., p. 33.

20 C. Greenberg, 'Review of an Exhibition of Joan Miro', *The Nation*, 7 June 1947, in O'Brian (ed.), *Clement Greenberg*, vol. II, pp. 153–4.

21 These are *Cut-Out Figure* (1948, oil on paper mounted on masonite, Private Collection Canada); and *Untitled* (1948, oil on canvas on paper mounted on board, Private Collection).

22 Fried was talking primarily about *Cut-Out* (1948); see *Three American Painters*, pp. 17–18.

23 C. Greenberg, 'Review of Exhibitions of Alberto Giacometti and Kurt Schwitters', *The Nation*, 7 February 1948, in O'Brian, *Clement Greenberg*, vol. II, p. 208.

24 Press release, 'Large Retrospective Exhibitio of Collages by Modern Europeans and Americans', MOMA, undated by Septembe 1948. There was no catalogue.

25 Margaret Miller, quotation in ibid.

26 C. Greenberg, 'Review of the Exhibition *Collage*', *The Nation*, 27 November 1948; i O'Brian (ed.), *Clement Greenberg*, vol. I, pp 260, 263.

27 C. Greenberg, 'The Present Prospects of American Painting and Sculpture', *Horizon*, October 1947, O'Brian (ed.), *Clement Greenberg*, p. 167.

28 C. Greenberg, 'Review of the Exhibition "Collage"', O'Brian (ed.), *Clement Greenberg*, vol. I, pp. 260–1.

29 ibid.

30 C. Greenberg, 'The New Sculpture', *Partisa Review*, June 1949; O'Brian, *Clement Greenberg*, vol. I, pp. 316–19.

31 C. Greenberg, 'Review of the Exhibition "Collage"', O'Brian (ed.), *Clement Greenberg*, vol. I, p. 260.

32 ibid., p. 262.

33 See Chapter 8 below, and especially n. 20.

34 Clark, *Farewell to an Idea*, p. 344.

35 J. Myers, 'Naming Pictures: Conversations between Lee Krasner and John Bemond Myers', *Artforum*, 23, Nov. 1984, p. 72.

36 The paintings were linked to Mondrian by Barbara Rose (*Krasner*, p. 72); to Irene Rice Pereira by Wagner (*Three Artists*, p. 166–7), and, most plausibly, to Krasner's friend and neighbour Giorgio Cavallon, by Landau (*Lee Krasner: Catalogue Raisonnée*, p. 123).

37 In fact Ashbery misquotes Gerturde Stein here. She had said through Alice Toklas tha 'Americans are like Spaniards, they are abstract and cruel. They are not brutal they are cruel': she is speaking about the origins of cubism in ritual. See Stein, *Autobiography of Alice B. Toklas*, p. 100. For Ashbery, see his 'A Place for Everything', *Art News*, March 1970, in the catalogue *Ann Ryan: Collages*, Washburn Gallery, New York, 1985.

38 C. Nemser, *Art Talk: Conversations with 12 Women Artists*, New York, 1975, pp. 93–4; Wagner, *Three Artists*, p. 172.

39 These are Landau, *Lee Krasner: Catalogue Raisonée*, 290–4 inclusive.

40 Reported by B. Robertson, 'Krasner's Collages' in *Lee Krasner: Collages*.

41 ibid.

42 Wagner, *Three Artists*, pp. 172–3.

43 B. Robertson, 'Krasner's Collages' in *Lee Krasner: Collages*.

44 A. Kaprow, 'A Statement' in Kirby, *Happenings*, pp. 44–5.

45 For Kaprow's argument that Pollock's freedom of movement and unorthodox materials led directly to Happenings, see his article 'The Legacy of Jackson Pollock', *Art News*, October, New York, 1958.

103 R. Motherwell, 'Beyond the Aesthetic' (1946), in *Robert Motherwell* (1965), p. 37

114 R. Ashbery, 'A place for everything'

apter 8: California Collage pp. 119–29

'Elmer Bischoff interviewed by Paul Kartshorn', 1977, Archives of American Art [AAA], p. 25, cited in Candida Smith, *Utopia and Dissent*, p. 88.

'Tape-recorded interview with Clay Spohn at his studio in Grand Street, New York', AAA, pp. 70–2; in Candida Smith, *Utopia and Dissent*, p. 111.

For these references and others, see R. Solnit, 'Heretical Constellations: Notes on California 1946–61', in *Beat Culture*, pp. 68–87.

Recollections of the photographer Charles Brittin interviewed by Sandra Starr in 1986, in *Lost and Found in California*, p. 73.

R. Duncan, 'The Homosexual in Society', New York, 1944; see Faas, *The Young Robert Duncan*, p. 150, cited by Watson, *Birth of the Beat Generation*, p. 201.

M. Auprey, 'An Interview with Jess', in Auprey, *Jess: A Grand Collage*, pp. 24–5.

ibid., p. 25.

ibid.

R. Creeley, 'On the Road: Notes on Artists and Poets 1950–1965', in *Poets of the Cities*, pp. 56, 58.

E-mail from Creeley to the author, 2003.

J. Clellan Holmes, 'This is the Beat Generation', *New York Times Magazine*, November 1952.

A. Ginsburg, in Plummer, *The Holy Goof*, p. 46; cited in Watson, *Birth of the Beat Generation*, p. 4.

The Beat film *Pull My Daisy* was made in six weeks and released in June 1959 (cinematogapher Robert Frank, narrator Jack Kerouac) to become a classic of American independent cinema.

Wally Hedrick interview no. 2, 1974, by Paul Karlstrom, AAA, pp. 7–10; cited by Candida Smith, *Utopia and Dissent*, pp. 202–3, and n. 53, p. 493.

This is *The Rose* (1958–1966, now in the collection of the Whitney Museum of American Art), which grew under added layers of plaster and paint to a weight of 2,300 pounds and had to be finally moved by cranes when DeFeo was evicted from her studio. The best account of the work and its history is B. Berkson, 'The Romance of the Rose', in *Jay DeFeo: Selected Works*, pp. 26–30.

The William Copley Gallery in Los Angeles had held a show of Max Ernst in 1948, as well as shows of work by Magritte, Tanguy, Cornell, Man Ray and Roberto Matta, all in the same year.

For *Semina*, see Candida Smith, *Utopia and Dissent*, pp. 232 ff.

See 'Bruce Conner: Interview with Mia Culpa', *Damage, 3*, Aug/Sept 1979, *Damage, 4*, January 1980; reprinted in Stiles and Selz (eds), *Theories and Documents*, pp. 326–33.

I am indebted to R. Solnit, 'Heretical Constellations: Notes on California 1946–61', in *Beat Culture*, pp. 71–2, and to the catalogue *2000 BC: The Bruce Conner Story Part II*.

C. Greenberg, 'The Pasted-Paper Revolution', *Art News*, September 1958; substantially rewritten to become 'Collage', *Art and Culture*, 1961.

Further north on the West Coast, Toni Onley and Al Neil in British Columbia made collage in the 1950s, largely unaware either of modern European art or the California assemblage movement. See Dikeakos, *The Collage Show*: including Dikeakos, Bill Bisselt, Gilles Foisy, Gary Lae-Nova, Michael Morris, Terry Reid, Jeff Wall and others.

Conner has described Mexican folk assemblages: 'I would go by an auto-repair garage and in the midst of greasy tools and objects on the wall would be a shrine to the Virgin of Guadalupe...right next to it might be a monkey wrench, and an electric light bulb, and plastic flowers, and a pinup of a half-naked girl. Pictures of family, souvenirs, all sorts of objects there', Boswell interview, 15 June 1983, in Boswell, 'Bruce Conner: Theatre of Light and Shadow', in *2000 BC: The Bruce Connor Story*, p. 44.

Both works aroused the ire of the top legal authority in Los Angeles, County Supervisor Warren Dorn, on the occasion of Kienholz's inaugural exhibition at the Los Angeles County Museum of Art in 1966. It was the occasion of Dorn's famous self-justification, 'My wife knows art, I know pornography'. See Candida Smith, *Utopia and Dissent*, pp. 318–29.

115 R. Creeley, 'On the road: notes on artists and poets 1950–1965', p. 56

116 C. Spohn, 'Tape recorded interview with Clay Spohn at his studio in Grant Street, New York'

119 'An Interview with Jess', in *Jess, A Grand Collage*, pp. 25–6

120 ibid., p. 25

Chapter 9: Later Surrealism pp. 131–43

1 *Les Prévert de Prévert: Collages*.

2 F. Woimant and A. Moeglin-Delcroix, 'Les Collages de Jacques Prévert', in *Les Prévert de Prévert: Collages*, p. 15.

3 P. Soupault, cited in *Bon Anniversaire Monsieur Bucaille*, p. 3.

4 Dubuffet wrote the preface for Chaissac's Galerie d'Arc en Ciel show, in which he positioned Chaissac as an 'outsider' about whom professional critics and academics would have nothing to say: 'There's practically nothing to Chaissac', Dubuffet wrote provocatively; 'there's practically nothing there. Thin pickings for the École de Paris critics ... I imagine our hot-shot art lecturers, art missionaries and weighty authorities – what can they say in front of a Chaissac? It's unthinkable ...', (a text that Chaissac would later describe as 'idiotic').

5 See S. Wilson, 'Gaston Chaissac: in situ', in *Gaston Chaissac: First London Exhibition*, pp. 5–9.

6 Chaissac, letter to Jean Paulhan, in Michaud, *Gaston Chaissac*, p. 136; Wilson, ibid., p. 7.

7 L. Alloway, 'Personal Statement', *Ark 19*, Spring 1957; reprinted in Robbins (ed.), *The Independent Group*, p. 165. See also Alloway's 'The Long Front of Culture', *Cambridge Opinion*, 17, 1959, as indicative of this continuity thesis.

8 Alison Smithson in conversation with Reyner Banham, n.d, recorded for *Fathers of Pop* but not used in the film; reprinted in Robbins (ed.), *The Independent Group*, p. 17.

9 R. Banham, 'Futurism for Keeps', *Arts Magazine*, 35, no. 3, December 1960, p. 33.

10 Minutes of the Meeting of the Sub-Committee on Lecture Policy and Programmes, 29 January 1952, p. 3, ICA Archives, London.

11 He told me he had to make his own (conversation with the author, 3 March 2000).

12 F. Whitford, 'Inside the Outsider', *Eduardo Paolozzi: Sculpture, Drawings, Collages and Graphics*, p. 14.

13 E. Paolozzi, 'Artificial Horizons and Eccentric Ladders', in *Eduardo Paolozzi: Artificial Horizons and Eccentric Ladders*, p. 11.

14 Henderson had met, among others, Duchamp on the occasion of his exhibition at Peggy Guggenheim's London gallery, of which Henderson's mother, Wyn, was for a time the manager.

15 See K. Hartley, 'Introduction', *Paolozzi*, p. 11.

16 A description of Roussel's method is available in Roussel, *Comment j'ai écrit certains de mes Livres*, a text which Paolozzi may have known.

17 E. Paolozzi, 'Artificial Horizons and Eccentric Ladders', in *Eduardo Paolozzi: Artificial Horizons and Eccentric Ladders*, p. 11.

18 The Krazy Kat Arkive is a sense-defying accumulation of some 20,000 comics, leaflets, magazines, objects, books of science-fiction, crime, encyclopaedias, mythology, space science, exploration, botany, technology, flying, electricity, wrestling, radiation, wildlife, monsters, travel, and sex. The objects run from an assortment of plastic ray-guns, aircraft kits, missile launchers (boxed), Noddy's car, space-rockets of all sizes and ambition, bombers, Donald the Demon, Dippy the Deep Diver, Manny the Reckless Mariner, Popeye, Batman, clockwork spacemen, and Field Marshall Flugel von Strudel – a toy plastic grotesque German Soldier, 136 mm high in his orange jackboots.

19 'Eduardo Paolozzi' in Robbins (ed.), *The Independent Group*, p. 192.

20 This and following passages are adapted from my 'Paolozzi's Aleatory Archive', *Archives de la critique d'art*, Rennes, Autumn 2004.

21 'Dorothy Morland', in Robbins (ed.), *The Independent Group*, p. 191.

22 From the series 'Ten Collages from Bunk!', Tate Gallery London numbering T01458–T01467.

23 A list of Paolozzi's sources is given in 'Some Sources for a Lecture by Eduardo Paolozzi, 24 June 1980', in Spencer (ed.), *Eduardo Paolozzi: Writings and Interviews*, Appendix II, pp. 345–6.

24 In Paolozzi's words, ' ... the invention of the impossible is achieved by manipulation and jumping beyond pre-conception ...', *Eduardo Paolozzi: Artificial Horizons and Eccentric Ladders*, p. 11.

25 E. Paolozzi, 'Collage, or a Scenario for a Comedy of Critical Hallucination', *Eduardo Paolozzi: Collages and Drawings*, [unpag.]. A friendship with the psychoanalyst Anton Ehrenzweig (Paolozzi taught him screen-printing at the Central School of Art in London) had alerted him to the debate about the artistic unconscious, and especially the investigation into 'surface' and 'depth' perception that Ehrenzweig pioneered in his book *The Psychoanalysis of Artistic Vision and Hearing*, London, 1953.

26 *Collages and Objects* took place 13–20 November, 1954. The overwhelming majority of the 'historical' pieces were from the collections of Roland Penrose, Lee Miller and E. L. T. Mesens.

27 In the recollection of R. Hamilton, in *The Expendable Icon: Works by John McHale*, Albright-Knox Art Gallery, 1984, p. 47.

28 L. Alloway, 'Dada 1956', *Architectural Design*, Nov. 1956; reprinted in Robbins (ed.) *The Independent Group*, p. 164.

29 L. Alloway, 'John McHale's Collages', 27 November–15 December 1956, ICA Library, Dover Street, London.

30 J. McHale, 'The Plastic Parthenon', *Dot-Zero Magazine*, Spring 1967, reprinted in Dorfles (ed.), *Kitsch*, pp. 98–110.

31 *The Times*, 2 May 1958, p. 7. The pretext for the article was the recent sale to the Guggenheim Museum of the 230 cm (seven-and-a-half foot) high *Jason I*, for the reputed sum of £1500. The broader case relating Independent Group enthusiasms to the ambitions of 'Tory Futurist renewal' is argued by D. Mellor, 'A "Glorious Technoculture" in Nineteen Fifties Britain: The Many Cultural Contexts of the Independent Group', in Robbins (ed.), *The Independent Group*, pp. 229–36.

32 These and following excerpts are from Paolozzi, 'Notes for a lecture at the ICA', *Uppercase*, vol. 1, 1958, unpaginated.

127 J. Laude, preface to *Le Scaphandrier des rêves*, 1950

129 C. Dotrement, preface to *Les Malheurs d'É*, Brussels 1949

131–4 E. Paolozzi, 'Artificial Horizons and Eccentric Ladders' (1996), pp. 10, 12

137 ibid., p 11

138 J. McHale, 'The plastic Parthenon' (1968), in Dorfles (ed.), *Kitsch*, p. 110

139 L. Alloway, 'John McHale's Collages' (1956)

Chapter 10: The Critique of Cities pp.145–63

1 The other artists of the Origine group were Mario Ballocco, Ettore Colla, Guiseppe Capogrossi. The 1949 show in Rome contained a short manifesto.

2 G. Celant, 'In Total Freedom: Italian Art 1943–68', in *The Italian Metamorphosis 1943–1968*, p. 8.

3 'Détournements et comportements de Rotella': conversation between Rotella and Giovanni Joppolo, *Opus International*, no. 81, Summer 1981, pp. 48–9.

4 M. Rotella, 'Statement, Rome 1957', reprinted in *Dufrêne, Hains*....

5 Burri did not exhibit in America until 1953, at the invitation of James Johnson Sweeney in 'Younger European Painters', Guggenheim Museum.

6 B. Buchloh, 'From Detail to Fragment: *Décollage affichiste*', *October*, 56, Spring 1991, pp. 107–8.

7 ibid., p. 108.

8 Villeglé, *Urbi et Orbi*, p. 32 and n. 3, p. 108.

9 Villeglé, *Un homme sans métier*, pp. 41–3.

10 Villeglé, *Urbi et Orbi*, pp. 109–10.

11 The so-called 'Rome Discourse' of 1953. For the comparison between Hains's *décollage* manner and Lacan's notions of *points de capiton* that 'upholster' language to the unconscious, see Nicolas Bourriaud, 'La Rhétorique Vécue: Langage et Comportement dans l'Oeuvre de Raymond Hains', in *Raymond Hains: Akzente 1949–1955*, pp. 49–50.

12 Villeglé and Hains, 'L'Intrusion du verre canelé dans la poésie', preface to *Hepérile Éclaté*, 1953; cited by Villeglé, 'Des Réalités Collectives', in *Dufrêne, Hains*..., p. 4.

13 Villeglé, 'L'Affiche Lacérée: ses successives immixtions dans les arts', *Leonardo*, vol. 2, 1969, p. 37. Hains had already made a film with Villeglé in 1949 entitled *Loi du 29 Juillet 1881* (16 mins).

14 Villeglé, in ibid., claims R. Hausmann's book *Courier Dada*, Paris, 1958, to have been for him the definitive statement. The precedent of Leo Malet they heard of later.

15 See the section on Albers in Duberman, *Black Mountain*, p. 56.

16 Statement by Rauschenberg for the exhibition *Scatole e Feticci Personali* [Boxes and Personal Fetishes], 3–10 March 1953, Galleria del Obelisco Rome.

17 Y.-A. Bois, 'Rauschenberg's Optimism', in *Robert Rauschenberg, Fotografie 1949–1985*, p. 7.

18 The debt to Rauschenberg's grandmother (on his mother's side) is referred to in Rose, *Rauschenberg*, [unpag.].

19 Steinberg, *Other Criteria*, 1972, pp. 88–90.

20 Lecture by Vostell with A. Kaprow, 'The Art of the Happening', delivered at the Cricket Theatre in New York, 1964, and transcribed in Becker and Vostell (eds), *Happenings*, p. 403.

21 It is said that Vostell only met the Parisians through the critic Jean-Jacques Levèque in 1960, and did not encounter Rauschenberg until 1961.

22 W. Vostell, statement in *Dufrêne, Hains*....

23 G. Hugnet, 'The Dada Spirit in Painting' [1932 and 1934], in Motherwell (ed.), *The Dada Painters and Poets*, pp. 159–61.

24 For an early account, see S. Simon, 'Wolf Vostell's Action Imagery', *Art International*, no. 12, May 1968, pp. 42 ff.

25 See Vostell, text for *Le Theâtre est dans la rue*, 1958. For a recent account of both it and *Cityrama* (1961), see C. Mesch, 'Vostell's Ruins: dé-collage and the mnemotechnic space of the post-war city', *Art History*, 23, 1, March 2000, pp. 88–115.

26 Dufrêne, 'Sur Les Dessous', in *Dufrêne, Hains*..., p. 2.

27 ibid., p. 6.

28 The reference is to C. Greenberg, 'Avant-Garde and Kitsch' [1939], reprinted in J. O'Brian (ed.), *Clement Greenberg: The Collected Essays and Criticism*, vol. 1, Chicago and London, 1986–93.

29 A. Jorn, 'Détourned Painting', in Sussman (ed.), *On the Passage of a Few People*, pp. 140–2.

30 An extension of *collage* aesthetics was provided by SI member Guiseppe Pinot-Gallizio who, also in May 1959, exhibited his *Caverna Dell'Antimateria* (Cavern of Anti-Matter) at the Galerie Réné Drouin, comprising vast lengths of canvas painted both by spray-machines and by hand, shorter lengths of which were then *découpée* and sold: the *collage* here consists of fragmenting his own mechanically-produced work and attaching it to the domestic space of display (in effect of course a parody of mass-production techniques increasingly dominating the commercial market). For the SI context, see P. Wollen, 'Bitter Victory: The Art and Politics of the Situationist International', in Sussman (ed.), *On the Passage of a Few People*, pp. 20–3.

31 See R. Fleck, 'Raymond Hains', in *Raymond Hains: Akzente 1949–1995*, pp. 63–4. The other Americans at the Paris Biennale – all under 30 – were Harold Altman, Fred Berger, Carmen Cicero, Helen Frankenthaler, Sonia Gechtoff, Nathan Oliveira, Billé Pritchard, Richards Ruben, Peter Voulkos,

John Paul Jones and Carol Summers. See *Première Biennale de Paris*, pp. 30–4.
32 Architects participating in *This is Tomorrow* included Theo Crosby, John Voelcker, J. D. H. Catleugh, Anthony Jackson, A. and P. Smithson, Erno Goldfinger, James Stirling, Richard Matthews, John Weeks, Peter Carter, Colin St John Wilson.
33 L. Alloway, 'Introduction: Design as a Human Activity', *This Is Tomorrow*, [unpag.].
34 UK couples were reported as spending one-eighth of their disposable income on HP; American couples one quarter. Hire Purchase, said *Picture Post*, 'would have horrified our grandfathers'. See 'Are We Enjoying Too Much of Tomorrow Today?, *Picture Post*, 28 April 1956, p. 15.
35 The date of Macmillan's speech at the Bradford football ground was 20 July 1957.
36 Statement reproduced in Hamilton, *Collected Words*, p. 24.
37 According to Booker, *The Neophiliacs*, p. 38.
38 Letter from Hamilton to A. and P. Smithson, 16 January 1957, in *Collected Words*, p. 28.
39 'About Collage: Peter Blake in conversation with Natalie Rudd', in *Peter Blake: About Collage*, p. 19.
140 E. Paolozzi, 'Notes for a lecture at the ICA' (1958)
142 M. Ballocco, 'Origine', *A.Z.Arte Oggi*, Milan, no. 6, Nov. 1950
143 P. Restany, 'Mimmo Rotella: Nouveau Réaliste' (1961), in *Mimmo Rotella: Antologica*, Pisa 2001, p 81
145 Villeglé, *Urbi et Orbi*, p. 109
151 W. Vostell, 'Dé/coll-age' in *Dufrêne, Hains...*
152 R. Rauschenberg, 'Untitled Statement' (1959), in Stiles and Selz (eds), *Theories and Documents*, p. 321
153 A. Jorn, 'Detourned Painting', p. 140
157 'Are We Enjoying Too Much of tomorrow Today?', *Picture Post*, 28 April 1956

Chapter 11: Collage in the Counter-culture
pp. 165–93
1 P. Restany, 'The New Realists', Galerie Apollinaire, Milan, 16 April 1960, in C. Harrison and P. Wood (eds), *Art in Theory 1900–2000: An Anthology of Changing Ideas* (new edn), London, 2002, pp. 724–5.
2 D. Spoerri, 'Trap pictures' [1960], in *Zero*, 3, 1961; Stiles and Selz (eds), *Theories and Documents*, p. 310.
3 B. Buchloh, 'From Detail to Fragment: *Décollage affichiste*', *October*, 56, 1991, p. 100.
4 Excerpting mass-media fragments has remained a primary technique of Blake's throughout a long career, even though the qualities of his more recent collages have been obscured by the popularity of his much-reproduced (and larger) paintings. His own collection of collage was shown as *Peter Blake: About Collage*, Tate Gallery, Liverpool, 2000–1.
5 Irwin's *Thornton Maximus* (1960) at some 3.7 x 4.9 metres (12 by 16 feet) would be one of the most startling works of the first *Situation* show in London in 1960: Alloway would describe it as comparable to the 'undulations of collapsing brickwork'; see his 'Situation in Retrospect', *Architectural Design*, February 1960, pp. 82–3.
6 A third factor in the decline of collage practice in London was the sharp increase in levels of awareness of new American art around 1960. Works by East-coast American artists such as Johns and Rauschenberg, and Happenings by Allan Kaprow, Jim Dine and Claes Oldenburg were conveyed instantly to young artists in Europe through magazines such as *Art News* and *Art in America*.
7 Or see the *Orange Scrapbook* of 1961–2, in which, not collaged, we find the first three pages of Camilla Gray's article 'From Painting to Photography: Experiments of the 1920s', with illustrations by Schwitters, Hausmann, Moholgy-Nagy, Prampolini, Lissitzky, Klutsis, Rodchenko, Stepanova, Stenberg and Man Ray, the last page of which is obscured by a garishly coloured magazine image of an electrical component from the Westinghouse Corporation.
8 R. Hamilton, Catalogue entry for the *Interior* series in *Richard Hamilton: Paintings Etc '56–64*.
9 Seitz, *The Art of Assemblage*, 'Introduction' and n. 5, p. 150. In 1953 Dubuffet had applied the term 'assemblage' to collages made of cut and pasted coloured paper, then transferred to litho ('assemblages d'empriente*s*'), then in 1954 extended it to objects 'made for the most part of *assemblages* of fragments and natural elements' such as wood, sponges, *papier-mâché* and debris (*Art of Assemblage*, p. 93).
10 ibid., pp. 89, 76 [my emphasis].
11 Lebel considered that his works helped precipitate the rebellion of May 1968. For an account of the Surrealist 'Tracts' published against him, see A. Mahon, 'Outrage Aux Bonnes Moeurs: Jean-Jacques Lebel and the Marquis de Sade', in *J-J Lebel*, pp. 96–9.
12 A. Breton, 'Enrico Baj' [1963], reprinted in A. Breton, *Surrealism and Painting* [1928] (trans. S. W. Taylor), London, 1965, pp. 395–400.
13 I once asked Rauschenberg about his dyslexia: he confirmed that it probably played a part (and that no one had asked him about it before). The occasion was the Guggenheim Museum retrospective, Bilbao Guggenheim, 1998.
14 O'Doherty, 'Rauschenberg', in *American Masters*, pp. 194–8. Though this remains the essential early commentary on Rauschenberg, I still believe O'Doherty was mistaken in thinking that the 'vernacular glance' was also mode of perception which the works encouraged towards themselves. On the contrary, a form a slowed-down 'museum' perception is surely essential if we are to accomplish what O'Doherty elsewhere suggests, namely a 'recovery' of the first moment of displacement and nonspecificity that the works rapidly lose – and have lost – under the weight of iconographical and curatorial fascination. A shorter version of O'Doherty's essay was published as 'Rauschenberg and the Vernacular Glance', *Art in America*, Sept.–Oct. 1973, pp. 82–7.
15 A. Kaprow, '18 Happenings in 6 Parts', in Kirby (ed.) *Happenings*, p. 60.
16 The first true cut-ups were published in S. Beiles, W. Burroughs, G. Corso and B. Gysin, *Minutes to Go*, Paris, 1960, as cut-and-paste collaborative texts. See also Burroughs, 'The Cut-Up Method of Brion Gysin' [1959], in W. Burroughs and B. Gysin, *The Third Mind*. For Burroughs and the visual arts, see Sobieszek, *Ports of Entry*.
17 See T. Crow, 'Saturday Disasters: Trace and Reference in Early Warhol', *Art in America*, 1987; reprinted in *Modern Art in the Common Culture*, pp. 49–65, and M. Livingstone, 'Do It Yourself: Notes on Warhol's Technique', in K. McShine (ed.), *Andy Warhol: A Retrospective*, Museum of Modern Art, 1989, pp. 63–70.
18 G. Ulmer, 'The Object of Post-Criticism', in Foster (ed.), *The Anti-Aesthetic*, p. 108.
19 See G. Ballo, 'Emulsified Canvases: Mec Art'; in *Mimmo Rotella: Lamière*, pp. 29–31.
20 Rauschenberg, 1965 statement to Dorothy Gees Seckler, cited in *Robert Rauschenberg: A Retrospective*, exh. cat., Guggenheim Museum, New York, 1998, p. 561. It should be noted that Rauschenberg had been experimenting with transferring photos with lighter fuel onto paper and lithostone since at least the spring of 1962. Warhol had been experimenting with 'anonymous' methods of image transfer, including collage, at least since 1960. See M. Livingstone, 'Do It Yourself: Notes on Warhol's Technique', in K. McShine (ed.), *Andy Warhol: A Retrospective*, Museum of Modern Art, 1989.
21 A. Michelson, 'Paris Letter', *Art International*, May 1964, p. 48.
22 Interview by Peter Boswell, 20 July 1983; interview by Bruce Jenkins and Peter Boswell, 1 June 1996, from P. Boswell, 'Bruce Conner: theatre of light and shadow', *2000 BC: The Bruce Conner Story Part II*, p. 28.
23 T. H. Garver, *The Prometheus Archive*, Newport Harbour Art Museum, 1979, p. 18.
24 Starr, *Lost and Found in California*, p. 99.
25 The 'Dennis Hopper One-Man Show' collages were finally exhibited as photo-etchings at the James Willis Gallery, San Francisco, and the Texan Gallery, Houston in 1973. See J. Rothfuss, 'Escape Artist', in *2000 BC: Bruce Conner Story Part II*, p. 163.
26 The phrase 'return to reality' is Hopper's. See D. Hopper and H. T. Hopkins, 'The Seductive Sixties', in *Dennis Hopper: A System of Moments*, p. 30.
27 V. Burda, 'A Conversation with Jiří Kolář Concerning "Evident Poetry"', *Jiri Kolar: L'Arte Come Forma Della Libertà*, p. 66.
28 Jiří Kolář, 'On Modern Poetry and On Himself', n.d., unpublished MS, cited in C. Kotik, in *Jiří Kolář: Transformations*, p. 8.
29 Cited by W. Schmied, 'Der Weg des Jiří Kolář', essay for Kolář exhibition at Kestner-Gesellschaft, Hanover, 1969.
30 Jiri Kolář, 'On Modern Poetry and On Himself', in catalogue for Kolář exhibition at Kestner-Gesellschaft, Hanover, 1969.
31 Jiri Kolář, 'Perhaps Nothing, Perhaps Something', *Jiří Kolář: L'Arte Come Forma della Libertà*, p. 49.
32 Kolář, cited in C. Kotik, in *Jiří Kolář: Transformations*, p. 9.
33 A. Breton, 'Surrealist Situation of the Object' [1935], in Hulten (ed.), *Surrealists Look at Art*, Venice (Calif.), 1990, p. 159.
34 Svankmeyer's animated collage films include *Picnic with Weismann* (13 mins, 1968), *Jabberwocky* (12 mins, 1981), *Meat In Love* (1 mins, 1989), *Death of Stalinism in Bohemia* (14 mins, 1990) as well as, more recently, some feature-length films.
35 Andreotti, 'Play-tactics of the Internationale Situationiste', *October*, 95, 2000, pp. 42–7.
36 ibid., p. 44, and n. 12; 'Position du Continent Contrescarpe', *Les Lèvres Nues*, 9, 1956, p. 40.
37 A. and P. Smithson, 'The "As Found" and the "Found"', in D. Robbins (ed.), *The Independent Group: Post-War Britain and the Aesthetics of Plenty*, Cambridge (Mass.), 1999, p. 201.
38 A.and P. Smithson, *Without Rhetoric*, p. 12.
39 P. Cook, quoting from *Archigram* I, May 1961, in Cook (ed.), *Archigram*, p. 8.
40 D. Green, 'Living Pod', in Cook (ed.), *Archigram*, p. 52.
41 R. Herron, 'Walking City', in *Ron Herron: 20 Years of Drawing*, [unpag.].
42 R. Herron, 'Tuned Suburb', in *Ron Herron: 20 Years of Drawing*, [unpag.].
43 'Manzak and Electronic Tomato', in Cook (ed.) *Archigram*, p. 124.
44 W. Chalk, 'Touch Not', in Cook (ed.), *Archigram*, p. 138.
160 D. Spoerri, 'Trap Pictures' (1960), in Stiles and Selz (eds), *Theories and Documents*, p. 318
163 P. Restany, 'Images more real than myth', *XXXII Venice Biennale*, 1964
170 W. Vostell, 'Manifesto' (1963), in Stiles and Selz (eds), *Theories and Documents*, p. 725
174 D. Hopper and H. T. Hopkins, 'The Seductive Sixties', *Dennis Hopper: A System of Moments*, MAK Vienna 2001, p. 30
175 J. Kolař, *Dictionary of Methods*, entry for *confrontage*
176 ibid., entry for *rollage*.
177 ibid., entry for *intercollage*.
179 I. Medek, letter to the author, 2004-05-28
181 G. Debord et al., 'Ordre de Boycott' (1956), in E. Sussmann (ed.), *On the Passage of a Few People through a Rather Brief Moment in Time: The Situationist Internaitonal*, Cambridge (Mass.), 1989, p. 144.

Chapter 12: Collage after Collage
pp. 195–213
1 Readers may refer to my *Art Today*, 2005.
2 Cited by C. Lanchner, 'The later adventures of Dada's "Good Girl": the photomontages of Hannah Höch after 1933', in *The Photomontages of Hannah Höch*, exh. cat., Walker Art Centre, 1996, p 147. .
3 Conversation with the author, May 1999.
4 R. Bearden, 'Rectangular Structure in My Montage Paintings', *Leonardo*, vol. 2, 1969, pp. 11–19.
5 Lee Krasner to Barbara Novak, TV Station WGBH Boston, 1979; E. Landau, *Lee Krasner: Catalogue Raisonée*, New York, 1995, p 146.
6 J. Myers, 'Naming Pictures: Conversations between Lee Krasner and John Bernard Myers', *Artforum*, 23, Nov. 1984, p. 71.
7 ibid., p. 71.
8 ibid., p. 73.
9 ibid., p. 73.
10 'Anomie' [Greek], literally 'without law', was first used to characterize the psychology of modern urban man by the French sociologist Emile Durkheim, *Suicide: A Study in Sociology*, 1897. See Buchloh, 'Gerhard Richter's Atlas: The Anomic Archive', in B. Buchloh et al., *Photography and Painting in the Work of Gerhard Richter*, pp. 11–30.
11 Both Gushchin and Serebriakova are treate more fully in my catalogue essay 'Learning From the *Luriki*', in *PhotoReclamation*.
12 P. Kennard, 'Piecing together the truth', *Th Guardian*, London, 27 March 1991, p. 12.
13 W. Benjamin, 'The Author as Producer' [1934], reprinted in Burgin, *Thinking Photography*, p. 24.
14 'Klaus Staeck: Interview by George Jappe', *Studio International*, March/April 1976, pp 137–40.
15 See T. Atkinson, 'Notes: Communities, Artists, Modernism', *Studio International*, March/April 1976, pp. 112–16.
16 Debord's *La Société du Spectacle* [1967] was first translated into English in 1970; Henri Lefebvre's *Critique de la Vie Quotidienne* appeared as *Everyday Life in the Modern World*, Harmondsworth, 1971 On Vaniegem and others, see Gray, *Leavin the 20th Century*.
17 Marcus, *Lipstick Traces*, p. 170.
18 On Vaucher, see P. Kennard, 'Foreword', *Gee Vaucher: Crass Art*, p. i.
19 Bürger, *Théorie der Avant-Garde*.
20 F. Jameson, 'Postmodernism and consume society', in H. Foster (ed), *The Anti-Aesthetic: Essays on Postmodern Culture*, Washington, 1983, p. 124.
21 W. Benjamin, 'The Author as Producer' [1934], reprinted in Burgin, *Thinking Photography*, pp. 28, 29.
22 J. Berger, 'Seeing through lies', *Sanity*, no. 2, 1981.
23 Lyotard, *The Post-Modern Condition*, pp. 73–6.
24 For a discussion of eclecticism in Polke, Sal and Schnabel, see my *Art Today*, chs 5, 6.
25 C. Metz, 'The Imaginary Signifier', in *Screen*, vol. 16, no. 2, 1975; as reprinted i Braudy and Cohen (eds), *Film Theory and Criticism*, p. 807.
26 L. Mulvey, 'Visual Pleasure and Narrative Cinema', *Screen*, vol. 16, no. 3, 1975; as reprinted in Braudy and Cohen (eds), *Film Theory and Criticism*, pp. 837–8.
27 Black, *Models and Metaphors*.
28 This early history is treated more fully in Berners-Lee, *Weaving the Web*.
29 For an artist's perception of these developments, see M. Rosler, 'Image Simulations, Computer Manipulations: Som Considerations', in Amelunxen et al. (eds), *Photography After Photography*, pp. 36–56
30 N. Burson, *Warhead I*, and *First Beauty Context*, both 1982.
31 V. Export, 'Digitale Fotografie' [1989], unpublished text supplied to the author.
32 J. Nechtvatel, correspondence with the author, 2003.
33 Paul, *Digital Art*, p 56–7.
34 A series of Stezaker's 'landscapes' first exhibited in 1999 are cut exactly down the middle and folded left-to-right so as to constitute a perfectly symmetrical image around the centre line. Situated at the far reaches of the technique we have come to know as collage, they in fact reprise a set c preoccupations first explored in 1920s Surrealism and then within the group around Bataille, Roger Caillois and Michel Leiris known as the Collège de Sociologie (College of Sociology) in Paris in the 1930s See Caillois, 'Mimicry and Legendary Psychaesthenia' [1935], *October*, 31, 1984 pp. 17–32.
35 *Kris Scholz: Landscapes, Portraits, Architectures, Flowers.*
36 Paul, *Digital Art*, p. 181.
187 D. Behrens, to the author, 1998
188 R. Bearden, 'Rectangular structure in my montage paintings', *Leonardo*, 1969
189 J. Myers, 'Naming Pictures' (1984), p. 71
196 L. Sterling, cited by L. O'Brien, 'The woman punk made me', in Sabin, *Punk Rock*, p. 19
197 R. Pincus Witten, 'Pure Pinter: An Interview with David Salle', *Arts Magazine*, 1985, p. 8
199 S. Lucas, in *Shaking and Stirring: An Introductory Guide to Sensation*, Royal Academy, London, 1997, p. 17
200 V. Export, 'Women's Art: A Manifesto' (1972), Stiles and Selz (eds), p. 756

BLIOGRAPHY

neral Works
es, D., *Photomontage*, London, 1976
erican Collage, Museum of Modern Art, New ork, 1965
gon, L., *Les Collages*, Paris, 1965
Aujourd'hui [special number on 'Collage'], eries 5, nos 2/3, March/April, 1954
erfield, J. (ed.), *Essays on Assemblage*, Museum of Modern Art [MOMA], New York, 992
gács, E., *Kollázs és Montázs*, Budapest, 1976
ffman, K. (ed.) (1989), *Collage: Critical Views*, nn Arbor and London
is, H., and R. Blesch, *Collage*, New York, 962
therwell, R. (ed.), *The Dada Painters and Poets*, New York, 1951
er on Paper, exh. cat., Museum of Modern rt, San Francisco, 1979
sted Pictures: Collage and Abstraction in the 0th Century, exh. cat., Knoedler Fine Art, New York, 2000
itische Collage: Kunstler aus Baden-Wurtemberg, exh. cat., Wurtemburger unstverein, Stuttgart, 1983
dari, F., *Collage: Pasted, Cut and Torn Papers*, New York, 1988
es, K., and P. Selz (eds), *Theories and Documents of Contemporary Art: A Sourcebook of Artist's Writings*, Berkeley Calif.), 1996
n der Collage sur Assemblage, exh. cat., nstitut für moderner Kunst, Nuremberg, 1968
ldman, D., *Collage, Assemblage and the Found Object*, London, 1992
escher, H., *Cinquante ans de collages*, exh. cat., Musée d'Art et d'Industrie, Saint-Etienne, 1964
–, *Collage*, New York and London, 1968
olfram, E., *History of Collage: An Anthology of Collage, Asemblage and Event Situations*, London, 1975

apter 1: Inventing Collage
dassari, A., *Picasso: Working on Paper*, London, 2000
ttington, D., *Cubism in the Shadow of War*, New Haven, 1998
usins, J., 'Documentary Chronology', in Rubin, *Picasso and Braque: Pioneering Cubism* (see below)
ix, P., *Dictionnaire Picasso*, Paris, 1995
ot, F., and C. Lake, *Life with Picasso*, London and New York, 1964
auss, R., *The Picasso Papers*, London and New York, 1998
ghten, P., *Re-Ordering the Universe: Picasso and Anarchism 1897–1914*, Princeton, 1989
onod-Fontaine, I., *David-Henry Kahnweiler, marchand, editeur, écrivain*, Paris, 1984
ggi, C., *In Defiance of Painting: cubism, futurism and the Invention of Collage*, New Haven, 1992
chardson, J., *A Life of Picasso*, vol. II: 1907–1917, New York, 1996
–, *Georges Braque*, London, 1959
bin, W., *Picasso in the Collection of the Museum of Modern Art*, New York, 1972
–, *Picasso and Braque: Pioneering Cubism*, MOMA, New York, 1989
– (ed.), *Picasso and Braque: A Symposium*, MOMA, New York, 1992
verini, G., *Tutta la vita di un pitore*, Rome, 1946
by, J. T., *Juan Gris*, MOMA, New York, 1958
ein, G., *Picasso*, London, 1938
llier, D., 'Braque; La Peinture et Nous', *Cahiers d'Art*, Paris, October 1954
arnod, J., *La Ruche & Montparnasse*, Paris, 1978
eiss, J., *The Popular Culture of Modern Art: Picasso, Duchamp and Avant-Gardism*, New Haven, 1994

apter 2: Paths to Construction
ldassari, A., *Picasso: Working on Paper*, London, 2000
is, Y.-A., *Painting as Model*, Cambridge and London, 1990
k, L., *Erinnerungen an Majakowski*, Munich, 1993
owling, E., and J. Golding, *Picasso: Sculptor/Painter*, London, Tate Gallery, 1994
iott, D. (ed.), *Alexander Rodchenko*, exh. cat., Museum of Modern Art, Oxford, 1979
Erlich, V., *Russian Formalism: History, Doctrine*, Gravenhage, 1955
Jakobson, R., *Selected Writings*, vol. III, The Hague, 1981
—, and K. Pomorska, *Dialogues*, Cambridge, 1983
Janacek, G., *The Look of Russian Literature: Avant-Garde Visual Experiment*, Princeton, 1984
Kahnweiler, D.-H., *Sculptures of Picasso* (trans. A. D. B. Sylvester), London, 1949
Khan-Magomedov, S., *Rodchenko: The Complete Works*, Cambridge, 1987
Lodder, C., *Russian Constructivism*, New Haven, 1983
Markov, V., *Manifesty i programmy russkikh futuristov*, Munich, 1967
Mayakovsky, V., *It*, Berlin, 1994
McCully, M. (ed.), *A Picasso Anthology: Documents, Criticism, Reminiscences*, London, 1982
Nakov, A., *Kazimir Malevich: Catalogue Raisonnée*, Paris, 2002
Noever, P. (ed.), *Rodchenko, Stepanova: The Future is Our Only Goal*, Munich, 1991
Paulhan, J., *La Peinture Cubiste*, Paris, 1970
Phillips, C. (ed.), *Photography in the Modern Era: European Documents and Critical Writings 1913–1940*, Metropolitan Museum, New York, 1989
Picasso, Dessins et papiers collés: Céret 1911–1913, exh. cat., Musée d'Art Moderne, Céret, 1997
Rubens: Drawing On Italy, exh. cat., National Gallery of Scotland, Edinburgh, 2002
Salmon, A., *L'Air de la Butte*, Paris, 1945
—, *La Jeune Sculpture Francaise*, Paris, 1919
Shklovsky, V., *Sentimental Journey*, Moscow and Berlin, 1923
Taylor, B., *Art and Literature under the Bolsheviks*, 2 vols, London, 1991 and 1992
Zervos, C., *Pablo Picasso*, 33 vols, Paris, 1932–78
Zhadova, L., *Tatlin*, London, 1984

Chapter 3: Dada Dialectics
Arp, H., *Arp 1886–1966*, Cambridge, 1986
—, *On My Way: Poetry and Essays 1912–1947*, New York, 1948
Ball, H., *Flight out of Time: A Dada Diary* [1915] (ed. J. Elderfield), Berkeley (Calif.), 1996.
Burchard, O. (Kunsthandlung), *Erste internationale Dada-Messe*, Berlin, 1920
Cardinal, R., and J. Elsner (eds), *The Cultures of Collecting*, London, 1994
Dietrich, D., *The Collages of Kurt Schwitters: Tradition and Innovation*, Cambridge, 1993
Elderfield, J., *Kurt Schwitters*, London and New York, 1985
Foster, S. C. (ed.), *"Event" Art and Art Events*, UMI Research Monographs, Michigan, 1988
Huelsenbeck, R. (ed.) *The Dada Almanac* [Berlin, 1920] (presented by M. Green), London, 1993
Jean, M. (ed.), *Arp on Arp: Poems, Essays, Memories*, New York, 1969
Lippard, L. (ed.), *Dadas on Art*, New Jersey, 1971
Ouelette, W., *Fantasy Postcards*, New York, 1975
The Photomontages of Hannah Höch, exh. cat., Walker Art Center, Minneapolis, 1997.
Richter, H., *Dada: Art and Anti-Art*, London and New York, 1964
Riha, K. (ed.), *Dada Berlin, Texte, Manifeste, Aktionen*, Stuttgart, 1977
Schwitters, K., *Das Literarisches Werk*, vol. 5: *Manifeste und Kritische Prosa* (ed. F. Lach), Cologne, 1981
Steinitz, K., *Kurt Schwitters: A Portrait from Life*, Berkeley and Los Angeles 1968

Chapter 4: Legacies of the Dada Mind
Adamowicz, E., *Surrealist Collage in Text and Image: Dissecting the Exquisite Corpse*, Cambridge, 1998
Benjamin, W., *One-Way Street* [1925–6], London, 1979
Camfield, W., *Max Ernst: Dada and the Dawn of Surrealism*, Munich, 1993
Dluhosch, E., and R. Švachá (eds), *Karel Teige 1900-1951: L'Enfant Terrible of the Czech Avant-Garde*, Cambridge (Mass.), 1999
Ernst, M., *Ecritures*, Paris, 1970
Friedrich Vordemberge-Gildewart: The Complete Works, exh. cat., Munich, 1996
Levinger, E., 'Rejection and Acceptance of Teige in the 1920s', in *Umění*, XLIII, Prague, 1995
Lippard, L. (ed.), *Surrealists on Art*, Princeton, 1970
Lomas, D., *The Haunted Self: Surrealism, Psychoanalysis, Subjectivity*, New Haven and London 2000
Spies, W., *Max Ernst: Collages*, London, 1991
Tanning, D., *Max Ernst: Beyond Painting*, New York, 1948
Tzara, T., *Seven Dada Manifestos and Lampisteries*, London, 1977

Chapter 5: The Surrealist Years
Aragon, L., 'La Peinture au défi', in *Exposition de collages*, exh. cat. (see below)
Breton, A., *Manifestos of Surrealism*, Ann Arbor, 1969
—, *Surrealism and Painting* [1928] (trans. S. W. Taylor), London, 1965
Císařová, M., 'Surrealism and Functionalism: Teige's Dual Way', *Rassegna*, 15, no. 53/1, 1993
Clifford, J., *The Predicament of Culture: Twentieth Century Ethnography, Literature and Art*, Cambridge (Mass.), 1988
Czech Collage, exh. cat., Narodny Gallery, Prague, 1997
Dluhosch, E., and R. Švachá (eds), *Karel Teige 1900-1951: L'Enfant Terrible of the Czech Avant-Garde*, Prague, 2001
Dupin, J., *Joan Miró: Life and Work*, New York, 1962
Effenberger, V. (et al.), *Výbror z díla*, 3 vols, Prague, 1966
Exposition de collages: Arp, Braque, Dalí, Duchamp, Ernst, Gris, Miro, Magritte, Man Ray, Picabia, Picasso, Tanguy, exh. cat., Galerie Goemans, Paris, 1930
Fer, B., *On Abstract Art*, London and New Haven, 1997
Gibson, I., *The Shameful Life of Salvador Dali*, London, 1997
Hugnet, G., *Pleins et Déliés: Souvenirs et Témoignages, 1926–1972*, Paris, 1972
—, *Dictionnaire du Dadaisme*, Paris, 1976
Hulten, P. (ed.), *The Surrealists Look at Art*, Venice (Calif.), 1990
The International Surrealist Exhibition, exh. cat., London, 1936
C. Lanchner, *Joan Miró*, exh. cat., MOMA, NEw York, 1993
Lomas, D., *The Haunted Self: Surrealism, Psychoanalysis, Subjectivity*, New Haven and London, 2000
Mundy, J. (ed.), *Surrealism: Desire Unbound*, exh. cat., Tate Modern, London, 2001
Nash, P., *Outline: An Autobiography and Other Writings*, London, 1944
Penrose, R., *Scrapbook: 1900–1981*, London, 1981
Roland Penrose, Lee Miller: The Surrealist and the Photographer, exh. cat., Scottish National Gallery of Modern Art, Edinburgh, 2001
Rémy, M., *Surrealism in Britain*, London, 1997
Rubin, W., *Miró in the Collection of MOMA*, New York, 1973
Srp, K., *Karel Teige*, Prague, 2001
—, *Toyen*, City Gallery, Prague, 2000
Štyrský, J., *Emilie Comes To Me In A Dream*, Ubu Gallery, New York, 1993
Sylvester, D. (ed.), *René Magritte: Catalogue Raisonnée*, Phillip Watson and the Menil Foundation, 1994
Teige, K., *Film*, Prague, 1925

Chapter 6: The Political and the Personal
Benjamin, W., *One-Way Street* [1925–6], London 1979
Chametzky, P., *Willi Baumeister: Zeichnungen, Gouachen, Collagen*, Edition Cantz, 1989/90
Evans, D., *John Heartfield: AIZ/VI 1930-38*, New York, 1992
Gombrich, E., *Aby Warburg: An Intellectual Biography*, London, 1970
Lavin, M., *Cut With the Kitchen Knife: the Weimar Photomontages of Hannah Hoch*, New Haven and London, 1993
Lehmann-Haupt, H., *Art Under a Dictatorship*, Oxford, 1954
Pachnicke, P., and K. Honnef (eds), *John Heartfield*, New York, 1992
Phillips, C. (ed.), *Photography in the Modern Era: European Documents and Critical Writings*, 1913–1940, New York, 1989
Teitelbaum, M. (ed.), *Montage in Modern Life 1919–1942*, Cambridge (Mass.), 1999

Chapter 7: New York Conversations
Carmean, E. (Jnr), *The Collages of Robert Motherwell*, Houston, 1972
Clark, T. J., *Farewell to an Idea: Episodes From a History of Modernism*, New Haven, 1999
Elderfield, J., *The Cut-Outs of Henry Matisse*, London, 1978
Greenberg, C., *Joan Miró*, New York, 1948
Guggenheim, P., *Out of this Century: Confessions of an Art Addict*, New York, 1979
Kirby, M., *Happenings: An Illustrated Anthology*, London, 1965
Landau, E., *Lee Krasner: Catalogue Raisonnée*, New York, 1995
Lee Krasner: Collages, exh. cat., Robert Miller Gallery, New York, 1986
O'Brian, J. (ed.), *Clement Greenberg: The Collected Essays and Criticism*, vols I–IV, Chicago and London, 1986–93
Phillips, L. *Frederick Kiesler*, Whitney Museum of American Art, New York, 1989
Robert Motherwell, exh. cat., MOMA, New York, 1965
Robert Motherwell, exh. cat., Albright-Knox Art Gallery, New York, 1983
Nemser, C., *Art Talk: Conversations with 12 Women Artists*, New York, 1975
Potter, J., *To a Violent Grave: An Oral History of Jackson Pollock*, New York, 1985
Rudenstine, C. (ed.), *The Peggy Guggenheim Collection, Venice*, New York, 1985
Stein, G., *Autobiography of Alice B.Toklas* [1933], Harmondsworth, 1966
Three American Painters, exh. cat., Fogg Art Museum, Harvard, 1965
Vail, K., *Peggy Guggenheim: A Celebration*, New York, 1998
Wagner, A., *Three Artists (Three Women): Modernism and the Art of Hesse, Krasner and O'Keefe*, Berkeley (Calif.), 1996

Chapter 8: California Collage
2000 BC: The Bruce Conner Story Part II, exh. cat., Los Angeles, Walker Art Center, Minneapolis, 1999
The Americans: The Collage, exh. cat., Contemporary Arts Museum, Houston, 1982
Auprey, M., *Jess: A Grand Collage 1951–1993*, Albright-Knox Art Gallery, New York, 1993
Beat Culture and the New America 1950–1965, exh. cat., Whitney Museum of American Art, New York 1995
Candida Smith, R., *Utopia and Dissent: Art, Poetry and Politics in California*, Berkeley (Calif.), 1955
Dikeakos, C., *The Collage Show*, exh. cat., Fine Arts Gallery, University of British Columbia, 1971
Greenberg, C., *Art and Culture* [1961], Boston, 1965
Jay DeFeo: Selected Works 1952-1989, exh. cat., Moore College of Art and Design, Philadelphia, 1996
The "Junk" Aesthetic: Assemblage of the 1950s and early 1960s, exh. cat., Whitney Museum of American Art, New York, 1989
Lost and Found in California: Four Decades of Assemblage Art, exh. cat., James Corcoran Gallery, Santa Monica, 1988
Plummer, W., *The Holy Goof: A Biography of Neal Cassady*, New York, 1981
Poets of the Cities: New York and San Francisco 1950–1965, exh. cat., Museum of Fine Arts, Dallas, 1974
Watson, S., *The Birth of the Beat Generation: Visionaries, Rebels and Hipsters 1944–1960*, New York, 1995

Chapter 9: Later Surrealism
Bon Anniversaire Monsieur Bucaille, Galerie 1900–2000, Paris, 1986
Dorfles, G. (ed.), *Kitsch: An Anthology of Bad Taste*, London, 1969
Eduardo Paolozzi: Artificial Horizons and Eccentric Ladders: Works on Paper 1946–95, exh. cat., British Council, London, 1996
Eduardo Paolozzi: Collages and Drawings, exh. cat., Anthony D'Offay Gallery, London, 1977
Eduardo Paolozzi: Sculpture, Drawings, Collages and Graphics, exh. cat., Arts Council of Great Britain, London, 1976
Ehrenzweig, A., *The Psychoanalysis of Artistic Vision and Hearing*, London, 1953
The Expendable Icon: Works by John McHale, exh. cat., Albright-Knox Art Gallery, 1984
Gaston Chaissac: First London Exhibition, exh. cat., Fischer Fine Art, London, 1986
Les Prévert de Prévert: Collages: Catalogue de la collection de l'auteur, Bibliothèque Nationale, Paris 1982

Max Bucaille: Collages et Oeuvres Diverses des Annees 30 et 40, Gallerie 1900–2000, Paris 1986

Michaud, D., *Gaston Chaissac: puzzle pour un homme seul*, Paris, 1974

Paolozzi, exh. cat., National Galleries of Scotland, Edinburgh, 1999

Robbins, D. (ed.), *The Independent Group: Post-War Britain and the Aesthetics of Plenty*, Cambridge (Mass.), 1999

Roussel, R., *Comment j'ai écrit certain de mes Livres*, Paris, 1963

Spencer, R. (ed.), *Eduardo Paolozzi: Writings and Interviews*, Oxford, 2000

Chapter 10: The Critique of Cities

Becker, J., and W. Vostell (eds), *Happenings: Fluxus, Pop Art, Nouveau Réalisme. Eine Dokumentation*, Reinbek bei Hamburg, 1965

Booker, C., *The Neophiliacs: A Study of the Revolution in English Life in the Fifties and Sixties*, London, 1969

Duberman, M., *Black Mountain: An Exploration in Community*, New York, 1993

Dufrêne, Hains, Rotella, Villeglé, Vostell: Decollagen: Plakatbrisse aus der Sammlung Cremer, Staatsgalerie Stuttgart, 1971

Hamilton, R., *Collected Words: 1953–1982*, London, 1982

Hausmann, R., *Courier Dada*, Paris, 1958

The Italian Metamorphosis 1943–1968, Guggenheim Museum, New York, 1994–5

Peter Blake: About Collage, exh. cat., Tate Gallery, London, 2000

Première Biennale de Paris, exh. cat., Musée d'Art Moderne de la Ville de Paris, 1959

Raymond Hains: Akzente 1949–1955, exh. cat., Musuem Moderne Kunst, Stiftung Ludwig, Vienna, 1995

Robert Rauschenberg, Fotografie 1949–1985, exh. cat., Galleria Laurence Rubin, Milan, 1999

Rose, B., *Rauschenberg: An Interview with Rauschenberg*, New York, 1987

Steinberg, L., *Other Criteria*, London and New York, 1972

Sussman, E. (ed.), *On the Passage of a Few People through a Rather Brief Moment in Time: the Situationist International*, Cambridge (Mass.), 1989

This Is Tomorrow, exh. cat., Whiechapel Art Gallery, London, 1956

Villeglé, J.de la, *Urbi et Orbi*, Mâcon, 1986

——, *Un homme sans métier*, Paris, 1995

Chapter 11: Collage in the Counter-culture

2000 BC: The Bruce Conner Story Part II, exh. cat., Walker Art Centre, Minnesota, 1999

Asger Jorn, exh. cat., Fundació Antoni Tàpies, Barcelona, 2002

Beiles, S. (et al.), *Minutes to Go*, Paris, 1960

Burroughs, W., and B. Gysin, *The Third Mind*, New York, 1979

Cook, P. (ed.), *Archigram*, London, 1972

Crow, T., *Modern Art in the Common Culture*, New Haven and London, 1996

Dennis Hopper: A System of Moments, exh. cat., MAK, Vienna, 2001

Foster, H. (ed.), *The Anti-Aesthetic: Essays on Postmodern Culture*, Washington, 1983

Jiří Kolář: L'Arte Come Forma Della Libertà, exh. cat., Galeria Schwarz, Milan, 1972

Jiří Kolář: Transformations, exh. cat., Albright Knox Art Gallery, Buffalo, New York, 1978

Jiří Kolář, Dictionaire des Méthodes, Alfortville, 1991

J-J Lebel: Bilder, Skulpturen, Instalationen, exh. cat., Museum Modernere Kunst, Stiftung Ludwig, Vienna, 1998

Kirby, M. (ed.), *Happenings: An Illustrated Anthology*, New York, 1966

McShine, K. (ed.), *Andy Warhol: A Retrospective*, MOMA, New York, 1989

Mimmo Rotella: Lamière, exh. cat., Studio Marconi, Milan, 1989

O'Doherty, B., *American Masters: The Voice and the Myth*, New York, 1974

Richard Hamilton: Paintings Etc '56–64, exh. cat., Hanover Gallery, London, 1964

Ron Herron: 20 Years of Drawing, exh. cat., Architectural Association, London, 1980

Seitz, W., *The Art of Assemblage*, MOMA, New York 1961

Smithson, A. and P., *Without Rhetoric: An Architectural Aesthetic 1955–1972*, London, 1973

Sobieszek, R. A., *Ports of Entry: William S.Burroughs and the Arts*, Los Angeles County Museum of Art, 1996

Starr, S., *Lost and Found in California: Four Decades of Assemblage Art*, Santa Monica, 1988

Chapter 12: Collage after Collage

Amelunxen, H. von, et al. (eds), *Photography After Photography: Memory and Representation in the Digital Age*, Munich, 1996

Berners-Lee, T., *Weaving the Web: The Origins and Future of the World Wide Web*, London, 1999

Black, M., *Models and Metaphors*, Ithica, New York, 1962

Braudy, L., and M. Cohen (eds), *Film Theory and Criticism: Introductory Readings*, Milton Keynes, 1999

Buchloh, B., (et al.), *Photography and Painting in the Work of Gerhard Richter*, MACBA, Barcelona, 1999

Bürger, P., *Theorie der Avant-Garde*, 1974

Burgin, V., *Thinking Photography*, London, 1982

Debord, G., *La Société du Spectacle*, 1967

Gee Vaucher: Crass Art and Other Pre-Post-Modernist Monsters, exh. cat., Edinburgh and San Francisco, 1999

Gray, C., *Leaving the 20th Century: The Incomplete Works of the Situationist International*, London 1998

Kris Scholz: Landscapes, Portraits, Architectures, Flowers (intro. by C. Terstappen), exh. cat., Munich, 2002

Lefebvre, H., *Critique de la Vie Quotidienne* (*Everyday Life in the Modern World*), Harmondsworth, 1971

Lyotard, J.-F., *The Post-Modern Condition: A Report on Knowledge* [1979], Manchester, 1984

Marcus, G., *Lipstick Traces: A Secret History of the Twentieth Century*, London, 1989

Paul, C., *Digital Art*, London and New York, 2003

PhotoReclamation: New Photography from Moscow and St Petersburg, exh. cat., Photographers Gallery, London, 1994

Reid, J., *Up They Rise: The Incomplete Works of Jamie Reid*, London, 1987

Sabin, R., *Punk Rock: So What? The Cultural Legact of Punk*, London, 1999

Taylor, B., *Art Today*, Prentice Hall, 2005

LIST OF ILLUSTRATIONS

Measurements are given in centimetres (with inches in brackets).

Collage and photomontage, 31.7 x 22.5 (12½ x 8⅞). Private Collection. © ADAGP, Paris and DACS, London 2004

Opening of the First International Dada Fair, Burchard Gallery, Berlin, June 1920. Photograph

Kurt Schwitters, *Abstraction 9: The Bow Tie*, 1918. Oil on board, 73.5 x 56.8 (28⅞ x 22⅜). Kurt Schwitters Archive at the Sprengel Museum, Hanover. Photo Michael Herling/Aline Gwose. © DACS 2004

Kurt Schwitters, *The Worker Picture* (*Das Arbeiterbild*), 1919. Assemblage, 125 x 91 (49¼ x 35⅞). Photo Moderna Museet, Stockholm. © DACS 2004

Kurt Schwitters, *Merz 19*, 1920. Paper collage, 18.5 x 15 (7¼ x 5⅞). Yale University Art Gallery. Gift of Collection Société Anonyme. © DACS 2004

Kurt Schwitters, *Merz 151: The Knave Child* (*Das Wenzelkind*), 1921. Paper collage, 17.1 x 12.9 (6¾ x 5⅛). Sprengel Museum, Hanover. © DACS 2004

Kurt Schwitters, *Forms in Space* (*Formen in Raum*), 1920. Paper and fabric collage on cardboard, 18 x 14.3 (7⅛ x 5⅝). Kunstsammlung Nordrhein-Westfalen, Düsseldorf. © DACS 2004

Hannah Höch, *Dada Panorama* (*Dada Rundschau*), 1919. Photomontage with gouache and watercolour on cardboard, 43.7 x 34.5 (17¼ x 13⅝). Berlinische Galerie, Landesmuseum für Moderne Kunst, Photographie und Architektur, Berlin. © DACS 2004

Hannah Höch, *Dada-Ernst*, 1920–1. Photomontage, 18.6 x 16.6 (7⅜ x 6½). Collection Arturo Schwarz, Milan. © DACS 2004

Hannah Höch, *Untitled*, 1921. Photomontage, 35.6 x 30.5 (14 x 12). Mr. and Mrs. Morton G. Newman Collection. © DACS 2004

Max Ernst, *Fruit of a Long Experience* (*Fruit d'une longue expérience*), 1919. Painted wood and metal wire relief, 45.7 x 38 (18 x 15). Private Collection, Geneva, Switzerland. © ADAGP, Paris and DACS, London 2004

Johannes Baargeld, *Anthropophiliac Tapeworm*, 1920. Assemblage sculpture, dimensions and whereabouts unknown. Reproduced in *Die Schammade*, 1920

Johannes Baader, *Plastic-Dada-Dio-Drama*, 1920. Assemblage sculpture, dimensions and whereabouts unknown

Max Ernst, *Little Machine Constructed by Minimax Dadamax Himself* (*Von minimax dadamax selbst konstruirtes maschinchen*), c. 1919–20. Hand printing, pencil and ink frottage, watercolour and gouache on paper, 49.4 x 31.5 (19½ x 12⅜). Peggy Guggenheim Collection, Venice (Solomon R. Guggenheim Foundation, NY). © ADAGP, Paris and DACS, London 2004

Physics apparatus from *Biblioteca Paedagogica*, 1914, p. 756

Max Ernst, *Hydrometric Demonstration of Killing by Temperature*, 1920. Gouache, ink and pencil on printed reproduction, 24 x 17 (9½ x 6¾). J. Tronche Collection, Paris. © ADAGP, Paris and DACS, London 2004

Max Ernst, *The Swan is Very Peaceful...*, 1920. Collage with photograph fragments, 8.3 x 12 (3¼ x 4¾). Yokohama Museum of Art. © ADAGP, Paris and DACS, London 2004

Gerrit Rietveld, *Shroeder House, Utrecht*, 1924–5. Photo Francis Carr © Thames & Hudson Ltd., London. © DACS 2004

Theo van Doesburg, *Space-Time Construction II*, 1924. Gouache on paper, 47 x 40.5 (18½ x 16). © Museo Thyssen-Bornemisza, Madrid

Karel Teige, *Departure for Cythera*, 1923–4. Picture-poem. Prague Municipal Gallery

Man Ray, *(Paper Circle and Tongs) No. 1* from *Les Champs Délicieux: Album de photographies*, Paris, 1922. One of 12 gelatin silver photographs, 36.6 x 29 (14⅜ x 11⅜). National Gallery of Australia, Canberra. Purchased 1982. © Man Ray Trust/ADAGP, Paris and DACS, London 2004

Jindrich Štyrský, *Souvenir*, 1924. Photomontage on paper, 23.9 x 30,2 (9⅜ x 11⅞). National Gallery, Prague

60 Kurt Schwitters, *Blue* (*Blau*), 1923–6. Relief construction, 53 x 42.5 (20⅞ x 16¾). Galerie Gmurzynska, Cologne. © DACS 2004

61 Friedrich Vordemberge-Gildewart, *Composition No. 48, Architecture – no optical valuation*, 1928. Collage, 35.5 x 26 (14 x 10¼). Collection Musée de Grenoble, France. Copyright Friedrich Vordemberge-Gildewart Foundation

62 Max Ernst, 'Let's go. Let's dance the Tenebreuse...', page from *Rêve d'une petite fille qui voulut entrer au Carmel* (A Little Girl Dreams of Taking the Veil), 1930 (trans. by Dorothea Tanning). Collage. © ADAGP, Paris and DACS, London 2004

63 André Breton, Jacqueline Lamba and Yves Tanguy, *Cadavre exquis*, 1938. Engraving on paper. Musée d'Unterlinden, Colmar. Photo O. Zimmermann

64 Pablo Picasso, *Guitar*, 1926. Assemblage of cardboard, tulle and string with pencil on cardboard, 10.3 x 12 (4⅛ x 4¾). Musée Picasso, Paris. © Photo RMN – Béatrice Hatala. © Succession Picasso/DACS 2004

65 Pablo Picasso, *Guitar*,1926. Assemblage of canvas, nails, string and knitting needle on painted wood, 130 x 97 (51¼ x 38⅛). Musée Picasso, Paris. © Succession Picasso/DACS 2004

66 Salvador Dalí, *Accommodations of Desire*, 1929. Oil and collage on board, 22 x 35 (8⅝ x 13¾). Jacques and Natasha Gelman Collection, The Metropolitan Museum of Art, New York. © Salvador Dalí, Gala-Salvador Dalí Foundation, DACS, London 2004

67 Salvador Dalí, *The First Days of Spring*, 1929. Oil and collage on panel, 50 x 65 (19¾ x 24⅝). © Salvador Dalí, Gala-Salvador Dalí Foundation, DACS, London 2004

68 René Magritte, *A Taste for the Invisible*, 1927. Oil on canvas, 73 x 100 (28½ x 39). Collection Mme. Jean Krebs, Brussels. © ADAGP, Paris and DACS, London 2004

69 René Magritte, *Untitled*, 1930. Cardboard and collage on canvas. Whereabouts unknown. © ADAGP, Paris and DACS, London 2004

70 Joan Miró, *Un oiseau poursuit une abeille et la baisse*, 1927. Oil and feathers on canvas, 83.5 x 102 (32⅞ x 40¼). Private Collection. © Succession Miró, DACS, 2004

71 Joan Miró, *Spanish Dancer*, 1928. Sandpaper, string, nails, hair, architect's triangle and paint on paper mounted on linoleum, 109.5 x 71 (43⅛ x 28). Morton G. Neumann Family Collection, USA. © Succession Miró, DACS, 2004

72 Joan Miró, *Collage*, 1929. Pastel, ink, watercolour, crayon and pasted papers on paper, 72.7 x 108.4 (28⅝ x 42⅝). The Museum of Modern Art, New York. James Thrall Soby Fund. © Succession Miró, DACS, 2004

73 Joan Miró, *Painting (Composition)*, 1933. Oil and acqueous medium on canvas, 130.5 x 163.2 (51⅜ x 64¼). Philadelphia Museum of Art, A.E. Gallatin Collection. © Succession Miró, DACS, 2004

74 Joan Miró, preparatory collage for *Painting*, 1933. Newspaper collage on paper, 47.5 x 63.2 (18⅝ x 24¾). Fundació Joan Miró, Barcelona. © Succession Miró, DACS, 2004

75 Joan Miró, *Drawing-Collage (Montroig)*, 1933. Conté and pasted paper on tan pastel paper, 106.7 x 69.9 (42 x 27½). The Morton G. Neumann Family Collection, USA. © Succession Miró, DACS, 2004

76 Toyen (Marie Čermínová) and Jindřich Štyrský, *How I Found Livingstone*, 1925. Collage, 40 x 30 (15¾ x 11¾). Private Collection, Prague. © ADAGP, Paris and DACS, London 2004 (for Toyen)

77 Georges Hugnet, *Une Nuit*, 1936. Collage, 32.4 x 24.8 (12¾ x 9¾). Zabriskie Gallery, New York. © ADAGP, Paris and DACS, London 2004

78 Toyen (Marie Čermínová) , *Fata Morgana*, 1926. Oil on canvas, 100 x 73 (39⅜ x 28¾). Ales South Bohemian Gallery, Hluboká nad Vlatova, Czech Republic. © ADAGP, Paris and DACS, London 2004

79 Jindřich Štyrský, *Sexual Nocturne*, 1931. Collage and ink on paper, 18.5 x 14 (7¼ x 5½). Private Collection

80 Jindřich Štyrský, *Untitled (maquette for Emilie Comes to Me in a Dream, No. 1 / Penis)*, 1933. Collage of silverprint and halftone cut-outs affixed to original mount, 24.4 x 18.7 (9⅝ x 7⅜). Courtesy Ubu Gallery, New York

81 Jindřich Štyrský, collage from *Portable Cabinet*, 1934. Collage on paper, 25 x 19 (9⅞ x 7½). Private Collection, Garches

82 Karel Teige, *Collage No. 23*, 1936. Paper, 24.5 x 16.5 (9⅝ x 6½). Památník národního písemnictví, Prague (77/72 – 198)

83 Jiří Kroha, *Sociological Elements of Living (Hygiene of Clothing and Underclothes)*, 1930–2. Collage on pasteboard, 70 x 99 (27½ x 39). Muzeum města Brna. Photo Karel Šabata

84 Karel Teige, *Collage No. 358*, 1948. Paper, 21.6 x 15.9 (8½ x 6¼). Památník národního písemnictví, Prague (77/72 – 478)

85 Paul Nash, *Swanage Surrealism*, c. 1936. Pencil, watercolour and photographic collage on paper. © Tate, London 2004

86 Roland Penrose, *Real Woman*, 1937. Paper, collage, decalcomania, frottage and pencil on card, 43.3 x 69 (17 x 27⅛). Copyright © The Roland Penrose Estate. All rights reserved

87 Eileen Agar, *Head*, 1937. Pasted papers. Collection Arthur Murray, London

88 Roland Penrose, *Elephant Bird*, 1938. Pasted postcards, chromo map, coloured papers and string, 81.3 x 54.6 (32 x 21½). Copyright © The Roland Penrose Estate. All rights reserved

89 El Lissitzky, Sergei Senkin and Gustav Klutsis, *The Task of the Press is the Education of the Masses*, 1928. Photofrieze at the International Press Exhibition ('Pressa') , Cologne.

90 Gustav Klutsis, *Millions of Workers Take Part in Socialist Competition*, 1927–8. Poster, photomontage. State Museum of the Revolution, Riga, Latvia (Inv. No. 9341/550-11)

91 Boris Klinch, *Our Enemy: Churchill*, photo-caricature for the 15th anniversary of the October Revolution *Proletarskoe foto*, November 1932. Photomontage

92 Aleksandr Rodchenko, page from the magazine *SSSR na Stroike* (USSR In Construction), no. 7, 1940, a special commemorative issue on Vladimir Mayakovsky. Gravure, 40.7 x 58.5 (16 x 23). © DACS 2004

93 Anonymous, photomontage before the Hall of Honour at the 'Deutschland' exhibition, Berlin, 1936

94 John Heartfield, 'The Peaceable Fish of Prey', *Volks-Illustrierte (VI, Prague)*, May 12, 1937, p. 307. 38 x 27 (15¼ x 10¾). © The Heartfield Community of Heirs/VG Bild-Kunst, Bonn and DACS, London 2004

95 Kasimir Malevich, *Analytical Chart*, c. 1924–7. Collage with pencil on transparent paper, pen and ink, 63.5 x 82.6 (25 x 32½). The Museum of Modern Art, New York

96 Hugo Gellert, 'What's It All About?', 1928. Collage in *New Masses*, July 1928, p. 16.

97 Aby Warburg, panel 79 from *Mnemosyne Atlas*, 1928–9. The Warburg Institute Archive, London

98 Hannah Höch, *Sammelalbum*, 1933. Page from collage book. Berlinische Galerie, Landesmuseum für Moderne Kunst, Photographie und Architektur, Berlin. © DACS 2004

99 Hannah Höch, *Der Kleine P (The Small P)*, 1931. Photomontage, 45 x 32 (17¾ x 12⅝). Collection Staatsgalerie Stuttgart, Germany. © DACS 2004

100 Hannah Höch, *The Eternal Folk Dancers* (*Die Ewigen Schuhplattler*), 1933. Photomontage and watercolour, 25.2 x 26 (9⅞ x 10¼). Collection Thomas Walther, New York. © DACS 2004

101 Willi Baumeister, *Arno Breker's Der Rächer (The Avenger) with Head drawn by Willi Baumeister*, c. 1941. Head, 5 x 4.5 (2 x 1¾). Baumeister Archive, Stuttgart. © DACS 2004

102 Paul Nash, *Dive Bomber. Parachute Trap*, c. 1940. Photomontage. © Tate, London 2004

103 Robert Motherwell, *Surprise and Inspriation* (originally titled: *Personage (Autoportrait)*), December 9, 1943. Paper collage, gouache and ink on board, 103.8 x 65.9 (40⅞ x 26). Peggy Guggenheim Collection, Venice (Solomon R. Guggenheim Foundation, NY). © Dedalus Foundation, Inc./VAGA, New York/DACS, London 2004

104 Joseph Cornell, *Medici Slot Machine*, 1942. Objects with pasted photographs and architectural plans, 39.4 x 31.8 x 11.1 (15½ x 12½ x 4⅜). Private Collection, Courtesy The Menil Foundation, Houston. © The Joseph and Robert Cornell Memorial Foundation/VAGA, New York/DACS, London 2004

105 Robert Motherwell, *View from a High Tower*, 1944. Collage of oil and paper on board 74.3 x 74.3 (29¼ x 29¼). Private Collection. © Dedalus Foundation, Inc./VAGA, New York/DACS, London 2004

106 William Baziotes, *The Drugged Balloonist*, c. 1942–3. Collage of printed paper, ink and graphite pencil on paperboard, 46.4 x 61 (18¼ x 24). The Baltimore Museum of Art: Bequest of Saidie A. May, BMA 1951.266. © Estate of William Baziotes

107 Henri Matisse, *Oceania, The Sky*, 1946. Stencil on linen, after a paper cutout maquette made in Paris, boulevard du Montparnasse, 177 x 370 (69⅝ x 145⅝). Centre Georges Pompidou, Paris. © Succession H. Matisse/DACS 2004

108 Jackson Pollock, *Cut Out*, 1948-50. Oil on cut-out paper mounted on canvas, 77.3 x 57 (30½ x 23½). Ohara Museum of Art, Kurashiki, Japan. © The Pollock-Krasner Foundation. © ARS, NY and DACS, London 2004

109 Jackson Pollock, *Out of the Web (Number 7)*, 1949. Oil and enamel paint on masonite, cut-out, 122 x 244 (48 x 96⅛). Collection Staatsgalerie Stuttgart, Germany. © The Pollock-Krasner Foundation. © ARS, NY and DACS, London 2004

110 Installation view of the exhibition 'Collage', MoMA, New York, 1948. Photo © Scala, Florence 2004/The Museum of Modern Art, New York

111 Ann Ryan, *Untitled (No. 234)*, 1948–54. Collage, 19.1 x 14 (7½ x 5½). Estate of the Artist, Courtesy Joan T. Washburn Gallery, New York

112 Lee Krasner, *The City*, 1953. Oil and paper collage on masonite 121.9 x 91.4 (48 x 36). Private Collection. © ARS, NY and DACS, London 2004

113 Lee Krasner, *Bald Eagle*, 1955. Oil, paper and canvas collage on linen, 195.6 x 130.8 (77 x 51½). Private Collection. © ARS, NY and DACS, London 2004

114 Allan Kaprow, *Caged Pheasant No. 2*, 1956. Collage and paint on canvas. Collection the Artist. Courtesy Research Library, Getty Research Institute, Los Angeles (980063)

115 Jess (Burgess Collins), *Paranoiac Portrait of Robert Creeley*, 1955. Collage, 66 x 55.9 (26 x 22). Courtesy Odyssia Gallery, New York

116 Clay Spohn, *Precious Objects*, 1949. Mixed media assemblage, 31.8 x 19.7 x 19.7 (12½ x 7¾ x 7¾). Oakland Museum of California, Gift of the Artist. Photo M. Lee Fatherree

117 Wallace Berman, *Veritas Panel*, c. 1952–6. Wood, photos, paper, metal. Destroyed. Photo Charles Brittin. © Wallace Berman Estate

118 Jess Collins, *Feature F*, 1953. Collage, 50.8 x 38.1 (20 x 15). Private Collection. Courtesy Odyssia Gallery, New York

119 Jess (Burgess Collins), *The Mouse's Tale*, 1951–4. Collage, 119.4 x 81.3 (47 x 32). San Francisco Museum of Modern Art. Gift of Frederic P. Snowden. Courtesy Odyssia Gallery, New York

120 Jess (Burgess Collins), *Tricky Cad, Case I*, 1954. Notebook of 12 collages with handwritten title page and blank end page, each 24.1 x 19.1 (9.5 x 7.5). Whitney Museum of Modern Art, New York. Courtesy Odyssia Gallery, New York

121 Wally Hedrick, *Xmas Tree*, 1955. Mixed media, 213.4 x 137.2 (84 x 54). Courtesy Linc Real Art, San Francisco

122 Jay DeFeo, *Blossom*, 1956. Photocollage, 111.8 x 88.9 (44 x 35). Museum of Modern Art, New York. © ARS, NY and DACS, London 2004